T-LEVELS
THE NEXT LEVEL QUALIFICATION

EDUCATION & CHILDCARE

ASSISTING TEACHING

Louise Burnham
Penny Tassoni
Janet King

Resource
rsed by
cfe.

HODDER
EDUCATION
AN HACHETTE UK COMPANY

'T Level' is a registered trade mark of the Institute for Apprenticeships and Technical Education.

The T Level is a qualification approved and managed by the Institute for Apprenticeships and Technical Education.

Although every effort has been made to ensure that website addresses are correct at time of going to press, Hodder Education cannot be held responsible for the content of any website mentioned in this book. It is sometimes possible to find a relocated web page by typing in the address of the home page for a website in the URL window of your browser.

Hachette UK's policy is to use papers that are natural, renewable and recyclable products and made from wood grown in well-managed forests and other controlled sources. The logging and manufacturing processes are expected to conform to the environmental regulations of the country of origin.

Orders: please contact Hachette UK Distribution, Hely Hutchinson Centre, Milton Road, Didcot, Oxfordshire, OX11 7HH. Telephone: +44 (0)1235 827827. Email education@hachette.co.uk Lines are open from 9 a.m. to 5 p.m., Monday to Friday. You can also order through our website: www.hoddereducation.co.uk

ISBN: 978-1-3983-1941-7

First published in 2021 by
Hodder Education,
An Hachette UK Company
Carmelite House
50 Victoria Embankment
London EC4Y 0DZ

www.hoddereducation.co.uk

Impression number 10 9 8 7 6 5 4 3 2 1

Year   2025 2024 2023 2022 2021

Cover photo © Jules Selmes Photography

Illustrations by Integra Software Services Pvt. Ltd., Pondicherry, India.

Typeset in India by Integra Software Services Pvt. Ltd., Pondicherry, India.

Printed in Slovenia

A catalogue record for this title is available from the British Library.

Contents

THE CORE

ASSISTING TEACHING

Acknowledgements

We would like to thank all the teachers who have given their feedback to us during the development of this textbook, including: Fiona Craig, Grimsby Institute, TEC Partnership; Dawn Hiscox, Peter Symonds College; Penny Muka, Uxbridge College; Bernadette Turner, Dudley College of Technology; and Jill Clausen, Havant & South Downs College.

Penny Tassoni

I would like to thank my great friend and co-author, Louise Burnham, for her support during this project. I would also like to thank my other co-author as well as Rachel Edge, Ruth Murphy and Emma Coopshon for their work. My thanks also go to the numerous practitioners and teachers whose dedication to children has inspired me. Finally, I need to thank my family, and especially Sofia and Olivia, who are helping me to maintain a 'hands on' approach to my writing.

Louise Burnham

I would like to thank Gemma Kirby, Nadeem Qureshi and Paul Showell for their advice around secondary assessments, Heather Rouse for information on the EYFS to Year 1 transfer, and Luke Burnham for information about iGCSEs.
I would also like to thank Rachel Edge and Ruth Murphy at Hodder Education and my co-authors, Penny Tassoni and Janet King, for all their support during this process.
Thank you to Unicorn Primary School for the use of their planning format.

Janet King

With thanks to Hodder Education and my co-authors for their positive encouragement and support. To all the wonderful colleagues and students, both past and present, that I have had the pleasure and privilege to work with, and to all education and childcare students and staff for the difference that they make to babies, children, and young people every single day. With love to my family.

Photo credits

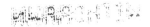

The Publishers would like to thank the following for permission to reproduce copyright material.

Page 1 © Jules Selmes/Hodder Education; page 4 © JulesSelmes/Hodder Education; page 8 © fizkes - stock. adobe.com; page 10 © Jules Selmes/Hodder Education; page 11 © JulesSelmes2014; page 12 © Getty Images/ iStockphoto/Thinkstock; page 14 © Monkey Business / stock.adobe.com; page 15 © Robert Read / Alamy Stock Photo; page 17 © Jules Selmes/Hodder Education; page 22 © Monkey Business/stock.adobe.com; page 25 © Jacob Crees Cockayne/Hodder Education; page 27 © Jules Selmes/Hodder Education; page 32 © Penny Tassoni; page 41 © Blend Images / Alamy Stock Photo; page 43 © Monkey Business/stock.adobe.com; page 47 © Monkey Business - stock.adobe.com; page 55 © Shutterstock / Monkey Business Images; page 62 © ilona75/123RF.com; page 68 © Jules Selmes/Hodder Education; page 73 © Monkey Business - stock.adobe.com; page 82 © Jacob Crees Cockayne/Hodder Education; page 83 © Jules Selmes/Hodder Education; page 91 © Africa Studio - stock. adobe.com; page 96© Africa Studio - stock.adobe.com; page 99 © Thinglass - Shutterstock.com; page 100 l © PicsArt - stock.adobe.com, r © Maryna - stock.adobe.com; page 101 © Jules Selmes/Hodder Education; page 106 © Jules Selmes/Hodder Education; page 110 © Jacob Crees Cockayne/Hodder Education; page 111 © Jacob Crees

Guide to the book

The following features can be found in this book.

Learning outcomes

Core knowledge outcomes that you must understand and learn.

Key term

Understand important terms.

Reflect

Tasks and questions providing an opportunity to reflect on the knowledge learned.

In practice

Tasks and questions designed to apply knowledge in workshops and simulated working environments.

Test yourself

A knowledge consolidation feature containing questions and tasks to aid understanding and guide you to think about a topic in detail.

Research

Research-based activities – either stretch and challenge activities, enabling you to go beyond the course, or industry placement-based activities encouraging you to discover more about your placement.

Practice points

Helpful tips and guidelines to help develop professional skills during the industry placement.

Good to know

Highlights knowledge content that will be useful to you when completing your OS synoptic assessments.

Case study

Placing knowledge into a fictionalised, real-life context. Useful to introduce problem solving and dilemmas.

CORE Chapter 1:
Wider Context

In this chapter, we will be looking at the scope of provision in education and childcare, the features and functions of the services available for babies, children and young people and their families, and how these support them.

As well as exploring this vast and diverse range of service provision, you will be introduced to the different occupational roles that exist across the education and childcare sector, and learn about the responsibilities that staff working in these roles hold.

Learning outcomes

This chapter covers the following knowledge outcomes for Core Element 1:

1.1 Understand the differences between a range of childcare and education provision, 0–19 years

1.2 Understand the different responsibilities of a range of roles, the entry requirements and possible career progression routes in the sector

1.1 Childcare and education provision from birth to 19 years

As you learn about the service provision and the diverse roles and responsibilities held by staff, you will also increase your own knowledge and understanding of the diverse employment opportunities open to you. Before we start to explore the different types of setting it will be useful to introduce some terms.

Types of setting

▶ **Voluntary:** This means provision that has been set up and funded by donations and voluntary contributions. It may, for example, be run by a charity or church group in the local community, and parents may have to pay a donation to help cover costs. In some cases, parents or carers may stay and supervise their children so that they can socialise with others, but the ways in which these settings operate vary. If children are left with staff, the setting will need to be registered with and inspected by **Ofsted**.

▶ **Private:** This means that parents need to pay for the provision as it is run privately. This may include settings such as a crèche, a workplace nursery, private day nursery or a childminder's home. These settings will need to be registered with and inspected by Ofsted if they are providing regular care and education for children. For example, a childminder will need to be registered and inspected, but a crèche that may just provide care from time to time does not.

▶ **Statutory/maintained:** This term is used for settings that are government-funded as they have to be available by law, such as schools. They will be registered and inspected by Ofsted. They may also be known as 'maintained' settings.

▶ **Independent:** This term is usually used for independent schools that are not paid for by government or state funding, so parents will be charged for them. Independent schools will still have to follow the Early Years Foundation Stage (EYFS) Framework and are also inspected by Ofsted.

> **Key term**
>
> *Ofsted:* stands for the Office for Standards in Education, Children's Services and Skills. Ofsted inspects and regulates services providing education and skills for learners of all ages, including those who care for babies, children and young people.

Childcare provision

Let's begin by considering the range of childcare and education provision that may be accessed by babies, children and young people, their features and how they operate so that similarities and differences can be identified.

In their early years, children may be cared for by a range of different services across childcare provision, including:

▶ childminders
▶ nannies
▶ nurseries
▶ pre-schools.

Childminders

Childminders work in their own homes and look after other people's children, often combining this with caring for their own children. Lone working can be demanding and challenging as there will be no one else to lend a hand. However, childminders can choose the hours they work and the services they provide.

Childminders will care for children's welfare, learning and development, and develop trusting professional relationships with parents, carers and others as required. Childminders are professionals providing **holistic** care and educational learning experiences. They need to plan for and resource diverse play provision for babies and children, often across a range of ages, provide food and drinks (or prepare them if they are provided by parents/carers), and promote physical care routines such as nappy changing and toileting, rest and sleep provision, and outdoor experiences.

> **Key term**
>
> *Holistic:* overall or all round; the idea that the parts of something are interconnected so looking at the whole rather than each individual part. Here, it means all-round care needs, with an appreciation of the contribution of each care need to overall wellbeing.

Good to know

'Anyone who looks after one or more children under the age of eight years in England or under the age of 12 years in Wales, to whom they are not related, on domestic premises, for reward, and for a total of more than two hours in any day must register as a childminder.'

(Source: Professional Association for Childcare and Early Years (PACEY) **www.pacey.org.uk**)

Childminders who do not register may receive a fine or even a prison sentence if they do not register with Ofsted.

Good to know

Childminders must be aware of ratios. The ratios will inform them how many children, and their age ranges, they can care for at any time. The Early Years Statutory Framework will guide childminders with regard to their role, including up-to-date information about ratios.

What do nannies do?

Nannies usually care for babies and children belonging to one family in the parents'/carers' own home. Sometimes, a nanny will be 'live in', but they can also live outside the home and travel to work. Nannies typically work alone to meet the needs of the babies and young children they care for. They may also be employed to work overseas. A professional nanny will carry out similar roles to a childminder, but typically for the children of one family in the family's home.

Nanny agencies may be able to support both the nanny and the family, and will be able to offer advice on important issues such as:

▶ **placement** – bringing the nanny and family together, and supporting both parties to maintain a positive relationship
▶ **contract** – nanny contracts can be essential in ensuring the nanny has a valid and reasonable job description and terms of employment
▶ **suitability checks** – the nanny agency may undertake recruitment safety checks such as a Disclosure and Barring Service (**DBS**) check, paediatric first aid, training and qualifications, as well as employment history; some nanny agencies may be able to support nannies with any training requirements
▶ **legal obligations** – the agency may be able to offer advice around contracts, pensions and taxation.

Registered childminders are typically self-employed and run their own business from home, or they may register through a childminding agency. It is not unusual for childminders to employ childminding assistants as their business grows, and this allows them to care for more children at any given time.

In England, the **childminder ratios** identifying the number of children that a childminder can care for, and the safeguarding and welfare requirements that must be in place, are included within the **Early Years Statutory Framework**.

You will learn more about the areas of learning and how the Early Years Statutory Framework is arranged in other chapters, specifically on pages 16–18. If you take the Early Years occupational specialism you will spend more time exploring its requirements.

There is pre-registration training and guidance that childminders need to undertake, and continuing professional development (CPD) is always recommended.

A childminder may apply for different types of registration:

▶ The **Early Years Register** is for those caring for children from birth to the 31 August after their fifth birthday. All registered childminders in England on the Early Years Register are inspected against the requirements of the Early Years Statutory Framework.
▶ The **Childcare Register**, which has two parts: compulsory registration for childminders that are caring for children aged from five up to eight years, and voluntary registration for childminders caring for children aged eight and over.

Many childminders are on both registers to enable them to care for a wide age range of children, but the appropriate ratios must be maintained for the age group (see Good to know).

Key term

DBS: stands for Disclosure and Barring Service, part of the suitability checks that must be made on individuals in the UK involved in the care of children and young people under 18 years of age. These specifically look at any criminal convictions recorded against an individual and are an important feature of safeguarding. You will find out more about DBS processes as you prepare for placement, as it is likely you will be required to undertake a DBS check yourself.

For more on safeguarding, see Core Chapter 3.

The nanny agency may also be able to promote social networks for the nanny, which is very important, especially if he or she is living away from home.

Research

Visit the **bapn.org.uk** website to find out more about what it is like to work as a professional nanny.

Nursery provision

▲ Can you think of different types of early years settings?

There are two main types of nursery provision: day nursery and statutory/maintained nursery school or class. The latter is usually attached to a primary school. Independent nursery settings are also available.

Day nursery provision caring for children from birth to five years of age

This is usually a private provision and parents/carers will pay for their child to have a place at the nursery. There are, however, government-funded free childcare places that certain children are entitled to if they meet particular criteria. The day nursery is usually open all year round and for most of the day, from early morning to early evening. The day nursery will be registered with and inspected by Ofsted. The day nursery must meet the requirements set within the Early Years Statutory Framework.

Staff working in a day nursery work in ratio according to their training and qualifications, and meet the holistic care needs of children, including physical, cognitive, speech, language and communication, social and emotional.

Qualifications that staff hold will vary from Level 2 to Level 7 (master's level), and the roles are equally diverse, but everyone is likely to be involved in observing children and planning for their next steps in line with the statutory framework. Day nurseries are often accessed by students for practical work placements following an early years specialism.

Statutory/maintained nursery schools or classes are local authority funded schools, with a head teacher and qualified teachers leading a team of specialist early years staff, providing education and care for three to four year olds (and increasingly for two year olds).

A **nursery class** is usually part of a primary school and will typically be led by a nursery teacher. Parents do not pay for their child/children to attend. Children are typically aged three to four when they attend, but some may be younger. The nursery will be open in term time only. Children will usually move on to the primary school and the head of the primary is the head teacher for the nursery class too. The nursery will be inspected by Ofsted and follow the requirements of the Early Years Statutory Framework.

A **nursery school** will function in the same way as a nursery class but statutory maintained nursery schools are not typically part of a primary school and will have their own head teacher. Nursery schools can be statutory/maintained or independent. Examples of independent nursery schools include Montessori nursery schools.

Research

▶ Look up independent Montessori nursery schools and statutory/maintained nursery schools to find out more about them.
▶ Summarise information regarding their approaches, and any similarities and differences in the services they offer.
▶ Present your findings as a chart or table.

Pre-schools

Pre-schools are classed as voluntary settings. This implies that there is no cost. In practice, though, costs usually do apply, however, these costs are low. Pre-schools often provide three hours of sessional care for children. Children attend pre-schools at around the age of two years, and provision is similar to the staffing and regulatory requirements of day care. Parents are often actively involved in pre-school settings.

Good to know

'[In England] Children must start full-time education once they reach compulsory school age. This is on 31 December, 31 March or 31 August following their fifth birthday – whichever comes first.'

(Source: **www.gov.uk /schools-admissions/school-starting-age**)

Reflect

To help you to consolidate your knowledge and understanding:
- Compare and contrast the forms of early years sector provision listed above.
- What similarities can you find?
- What are the differences between the types of sector provision?

Read the following case study and reflect on the discussion points.

Case study

Anita is the mother of two children under five years of age: Shelley is 18 months and Lola is four. Anita is planning to return to full-time work in the next two months and is considering the childcare options available to her.
- Work in small groups to identify the range of provision Anita and her children could use.
- Compare and contrast the provision identified.
- In your group, discuss any advantages or disadvantages to different types of childcare available and share your thoughts with your peers.

School provision

There are many different types of school in the UK, educating children from age five up to age sixteen. Ofsted inspects services providing education and skills for pupils of all ages.

Maintained schools

Maintained schools, providing both primary and secondary education, are a common category. They include:
- community schools
- voluntary controlled schools
- voluntary aided schools (usually church or faith schools)
- foundation schools
- trust schools.

Good to know

Children may formally leave school on the last Friday in June if they are 16 by the end of the summer holidays. They must then do one of the following until the age of 18:
- stay in full-time education, for example, at a college
- start an apprenticeship or traineeship
- spend 20 hours or more a week working or volunteering, while in part-time education or training.

As mentioned earlier in this chapter, statutory maintained schools are those funded by the local authority. Parents/carers do not need to pay for their child/children to attend. As you can see from the list below, there are different types of schools that fall into the maintained category.

- **Maintained community schools** are state funded, are not influenced by business or religious groups, and must follow the National Curriculum. Teaching and learning is led by head teachers, teaching staff and teaching assistants/learning support mentors. The school staffing structure includes non-teaching staff and an active governing body.
- **Voluntary controlled schools** usually have foundation or trust status, for instance, connected to a Christian denomination, that has some influence in the running of the school but makes no financial contribution. The teaching and learning, as well as the regulatory body, remain the same as for community schools.
- **Voluntary aided schools** – as with voluntary controlled schools, there is influence from the foundation or the trust. However, in a voluntary aided school the foundation or trust contributes financially to the upkeep of the school.
- **Foundation schools** function in the same way as a maintained school, with greater responsibility placed on the governing body, which is sometimes supported by representatives from religious groups in the running of the school.
- **Trust schools** function as foundation schools, supported by a charitable foundation (the charitable foundation is known as a trust).

For more on pupils with special educational needs, see Core Chapter 11.

> **Good to know**
>
> Maintained schools in England must follow the National Curriculum. They may focus on specific subjects (such as RE in a church school) but the curriculum must be followed appropriately at each key stage. Maintained schools must also follow the SEN Code of Practice.

Non-maintained schools

Just because maintained schools are funded by the local authority, this does not mean that all non-maintained schools are not (i.e. charge fees to attend). Non-maintained schools are divided into:

▶ academies (including free schools)
▶ private schools (including independent special schools).

Academies and free schools

These types of school receive their funding direct from the government (the Education Funding Agency) and are an initiative intended to drive up standards and improve achievement. This funding arrangement is different to that in place for maintained schools. Such schools are run by a charitable trust; **academy schools** are, therefore, often referred to as **academy trusts**. Some academy schools work with others to form a **multi-academy trust (MAT)**.

An academy does not need to follow the National Curriculum, but the pupils will need to sit National Curriculum assessments. Academy schools and free schools have the same funding arrangements: the funding is not from local authority but from central government. All academies, including free schools, have greater control over their curriculum delivery and finances than do maintained schools.

Private schools

Private schools (also known as independent schools) charge fees to attend and do not receive general government funding. Similar to academies and free schools, pupils do not have to follow the National Curriculum. All private schools must be registered with the government and are inspected regularly.

Under the Children and Families Act 2014, an **independent special school** is an independent school that is organised to make **special educational provision (SEP)** for pupils with special educational needs. There may be circumstances when the local authority must pay a pupil's fees – for example, if the independent school is named in the pupil's **education, health and care (EHC) plan**, which means the local authority then has a financial responsibility.

Home schooling

Parents have the right to educate their children at home. In this case, children must have access to a full-time curriculum. They do not need to follow the National Curriculum, however, learning will be monitored by the local authority. Children with SEND or a school attendance order must be given consent from the local authority for home schooling.

> **Research**
>
> Find out more about independent special schools on the government website: **www.gov.uk/government/publications/independent-special-schools-and-colleges**

> **Key term**
>
> *Education, health and care (EHC) plan:* an EHC plan is for children and young people aged up to 25 who need more support than is available through special educational needs support; it is drawn up to outline provision for a child or young person following an assessment of special educational needs. EHC plans identify educational, health and social needs, and set out the additional support to meet those needs. Find out more here: **www.gov.uk/children-with-special-educational-needs/extra-SEN-help**
>
> For more on assessment of special educational needs, see Core Chapter 11, page 178.

> **Good to know**
>
> Students aged 16–25 can request a SEND assessment themselves. For example, an individual may request a diagnosis for dyslexia. Find more information here: **www.gov.uk/children-with-special-educational-needs/extra-SEN-help**

> **Test yourself**
>
> Produce a chart including the maintained and non-maintained school provision talked about in this section. In the chart, identify as many features and functions for each provision as you can. Next, highlight the similarities and summarise any differences.

Post-16 provision

Of course, educational opportunities continue after the age of 16 and there is a diverse range of provision available for students in England once they have turned 16 years of age. There are different categories of qualifications and courses of study. This includes a more 'academic' path, studying for A-levels, Applied General Qualifications or the International Baccalaureate, or a wide range of more 'vocational' courses, including apprenticeships and traineeships for competence-based, work-related employment training, and technical education that allows students to prepare for specific occupational roles, as well as support with progression to higher education.

Let's take a look at the different settings where students can undertake the variety of training options open to them:

▶ school sixth forms
▶ sixth-form colleges
▶ general further education and **tertiary colleges**
▶ private, independent and voluntary providers (publicly funded)
▶ employers
▶ special colleges (including agriculture and horticulture colleges)
▶ art, design and performing arts colleges
▶ higher education institutions (HEIs).

School sixth forms

School sixth forms are based in schools and cater for students aged 16–19. This period of study is also referred to as Key Stage 5, or Years 12 and 13. While studying in sixth form, students typically prepare for A-level, International Baccalaureate or technical qualifications. A student can be in sixth form in a maintained school or in a private school.

Sixth-form colleges

Sixth-form colleges are generally larger than a school sixth form, but smaller than a further education college. The range of courses offered is, therefore, likely to be more diverse than that of the school sixth form.

Further education colleges

Further education (FE) colleges generally offer a wider provision than sixth form. For example, as well as A-level, International Baccalaureate or technical qualifications at Key Stage 5, the student will be able to find a course that is set at various levels, often beginning at Level 1 and stretching to Level 5, including higher-level apprenticeships and foundation

degrees. Some colleges work in partnership with HEIs (universities) to deliver degree programmes too. FE colleges prepare students for the world of work as well as for study at higher level. Students accessing FE colleges are diverse, including adult students and students with special educational needs.

> ### Key terms
>
> *Tertiary college:* an institution that provides general and vocational FE for students aged 16–19. Such colleges provide the next stage of education, after primary and secondary. They are distinct from general FE colleges in that they cater for a specific age group, and offer a less extensive and varied curriculum.
>
> *Further education colleges:* include general FE and tertiary colleges, sixth-form colleges and specialist colleges, as well as adult education provision. You can find out more on the government's website.

Private, independent and voluntary providers (publicly funded)

Students may train and work within the private, independent and voluntary sector. For example, you may complete your study with a private training company rather than in a school or college. Apprentices may complete their training under the supervision of private, independent and voluntary provision – for example, a private day nursery, an independent school, or within a charitable or not-for-profit organisation.

Employers

Certain employers have worked with the Institute for Apprenticeships and Technical Education in the production of apprenticeship standards. Employers have significantly influenced the standards for education and training due to their leadership in their sectors.

Special colleges (including agriculture and horticulture colleges)

Special colleges sometimes offer residential facilities and usually focus on a particular specialist area, such as music. They have a wealth of expertise to meet the needs of children and young people with special educational needs and disabilities from secondary age and beyond.

Art, design and performing arts colleges

Art, design and performing arts are specialist areas of study where students can develop the skills needed to work in a range of roles relating to this sector.

Higher education institutions

These institutions (HEIs) offer university-level programmes. At university, students can study undergraduate and then postgraduate programmes after taking most Level 3 general or technical qualifications (such as this one). As an undergraduate, you will study towards a foundation or full degree (Level 5–6 qualification); as a postgraduate, you may study towards a master's (Level 7) or even a doctorate (Level 8).

▲ Can you think of any learning benefits from collaborating with peers?

How and when education became compulsory in England and Wales, and how this has changed over time

Educating children has not always been a legal requirement or open to all, and the law in the UK has evolved regarding at what age children must start and finish their schooling. The table below shows the most significant dates in this process.

Year	Change in education law	
1870	Introduction of compulsory education	For the first time, the government mandates the provision of elementary education for children aged 5–13 years of age under the Elementary Education Act 1870. Attendance is compulsory for boys and girls aged 5–10 years of age until attainment of the 'educational standard'.
1893–1921	School leaving age raised	The school leaving age is raised to 11 in 1893, 12 in 1899 and to 14 in 1921.
1944	The Education Act 1944	State education is now free for all children. The act created separate primary schools (for children aged 5–11) and secondary schools (11–15). Local education authorities (LEAs) also had to ensure nursery provision, disability provision and boarding. The compulsory school age was raised to 15, then 16 in 1972.
1972	Compulsory education raised to age 16	Preparation for raising the school leaving age started in 1964 and was established in 1972 in preparation for school leavers the following June.

Year	Change in education law	
1988	The Education Reform Act 1988	This act introduced a compulsory National Curriculum consisting of 14 subjects.
		Teachers were no longer in charge of the curriculum but were accountable for it through the introduction of compulsory standardised assessments at ages 7, 11, 14 (SATs) and 16 (GCSE).
2008	The Education and Skills Act 2008	Government statistics showed that 11% of 16 to 18 year olds were neither continuing their education after completion of their GCSEs, nor in full-time employment or an apprenticeship. This led to increased unemployment rates.
		As education is an area managed in Wales by the Welsh Government, the law regarding school leaving age differs between England and Wales, as follows:
		England: A child may leave school on the last Friday in June if they will be 16 by the end of the summer holidays. They must then do one of the following until they are 18: • stay in full-time education, for example, at an FE college • start an apprenticeship or traineeship • spend 20 hours or more a week working or volunteering, while in part-time education or training.
		Wales: A child may leave school at 16, but it is not compulsory to stay in training or full-time education.

▲ How UK law has evolved regarding the age at which children must start and finish schooling

Regulation

In this section, we are going to find out a little bit more about regulation and how regulation contributes to education and childcare specifically, including:

▶ Department for Education (DfE)
▶ Office for Standards in Education, Children's Services and Skills (Ofsted)
▶ Office of Qualifications and Examinations Regulation (Ofqual)
▶ Office for Students (OfS).

Department for Education (DfE)

The **Department for Education** is the part of government responsible, in England, for Children's Services and education, including early years, schools, higher and further education policy, apprenticeships and wider skills.

The DfE has key responsibilities for teaching and learning in education. It also produces statutory guidance around legislation to influence how we work within education and childcare. This guidance is produced through the development of policies and procedures intended to keep babies, children and young people safe, healthy and well.

Many key publications, such as *The Early Years Statutory Framework* and *The National Curriculum*, are published by the Department for Education.

Office for Standards in Education, Children's Services and Skills (Ofsted)

We have already discussed **Ofsted** in this chapter (page 2), including a key term and examples of the role of Ofsted. Ofsted works to keep babies, children and young people safe, and to promote high standards in education and childcare.

Ofsted inspects and regulates registered settings in education and childcare to raise standards, and ensure that babies, children, young people and adults who are accessing education receive the best possible teaching and learning. Inspections are carried out regularly to maintain standards, set action plans and support quality in practice (**www.gov.uk/government/organisations/ofsted**).

Office of Qualifications and Examinations Regulation (Ofqual)

The **Office of Qualifications and Examinations Regulation (Ofqual)** regulates qualifications, examinations and assessments in England.

Regulated qualifications include general education, such as GCSEs and A-levels, technical qualifications and others that have been submitted by awarding organisations (exam boards) for regulation. This means that Ofqual has a responsibility to check that the qualifications meet appropriate standards, that they prepare the students taking them for work or further study, and that teachers and students have all the information they need to deliver the qualification successfully.

Ofqual will also consider how well the qualifications prepare students for the next stage; this is sometimes referred to as how 'fit for purpose' the qualifications are. Regulation by Ofqual reassures everyone involved that qualifications have been thoroughly considered for validity and reliability (**www.gov.uk/government/organisations/ofqual**).

Office for Students (OfS)

The **Office for Students** works in a similar way to other regulators in that it is in place to make sure standards are being maintained, to raise concerns and action-plan where they are not, and track and monitor any action implemented to deal with this. The OfS is the independent regulator of higher education in England. This means that it is concerned with teaching and learning in universities or training centres delivering undergraduate or postgraduate programmes. Its aim is to support and ensure quality in all HE students' experience of higher education (**www.officeforstudents.org.uk**).

1.2 Occupational roles in education and childcare

This section looks in more detail at the different responsibilities of the diverse roles that exist in education and childcare, to help you consider the specific entry requirements for particular occupations and understand possible career progression routes in the sector.

To help us to categorise the occupational roles let's consider them as general roles and specialist roles. Bear in mind, however, that it is possible that an individual identified as working in a general role will also be responsible for a specialist role – for example, a teacher may also be a designated safeguarding officer/lead person.

General roles in education and childcare

These can be categorised as follows:
▶ early years practitioner
▶ early years educator
▶ room leader
▶ teaching assistant
▶ teacher/lecturer
▶ head teacher.

Early years practitioner

This is a designated occupational role within the early years workforce. The **early years practitioner** will be qualified at Level 2 in early years care and education, and will work alongside the Level 3 early years educator.

The qualification that the early years practitioner holds means they meet the criteria required to work within this occupational role. The responsibilities they hold are diverse, and they will be involved in all aspects of caring for babies and young children from birth to five, as identified in the Early Years Statutory Framework.

Their daily routine is likely to include most or all of the following duties:
▶ meeting the individual physical care routines of children
▶ observing and planning
▶ working with others
▶ including parents/carers, colleagues and other professionals
▶ record keeping and reporting
▶ promoting effective playful interactions with babies and young children.

▲ How is this adult enhancing the children's experiences?

Early years educator

The **early years educator** is a designated occupational role within the early years workforce. They will be qualified at Level 3 and will work within the ratios specified in the Early Years Statutory Framework. A Level 3 early years educator, once qualified, will be able to progress within the early years workforce to take a position such as room leader, and may also take up leadership, deputy management and management roles.

The early years educator will undertake all the duties of the early years practitioner, but will hold greater responsibility and accountability for intervention and quality as appropriate. The early years educator will take an active role as a key person, observing and planning for next steps effectively, liaising with parents/carers and other professionals to ensure the best outcome for children in their care, while maintaining the requirements of the Early Years Statutory Framework to keep children safe, healthy and well.

▲ Some teaching assistants may work one-to-one with pupils

Case study

Anya is 15 years old. She is making good progress with her academic studies and has discussed being a primary school teacher with her tutor. Following the half-term break, Anya has been late arriving at school and sometimes not attending all of her classes. She is not socialising with her usual group of friends and they are concerned about her welfare, reporting that she is not eating during the day and that she is exercising in the gym all the time. Anya's parents have come in to the school voluntarily as they are concerned for her emotional wellbeing.

▶ Summarise the situation.
▶ How can the school support Anya and her parents?
▶ What other professionals may be able to offer support to Anya and her parents at this anxious time?

Reflect

Nannies and childminders make a valuable contribution to the early years workforce; there is information about these significant roles earlier in this section. Take the opportunity to look back at the role of the professional nanny and childminder to give you a broader insight into the occupational roles that exist within the early years workforce.

Good to know

Occupational maps can be found on the CACHE website. The link below leads to a career progression map, which will give you the opportunity to think about different career pathways in education and childcare. The CACHE website also has case studies to read through that may inspire your own career aspirations.

www.cache.org.uk/news-media/early-years-career-progression-map

Room leader

The **room leader** will be an experienced early years educator and, as such, all of those responsibilities will apply to this occupational role too. The room leader will be responsible for the running of a room – for example, a pre-school room with children aged three to four, or a baby room with children under two years. Although each setting will decide on the age ranges of its different rooms, children usually tend to be cared for in age ranges with time to come together as larger groups, particularly at quieter times of the day or at mealtimes.

The room leader's responsibility may extend to managing budgets and ordering resources/equipment, as well as making sure that child ratios and other legislative requirements within the Early Years Statutory Framework are met. The room leader may have responsibility for undertaking peer observations, appraisals and performance management of colleagues, such as early years practitioners or students.

Teaching assistant

The **teaching assistant** will support teaching and learning for individuals or for groups of pupils, working closely with the class teacher. The teaching assistant may work one-to-one with a single pupil or with a small group of children with special educational needs and disabilities (SEND) to carry out the teacher's lessons in a **differentiated** way to meet their needs (see Core Chapter 2, page 22).

For more about SEND, see Core Chapter 11.

Teaching assistants will also update, record and monitor progress, and undertake activities such as guided reading. They will be expected to support planning and attend meetings as appropriate. There are opportunities for the teaching assistant to progress to higher level teaching assistant (HLTA) status, and in this role they will be able to undertake more responsibilities working with pupils, such as leading some lessons. A teaching assistant may also choose to undertake a graduate programme to train as a teacher.

Good to know

More information about the role of the teaching assistant and the qualifications that can support this pathway can be found on the CACHE website: **www.cache.org.uk/our-qualifications-and-services/ supporting-teaching-and-learning**

You can find out more about higher level teaching assistant standards at the HLTA website: **www.hlta.org.uk**

▲ What does this photo tell you about the level of engagement between the teacher and the children?

Teacher/lecturer

Teachers and lecturers usually have similar responsibilities. For example, both are involved in advancing teaching and learning through planning, team collaboration and significantly raising students' knowledge, understanding and skills through effective strategies. The qualifications and the journey the teacher and lecturer may take may vary, however.

▶ The **teacher** is likely to work in school environments and will be a qualified teacher (QTS). Their training will have included study at higher education level in order to achieve QTS.

▶ The **lecturer** is likely to work in further or higher education and, as well as academic qualifications, may also have significant industry experience. For example, a lecturer in early years may have worked extensively in the early years workforce. To teach in higher education, universities often require postgraduate qualifications and a commitment to ongoing research.

Head teacher

The head teacher will be responsible for the day-to-day running of the school. Being a head teacher is a challenging and responsible position. Some of the responsibilities required of this role are:

▶ liaise with the governing body
▶ engage with the school ethos and values/mission in partnership with pupils, staff, parents and carers
▶ lead teaching and learning
▶ staff recruitment, appraisal and disciplinary procedures.

Good to know

Various pathways to head teaching are outlined on the UCAS website: **www.ucas.com/ucas/after-gcses/find-career-ideas/explore-jobs/job-profile/ head-teacher**

Specialist roles

Some of the specialist roles that exist within education and childcare include:

▶ special educational needs and disabilities coordinator (SENDCo)
▶ safeguarding officer/designated person
▶ mental health lead
▶ mentor/pastoral support
▶ physical activity and nutrition coordinator (PANCo)
▶ counsellor
▶ careers advisor.

Individuals holding a general role within education and childcare may also be responsible for some of the specialist roles that are listed here.

Special educational needs and disabilities coordinator (SENDCo)

Each setting, whether an early years setting or a school, will have a **SENDCo** in place. The SENDCo will be responsible for liaising with parents/carers, colleagues and other professionals to ensure that individual children's needs are met, and resources and equipment provided in line with organisational policy and procedures, and in adherence with the Special Educational Needs Code of Practice.

In an early years setting, an experienced early years educator usually takes this role. There are qualifications that can be taken at Level 2, Level 3 and Level 4 to support the SENDCo to manage their responsibilities efficiently. In a school, a class teacher will undertake the role of SENDCo and formal training will be required to hold this responsibility.

Safeguarding officer/designated person

Safeguarding babies, children and young people is everyone's responsibility. However, in education and childcare, a named member of staff will hold the position of **designated safeguarding officer** or **designated safeguarding lead**, in line with the Children Act 2004. Having a named member of staff holding responsibility for safeguarding means there can be clear leadership, guidance and professional partnerships.

The designated safeguarding officer/lead will undergo relevant training to be able to support staff in recognising signs and symptoms of need in babies, children and young people, and will advise staff, ensuring that processes for raising concerns are clear and straightforward. The designated safeguarding officer/lead will take a role in recording and reporting to ensure best practice.

Research

Statutory guidance is updated regularly to ensure the best possible outcomes for babies, children and young people.

Visit **www.gov.uk** to see the latest information and guidance around the role of the designated safeguarding officer/lead and summarise your findings.

Mental health lead

The emotional health and mental wellbeing of children and young people is significant to holistic health, development and learning. Working in education and childcare, mental health lead practitioners will support children, young people and their families, as well as supporting staff with appropriate strategies and approaches to promote positive wellbeing.

Research

The Mental Health Foundation Association has produced useful documents to support an understanding of the importance of recognising mental health in children and young people, and the significance of intervention for a child's holistic health and wellbeing.

Find out more about the important specialist role of the mental health first aider in education and childcare here: **https://mhfaengland.org**

Mentor/pastoral support

Mentoring supports staff to develop confidence and competence in education and childcare. A mentor is more experienced or more knowledgeable in a particular aspect of the occupational role and helps by guiding and supporting a less experienced or less knowledgeable person. This is often seen at the beginning of someone's career, where an experienced colleague mentors a new member of staff.

On placement, you may be mentored by an experienced colleague. Their specialist knowledge and skills can be invaluable in helping you to develop the knowledge, understanding and skills that are required in this type of work.

Pastoral support for children and young people in education and childcare is concerned with the child's or young person's overall health, welfare and wellbeing. This is a whole-school approach that is concerned with how children and young people are settling in to their environment. Mentoring programmes, such as 'buddy systems' that connect younger and more experienced pupils/students with one another, can make a positive difference during transition or when learning new skills.

Physical activity and nutrition coordinator (PANCo)

Many early years settings are striving to have a member of staff responsible for promoting physical exercise and nutrition in the setting. The **physical activity and nutrition coordinator (PANCo)** will have undertaken specific training at Level 4 in order to lead in this specialist role. They will advise staff and liaise with parents to improve the setting's approach in this area.

Counsellor

If staff in education and childcare are concerned about the welfare and wellbeing of children and young people they may consider specialist intervention. There are different professionals that can support in times of need – for example, an **educational psychologist** can carry out assessments to support individuals with possible learning difficulties, and may also support children with emotional problems that may impact self-esteem and behaviour. **Child and Adolescent Mental Health Services (CAMHS)** offers specialist support, including counselling. A **social worker** may be able to provide counselling services, especially where safeguarding and welfare concerns have been raised.

Careers advisor

Careers advisors in education are able to inform students about a diverse range of occupational roles, training and qualifications, study programmes and career journeys, such as opportunities for promotion. Careers advisors will also be able to support with administration issues such as writing a CV, applying for a job or for further study, and are skilled in using assessment tools such as psychometric testing.

▲ It is important for young people to be included in discussions involving them to help them reach informed decisions about their futures.

Assessment practice

1 Identify **two** features of maintained schools.
2 List **one** similarity and **one** difference between academy schools and maintained schools.
3 List **three** responsibilities held by an early years educator.
4 Summarise the role of Ofqual in education and childcare.
5 A local authority primary school is an example of:
   a) a private service
   b) a statutory service
   c) a voluntary service.
6 Which of the following do **not** need to follow the National Curriculum?
   a) academy schools
   b) voluntary aided schools
   c) state primary schools
   d) state secondary schools.
7 Describe the role of the designated safeguarding lead in education and childcare.
8 Explain the role of Ofsted in education and childcare.
9 Compare the role of the childminder with that of the professional nanny.
10 Analyse the role of the physical activity and nutrition coordinator for children's holistic health and wellbeing.

CORE Chapter 2:
Supporting Education

Supporting children's and young people's education is complex. In this chapter, we look at the education frameworks in England and also the skills that adults need to work effectively with children and young people, which include providing feedback. We consider different theories of how children and young people learn and also the factors that might affect their development, including the role of metacognition skills. This chapter looks at the role of technology in learning, and we also consider why some children and young people may find literacy and mathematics challenging.

Learning outcomes

This chapter covers the following knowledge outcomes for Core Element 2:

2.1 The origin and purpose of the Early Years Foundation Stage and the National Curriculum from Key Stage 1 to Key Stage 4

2.2 The skills and attributes that support children's and young people's education

2.3 The key concepts underpinning a range of theoretical approaches, the strengths and criticisms of each approach, and how they complement one another to inform practice

2.4 How metacognition supports children and young people to manage their own learning

2.5 How practitioners provide effective feedback and why it is important in supporting children's/young people's educational development

2.6 Why up-to-date and appropriate technology is important to effectively support children's/young people's educational development

2.7 How personal, educational and environmental factors may affect engagement and development in reading, literacy and mathematics

This chapter also includes one knowledge outcome from Assisting Teaching Performance Outcome 1. Text relating to Assisting Teaching is highlighted. Note that this content does not form part of the core assessments.

K1.1 The student must understand the requirements of each key stage of the school curriculum

2.1 The origin and purpose of the Early Years Foundation Stage and the National Curriculum from Key Stage 1 to Key Stage 4

The Early Years Foundation Stage

The Statutory Framework for the Early Years Foundation Stage is usually referred to as the EYFS. It was introduced in 2008 to improve opportunities for children aged from birth to five years (including the reception year) and also to ensure minimum safety and welfare standards were in place. There were revisions to it in 2012 and 2017, and further revision is expected in 2021. The EYFS built upon previous governments' curricula and requirements dating back to 1996, when funding for free or subsidised nursery places for specific age groups was first introduced for parents.

Early Learning Goals and Assessment

The EYFS has **Early Learning Goals**, which are outcomes that most children are expected to achieve by the end of their reception year. These outcomes are measured by teachers carrying out observations and then assessing children's progress. This measurement is known as the **Early Years Foundation Stage Profile (EYFSP)**. Results of the profile are passed on to the government via local authorities. At the time of writing, children will also have a communication and language assessment from 2021 when they first start in the reception class. This measurement is known as the **Reception Baseline Assessment (RBA)**.

Schools providing EYFS and National Curriculum

Some primary schools have a nursery as well as a reception class. When this is the case, they will be working with both curricula. They are required to provide the EYFS for nursery and reception, but then the National Curriculum for children once they start in Year 1.

Inspection of education settings

The inspection of most education settings, including childminders' and early years settings in England, is carried out by Ofsted. In private or independent schools, this work is done by a separate inspection body called the Independent Schools Inspectorate, whose work is monitored by Ofsted. Ofsted reports its findings to the Department for Education. It also publishes reports each year about overall trends in standards in education.

> See Core Chapter 1 for more on the inspection of education settings.

The scope of the Early Years Foundation Stage (EYFS)

The EYFS does not just look at early education, but also sets legal requirements for the safeguarding and wellbeing of children aged from birth to five years in early years settings and in the reception year. These requirements cover staffing ratios, outings and the administration of medicines. Inspections of early years settings look at both the quality of education and whether settings are meeting safeguarding and welfare requirements.

> **Research**
>
> Download the latest copy of the Statutory Early Years Foundation Stage Framework from the **gov.uk** website.
>
> Work out how many adults are needed to work in a day care setting without a qualified teacher for each of the following:
> - eight babies aged from birth to ten months
> - seven children aged two years
> - 12 children aged three to four years.

Learning and development requirements

There are seven areas of learning and development set out in the EYFS. Since 2012, they have been split into two sections: prime and specific. The prime areas of the EYFS are seen as the foundation for later learning and so are the focus for working with babies and toddlers.

There are three prime areas, as shown in the diagram and described below.

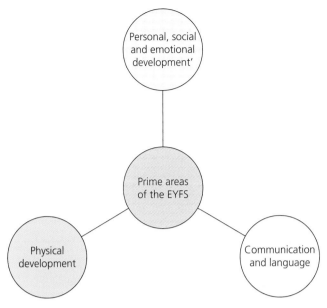

▲ The prime areas of the EYFS

1 **Personal, social and emotional development (PSED):** This area of learning and development is about children's emotional and social skills as well as their behaviour and attitudes.
2 **Physical development:** This area of learning and development is about children's physical skills. At the time of writing, it also includes learning about being healthy, but this may change with the revisions proposed for 2021.
3 **Communication and language:** This is about developing children's ability to talk, listen and understand. Learning new vocabulary is part of this.

The progress check at age two

When children are two years old, early years settings are required to do a check that looks at the progress children are making in the prime areas. This is often referred to by practitioners as the **progress check** or the 'two-year-old check'. This check was introduced in 2012 and the aim was that it would link to a health check of two year olds carried out by health visitors.

For more on the role of health visitors, see Core Chapter 6.

Specific areas of learning and development

In addition to the prime areas, there are four specific areas of learning and development. These link to later curriculum areas within the National Curriculum.
1 **Mathematics:** This area of learning and development looks at several aspects of mathematics including number, shape, size and measurement.

Research
► Look at a copy of the EYFS and read the section that outlines mathematics as an area of learning and development.
► Read the Early Learning Goals for mathematics.
► To what extent do the Early Learning Goals assess the entirety of the area of learning and development?

2 **Literacy:** This area of learning and development looks at children learning to read, write and understand texts. In the early years, this includes helping children to develop a love of books, poems and rhymes.

▲ How might sharing books with young children encourage a love of books later?

3 **Understanding of the world:** This area of learning and development focuses on children learning about their local community, nature, and also their personal history and that of others. In the current EYFS, this area also includes technology, but this is likely to be removed in the revised EYFS for 2021.
4 **Expressive arts and design:** This is a wide-ranging area that includes music, painting and modelling, but also role play and drama.

Characteristics of effective teaching and learning

To help early years settings understand how best to provide activities and opportunities for the areas of learning development, the EYFS gives three characteristics of how babies and young children learn:
1 Playing and exploring
2 Active learning
3 Creating and thinking.

These are known as the characteristics of effective teaching and learning, and Ofsted looks at them as part of its inspections.

The National Curriculum

The **National Curriculum** was introduced in England in 1988. Its aim was to make sure that all pupils were having the same opportunities to learn key subjects and also that there was a way of measuring standards. Before the National Curriculum was introduced, it was the responsibility of individual schools to decide what and how much to teach of any subject. As part of the National Curriculum, tests known as SATs (Statutory Assessment Tests) were also introduced at the end of each key stage.

Schools that are now academies no longer have to follow the National Curriculum, but they must ensure that their content and teaching is at least equivalent to the National Curriculum.

Key stages

The National Curriculum is divided into four stages. The table below shows the ages associated with each **key stage**.

Key Stage 1	5–7 years
Key Stage 2	7–11 years
Key Stage 3	11–14 years
Key Stage 4	14–16 years

▲ The ages associated with each key stage

The content of the National Curriculum is decided by the Department for Education. By law, the Department for Education is required to publish programmes of study for each National Curriculum subject. Schools can, however, organise how they teach the content provided that it is taught to all pupils. Subjects in the National Curriculum are split into **core subjects**, which are English, mathematics and science, and **foundation subjects**.

The table below lists the core and foundation subjects that are required at different key stages.

Key stages	1	2	3	4
Age	5–7	7–11	11–14	14–16
Year groups	1–2	3–6	7–9	10–11
Core subjects				
English	✔	✔	✔	✔
Mathematics	✔	✔	✔	✔
Science	✔	✔	✔	✔
Foundation subjects				
Art and design	✔	✔	✔	
Citizenship			✔	✔
Computing	✔	✔	✔	✔
Design and technology	✔	✔	✔	
Languages		✔	✔	
Geography	✔	✔	✔	
History	✔	✔	✔	
Music	✔	✔	✔	
Physical education	✔	✔	✔	✔

▲ The core and foundation subjects required at different key stages

Key Stage 4

Pupils in Key Stage 4 are preparing for GCSEs or other Level 2 qualifications, and so there is more flexibility since they have some choice over what they study. All pupils must still study English, mathematics and science; these are known as 'core' subjects. In addition, they must continue with computer science, physical education and citizenship, although they may not need to be assessed in these; these are known as foundation subjects. Pupils also have to take at least one subject from the following:

▶ arts (art and design, music, dance, drama and media arts)
▶ design and technology
▶ humanities (geography, history, religious education)
▶ modern foreign languages.

The EBacc (English Baccalaureate)

To encourage schools to offer pupils a spread of GCSEs that will give them a broad base of study, the government has introduced the **English Baccalaureate (EBacc)**. The EBacc is not a qualification in itself, but a performance indicator. Schools are measured on the number of pupils that take GCSEs in these subjects.

The EBacc is composed of:
▶ English language and literature
▶ maths
▶ the sciences (either two GCSEs that cover physics, chemistry and biology, or three single-science GCSEs, which might include computing science)
▶ geography or history
▶ a modern or ancient language.

Alternative options to GCSEs

Some schools will offer vocational qualifications alongside GCSEs. These may include technical qualifications in health and social care, business studies or travel and tourism.

> **Reflect**
>
> What subjects did you study at Key Stage 4?
>
> Which subjects did you take a GCSE or Level 2 vocational equivalent in?

Other requirements for schools

In addition to the National Curriculum, schools also have other teaching requirements, as described.

Worship and religious education

All state schools have to make provision for a daily act of collective worship – many schools will hold an assembly, for example. Schools must teach religious education to pupils at every key stage.

Relationships and sex education (RSE)

Primary schools are required to provide relationships education in Key Stages 1 and 2. Sex education is not compulsory in Key Stages 1 and 2, although primary schools will cover reproduction as part of the science curriculum. Where a primary school provides sex education, parents can choose to withdraw their child.

In Key Stages 3 and 4, schools must provide sex and relationships education. However, if they choose, parents can ask that their child be excused for all or some of the lessons.

Post-16 education: 16–19 (academic and technical)

After pupils have finished Key Stage 4, they have the following choices.
▶ Find a job.
▶ Begin an apprenticeship. Apprentices take a qualification while working for an employer. The apprentices are paid an apprentice wage, which is set by the government. Apprenticeships last between one and four years depending on the level of the qualification that is being taken.
▶ Take a traineeship. These are often short-term jobs with an employer that may later lead to an apprenticeship. The amount of training that takes place will depend on the employer.
▶ Study for a vocational qualification such as a T Level.
▶ Study for A-levels.

They may also combine work or volunteering (20 hours or more) with part-time education or training.

All young people must continue to study maths and English if they have not achieved Grade 4 in their GCSEs (or equivalent) as part of their post-16 education. They can either resit these GCSEs or take equivalents, e.g. in functional skills.

> **Reflect**
>
> ▶ Why did you choose to study a technical qualification?
> ▶ Did you consider any other post-16 routes?
> ▶ Do you know anyone who chose another route? How has this gone for them?

K1.1 The student must understand the requirements of each key stage of the school curriculum

We have seen above the requirements of the National Curriculum, how it is divided into four key stages and how some subjects are compulsory at different ages. We have also seen some of the other requirements for state schools such as the provision of religious and sex education. Other subjects that may be taught include personal, social and health education (PSHE) and citizenship at Key Stages 1 and 2, and modern foreign languages at Key Stage 1.

In this section, we look at the assessment requirements for each key stage.

Research

▶ Choose a key stage that links to a work placement.
▶ Look at the programme of study for English by visiting: **www.gov.uk/government/publications/national-curriculum-in-england-english-programmes-of-study**
▶ How does the programme of study link to the teaching on your work placement?

Assessments

To check that children and young people are making the expected progress, there are assessments at different stages. In Key Stages 1 and 2, these are referred to as Statutory Assessment Tests (SATS), and are in the core subjects of English, maths and science. Assessments are required by the Department for Education and the results of the assessments are shared with parents. In addition, the majority of data from the assessments is made public, although this data does not include details of individual children's attainment.

For more on assessments, see Core Chapter 8.

Phonics screening

In Year 1, there is a phonics assessment. This is to check that children have learned the sounds or phonics they will need in order to read.

See also synthetic phonics on page 46.

Research

You can find out more about the phonics test and look at a sample here: **www.gov.uk/government/publications/phonics-screening-check-sample-materials-and-training-video**

Key Stage 1

At the end of Key Stage 1, when children are in Year 2, there is a Key Stage 1 assessment. Children are assessed in mathematics, reading, writing and science. Some schools also choose to do tests in punctuation, spelling and grammar, but this is not compulsory. As well as the tests in reading and maths that are sent out to schools, teachers also have to assess children's progress using documents called teacher assessment frameworks. Parents are given the results of teacher assessments in a report. For mathematics, reading and writing, and science, children are judged to be one of the following:
▶ Working towards the expected standard
▶ Working at the expected standard
▶ Working at greater depth within the expected standard.

Research

Find out more about Key Stage 1 and 2 SATS at: **www.gov.uk/government/publications/key-stage-1-and-2-national-curriculum-tests-information-for-parents**

Key Stage 2

At the end of Key Stage 2, children are assessed on the subjects shown in the table below. Parents are given a report afterwards. The report includes either test results or teacher assessment judgements for each area.

Subject	Teacher assessed	Test
English grammar, punctuation and spelling		✔
English reading		✔
English writing	✔	
Mathematics		✔
Science	✔	

▲ How children are assessed at the end of Key Stage 2

As for Key Stage 1, parents are informed of their child's results for the test using the following judgements:

▶ Working towards the expected standard
▶ Working at the expected standard
▶ Working at greater depth within the expected standard.

The only exception is science, where there are only two judgements:

▶ Has not met the expected standard
▶ Is working at the expected standard.

At Key Stage 2 the range of scores in the tests is 80 to 120. Children who gain over 100 are working at or exceeding the expected standard. Children who gain under 100 are working below the expected standard. A score of below 100 should trigger more support for the child.

Key Stages 3 and 4

There are no formal assessments at the end of Key Stage 3, but teachers are required to track pupils' progress in Years 7, 8 and 9.

At the end of Key Stage 4, pupils will take GCSEs or Level 2 vocational qualifications such as Technical Awards or BTECs.

Research

Find out more about the standards that pupils need to achieve in Key Stages 1 and 2. Download a copy of a sample paper by typing 'Key Stage 1 assessments sample paper tests' into your browser. Look out for a website with **gov.uk** in its address.

What do you think about the difficulty of these papers?

2.2 How adults can effectively support children and young people in their education

There are many ways in which adults support children and young people with their education.

Involving children in planning their own learning

One of the ways that adults use to support children and young people is to involve them in planning for their own learning. This might mean asking pre-school children which resources and activities they might like. In a school setting, it might mean asking children or young people to choose projects to work on or decide on ways to present information. Involving children and young people is more likely to motivate them. This usually results in them concentrating harder, which means they are more likely to learn.

Reflect

In your placement, look at the ways in which adults give children and/or young people opportunities to plan their own learning.

What are the benefits of this approach?

Communicating clearly, using positive and appropriate language for age and stage of development

Being able to communicate well with children and young people is perhaps one of the most important

skills to master. To communicate well, you need to adapt what you are saying or how you are saying it to the individual child or young person. This means that the way an adult might communicate to a nervous three year old will be different to the communication style used with a confident fourteen year old. To communicate well you need to focus on the following elements.

Language level

You need to think about the language level of the child or young person. This is linked to their age and stage of development. It is worth remembering that some children and young people may be new to English. Some children and young people may have disabilities such as hearing loss, language delay or special educational needs that affect how easily they can understand spoken language.

See Core Chapter 12 for more on English as an additional language.

Facial expression and body language

Our faces and our bodies are important in communication. Positive communication such as smiling, using our hands or nodding when listening works well when providing information. On the other hand, when reprimanding or trying to prevent unwanted behaviour, adults may look sterner!

▲ Why is positive communication important in teaching young people?

Posture

Whether we stand, sit, kneel or squat makes a difference to communication. Positive communication is more likely when we are at the same level as the child or young person. This is particularly important to remember with young children. With older children and young people, there may be times when by standing rather than sitting you convey that you have authority. Standing over a child or young person is not, however, helpful when encouraging, coaching or supporting is our aim.

Proximity

Proximity refers to how close we are to the child or young person. Being at a distance can make it harder for a child or young person to pay attention. Ideally, for encouraging, supporting and coaching, you should aim to be fairly close, but not so close for it to feel threatening.

> **Reflect**
>
> Watch how adults in your placement setting communicate with children/young people.
> ▶ How do they hold their attention?
> ▶ How do they adapt their language and communication style to suit the situation or the individual they are working with?

Giving effective feedback and facilitating children's and young people's self-assessment

As part of being able to communicate with children and young people, we need to be able to provide them with feedback. We also need to help them analyse their own work and progress. This is called **self-assessment**. We look at feedback and self-assessment later in this chapter.

Managing your own and others' time

To work well with children and young people, you need to be organised. This includes time management: your own and other people's.

Managing your time

You need to be punctual, but also learn how long tasks take to do – for example, how long it takes to put up a display or set up a role-play area. Knowing how long things take means you can plan your time carefully. There are consequences when you do not manage your time. Children and young people who are waiting for things to be ready are more likely to show unwanted behaviour because they become bored. Colleagues and parents may also become frustrated with you and, over a period of time, may lose confidence in you.

Managing others' time

During lessons and activities, you need to keep an eye on the time and also judge how long it will take children and young people to do things. If adults do not do this well, there is a danger that children and young people will not have time to finish tasks and activities or tidy away. This can lead to children and young people feeling rushed or frustrated because they can never finish things. In some cases, the opposite can be true. Some children or young people may finish quickly and then become bored waiting. This is one reason why careful planning and differentiating activities is so important. Differentiating activities is about making sure that children and young people are given tasks that are matched to their level of skills and knowledge.

> **Practice points**
>
> Take the following steps to help you with time management.
> ▶ Wear a watch or keep a clock near you.
> ▶ Time how long it takes children and young people to do things such as collecting resources or tidying away.
> ▶ Allow more time when you are doing things for the first time.
> ▶ When planning activities and lessons always allow a little extra time.
> ▶ Watch how other adults manage their time.

Managing behaviour

Children and young people need adults to guide their behaviour so that they are able to learn. This is particularly important where children and young people are in groups. Disruptive behaviour can distract others from working and it may also prevent a child or young person from achieving their own potential.

> We look at ways of managing behaviour in Core Chapter 4.

Observing and assessing individuals

One of the ways we support education is to recognise the skills and knowledge that have been acquired by children and young people. This is done through observation and assessment, which are covered in Core Chapter 8.

As part of observing and assessing, we also need to identify where children or young people would benefit from having more support or teaching. **Early identification** is very important – the earlier we identify children and young people who need additional support, the better. This is because, otherwise, children may begin to believe that they are not capable and so lose motivation. The term **tailored intervention** is used to describe when we provide support that is designed to help children and young people develop a specific skill or piece of knowledge.

Key terms

Early identification: quickly recognising that a child or young person may need additional support.

Tailored intervention: designing support to help a child or young person pick up a specific skill or piece of knowledge.

Engaging disengaged children/young people by involving them in their own learning and assessment

Some children and young people can lose interest or motivation. As we saw a little earlier in this section, encouraging them to be involved in their learning and also assessment can be a good strategy.

Attributes that inform teachers'/practitioners' professional behaviour and why they are important to effectively support children's/young people's education

What makes a good teacher or practitioner? As well as using various skills, there are certain professional behaviours that are needed. The table below shows these professional behaviours and the reasons why they support children's and young people's education.

Approachability	When a child or young person needs more support or reassurance when they have a problem, they need an adult who looks friendly and kind.
Confidence	Children and young people need to feel secure. Adults who look and sound confident can help them feel safe.
Empathy	Adults need to understand how a child or young person might be feeling and then to show empathy.
Knowledge	Children and young people need adults who know about what they are teaching. For young children, it is important that adults also use accurate language.
Passion	Adults who work best with children and young people and love helping them, will love their work and want to be in the setting.
Patience	Children and young people learn things at different speeds. They may also work harder sometimes than others. Being patient is, therefore, essential.
Positivity	Adults who work well with children and young people manage to remain enthusiastic even when things are not going smoothly. They are positive with children and young people, but also with their colleagues and other adults.
Reflection	The ability to step back and think about a situation or a child's or young person's needs is essential. Being able to reflect can allow us to change how we are doing things, to make it easier for children and young people to learn.
Resourcefulness	Being able to think creatively and also think quickly is important for adults working with children and young people. It may be that a piece of equipment that was key to an activity is broken and we quickly have to come up with a new activity.
Respect for others	Adults who work well in education and childcare settings have respect for others. This shows in their relationships with colleagues, parents and also with children and young people. By showing respect for children and young people, we are also acting as role models for them in their relationships with others.

▲ Professional behaviours and how they support children's and young people's education

Chris is a Key Stage 2 teacher. He specialises in science teaching and takes different year groups across the school. The children respond well to him. He has a sense of humour, but can also be firm where necessary. He is kind and warm and goes out of his way to support children who need a little more time for their learning. One of the reasons why the children enjoy his teaching is that he surprises them with new experiments. He also follows children's interests and encourages them to be active in their learning. He looks at the outcomes that need to be taught and thinks about the best way to make them interesting for children. When it is his turn to teach a class, he arrives on time and has with him the resources he needs. His colleagues respect and like him because he is reliable, friendly and always ready to help out.

▶ What attributes does Chris show?
▶ How do these attributes help him to be an effective teacher?
▶ What impact might Chris have on children's education?

2.3 Theoretical approaches to learning

How do children and young people learn? Is learning linked to growth and development? How can adults support children's and young people's learning? These are the questions that people have been trying to answer for a long time. There are now a number of theories that influence practice in education and childcare settings. While some theories contradict one another, others complement one another. When looking at different theories, it is also worth looking at when they were developed. Some theories may now seem out of date because they were developed when society was different and also without the benefit of modern science.

Behaviourist approach

The **behaviourist** approach to learning suggests that we learn as a result of what happens to us. The term for this is **external stimuli**. A child looking at a book may associate books with pleasure if an adult praises them when they look at a book. A pupil might learn their times tables because a reward is offered if all of the answers are correct.

There are many criticisms of the behaviourist approach to children's learning. It is considered by many to be too passive and to suggest that the child or young person does not take responsibility for or shape their own learning. It also does not give an account of how children's and young people's logic changes over time as they grow and develop (**internal cognitive processes**).

For the purposes of this qualification, the key principles of the behaviourist approach are as follows:
▶ Behaviour is shaped by external stimuli, rather than internal cognitive processes.
▶ Positive and negative reinforcement can modify behaviour and learning (**operant conditioning** – see below).

▶ Continuity is central to long-term associations.

(While these are the principles listed for this qualification, it is important to note that they may not be recognised in other contexts.)

Different theories of behaviourism

Behaviourism is a term that covers theories that in practice are quite different to one another. There are, for example, two **theories of conditioning** that we will look at: classical and operant conditioning. In addition, there is **social learning theory**, which has an element of operant conditioning within it but is otherwise very different.

The difference between classical and operant conditioning

The key difference between classical and operant conditioning is the timing of the external stimuli. With **classical conditioning**, the external stimuli occurs before or at the time of the action. In operant conditioning, the external stimuli (sometimes a reward) occurs afterwards.

Classical conditioning

Two names are associated with classical conditioning: Pavlov and Watson. Classical conditioning is not normally used as a teaching strategy in education settings.

Ivan Pavlov, 1849–1936

Pavlov was a Russian physiologist. He is famous because of his work with dogs and his theory that became known as 'classical conditioning'. As a result of other research he was doing, Pavlov noticed that just before dogs were about to be fed, they produced a lot of saliva. He was interested in why this occurred. He devised an experiment where some dogs heard a buzzer before they were fed. He then noted that, after a while, these dogs produced saliva when only the buzzer occurred. He called this a 'conditioned reflex'.

Pavlov also looked at what would happen if the buzzer rang repeatedly and no food was offered to the dogs. He found that, gradually, the conditioned response (dogs salivating) became weaker until finally the dogs did not react to the buzzer at all. The term used by behaviourists when this happens is **extinction**.

Links to educational practice
▶ Pavlov's work was limited to animals.
▶ His work was built on by others and sparked interest in experiments that later became operant conditioning.

John B. Watson, 1878–1958

Pavlov's work was subsequently built on by Watson, who showed that it was possible to use classical conditioning on humans. In a famous experiment known as 'Little Albert', Watson was able to make a baby afraid of a white rat. The baby had previously shown no fear of rats. During the experiment, every time the baby tried to touch the rat, a loud sound was made. This alarmed the baby. After a short time, whenever the baby saw a rat or a furry animal, he would be frightened.

Links to educational practice
While, overall, this theory is not used in practice, it may help adults understand the responses of a child or young person who may show an 'irrational fear' of an object or situation because it is associated with a trauma they have experienced, e.g. a child who is frequently abused by being hit with a shoe may show fear when in nursery an adult starts to change their shoes.

Operant conditioning

Two names are particularly used in connection with operant conditioning: Thorndike and Skinner. Operant conditioning has developed over time and is now used as a way of modifying children's and young people's behaviour.

Edward Thorndike, 1874–1949

Thorndike showed through experiments with cats that the consequences of a behaviour would influence subsequent behaviour. He called this the **law of effect**.

In his experiments, hungry cats were put into a 'puzzle box', which had a lever that allowed the cats to escape. The cats could see from inside the box a piece of fish,

which they were able to eat every time they escaped. At first the cats took about five minutes to escape and did so the first time purely through trial and error. After this, they were able to reduce the time it took them to escape until it took less than five seconds.

Thorndike suggested that the cats learned to operate the lever because their behaviour had been rewarded, or 'stamped in', by being able to escape and in particular by eating the fish. His theory was later known as 'operant conditioning' and was the starting point for later work on human learning and behaviour.

B.F. Skinner, 1904–1990

Skinner adopted and furthered the work of Thorndike into the now accepted model of 'operant conditioning'. While Skinner accepted the work of Pavlov and Watson, he suggested, however, that most humans and animals learn through exploring the environment and then drawing conclusions based on the consequences of their behaviour. This means that we tend to be active in the learning process, which is an important difference from classical conditioning.

Skinner divided the consequences of actions into three groups:
1 Positive reinforcers
2 Negative reinforcers
3 Punishments.

Positive reinforcers are likely to make us repeat behaviour where we get something we desire – for example, we may buy a new food product after having tried and liked a free sample. Skinner suggested that using positive reinforcement was the most effective way of encouraging new learning. Positive reinforcers for children include gaining adults' attention, praise, stickers, sweets and treats.

▲ How might this sticker affect how this child behaves in the future?

Negative reinforcers are likely to make us repeat behaviour as well, but this is usually to stop something from occurring. If a parent continually nags a child to tidy up and the child gets tired of being nagged, they might tidy up in order to stop the nagging.

Punishers are likely to stop us from repeating behaviour – for example, we may learn to stay away from an electric fence after receiving a shock.

There are also **unexpected positive reinforcers**. For instance, Skinner found during his experiments that it was often hard to predict what would act as a positive reinforcer and that it was sometimes only after the event that this became clear – an example of this is when children sometimes deliberately behave badly in order to attract an adult's attention. If they manage to attract the desired attention, they are more likely to show the behaviour again despite being told off. Gaining the adult's attention in this case is the positive reinforcer even if they are being told off.

It is also worth noting that sometimes the action of the child or young person will in itself be the positive reinforcer – for example, a toddler might repeatedly climb on to a table because they have learned that they like the sensation of climbing.

There are some reinforcers that give us instant pleasure or satisfaction, or meet a need. These are referred to as primary reinforcers. Chocolate is a **primary reinforcer** because most people find that once they put it into their mouths, they enjoy the taste. **Secondary reinforcers** are different because they in themselves do not give us satisfaction, but we learn that they symbolise getting primary reinforcement. A good example of secondary reinforcement in our daily lives is money. Coins and notes in themselves do not give us reward, but we learn that they can be used to buy something that will give us primary reinforcement (e.g. food).

Star charts and systems where children and young people have to collect tokens or stickers in order eventually to get a reward are examples of secondary reinforcers. Secondary reinforcers require a certain level of cognitive development for them to be effective. A toddler, for example, may not understand how a sticker they have been given will lead to something else later. This means that, with young children, using primary reinforcers at the right time is more likely to be effective.

Skinner looked at the effect that giving positive reinforcements at different intervals (**frequency of reinforcement**) would have on behaviour. How long would behaviour be shown without a positive reinforcement before extinction took place? He found that if positive reinforcement stopped and did not return, over time the behaviour would cease. Interestingly, he found that unpredictable reinforcement works better than continual reinforcement. This would seem to work because it teaches the learner not to expect a reward or reinforcement every time, hence, they keep on showing the behaviour just in case a reinforcement is given.

In everyday life, this is one of the reasons why gamblers find it so hard to stop playing. They know that they will not win every time, but carry on just in case they get lucky.

> **Reflect**
>
> Using the theory of reinforcement, why might it be worth ignoring attention-seeking behaviour rather than responding to it?

Delaying positive reinforcement – for example, saying to a child that they can have a sticker at the end of the week – may weaken the effect of the reinforcement. Immediate positive reinforcements are the most effective, partly because the behaviour is then more strongly linked to the reinforcement.

Links to educational practice
- Rewards are often given for behaviour, but also for achievement.
- Star charts are often used to improve the behaviour of individuals, but also groups.
- Praise is given to encourage behaviour and also to encourage effort.
- Some behaviours are ignored so as not to reinforce them.

Criticisms of operant conditioning
- Children and young people should be encouraged to learn because they enjoy it, rather than to achieve rewards.
- Research suggests that self-motivation is more effective in the long term than short-term praise and rewards.
- This approach to education assumes that children and young people are passive learners and cannot take responsibility for or be involved in their own learning (see page 25).

Albert Bandura, born 1925

Bandura is known for recognising that children could learn by watching others, and devising an experiment to prove this. The term **modelling** is often used to explain the process by which children learn by copying others. The person doing the action is the 'role model'.

Bandura's theory was originally called social learning theory, but he later renamed it **social cognitive theory**. His theory is partly a behaviourist one because it argues that when children and young people see that some actions might be rewarded or punished, this influences their behaviour. However, his theory also suggests that children are active in their learning and that thought is needed: children need to extract and remember relevant information in order to learn. Bandura's theory also emphasises the social aspect of learning, as children learn while watching others.

In his famous 'bobo doll' experiment, Bandura showed three groups of children a film. The film showed the children an adult in a room with a bobo doll (a large inflatable doll). The three groups of children each saw a different variation on the behaviour of the adult.

▶ Group A saw the adult acting aggressively to the doll.
▶ Group B saw the adult being aggressive towards the doll, but at the end of the film the adult was rewarded with sweets and lemonade by another adult.
▶ Group C saw the adult being aggressive towards the doll, but at the end a second adult appeared and told off the first adult.

After the film, each child was shown in turn into a playroom where there was a variety of toys, including the bobo doll. The reactions of the children were recorded. Group C children were the least aggressive towards the doll, but there was little difference between groups A and B. This suggested that they were less influenced by the reward that had been offered to the adult.

A follow-up to the experiment asked the children if they could demonstrate how the doll had been attacked, and they were rewarded for doing so. There was little difference between the three groups of children, which showed that they could all imitate the behaviour they had seen.

Since his original experiment, Bandura has proposed that there are factors that affect whether or not a child will copy what they have seen.

▶ Attention: Whether the child is focusing on what the adult is doing.
▶ Retention: Whether and how much the child can remember of what they have seen.
▶ Reproduction: Whether the child has the skills to be able to repeat what they have seen.
▶ Motivation: Whether the child is keen to repeat what has been modelled and also whether they believe they have the capacity to do so (self-efficacy, see below).

Bandura's later work also considered a concept he called **self-efficacy**. This is linked to **self-concept** and the beliefs that children have about their capacity to learn. If children do not have strong self-efficacy, they may not have the motivation to learn a new skill.

> We look at self-concept in Core Chapter 4.

▲ How has the play of these children been influenced by adults?

It is worth noting that social cognitive theory complements other approaches to education we will look at later in this chapter. The element of children learning by being with others links to Vygotsky's and Bruner's work (see pages 33 and 34). In addition, the cognitive aspect of memory and analysis links to cognitive theories of learning.

Links to educational practice
▶ Children are more likely to show an interest in learning something when they see an adult doing it.
▶ Adults use this theory when teaching skills; they may demonstrate a skill, but then encourage children or young people to have a go for themselves.
▶ Adults working with children are seen as 'role models' and so are expected to show appropriate behaviours.

Criticisms of social cognitive theory

This theory is widely accepted as a way of understanding how children and young people may sometimes learn from others. That being said, as its focus is on external stimuli, such as children learning from things that they notice others doing, it does not focus on the child as an independent learner.

Case study

Nova is two years old. She is an active toddler. Today she has watched her father open the kitchen bin by pressing down on the lid. When he was not watching, she repeated his action. She is delighted with the way the lid flips up and the feeling she has when she presses it down again. She opens and closes the bin several times before her father tells her not to do it. Whenever she can, she goes over to the bin to open and close it.

▶ Using social cognitive theory, explain how Nova has learned to open and close the bin.
▶ Using Skinner's operant conditioning theory, explain why she is repeating this action even though she has been told to stop.
▶ Why might the immediate reinforcement provided by the lid flipping up make this behaviour stronger?

Cognitivist approach

The **cognitivist approach to learning** stresses the **cognitive** processes (i.e. thinking) that take place in the brain, such as memory and connecting new information to existing information. This approach is also known as the **information processing** model. The role of memory and how information is presented are considered to be particularly important.

For the purposes of this qualification, the key principles of the cognitivist approach are listed as:

▶ the act or process of knowing is driven by mental processes, rather than the environment
▶ individuals process new information by making links with prior knowledge
▶ learning is measured by a change in an individual's **schema** (see page 31, where we discuss the work of Piaget)
▶ instruction should be logical and well structured.

Key term

Schema: a pattern of thought or behaviour.

Note that these principles may not be recognised in other contexts.

Key theorists

For the purposes of this qualification, the theorists described below are linked to cognitivist theory. (Note that Bruner and Piaget are more commonly associated with the constructivist approach. We look at their work in that section, on pages 31 and 34.)

Robert Gagné, 1916–2002

Robert Gagné's work is based on information processing theory. It has been widely adopted for the instruction of military personnel and as such is sometimes referred to as **instructional theory**. Gagné's work suggests that there are different types of learning as well as different levels of learning. Teachers have to identify the type or types of learning that are involved in a task and tailor a programme accordingly. Gagné suggests that instruction is most effective if the teacher has identified detailed and clear objectives, and that learning should be a step-by-step process.

Gagné suggests that there are five broad types of learning:
1 Verbal information
2 Intellectual skill
3 Cognitive strategy
4 Attitude
5 **Motor skill**.

By identifying what type, or types, of skill is needed for new learning to take place, teaching can be more effective. Gagné uses the term **taxonomy**, meaning 'a system of identification and naming'.

Key term

Motor skills: physical movements.

As well as identifying different types of learning, Gagné also suggested that, for each type of learning, different **internal and external conditions** needed to be considered. Internal conditions are things that the learner already knows, feels or can do. External conditions are the things that the teacher needs to provide.

Once teachers have identified what the learning objective is and also the learning conditions, Gagné suggests that teachers or instructors need to structure their teaching. He outlined nine **instructional events** that form a clear process, as follows.

1 **Gaining attention:** Making sure that learners are ready to learn and are paying attention.
2 **Informing learners of the objective:** Telling learners about what they are going to be taught.
3 **Stimulating recall of prerequisite learning:** Reminding learners about skills or knowledge that will be important for this new skill or concept.
4 **Presenting the stimulus material:** Beginning the teaching and showing learners what they will need to do.
5 **Providing learning guidance:** Explaining or showing learners how to approach the task.
6 **Eliciting the performance:** Supporting or advising learners as they are completing the task.
7 **Providing feedback:** Giving learners comments about how they are doing or have done.
8 **Assessing the performance:** Assessing how well individual learners have managed the task.
9 **Enhancing retention and transfer:** Making sure that learners will be able to retain the information and apply it to new tasks.

Case study

The class needs to learn about measuring using millimetres. The lesson starts with the teacher laying out three items: a measuring tape, a metre stick and a ruler. The teacher says that by the end of the lesson they will be able to accurately measure something quite small. He reminds the class of how they measured objects rounding up to the nearest centimetre. The teacher then puts out some small objects and a ruler. He shows the children how they hold the ruler and line it up against the object. The children then choose something to measure. The teacher encourages each child and helps them where necessary. He then asks the children to each choose a new object and to measure it alone. The teacher observes which children have mastered this new learning. He then encourages the children to practise this skill. For homework, they have to choose three different sizes of items to measure.
▶ Which types of learning are used by children while learning to measure?
▶ For each stage of the lesson, can you map it to Gagné's nine instructional events?
▶ Can you explain why the step-by-step approach to learning this skill helped some children?

Links to educational practice
▶ This approach is rarely used in early years settings. However, many schools have adopted Gagné's method when planning the curriculum and also individual lessons.
▶ Most teachers now explain the objectives of a lesson to children.
▶ Step-by-step instruction and checking that children and young people have gained the requisite skills and knowledge are widely used as techniques for teaching.

Criticisms of Gagné's approach
▶ This approach does not allow for children and young people to lead their own learning.
▶ Some teachers use the nine-step instructional events in ways that make their lessons boring because they do not pick up on children's or young people's interests or spontaneous events. Interestingly, though, learners' motivation and interest is considered important by Gagné.
▶ Gagné does not focus on the emotional and social aspects of learning.

Carol Dweck, born 1946

Carol Dweck has proposed a concept sometimes known as **mind-set theory**. It focuses on the beliefs that children and young people have about intelligence. It does not consider the cognitive processes by which children and young people learn information. For the purposes of this qualification, Carol Dweck is in the list of cognitivist approaches, but it is worth noting that this will not be recognised in other contexts.

Carol Dweck is known for her work on **implicit intelligence** theory. This theory considers how children's thinking about intelligence affects how well they do. Some children think that intelligence is something they cannot change – they are either clever or not. This, in turn, may affect how much effort and practice a child puts in to their learning and also how they cope with any setbacks. A child who sees themselves as intelligent will work hard, believing that they are capable. A child who views themselves as not so clever may give up quickly. Dweck calls this a **fixed mind-set**.

Key term

Fixed mind-set: when a person believes that their intelligence and ability to learn cannot be altered.

The other mind-set that some children have is called a **growth mind-set**. These are children who believe that, with effort, practice and support, they will be able to achieve. Children and young people with a growth mind-set tend to persevere, seek help when needed and are ready to practise skills in order to master them. They do not expect instant success.

> ### Key term
>
> **Growth mind-set:** when a person believes that they can control their learning and outcomes through hard work, practice and by asking for help.

Dweck's work shows that some children and young people who are not doing so well can be helped by encouraging them to **develop a growth mind-set**. This can be achieved by teaching them a little about the brain and how it can change over time if skills and activities are practised. The role of praise, and what adults say to children and young people, matters. Comments such as 'well done, you are clever' are not seen as helpful under this theory because the role of effort and perseverance is not stressed.

Bandura's later work looks at **self-efficacy**, which we considered earlier (page 27). There are links between Bandura's work on self-efficacy (i.e. whether a child views themselves as essentially capable) and Dweck's work.

Links to educational practice

▶ Some children and young people give up quickly if they believe they cannot achieve. They may not even try something new. Adults should praise children and young people for the skills of perseverance and effort rather than their results.
▶ Teachers can help children and young people to develop a growth mind-set by supporting them to set themselves achievable goals and encouraging a step-by-step approach so that the goals are met.

Criticisms of mind-set theory

▶ This is a relatively new theory and it has been widely adopted by some schools. There are criticisms of this work, however. These include the point that the findings of Dweck and her colleagues cannot easily be reproduced.
▶ In addition, some studies have shown that it makes only a small difference to children's and young people's test scores.

> ### Case study
>
> Martha is 12 years old. She hates maths lessons. As soon as she enters the classroom, she feels stressed. She has stopped listening and working during maths lessons. When asked about this, she says that there is no point as she is no good at maths. Her parents also say that they were never any good at maths and so she thinks that it runs in families. Every time there is a test, she scores very badly. When she was younger, Martha wanted to be an architect. After finding out that maths was needed, she changed her mind and is thinking about going into the tourism industry.
> ▶ Explain why Martha's attitude towards maths is an example of a 'fixed mind-set'.
> ▶ How is this affecting her later options when it comes to careers?
> ▶ Why will it be important for teachers to work with her to develop a 'growth' mind-set?

Constructivist approach

There are two broad theories within this category: **constructivist** and **social constructivist**. Both agree that children are active learners and construct their thinking as a result of experiences. Social constructivists believe that interactions with adults, children or young people are significant.

Key principles

For the purposes of this qualification, the key principles of the constructivist approach are:
▶ Individuals create their own understanding by linking new information to previous experiences and cultural factors.
▶ Knowledge is constructed through interactions between teacher and student, in which the teacher **scaffolds** learning to encourage greater independence.
▶ Instruction is organised around problem solving, projects and cooperative learning.

While these are the principles listed for this qualification, it is important to note that they may not be recognised in other contexts.

> ### Key term
>
> **Scaffolding:** the way an adult supports children's and young people's learning through questions and comments.

John Dewey, 1859–1952

John Dewey was a philosopher, but also had strong views on children's education, founding his own school in the university where he worked. He believed that children can and should be active in their learning. He suggested that teaching should be based on real-life experiences and centred around children's interests and what is meaningful to them. Needing to measure something in real life, for example, would be the starting point of learning the concepts around measurement.

The term **experiential learning** is often linked with Dewey's work. This term refers to the idea that children learn from first-hand experiences and doing things rather than just hearing about them. The role of the adult was also important for Dewey. Adults would assist children in their problem solving rather than dictate how something should be learned.

Links to educational practice

▶ Children and young people have the capacity to learn for themselves.

▶ It is important to make things relevant to children and young people.

▶ Activities need to be based on what is meaningful and of interest to children and young people.

Jean Piaget, 1896–1980

Jean Piaget was originally a zoologist but became involved in intelligence testing of children. He soon became fascinated by the way that young children seemed to have their own logic and that quite often groups of children of the same age gave the same incorrect answers. Having observed his own children closely and also having carried out experiments with children of different ages, he created a theory that not only explains how children learn, but also how their cognitive development changes over time.

Piaget came to the conclusion that children develop patterns of actions and thinking that provide them with conclusions about the world. He called these **schemas**. A child might, for example, develop a schema that all trousers are blue because their trousers are blue. Piaget suggested that there come times when children are forced to adapt their conclusions. The child might be given a pair of dark-red trousers. Piaget gave specific terms to the process by which young children would need to develop or adapt new schemas, as shown in the diagram.

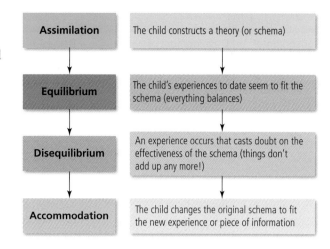

▲ Piaget's theory of how children develop or change existing schemas

The process of absorbing new information and then developing new schemas to accommodate the new information is why the term 'constructivist' is used to describe Piaget's theory: children and young people are 'constructing' their thoughts.

> **Reflect**
>
> Piaget suggested that schemas can be physical as well as ways of thinking about things. Think about how you brush your teeth. Do you always start in the same place? This would be an example of a physical schema.
>
> What other physical schemas are part of your daily routine?

> **Research**
>
> The concept of the child as an active learner is reflected in the Early Years Foundation Stage.
> ▶ Read the section of the EYFS relating to the characteristics of learning.
> ▶ How does this relate to Piaget's view that children learn using their experiences?

Piaget also suggested that, as children develop and have more experiences, this is reflected in their thinking. He grouped children's cognitive development into four broad stages. Each stage has certain features. The table below outlines these **stages of cognitive development**.

Stage	Features	Explanation of features
Sensorimotor (0–2 years)	Development of object permanence Child begins to use symbols, e.g. language	Babies' first schemas are physical ones; they learn to repeat movements and control them. By 8–9 months, babies gain the concept of **object permanence**. This means they search for objects that have been hidden rather than accept that they have 'disappeared'. Babies start to understand that words have meanings – thus they are starting to use symbols.
Preoperational (2–7 years)	Child uses symbols in play and thought Egocentrism Animism Inability to conserve	Children become active users of symbols, especially in their play (e.g. a cardboard box is used as an oven). Children assume that their experiences and preferences are shared by everyone else. Piaget called this **egocentrism**. They talk about or draw objects as if they had feelings too (e.g. a sun with a happy face). Piaget called this **animism**. Children have not yet understood conservation (see below).
Concrete operations (7–11 years)	Ability to conserve Children begin to solve mental problems using practical supports such as counters and objects	Children understand that just because objects may have been reordered, the quantity remains the same: ten counters in a circle is the same as ten counters in a straight line. Piaget called this **conservation**. Children understand the importance of rules and enjoy games that have rules. They also impose rules on others (e.g. 'You can't put that there!'). They use everyday objects and their own experiences to help them solve and think about problems (e.g. a child makes a bridge that looks like one that they have seen).
Formal operations (11–15 years)	Solving abstract problems without props Ability to analyse and hypothesise	Young people are now able to manipulate thoughts and ideas to solve problems without needing practical props (e.g. reading a map). They are able to hypothesise about situations in a realistic way (e.g. 'What would you do if someone gave you £1000 to do badly in an exam?'). Interestingly, Piaget suggested that formal operations did not develop automatically and that, later in life, experience and training may be needed in some areas.

▲ Piaget's stages of cognitive development

▲ How is the child showing animism in this drawing?

Conservation

It is interesting to repeat one of Piaget's tests with children. Ask your placement supervisor if you can observe a child in your setting aged four years. Set out eight buttons in a row. Count the buttons with the child. Agree that there are eight buttons there. Move the buttons around to form a close group. Ask the child if there are still the same number.

Links to educational practice

▶ Young children may not be cognitively ready to learn abstract concepts.

▶ Young children can learn from doing and are active learners.

▶ Recognition that the environment is important in children's learning.

▶ Children's thoughts and logic may be different from adults'.

Criticisms of Piaget's work

▶ There have been many criticisms of Piaget's work, although some elements such as 'animism' and 'egocentrism' are generally recognised.

▶ The main criticism is that he may have underestimated what children can do. With instruction, but also repeated experience, children may be able to understand more.

▶ Piaget did not emphasise the role of the adult in supporting children's learning. This meant in the early days of his theory being adopted, many education settings felt that a stimulating environment would be sufficient for children to learn from.

▶ Waiting for children to be ready before exposing them to a concept may hold them back.

Social constructivist approach

Like the constructivist approach, social constructivist theory agrees that children are active learners and construct their thinking as a result of experiences. In addition, social constructivists believe that interactions between the child and adults or older children are significant.

Key theorists

Vygotsky and Bruner are known for their interest in social interactions and how these enable children to learn and develop. While Piaget did not focus on the role of the adult or teacher, social constructivists view the role of the adult as essential in children's learning.

Lev Vygotsky, 1896–1934

Lev Vygotsky, a Russian who was working at around the same time as Piaget, also came to the view that children were active in their learning. He suggested, however, that the role of interaction between adults (or older children) and the child was of great significance. Young children were in effect apprentices learning from watching, interacting and being coached by adults or older children.

His theory is, therefore, sometimes referred to as a **social constructivist model**. Value is placed on the social dimension of learning. According to Vygotsky, children developed more sophisticated thinking and reasoning through interactions that he referred to as **higher-level thinking**.

One of the most influential parts of Vygotsky's theory is the **zone of proximal development**. The zone of proximal development is a term that Vygotsky used to describe the way in which children's cognition develops through adult interaction. It refers to the potential difference between a child's current abilities and what they might be able to achieve given adult encouragement and interaction. To understand this, it is worth looking at an example of what it means in practice, as shown in the illustration.

1) The adult observes that the child is able to count objects one by one.

2) The adult shows the child how to count in pairs.

3) Eventually, the child learns how to do this alone.

▲ The zone of proximal development in practice

In the example shown, the child could count, but had not seen or discovered how to count in pairs. With the adult's help, the child's development has been extended.

Links to educational practice

▶ Vygotsky's work has had a significant influence in education settings, especially in early years.
▶ Observing and assessing children in order to work out their 'next steps'.
▶ Encouraging mixed-aged groups and mentoring so younger children learn from older ones.
▶ Groups of children and young people working together.

Jerome Bruner, 1915–2016

Jerome Bruner was influenced by Piaget and especially influenced by the work of Vygotsky. His work has several aspects. First, he suggested that there are different modes of thinking. As adults we are able to access all of them, but children acquire them over time, as shown in the following table.

Enactive 0–1 years	Learning and thought takes place because of physical movements
Iconic 1–6 years	Thoughts are developed as mental images (e.g. a child thinks about milk and sees in their head a picture of it)
Symbolic 7 years +	Thinking can be encoded using symbols such as language or numbers (e.g. a child can write down their thoughts)

▲ How children acquire different modes of thinking over time

Like Vygotsky, Bruner believed that adults play a vital role in children's development. He suggested that children could learn anything provided the information was sufficiently simplified and presented to them in a way they could access. He proposed that a **spiral curriculum** would be an effective way of teaching children: they would learn something at a simplified level, then it could be repeatedly covered in increasing depth. While Bruner suggested that information had to be presented at the right level, he felt that children learned best when they were able to discover things for themselves. This has been called 'discovery learning'. He was opposed to rote learning and saw the role of the adult as that of facilitator.

Bruner also valued play as a tool for children's learning, but suggested through his research that adults are able to enrich and develop children's learning if they join children in play. He showed, through observing children in a range of different play settings, that when children played without any adult input, their play and ideas were less sophisticated than when adults were involved.

Links to educational practice

▶ Inquiry-based education where children are supported to learn for themselves.
▶ Adults involved in children's play.

Criticisms of social constructivist approaches

▶ Children and young people may not make sufficient progress due to lack of formal instruction.
▶ Social constructivist approaches in practice require higher adult–child ratios than is possible in education settings.

Humanist approach

Humanism is a type of philosophy that views people as essentially good and capable. The humanist approach to education focuses on the feelings, attitudes and welfare of the child or young person. There is a belief that humans have a thirst for knowledge and learning, and that the role of the adult is to provide the right conditions for children and young people, who should be trusted with their own learning.

Key principles

For the purposes of this qualification, the key principles of the humanist approach are as follows.

▶ Learning is a holistic experience in which individuals construct knowledge in the context of their own unique feelings, values and experiences.

▶ Feelings are as important as knowledge in the learning process.

▶ Teachers facilitate personalised, student-led education.

While these are the principles listed for this qualification, it is important to note that they may not be recognised in other contexts.

For this qualification, the following theorists are linked with this approach:

▶ Bronfenbrenner
▶ Knowles
▶ Maslow.

Urie Bronfenbrenner, 1917–2005

Bronfenbrenner is known for his **ecological systems** theory, later renamed **bioecological system**. He argued that children's and young people's development is influenced by a wide range of environmental factors: their parents and teachers, but also their community and, in turn, the wider society and culture in which they live.

His theory is often presented as a diagram like that shown here.

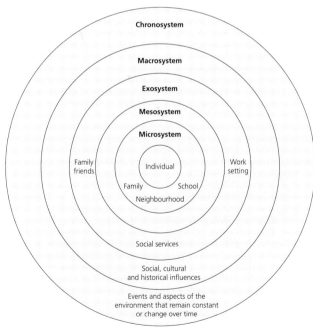

▲ Bronfenbrenner's ecological systems theory

Bronfenbrenner's 'ecological (or bioecological) system' is composed of the following parts.

▶ **Microsystem:** This refers to the child's immediate environment such as parents, siblings, teachers and friends.

▶ **Mesosystem:** This looks at the relationship between different elements of the microsystem, e.g. if a parent disagrees with another family member, both in the child's microsystem, their conflict may affect the child's learning and development. When a teacher and a parent have a good relationship and share information, on the other hand, this is likely to have a positive effect on the child's learning and development.

▶ **Exosystem:** This looks at how events, people and places that the child is not directly connected to can still have a direct influence on their learning and development. The closure of a local Jobcentre, for instance, may affect how easily the child's parent can look for work. This, in turn, affects the stress levels of the parent and their interactions with the child.

▶ **Macrosystem:** This is the wider environment and context in which the child or young person lives. It includes the culture, religious values, economy and politics of the country in which the child or young person lives. A child who grows up in a prosperous country may have free education for longer and access to better health services.

▶ **Chronosystem:** These are the events that occur during the child's or young person's life that may have an effect on their development, such as growing up in a time of war. Recently, for example, children and young people have been living during a pandemic; their own lives and the lives of their family members will have been changed as a result.

Links to educational practice

▶ An understanding that wider issues such as poverty and attitudes in the community may affect children's and young people's learning and development.

▶ Increased involvement of parents and local communities in some education settings.

Criticisms of Bronfenbrenner's theory

▶ The theory is difficult to prove or disprove.

▶ It does not explain how some children growing up in the most difficult circumstances may still manage to succeed.

Rufus lives with his parents and older sister in a comfortable neighbourhood. They have a garden and his grandparents live close by. Rufus's parents are both employed and have good jobs. Rufus is looked after by a local childminder, who is a friend of the family, and also by his grandparents. Since his older sister's birth, Rufus's parents have been part of a parenting network. The parents in the group often message one another, share photographs and offer one another advice. They often all meet up for barbecues.

Recently, Rufus's mother's employer has offered her the chance to study for a degree, thanks to a scheme set up by the government, which is keen to improve education for adults in the workforce, in the hope that a more educated workforce will help the economy out of recession. Rufus's mother is enjoying studying, but it has meant she has had less time to spend with Rufus and sometimes she becomes quite stressed.

▶ What are the direct influences on Rufus? Using Bronfenbrenner's theory, identify some of the indirect influences on Rufus.

▶ Why is it important for adults working with children to think about the context in which children live?

Malcolm Knowles, 1913–1997

Malcolm Knowles focused on adult education in his research. He believed that adults learn differently to children and young people, developing a theory that is referred to as **adult learning theory**. This theory does not look at the cognitive process that takes place during learning, but instead looks at how to provide the best conditions for adults to learn. This includes assumptions about adults that the teacher or trainer needs to consider. Since developing his original ideas in the 1960s, Knowles has revised and added to the theory.

Knowles suggested that the starting point for the teacher or tutor is to recognise that adults have different attitudes, experiences and knowledge from children or young people. He proposed five **key assumptions** that teachers or tutors need to make:

1   **Self-concept:** Adults who come to learn are aware of their strengths and weaknesses and so are more likely to be confident.
2   **Adult experience:** Adults as learners already come to the lecture hall or classroom with life experiences and sometimes prior knowledge. This needs to be recognised by the tutor or teacher.

3   **Readiness to learn:** Adults who come to learn have chosen to do so, and are ready and willing to learn. This differs from the case with children and young people, where school or lessons are compulsory.
4   **Orientation to learning:** Adults who come to learn have reasons for doing so and a good idea of what they want to learn. Teachers or tutors need to understand what an individual adult wants from her or his learning.
5   **Motivation to learn:** Adults have a strong inner motivation to learn. Stickers and praise that might work with children or young people will not be effective, and will be seen as patronising to an adult.

Based on these assumptions, Knowles suggested that there were four principles that tutors and teachers should consider when **designing courses** and **delivering sessions**.

1   **Involvement:** Adults have to be involved in decisions about their learning. Unlike children and young people, where schools make all the decisions about what is to be taught, adults like to be part of the process.
2   **Experiences:** Adults like to learn by drawing on and building upon their experiences. Teachers and tutors need to consider this.
3   **Relevance:** As adults have a clear idea of what they want to learn, it is important that material is relevant. They need to understand why what they are learning is directly useful for them to know.
4   **Problem solving:** Hands-on and problem solving approaches are preferred by adults, rather than just being lectured with content.

Links to educational practice

▶ Knowles' work has influenced a range of organisations that create materials and training for adults.
▶ Many trainers and lecturers use this approach to develop their courses and to deliver training.
▶ Group discussions and tasks are often used as a way of sharing and developing best practice in a variety of sectors.

Criticisms of adult learning theory

▶ Not all adults come to learning by choice. They may be sent by an employer or may need to gain a qualification.
▶ Some adults may find it hard to motivate and organise themselves if they have not developed these skills.

Abraham Maslow, 1908–1970

Maslow was a well-known humanist. He is particularly known for suggesting that humans have a hierarchy of needs: **physiological needs**, **safety needs**, **love and belonging**, **esteem** and **self-actualisation**. Each need has to be met in order for humans to be able to realise their potential. Maslow's hierarchy of needs is a theory of motivation and has been widely adopted by industry as well as education. His original work was in text format but a diagram has since been developed that helps to explain his theory, as shown here.

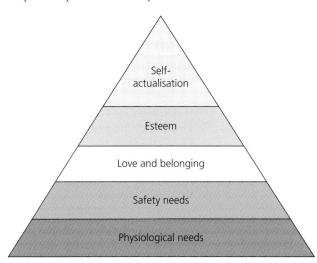

▲ Maslow's hierarchy of needs

> ### Key terms
>
> *Physiological needs:* things that the human body needs to survive, including clean water, shelter, food and also being at a comfortable temperature.
>
> *Safety needs:* people know that they are not in danger.
>
> *Love and belonging:* feeling part of a group, having family and friends; for adults, this may include a life partner.
>
> *Esteem:* having a positive self-concept and having feelings of competence. Feeling recognised and valued by others.
>
> *Self-actualisation:* the ability to think and be creative without worrying what others might think.

Maslow suggested that humans have needs that can be put into an order. Until each of the more basic needs is met, humans cannot focus on the highest need: self-actualisation. Self-actualisation is where humans can discover and achieve their potential. To understand this, think about a person who is living somewhere that has been devastated by war. There is no running water or anywhere to live. Is that person likely to paint a masterpiece or to go out to find water and food, and look for shelter?

Links to educational practice
▶ It is essential to create environments that are comfortable and safe for children and young people.
▶ Helping children and young people feel part of a group and cared for by adults comes before learning.
▶ Adults need to try to develop positive self-esteem in children and young people.

Criticisms of Maslow's hierarchy of needs
▶ Research has not always proved Maslow's theory to be correct.
▶ It does not explain how some adults who have not had their love and belonging needs met have still managed to achieve.

Connectivist approach

The **connectivist approach** is a response to modern technology, particularly the internet, browsers and social media. The idea behind this approach is that children and young people are no longer reliant on teachers and adults as their only sources of information. Using technology, they can connect with others and also find a range of sources from which to gain information.

Key principles

For the purposes of this qualification, the following key principles are given:
▶ Technology has created new ways for people to share knowledge and learn from others.
▶ Teachers facilitate students in independently seeking out new information online.
▶ Students learn outside of traditional classrooms through peer learning networks and massively open online courses (MOOCs).

Stephen Downes, born 1959, and George Siemens, born 1970

These are two names associated with the connectivist approach. They have worked together, but also separately, and have lectured and produced materials about how connectivism could work.

Connectivism was referred to by George Siemens as 'a theory of learning in the digital age'. The key point of this approach is an understanding that different pieces of knowledge are held in many places and can be accessed by many people. It means that the boundaries of knowledge, which previously were restricted to teachers or even textbooks, are no longer there provided that children and young people can have access to the internet. An example of this approach is the way that Siemens pioneered free and open online courses that are openly shared. These are known as **massively open online courses (MOOCS)**.

As knowledge in the digital age can constantly be updated due to new information being shared, Siemens and Downes suggest that, unlike traditional approaches to education, the focus is less on knowledge itself, but more on learning and knowing what to learn. The skill for children and young people is to know where to find as well as share accurate and relevant information, with whom and how to connect, and how to analyse the information gained.

In 2005, Siemens outlined the following principles of connectivism:

▶ Learning and knowledge rest in diversity of opinions.
▶ Learning is a process of connecting specialised nodes (information sources).
▶ Learning may reside in non-human appliances.
▶ Capacity to know more is more critical than what is currently known.
▶ Nurturing and maintaining connections is needed to facilitate continual learning.
▶ Ability to see connections between fields, ideas and concepts is a core skill.
▶ **Currency** (accurate, up-to-date knowledge) is the intent of all connectivist learning activities.
▶ Decision making is itself a learning process. Choosing what to learn and the meaning of incoming information is seen through the lens of a shifting reality. While there is a right answer now, it may be wrong tomorrow due to alterations in the information climate affecting the decision.

> (Source: Siemens, 2005, Connectivism: a learning theory for the digital age, **https://jotamac.typepad.com/jotamacs_ weblog/files/Connectivism.pdf**)

Links to educational practice

▶ Some adults, including parents, now recognise that they need to guide and facilitate children and young people in learning from digital sources of information.
▶ Children and young people are increasingly being encouraged to gain information and to extend their knowledge through the use of technology.
▶ Many schools have adopted online learning courses.

Criticisms of the connectivist approach

▶ Connectivism is not recognised as a theory by some as there is a lack of data and experiments – although it is seen as an approach to learning.
▶ The technology is new and so this approach cannot yet be fully evaluated.

How these theoretical approaches are applied through teacher- and student-led pedagogical strategies

When looking at how children and young people are taught, we may see that there are times when adults take a significant role and direct children and young people. This is referred to as **teacher-led** or **adult-led learning**.

Teacher-led or adult-led learning

For the purposes of this qualification, the characteristics of teacher-led learning are considered to be as follows.

▶ The teacher is at the centre of the learning process, relying on traditional methods of instruction, and a closely controlled environment and curriculum.

For the purposes of this qualification, the following approaches are linked to 'teacher-led' learning:
▶ behaviourism
▶ cognitivism
▶ constructivism (scaffolding).

Student-led or child-centred learning

Another approach to teaching children and young people is known as **student-led** or **child-centred learning**. This approach encourages children or young people to explore their own interests, and the role of the adult is to facilitate and encourage.

For the purposes of this qualification, student-led learning is considered to:
▶ Position the student in a more active role where they are using their own prior knowledge and problem solving skills to collaborate, discuss and create new understanding, with the teacher as facilitator.

For the purposes of this qualification, the following approaches are linked to student-led learning:
▶ cognitivism
▶ constructivism
▶ humanism
▶ connectivism.

A combination approach

Teacher-led and student-led approaches are often combined. In many education and childcare settings, the two approaches are used side by side. A child or young person might be taught a skill using an 'adult-led' approach, but is then encouraged to use the skill to explore something of interest to themselves.

2.4 How metacognition supports children and young people to manage their own learning

Have you ever been in a lesson when your mind has drifted and then you have made yourself concentrate more? The skill that you used is known as metacognition. Metacognition is the ability to understand, be aware and then try to control one's own mental processes.

The importance of metacognition

Metacognition is a broad term and includes the wide range of strategies that we can use to improve our concentration, learning and memory. Here are some of the ways that children and young people could use metacognition to manage their learning:

▶ **Identifying the strengths and areas for development in their own learning:** Metacognition skills can help children and young people to think about what they find easy and difficult. This is important in learning because to make progress in areas where you are weak, you first need to work out what they are. While adults can do this for children and young people, it is always more effective when children and young people can do this for themselves.

▶ **Using cognitive strategies to 'construct' knowledge:** One of the ways that we learn is to connect different pieces of knowledge. We may, for example, know that clouds are needed for rain; we may also know that there can be clouds without any rain. A metacognition skill would be to find out what colour clouds are associated with large amounts of rain. By doing this, new knowledge could be developed.

▶ **Using metacognitive strategies to regulate and evaluate their own learning:** Children and young people can use their metacognition skills to 'make' themselves try hard, practise again or seek help. They can use metacognition skills to recognise what they have found easy or difficult, and what they need to do next.

How metacognition positively impacts on children's and young people's education and achievement

Children and young people who have developed good metacognition skills have significant advantages when it comes to education and achievement. It is worth recognising first that these skills develop over time. Metacognition is linked to the development of memory and the ability to analyse and use information, so young children have less developed metacognition skills. Metacognition skills develop over time, with older children and young people being able to access some of them.

Adults can help with metacognition skills by sharing some of the strategies they use. These might include highlighting text that needs to be memorised, testing yourself to check what you know or thinking about the last place you used something that you have lost. Adults can also encourage metacognition skills by asking children and young people what they think – for example, 'What are you happy with? What do you need to concentrate on next?'

Ways in which metacognition skills can positively impact on education achievement

▶ **Building up a set of transferable strategies and skills that they can apply to new subjects and situations:** Children and young people with strong metacognition skills are able to consciously think about strategies and skills that they have experienced in the past and use them in new situations. This can help them solve new problems.

▶ **Better preparation for assessments:** Many assessments require that children and young people spend time revising knowledge or practising skills. Those who have strong metacognition skills do better in assessments. This is because they are able to analyse where they need to put in more effort and they are also able to develop strategies to help them remember things, such as thinking about a professor who has lost a finger to remember that there is only one 'f' in 'professor'.

Case study

Shona and Rahima are both in Year 6. Each week they have a spelling test. Each week, Shona does badly while Rahima normally does very well. Shona looks at the words the night before. Rahima looks at the words on the day they are given by the teacher. She works out which ones she already can spell. She then divides the rest of the words into three groups. Each night, she writes out one group of words and plays games with them. She also writes out the hardest words and displays them on her wardrobe door. The day before the test, she asks her parent to call out the words so she can practise spelling them. She has learned these strategies because her mother used to do them with her when she was younger.

When asked about their test results, Shona says that she has looked at the words, but she has been unlucky.

▶ Who has the most developed metacognition skills?
▶ How do these skills affect the result of the test?
▶ What has been the role of the adult in developing metacognition skills?

▶ **Monitoring their own understanding:** If children and young people have good metacognition skills they are able to ask themselves about whether or not they have understood a specific piece of information, task or skill. They should also be able to analyse the best way of doing something about it – for example, finding a new resource, asking a friend/adult for help, or rereading or repeating the task.
▶ **Identifying barriers to their own learning and actively minimising them:** Children and young people can use their metacognition skills to work out how they learn and remember information best, and also what affects their learning. This might include recognising that they find it hard to concentrate when it is noisy or when they are tired. Using this analysis, they can actively look for ways to improve their learning.
▶ **Learning from mistakes in order to avoid them in the future:** Children and young people who have good metacognition skills can accurately analyse information from their mistakes in order to improve their performance.

▶ **Adapting their learning strategies as appropriate to the task:** When children and young people have strong metacognition skills they can think about how best they learn and choose strategies that are suited to both them and the task.

2.5 How practitioners provide effective feedback and why it is important in supporting children's/young people's educational development

In the past, adults often looked at schoolchildren's work and just said 'well done' or 'good'. This did not really help children know what they needed to do more of or how to improve. Today, we know that by providing feedback to children and young people we can help them reflect on their work, guide them and so support them to make progress in their learning. The term 'formative feedback' is sometimes used to describe this process.

As well as learning, feedback can also be used to support children's and young people's behaviour (see Core Chapter 4).

Here are some key points in relation to feedback. It should be:
▶ **Timely:** Having a conversation with an adult or written feedback works better during or soon after the task or activity. This is because the child or young person is more likely to retain the information. It also matters because during or soon after an activity or task, a child or young person is more likely to be interested and motivated.
▶ **Clear and detailed:** Effective feedback helps children and young people know exactly what they have done well, but also what they need to do to improve.

▶ **Relevant to criteria:** While young children need simply to enjoy their learning and experiences, later on, children and young people will be preparing for assessments or qualifications. These might include swimming certificates and music exams, but also qualifications. When this is the case, adults need to help children and young people understand what they need to do to achieve the assessment or qualification. They need to know how they are doing and also what they need to do to meet the requirements. This might mean giving young people the qualification syllabus and encouraging them to check their own work against it.

▶ **Action-orientated:** Effective feedback helps children and young people know what they need to do next and provides them with goals for the future. This helps them to plan their next tasks or approaches. **Action-orientated feedback** might focus a child on checking punctuation or a young person on researching the meaning of a word. It might also help children and young people prioritise what they need to do first. This might help prevent them becoming overwhelmed. As well as helping children and young people understand what actions they need to take next, action-orientated feedback may also help them to understand what they need to continue to do.

▶ **Ongoing:** Effective feedback is continuous. This can help children and young people to be guided towards outcomes and also to avoid learning skills or knowledge incorrectly. Continuous feedback can also be motivating as children and young people know that their work and effort is being valued. As we have already seen, children and young people need to be involved in their feedback. If this process is continuous, they can develop the skills they need in order to learn self-evaluation and reflection.

▶ **Interactive:** Effective feedback is interactive. We might ask questions to find out what the child or young person thinks, or to help them see something from a different perspective – for example, 'What would happen if …?' If we make sure that effective feedback is interactive, children and young people are more likely to feel positive and motivated.

▲ These young people are learning about catering. Why is it important that they are given action-orientated feedback?

2.6 Why up-to-date and appropriate technology is important to effectively support children's/young people's educational development

These days, it is rare to find an educational setting that does not use technology in some way to support children's and young people's learning. In early years settings, the use of technology with babies and young children is usually kept to a minimum, as first-hand experiences and physically playing with objects are thought to offer the best way for this age group to learn. Early years practitioners, on the other hand, will use technology to share information with parents and professionals, and also to help them record progress.

As they develop, technology is increasingly introduced as a way for children and young people not only to find knowledge, but also to develop their skills and understanding of technology. The National Curriculum now includes learning how to use code for programming.

Here are some of the ways in which you may find technology being used:

▶ **Tracking children's/young people's progress:** Many settings have software that tracks progress or adults input information into systems that can be accessed by colleagues.

▶ **Ease of sharing information:** Many settings use technology to share information. They may do so with the local authority about national assessments, for example. Most settings will also communicate and share information with parents. A setting may have its own website, for example. In early years, parents can often access their child's 'learning journey' online.

▶ **Using a variety of media to introduce and explore a topic:** Many settings will use technology to gain children's and young people's interest. They may show a photo, play a film clip or music, or a podcast. In addition, many settings will encourage children and young people to follow up on something that they have seen or done by going online.

▶ **Planning and designing suitable online and offline learning materials and assessments:** In schools, many adults use technology to find and also create offline and online activities and materials to use with children and young people. Some materials can also be used for assessment purposes. One of the advantages of some online resources is that they have already been mapped to the National Curriculum. A disadvantage of online resources is that they may not link to children's and young people's interests or level of development.

▶ **Equipping children/young people to navigate a vast amount of information and evaluate the validity of sources:** We have seen from the early approach to learning known as connectivism (page 37) that children and young people must learn how to navigate information that is online. Using technology alongside children and young people can help them develop the skills to recognise when information may be inaccurate or biased.

▶ **Making learning accessible for children/young people with special educational needs and disabilities (SEND):** Some aspects of technology, such as voice-activated typing, can make a significant difference to children and young people with SEND. Here are some simple ways in which technology can make a difference:
  – Using a screen and changing the size of the font to help children and young people with visual impairment.
  – Using touchscreen technology to help children and young people to access activities such as drawing if they have difficulty with motor skills.
  – Using audio books to help children and young people who find reading difficult.

  – Using online programs that allow children and young people to learn at their own pace and repeat lessons.

▶ **Communicating and collaborating safely with children/young people online:** Online technology means that children and young people can meet other children and young people online. This can be an exciting learning opportunity, especially where they connect with other children and young people from different countries and cultures. They can talk about their lives, schooling and also share aspects of their lives that are important to them. The role of the adult is to help children and young people learn how to do this safely. Also, as children and young people are increasingly connected to one another via social media, adults also have to teach them how people tend to show only 'their best selves' online.

Research

Choose a National Curriculum subject and key stage or an area of learning and development from the EYFS.

Using one of these websites, evaluate the quality of resources on offer:
▶ www.bbc.co.uk/bitesize
▶ www.twinkl.co.uk
▶ www.hamilton-trust.org.uk

Case study

Sofia is four years old. She is with her childminder. It is first thing in the morning and the other children are not due to arrive for a while. They go into the garden to water the seeds they have planted. Sofia spots a 'lizard' on a plant. The childminder takes a photograph of it. They spend some time looking at it. The childminder suggests that they can go inside and find out more about what they have seen. Using the photograph, they compare it to similar images online. The childminder prints out the photograph and together they write a caption. Sofia tells her mother later in the day that they have seen a newt.
▶ Explain why this is a good example of how technology can build on first-hand experiences.
▶ How is technology supporting Sofia's literacy skills?
▶ Why is it important Sofia learns that technology can be used to find out things?

▲ Why is it important for adults to guide young people to ensure their safety online?

▶ **Modelling legal, ethical and secure methods of accessing/using online data and media:** By using technology and guiding children and young people, we can show them how to use the internet and associated technology safely. With young people, this includes ethical and legal aspects such as illegal streaming of films, sporting activities and music. It is also important for children and young people to be taught the importance of privacy and protecting their personal information.

▶ **Helping to prepare children/young people for future careers and digital citizenship:** Technology is now an everyday part of life and is likely to remain so. For children and young people, it is now an essential part of an educational programme to know how to use and benefit from it.

2.7 How personal, educational and environmental factors may affect engagement and development in reading, literacy and mathematics

Reading, writing and mathematics are considered to be essential for children and young people to master. Unfortunately, some children and young people can lose motivation or find learning literacy and mathematics difficult. There are many factors that can affect children's and young people's engagement and development in these areas. For the purposes of this qualification, we are dividing them into three broad areas: personal factors, educational factors and environmental factors.

Personal factors

Some of the personal factors that may affect engagement and development in reading, literacy and mathematics are described in the table below.

Level of cognitive and language development	In order for young children to learn to read and begin to write, they must have fluent language. Later, children and young people who have good vocabulary levels are likely to find reading more enjoyable and produce higher levels of writing. Language is also needed for mathematics and problem solving. Children and young people need to analyse and retrieve information, and this is linked to both cognitive development and language development.
Physical health and wellbeing	Children and young people who are in good health are more likely to have higher attendance in early years settings and schools. This means they do not miss out on experiences and teaching.
Special educational needs and disabilities (SEND)	Some types of SEND may cause children and young people to have delays in development. This might be because they have learning difficulties and need longer to learn concepts. It may also be because their disability causes them to have absences.
Motivation and interest	How much a child or young person wants to learn can affect their progress in literacy and mathematics. As we will see, motivation is also linked to how things are taught and the encouragement available.
Confidence to try without fear of failure	Mistakes are part of learning. When children and young people are fearful of making a mistake, they may miss out on opportunities to learn.
Socio-economic circumstances	Children and young people from poorer families may sometimes be at a disadvantage. They may not have time or space to do their homework. They may also not have had the same opportunities to see and apply literacy and mathematical concepts (e.g. a trip to the zoo may involve reading the signs, being aware of space and size, and paying for an entrance ticket).
Bilingualism: English as an additional language (EAL)	Children and young people who have more than one language may not always have the vocabulary needed to talk and use concepts in mathematics. If they are new to English, they may also need more support to help them learn how print works in English (see Core Chapter 12).
Previous experiences or support	How much a child or young person has enjoyed looking at books, reading, writing and doing mathematics will influence their attitude towards it. Positive experiences will help children and young people to persevere.

▲ Personal factors that may affect engagement and development in reading, literacy and mathematics

Educational factors

Educational factors are those factors that relate to what happens when children and young people are in education settings. Early years settings and schools can differ widely. A child or young person who thrives in one may not do so well in another. Some children and young people also attend private education, where the adult–pupil ratio may be more favourable. Here are some educational factors that might make a difference to children's and young people's learning and engagement in literacy and mathematics.

The quality of teaching and support at varying stages of development

Children and young people can benefit from adults who enjoy teaching and supporting learning. Being with an adult who is skilful and with whom they have a good relationship really matters to children's and young people's life chances. Here are some examples of ways in which high-quality teaching can make a difference at varying stages of development.

Early years settings

▶ **Reading:** Adults take time to share books with individual children. They choose books that they know are right for the child's language level and that will be enjoyable. They encourage children to talk about the story and, when children are developmentally ready, they draw their attention to print. Young children associate books with pleasure and are keen to learn to read when they start school.

▶ **Writing:** Adults provide interesting activities that will encourage young children to make marks using paint, crayons and sensory materials. Adults often write in front of children and so act as role models. They show those children who are ready how to make letter shapes. By the time the children start school, they are motivated and confident to make letter shapes and marks.

▶ **Mathematics:** Adults talk to children as they play, and draw their attention to concepts such as size and shape. Adults look for opportunities during daily routines to count objects and actions with children. Children start school already having words to describe size, shape, time and measure. They also enjoy counting with adults and may recognise a few numbers.

School settings

▶ **Reading:** When children are learning to read, adults are supportive and encouraging when mistakes are made. They also teach methodically so that children acquire knowledge about reading systematically. At all ages, they choose a wide range of books and texts to help pupils become confident readers. Later they help young people to analyse stories, poems and texts, and to discuss them.

▶ **Writing:** When children are learning to write, adults make them feel confident so that they are not afraid of making mistakes. As children develop their writing skills, adults may show them spelling strategies, and provide information about punctuation and grammar. They encourage children to enjoy writing and look for ways of building their confidence. With young people, adults encourage them to reflect on their writing.

▶ **Mathematics:** Adults look for activities that will build children's and young people's confidence and skills in mathematics. They try different approaches when a child or young person does not understand a concept. Adults use assessment to make sure that a child or young person has acquired a concept before building on it. They try to make mathematics relevant, and encourage children and young people to ask questions and to seek support.

> **Reflect**
>
> As a child or young person, did you experience some good teaching that helped you with literacy and mathematics? What was it?

Age- and stage-appropriate materials

Resources can play a part in children's and young people's engagement in literacy and mathematics. A well-resourced setting can provide children and young people with plenty of opportunities to inspire their learning and can also help them apply their learning. At all ages, a wide range of books that are of interest to children and young people can make a difference to engagement in reading. Resources and materials are effective only when they are age appropriate and when they are combined with good teaching.

Use of aids and adaptations

Some children and young people with a disability or learning needs may need physical resources that help them with their learning in literacy and mathematics. An example of this might be audio books for children and young people who cannot see print or who struggle with reading.

Use of synthetic phonics (reading and literacy)

Synthetic phonics is an approach to learning to read and write. The idea is that sounds in words are broken down to their smallest component (e.g. c-a-t). Synthetic phonics is currently the approach used in English schools, although it is worth noting that there are other approaches. It is a systematic approach, meaning teachers follow a highly structured programme. This means, for example, that all children begin by learning the same six sounds: S-A-T-P-I-N. In theory, children are not meant to move on to other letter sounds until they have mastered these. This structured approach is thought to help many children learn to read.

> ### Research
>
> If you have a placement in a primary or infant school, find out whether it uses synthetic phonics with its reception and Year 1 children.
>
> If so, does it also use other methods alongside synthetic phonics?

Environmental factors

Where children and young people grow up and what they experience can not only make a difference to their learning generally, but also to their interest in literacy and mathematics. Here are some examples of environmental factors:

▶ **Exposure to a stimulating, language-rich environment and resources:** In the early years of a child's life, interaction with parents and family members makes a significant difference to their later literacy and mathematical skills. The term 'language-rich environment' is used to describe opportunities to talk, listen and engage with others. For older children and young people, a language-rich environment can still make a difference. Some families seem naturally to discuss and debate topics. This, in turn, can help children and young people learn how to argue, negotiate and use language for thinking.

▶ **Opportunities to practise and apply knowledge:** Children and young people are often given homework. Homework helps them to practise and consolidate knowledge and skills. Not all children and young people have quiet spaces where they can do their homework, however, and so can miss out on time to learn and practise skills. In addition, some children and young people have more opportunities than others to apply their knowledge. A young person may, for example, help out in a family's business and so learn about accounts or handling money. This, in turn, can support their mathematical skills.

▶ **Support and involvement from parents or carers, peers and other professionals:** We have seen that good teaching makes a significant difference to children and young people. So, too, do the other people in their lives. Children and young people not only need encouragement, but also sometimes advice. This can come from their family members, friends or a neighbour, or from other professionals such as counsellors.

> ### Assessment practice
>
> 1. Outline the positive effects on learning if a humanist approach is taken.
> 2. Explain what is meant by modelling in the context of social learning theory.
> 3. Identify **two** criticisms of operant conditioning when used in relation to teaching children and young people.
> 4. Why might having a closed mind-set affect a young person's progress in mathematics?
> 5. Explain what is meant by a connectivist approach to learning.
> 6. Give **one** example of a metacognition skill that would help a young person to learn.
> 7. Explain why feedback needs to be clear and detailed when working with young people.
> 8. Why do children who are in language-rich home environments have an advantage in literacy activities?

CORE Chapter 3: Safeguarding, Health and Safety and Wellbeing

An important aspect of your role is to know and understand how to safeguard children and young people. You will need to know about the legislation and guidelines that exist for safeguarding their welfare, as well as understand how your own school's or early years setting's policies reflect these. You should also know about the factors that may indicate a child or young person may be at risk from abuse or harm, and how abuse may affect their development and behaviour. Finally, you should know what action to take if you have concerns about a child's or young person's wellbeing.

Learning outcomes

This chapter covers the following knowledge outcomes for Core Element 3:

3.1 The legal requirements and guidance relating to security, confidentiality of information, safeguarding, health, safety and wellbeing

3.2 How statutory guidance informs settings' safeguarding policies and procedures

3.3 How legislation informs organisational policies and procedures for recording, storing and sharing information on children's and young people's progress, needs and welfare

3.4 The importance of children's and young people's emotional health and its impact on their overall wellbeing, and how early years settings, schools and colleges can support children's and young people's emotional health and wellbeing

3.5 The difference between a child or young person 'at risk' and a child or young person 'in need', and the reporting requirements of each

3.6 The factors that may indicate that a child/young person is in danger or at risk of abuse

3.7 What constitutes a position of trust, and how power and influence can be used and abused when working with children and young people

3.8 A range of indicators that an adult in the setting may have inappropriate relationships with children and young people, and how to deal with this

3.9 How abuse, neglect, bullying, persecution and violence may impact on children's and young people's development and behaviour

The knowledge from this chapter corresponds with Assisting Teaching knowledge. Text relating to Assisting Teaching is highlighted. Note that this content will not form part of the core assessments.

K3.2 Why it is important to share relevant information in a timely manner with the safeguarding lead

3.1 The legal requirements and guidance relating to security, confidentiality of information, and safeguarding health, safety and wellbeing

Legislation	Description of responsibilities	Relevance to practice
Health and Safety at Work Act 1974	This key legislation affects the management of health and safety in all organisations and work settings.	Under this act, all those who work in schools or colleges will have responsibility for health and safety, which includes: • reporting hazards • following the policies and procedures of the setting for health and safety • using safety equipment and PPE (personal protective equipment) where needed • ensuring all materials, equipment and resources are safe • not harming themselves or others by their actions.
Children Act 1989/2004	This act outlines the responsibilities of parents and all those who work with children and young people. It includes two specific sections that focus on **safeguarding**: 1 Section 17 – this states that services must be put in place by local authorities to 'safeguard and promote the welfare of children within their area who are in need' 2 Section 47 – this states that the local authority has a duty to investigate instances where it has 'reasonable cause to suspect that a child is suffering, or likely to suffer, significant harm'.	The act was amended in 2004 to reinforce the message that all organisations that work with children and young people have a duty to help safeguard and promote the welfare of children. This amendment also created the posts of separate Children's Commissioners for England, Northern Ireland, Scotland and Wales, and new **Local Safeguarding Children Boards** (now Local Safeguarding Partnerships) to allow the function to investigate and review all children's deaths in a local area.
Care Standards Act 2000	This act was brought in to regulate social care, early years and social services, and to ensure that all providers are competent in their duty of care.	It is particularly relevant to children's homes and childcare settings, and to those providing childminding or day care services. It also means that Ofsted Early Years has a duty to register and inspect childcare services for day nurseries, playgroups, after-school clubs and holiday play schemes, and childminders. The Care Standards Act also established a National Care Standards Commission, to promote improvement in public health. This has since changed to the **Care Quality Commission**.

➡️

Key term

Safeguarding: action taken to promote the welfare of children and protect them from harm (as defined by the NSPCC, 2018).

Legislation	Description of responsibilities	Relevance to practice
Female Genital Mutilation (FGM) Act 2003	This act makes it an offence to carry out or assist in performing FGM, whether or not this takes place in or outside the UK. FGM is a form of abuse and can cause long-term mental health and physical problems for the victim. Under this act, it is also an offence to fail to protect a girl from risk. All those working with children and young people have a responsibility to be vigilant and should know the signs to look out for, which include: • excitement about going to a 'special' holiday home • extended school absence, which is repeated • withdrawn behaviour or anxiety • having difficulty walking, sitting or moving around.	FGM is more likely to originate from certain communities in north-eastern, eastern and western regions of Africa, as well as some parts of Asia, and some communities in Southeast Asia and the Middle East. This means that girls who live in the UK but whose families are from a community that practises FGM are at greater risk. Any professional working with children and/or young people should follow their setting's procedures for reporting any suspected or potential cases of FGM. Where potential cases are suspected, protection orders can be put in place. Both the NSPCC and NHS websites have more information on FGM. See www.nspcc.org.uk and www.nhs.uk
Safeguarding Vulnerable Groups Act 2006	This act was passed to prevent unsuitable people from working with children and young people, and vulnerable adults. It aimed to do this through setting up a checking and barring scheme, initially known as the Criminal Records Bureau (CRB) check.	The DBS (Disclosure and Barring Service) check is now a legal requirement for working with children and young people. It applies to the health and social care sectors as well as those working in education and early years.
Childcare Act 2006	This act places a duty on settings and local authorities to help improve wellbeing for children and to reduce inequalities. It is exclusively for early years and childcare, and requires local authorities and private, voluntary and independent childcare providers to work together to ensure that there is enough childcare to meet the local need. It also provides the legislative framework for registering childminders and other childcare providers, which are monitored and inspected by Ofsted.	Under this act, all settings caring for children up to age five are now required to register and deliver the Early Years Foundation Stage (EYFS). They are expected to provide adequate information to parents and to ensure that this is accessible to all. For a version of this act with explanatory notes, search for Childcare Act 2006 at www.legislation.gov.uk
Equality Act 2010	The Equality Act 2010 is key legislation for equality and diversity in the UK, and replaced all previous equality laws. It is designed to protect the rights of individuals, and ensure that they are protected from unfair treatment in the workplace, when using public services, healthcare or transport, and when	Under this act, no one should be treated unfavourably because of one of the **protected characteristics** listed below. This includes all children and young people, parents and carers, staff and visitors: • age • disability • gender reassignment • marriage and civil partnership • pregnancy and maternity

Legislation	Description of responsibilities	Relevance to practice
Equality Act 2010 (cont.)	communicating with organisations or public bodies. It, therefore, applies to everyone in schools and early years settings.	• race • religion or belief • sex • sexual orientation. You will need to ensure that you treat everyone you meet in the setting fairly, and demonstrate **inclusive practice** in your work with children and young people. The Equality Act also requires that reasonable adjustments are made to accommodate different needs. In school and education settings, this will apply particularly to children with SEND. For more on the Equality Act, see Core Chapter 10.
Children and Families Act 2014	This act aimed to improve services for vulnerable children. It is another key piece of legislation for child welfare and family law, and is divided into nine areas.	When working in schools and early years settings, you need to know about the following aspects. • Children and young people with SEND: The largest of these areas is also closely linked to the SEND Code of Practice, which is about the law for children and young people who have special educational needs and disabilities. It gives families more control over their child's welfare and establishes the requirement for an education, health and care (EHC) plan setting out the SEN assessment and provision for children and young people under 25. For more on this, see Core Chapter 11. • Childcare: This part of the act established agencies for registered childminders, to enable them to access training and advice, although it is not a requirement for them to be registered with them. • Children's Commissioner: The role of the Children's Commissioner for England changed from representing the views and interests of children to promoting and protecting their rights. • Working rights: Families have more rights to flexible working and parental leave around the birth of a child, and adoptive parents have the right to time off to attend meetings before a placement.
Children and Social Work Act 2017	This act was brought in to protect the support for children and young people in care, and to promote safeguarding and welfare. It also brought in regulation for social workers and established a Child	With the introduction of this act, all primary schools were asked to provide relationships education, and all secondary schools relationships and sex education.

Key term

Inclusive practice: developing an approach that recognises the diversity of children and young people, and promotes positive attitudes, differentiation and respect.

Legislation	Description of responsibilities	Relevance to practice
	Safeguarding Practice Review Panel, in order to look at serious safeguarding issues. It has three main elements: 1 To introduce **Corporate Parenting Principles**, to ensure that the council is the best possible parent to children in its care, or 'looked after children', and provides a local offer for those leaving care and preparing for adulthood. State schools and academies must also have a staff member who is responsible for promoting the educational achievement of children in care and looked after children. 2 To introduce professional standards and regulation for social workers under a new body called Social Work England. 3 To change local and national safeguarding arrangements. Local Safeguarding Children Boards (set up in 2004 under the Children Act) were abolished and replaced by Local Safeguarding Partners and Child Death Review Partnerships. These are the Chief of Police, the local authority and local Clinical Commissioning Groups, and are to respond specifically to the needs of local children and young people. Two or more areas can also combine where needed. On a national level, a new Child Safeguarding Practice Review Panel was established, to identify and review cases of national significance.	
General Data Protection Regulations (GDPR) 2018	The Data Protection Act 2018 is the UK's implementation of the GDPR legislation from the EU. It replaces the Data Protection Act 1998, and informs the policies and procedures organisations must have around recording, storing and sharing information. This includes personal information on all staff and pupils. For example: • names, addresses, dates of birth • photographs • National Insurance and bank details of staff • information about medical conditions, needs or allergies, details of GPs • progress reports on pupils, and exam results • information on pupils' needs and welfare, including SEN assessments • information on the safeguarding of pupils • staff development reviews.	Under the GDPR, all those who keep and use personal data on individuals must follow these seven principles with regard to the information: 1 Obtain and keep it fairly, lawfully and transparently. 2 Use it only for the specified purpose and inform people what this is. 3 Collect only the minimum amount of data needed. 4 Do not store old information, and ensure the safe disposal of inaccurate personal data. 5 Ensure it is accurate and up to date, and do not keep it for longer than necessary. 6 Handle it in a secure way to prevent unauthorised use, access, loss or damage. 7 Keep documentation and policies regarding data collection within the principles of GDPR.

(→)

Legislation	Description of responsibilities	Relevance to practice
Keeping Children Safe in Education 2019	This statutory guidance was introduced to promote the safeguarding and welfare of children and young people. It applies to all schools and colleges in England, and to maintained nursery schools.	New safeguarding partner arrangements were put in place (as defined by the Children and Social Work Act 2017, described previously). Schools are to consider opportunities to teach safeguarding as part of the curriculum, through relationships or sex and relationships education. Ofsted will inspect and report on the effectiveness of safeguarding arrangements. Updated DBS checks during recruitment of staff and on existing staff. **Upskirting** is made a criminal offence.
Guidance for Safer Working Practice 2019	This non-statutory guidance from the Safer Recruitment Consortium should be read alongside the DfE Statutory Guidance 'Keeping Children Safe in Education'. For more on this document, see Section 3.2.	The guidance refers to the requirement for a staff code of conduct. It also sets out practical advice to schools, colleges and early years settings around the standards of behaviour that are expected of all those who work with children and young people, and outlined at staff induction. This should include, for example: • acceptable use of technologies • staff–pupil relationships • use of social media • transporting pupils • photographing pupils.

▲ The legal requirements and guidance relating to security, confidentiality of information, and safeguarding health, safety and wellbeing

Key term

Upskirting: taking a photo up a person's skirt or dress without their knowledge or consent.

Test yourself

1 Which four key areas do you need to know about concerning the Children and Families Act 2014?
2 What are the nine protected characteristics under the Equality Act 2010?
3 What are your responsibilities under the Health and Safety at Work Act 1974?

Research

Find out more about any three of the pieces of legislation listed on the previous pages.
▶ How do they affect what you or others in your setting do in the workplace?
▶ Why is it important for schools and early years settings to be up to date with their policies and procedures?

3.2 How statutory guidance informs safeguarding policies and procedures

By law, all organisations working with children and young people up to the age of 18 need to have guidelines, policies and procedures to make sure they are protected and kept safe from harm. The following statutory guidance should support and inform safeguarding policies and procedures in your school or early years setting.

Prevent Duty Guidance 2015

This guidance outlines all key areas that staff should be aware of in the context of safeguarding. It refers to the Counter-Terrorism and Security Act 2015. All those working with children and young people should understand and be aware of the guidance, and of their responsibilities to 'prevent people from being drawn into terrorism'. Their safeguarding policy should outline the level of risk, which will vary considerably between organisations and locality.

Supervision of activity with children

This document gives guidance to settings that have volunteers and employees who are working with children or young people in **regulated activities**. All those who are working in this way are required to have an Enhanced DBS check. However, if they are supervised at all times when with children or young people, this does not apply.

> **Key term**
>
> *Regulated activity:* unsupervised activities when teaching, training, instructing, caring for or supervising children.

Special Educational Needs and Disability Code of Practice: 0 to 25 years 2015

This statutory guidance is linked to the Children and Families Act 2014, and sets out the requirements for settings as regards children and young people who have special educational needs. It states that they require 'additional consideration' due to their needs if they:

▶ are looked after or care leavers
▶ have social care needs, or are 'in need'
▶ are educated in alternative provision or out of area
▶ are children of service personnel (in the armed forces)
▶ are in youth custody.

The Code of Practice sets out what schools and early years settings must have in place for these children and young people, as well as staff responsibilities for safeguarding and wellbeing.

> For more on this guidance and how it impacts working with children and young people with SEND, see Core Chapter 11.

Supporting pupils at school with medical conditions

This guidance is specifically for schools; early years settings should refer to the EYFS guidance. Although its main purpose is around ensuring that pupils with medical conditions are properly supported and cared for alongside their education, it also points out that these pupils may be vulnerable due to their conditions, and highlights that there may be social and emotional implications for them, particularly if their needs are complex. The school's safeguarding policy should highlight staff responsibilities and procedures for implementing and reviewing healthcare plans.

Multi-agency statutory guidance on female genital mutilation

This statutory guidance document provides information, guidance and support for all those who have a responsibility to safeguard girls from FGM. It sets out the requirements of the legislation, which places a mandatory duty on all healthcare, education and medical professionals to report concerns immediately to the police.

Keeping Children Safe in Education Part 1

This guidance is for all schools and colleges and also includes maintained nursery schools. The safeguarding information in Part 1 outlines the role of education staff and how they should protect children and young people. This document should be referred to when writing safeguarding policies as it sets out very clearly what constitutes abuse, what staff should do if they have concerns about a child or young person, and how educational settings should refer on to social care and/or the police.

Sexual Violence and Sexual Harassment Between Children in Schools and Colleges (guidance document) 2018

This DfE guidance is for schools and colleges, and is advice for head teachers and safeguarding leads that covers children of all ages in both primary and secondary schools. It reinforces the need for all organisations to safeguard and promote the welfare of children and young people, and ensure that they do all they can to promote 'healthy and respectful relationships'. It sets out what staff should do in situations of sexual bullying, sexting, sexual violence or harassment between children and young people.

Working Together to Safeguard Children

This guidance informs safeguarding policies as it sets out how different agencies such as healthcare professionals, adult social care and educational practitioners should work together in order to protect children and young people and promote their welfare. It puts the child or young person at the centre of all decisions that are made and highlights the importance of early help.

3.3 How legislation informs organisational policies and procedures for recording, storing and sharing information on children's and young people's progress, needs and welfare

All legislation that is concerned with data and record keeping will influence how information on children's and young people's progress is recorded, stored and shared in your organisation. Your school, college or early years setting will have a range of policies and procedures that set out what is required by law, and all those who are responsible for keeping information should be aware of them.

Freedom of Information Act 2000

This legislation was brought in to allow public access to information that is held by public authorities – for example, state schools, the police or the NHS. It means that these public bodies must ensure that they have policies and procedures in place for recording, storing and sharing information on individuals.

Alongside the General Data Protection Regulations (GDPR) (see below), it sets out how organisations should keep official information and how individuals can apply for it if needed through a Freedom of Information request. Therefore, schools, early years settings and colleges are required to store the information safely and be able to access it when required.

Data Protection Act 2018/General Data Protection Regulations (GDPR) 2018

Refer to the table in Section 3.1 for more information about this legislation and how it informs policies and procedures.

In practice

▶ Look at three of the following policies within your organisation:
   – record-keeping policy
   – assessment policy
   – confidentiality policy
   – special educational needs policy
   – safeguarding policy.
▶ What do these policies say about recording, storing and sharing information?
▶ How does this relate to the legislation above?

3.4 The importance of children's and young people's emotional health and its impact on their overall wellbeing

The emotional health of children and young people has been recognised by mental health organisations as having a direct influence on their cognitive development and wellbeing. In addition, statistics released by NHS Digital in 2018 showed that one in nine children aged from five to fifteen had a diagnosed mental health disorder, a rise from one in ten in 2004 (source: **https:// digital.nhs.uk/data-and-information/publications/ statistical/mental-health-of-children-and-young-people-in-england/2017/2017**).

All those who work with children and young people need to be aware of how emotional health impacts not only on learning and development but also on children's later resilience and outcomes as adults. Public Health England lists the kinds of mental health problems that are common in children and young people as a result of this, such as depression, self-harm, eating disorders, generalised anxiety disorder (GAD) and post-traumatic stress disorder (PTSD).

In addition, it lists the types of factors that will give children and young people greater ability to cope, and that will help their emotional health and wellbeing:

▶ feeling loved, valued and protected
▶ being part of a family and having a sense of belonging at home, in school and within their community
▶ being in good health, and having a balanced diet and exercise
▶ having the freedom to play and enjoy themselves
▶ being hopeful and optimistic
▶ going to a school that looks after pupil wellbeing
▶ having a voice and a sense of control over their own life
▶ having resilience and the ability to problem solve.

▲ Why is it important for young children to be able to play together?

How early years settings, schools and colleges can apply Public Health England's eight principles to support emotional health and wellbeing

These eight principles to support children's and young people's emotional health and wellbeing (see illustration below) were published by Public Health England in 2015 to support schools and colleges. Each strand or heading in the document outlines ways in which this can be achieved. Although it was not written with early years settings in mind, many of the principles can still be applied. The majority of these principles are also linked to the list of factors above.

▲ Eight principles to promoting a whole-school and college approach to emotional health and wellbeing

Source: Public Health England, *Promoting Children and Young People's Emotional Health and Wellbeing*

In detail, these eight principles are as follows:
1 **An ethos and environment that promotes respect and values diversity:** The setting's physical, social and emotional environment, and positive relationships between children, young people and adults, are a critical part of promoting student wellbeing. This is because they are linked to the important sense of belonging.

2 **Curriculum, teaching and learning to promote resilience and support social and emotional learning:** There should be a programme of social and emotional learning for children and young people, and opportunities through the wider curriculum to link and support their experiences. For example, schools and early years settings will spend time talking about and doing work before periods of potential anxiety, such as moving to primary or secondary school. They should also use opportunities to talk through issues such as problem solving, conflict resolution, understanding feelings and collaborative working. Personal, social and emotional development (PSED) is one of the EYFS's prime areas of learning and development, and personal, social and health education (PSHE) is a National Curriculum subject in schools.

3 **Enabling student voice to influence decisions:** Children and young people need to feel listened to and valued by adults, and there should be opportunities for them to put forward their own ideas and solutions. Most primary and secondary schools now have a school council or pupil parliament with pupil representatives from each year group. This enables children and young people to make their voices heard on a range of issues, including environmental, teaching and learning, behaviour, and so on. In the early years, the EYFS places importance on listening to children's needs and interests so that provision can be made more meaningful to them, and their development and learning can be enhanced.

4 **Staff development to support their own wellbeing and that of students:** For children and young people to achieve emotional wellbeing, staff need to be aware of its importance. They should also be able to identify the kinds of indicators of mental health difficulties in children and young people, as well as ways of accessing support when it is needed. Staff too should be included in the setting's ethos of wellbeing, by making it an item in staff meetings and training, and through a culture of open communication and making them feel valued.

5 **Identifying need and monitoring impact of interventions:** As well as being aware of its importance, staff will also need to be able to measure the emotional health and wellbeing of children and young people in their setting, so that they can put steps in place to support them. Children and young people may need intervention for their wellbeing through targeted support, which will need to be monitored (see below). Depending on the age of the children or young people, schools and early years settings may use different methods to find out about emotional health and wellbeing:

– younger children using smiles or frowns on a chart to indicate how they are feeling each day, at different times of day

– the **Stirling Children's Wellbeing Scale** – an exercise for education professionals to use to measure emotional and psychological wellbeing in eight to fifteen year olds

– the **Warwick-Edinburgh Mental Wellbeing Scale** – an exercise for pupils aged 13 or over.

The kind of interventions that may be offered could include:

– **Early Help Assessments (EHAs)**
– counselling sessions for older pupils
– mentoring programmes
– talking or 'chatterbox' clubs for younger children in a safe space
– promotion of school-based and other sources of information and support, such as Childline or Barnardo's.

Key term

Early Help Assessments (EHAs): a tool to identify and discuss support for children and families with local partners.

Case study

Kamal is just going into Year 11 where he will be taking his GCSEs. He has always been quiet but you notice that in the last few weeks he has become withdrawn from his friends and has been absent from school more often.

▶ Would you say anything and, if so, to whom?
▶ Are there any other steps you should take?

---

6 **Working with parents/carers:** Schools, colleges and early years settings should ensure that they work with parents as much as possible in order to support children's and young people's emotional health and wellbeing. The Public Health England document states that there is strong evidence that where providers work with parents there are social as well as economic benefits. From Ofsted requirements to information about school policies, and supporting parents with their parenting skills, as well as activities in the wider community, these can have a positive influence.

See also Core Chapter 6 Working with others.

7 **Targeted support and appropriate referral:** Some children and young people will be more vulnerable to mental health issues – for example, those from a deprived background, excluded pupils, asylum seekers and refugees, or those with SEN. Schools and colleges may need to refer a child or young person for further support.

8 **Leadership and management that supports and champions efforts to promote emotional health and wellbeing:** At the centre of all these principles is effective leadership that promotes and highlights the importance of emotional wellbeing to children and young people. This should be shown through the way in which social and emotional wellbeing is monitored and evaluated through the organisation.

For more information, visit **www.gov.uk**, search for 'Promoting children and young people's emotional health and wellbeing' and you will find a PDF of the document that you can download.

3.5 The difference between a child or young person 'at risk' and a child or young person 'in need'

It is important that you know the difference between these two terms. A child or young person **at risk** is one who is in a position of vulnerability to abuse or harm. This means that the abuse or harm may be happening (but may also not be), or is at risk of happening; this might be due to a range of factors, such as those discussed in Section 3.6.

A child or young person **in need** is defined by law as a person under 18 who needs extra support to improve their opportunities through the services of the local authority, whether this is due to their personal circumstances or a medical or physical need. This means that they may be in social care, such as **looked after children**, children with disabilities, or those with other safeguarding and welfare needs.

> **Key term**
>
> *Looked after child (LAC):* a child who has been in the care of their local authority for more than 24 hours, sometimes also referred to as children in care. This can include children living with foster parents, in a residential children's home, hostel or secure accommodation.

> **Reflect**
>
> Anna is six and lives with her mum and stepdad. She is in school every day and her parents are always involved in school-based events. Staff have noticed that recently Anna is very quiet and has become quite withdrawn. Lunchtime staff have also said that she is not eating. They have mentioned this to her mum but have been told that she is upset because they have had to cancel their holiday.
>
> Roman is 15 and lives with his mum. He is her carer as she has multiple sclerosis and limited independence, as well as depression. The family have a designated social worker, but Roman is regularly absent from school.
>
> ▶ Which of these children might be considered at risk and which in need?
> ▶ Would you do anything in either situation?

The mandatory reporting requirements to escalate concerns that a child or young person is in need or at risk

> See Sections 3.2 and 3.3, and also Assisting Teaching K3.1.

In order to comply with legislation, policies and procedures, it is a responsibility of all those who work with children and young people to keep them safe and free from harm. As educators we are also responsible for ensuring that we support children and young people to achieve the best possible outcomes. This means that we as professionals must, by law, report any concerns that a child or young person is in need or at risk.

If you suspect that a child or young person in your school or early years setting is in need or at risk, you must follow the correct policies and procedures that are in place in your organisation as soon as possible. You should receive training in your organisation's safeguarding or child protection policy at induction or through ongoing staff continuing professional development (CPD). This will outline the indicators of concern or abuse and set out in a clear way the steps you should follow.

In most cases, you would be obliged to share your concerns immediately with your **designated safeguarding lead (DSL)**, outlining why and what has happened or been said; they would then take your concerns further. The procedures the organisation has put in place should be clear and easy to follow. In some cases, organisations may have a flowchart that details what to do at each stage, and how to proceed if you are not happy with the response or action that is taken.

If a child or young person has confided in you, safeguarding is one of the cases in which you have to tell them that you cannot keep the information to yourself, as you need to protect their safety. All information shared with the DSL should be confidential – they will decide if the concerns should be referred on to other professionals on a 'need to know' basis.

> ## Key term
>
> **Designated safeguarding lead (DSL):** the person in a school or early years setting who is responsible for all safeguarding issues.

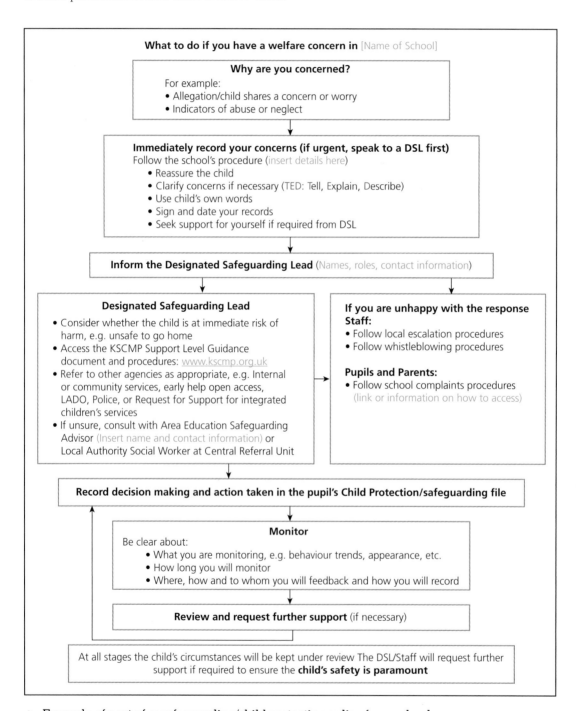

What to do if you have a welfare concern in [Name of School]

Why are you concerned?
For example:
- Allegation/child shares a concern or worry
- Indicators of abuse or neglect

Immediately record your concerns (if urgent, speak to a DSL first)
Follow the school's procedure (insert details here)
- Reassure the child
- Clarify concerns if necessary (TED: Tell, Explain, Describe)
- Use child's own words
- Sign and date your records
- Seek support for yourself if required from DSL

Inform the Designated Safeguarding Lead (Names, roles, contact information)

Designated Safeguarding Lead
- Consider whether the child is at immediate risk of harm, e.g. unsafe to go home
- Access the KSCMP Support Level Guidance document and procedures: www.kscmp.org.uk
- Refer to other agencies as appropriate, e.g. Internal or community services, early help open access, LADO, Police, or Request for Support for integrated children's services
- If unsure, consult with Area Education Safeguarding Advisor (Insert name and contact information) or Local Authority Social Worker at Central Referral Unit

If you are unhappy with the response
Staff:
- Follow local escalation procedures
- Follow whistleblowing procedures

Pupils and Parents:
- Follow school complaints procedures
(link or information on how to access)

Record decision making and action taken in the pupil's Child Protection/safeguarding file

Monitor
Be clear about:
- What you are monitoring, e.g. behaviour trends, appearance, etc.
- How long you will monitor
- Where, how and to whom you will feedback and how you will record

Review and request further support (if necessary)

At all stages the child's circumstances will be kept under review The DSL/Staff will request further support if required to ensure the **child's safety is paramount**

▲ Example of part of a safeguarding/child protection policy for a school
Source: KELSI **www.kelsi.org.uk/__data/assets/pdf_file/0020/66008/Child-Protection-Exemplar-Policy-for-schools.pdf**

K3.2 Why it is important to share relevant information in a timely manner with the safeguarding lead

The reasons for sharing information as soon as possible are to:
- ensure that pupils are kept safe and free from harm
- ensure effective identification and appropriate provision is put in place
- comply with policies, procedures and legislation.

Reason to share information with DSL	Why it is important
Ensuring that pupils are kept safe and free from harm	This is the most critical reason to share information immediately. It is the responsibility of all adults in the setting to keep children and young people safe and free from harm.
Ensuring effective identification and appropriate provision is put in place	All relevant information must be shared with the DSL so that they can build a clear picture of the situation. This will help them to take appropriate action as soon as possible.
Complying with policies, procedures and legislation	The DSL should ensure that policies, procedures and legislation are followed so that there is a clear line of action from the point of concerns being raised. This will also help them to show that they are acting in line with their responsibilities.

▲ Reasons to share information with the designated safeguarding lead, and why this is important

3.6 The factors that may indicate that a child/young person is in danger or at risk of abuse

You should know about the different kinds of abuse that children and young people may be vulnerable to. This is very important, as you will be responsible for reporting any concerns you might have, as discussed in Section 3.5.

Abuse is normally categorised as follows:
- Physical abuse – when someone is physically hurt or harmed
- Emotional abuse – when someone is continually emotionally mistreated
- Sexual abuse – when sexual activity is forced upon someone – including child sexual exploitation (CSE)
- Neglect – when a baby's or child's basic needs are persistently not met
- Domestic abuse – when there is violent behaviour within a relationship
- Bullying and cyber bullying – when a child is bullied by their peers
- Child criminal exploitation (CCE) – when a child is trafficked or exploited and made to commit crimes, for example, as part of a gang.

(Note that an individual may be subject to more than one type of abuse.)

> For more on the different types of abuse, how to recognise them and who to report to, see also Assisting Teaching K3.1.

You should also know about factors that may indicate that a child or young person is more in danger or at risk of abuse. According to the World Health Organization (WHO), research has shown that there is often a link between abuse and certain characteristics of the child and their environment. Some of these are outlined briefly in the following table.

Individual factors	Reasons
Physical or developmental disability	Children and young people who have a physical or developmental disability may be more vulnerable to abuse for a number of reasons: • they may be unable to stop the abuser • they may have less of an understanding of what is happening • they may be less likely to tell others about the abuse.
Child is product of an abusive relationship	If the child or young person is the product of an abusive relationship, they will be more likely to suffer abuse themselves as it will already be in the home.
Lack of secure attachment with parent/carer	If a child or young person does not have a secure and loving attachment with a parent or carer, this may increase the likelihood of abuse.
Parental factors	**Reasons**
Parent has already abused a child/been abused	Parents who have been abused themselves or who are already known to have abused a child or young person may be more likely to abuse a child or young person.
Single parent with low education	A parent who has a low level of education or understanding of the impact of what they are doing, or who is a lone carer for a child or young person, may be more likely to abuse a child or young person.
Unrealistic expectations of parents/lack of skills	Parents who are uninformed, or who do not know about child development or may not have appropriate parenting skills may be more likely to abuse. They may not know how to manage conflict situations or understand ways in which they can support their children more effectively.
Parental isolation	Parents who are more socially isolated or who have limited support from family and friends or the local community may be more likely to abuse children and young people.
Parental mental illness/drug or alcohol abuse	According to the WHO research, parents who have mental health issues, poor self-esteem or self-control, or who are using drugs or alcohol are more likely to abuse their children.
Environmental factors	**Reasons**
Overcrowding in the home, poverty or lack of opportunity to improve	High rates of poverty or overcrowding are more likely to increase stress levels in the home, which can lead to abuse.
Domestic violence	Where there is already violence in the home, children and young people are likely to be subject to it themselves. In addition, children witnessing domestic violence is also a form of abuse.
Non-biologically related adult in the home	Adults who are not biologically related to a child or young person are statistically more likely to be abusers.

▲ Factors that may indicate more risk of abuse

Case study

You are working in a Year 3 class in a school that is in a deprived area. You have noticed that a new child in your class, Jack, rarely speaks to anyone and is unable to stay focused on any activity. He is brought to school by his grandmother and you know that he is a child who receives free school meals and has a social worker. He is also regularly without the appropriate clothing for the weather and is the last to respond to any communications the school sends home.

▶ Outline any concerns you might have about Jack.
▶ Do you think these factors mean that Jack is being abused?
▶ What would you do in this situation?

3.7 The legal definition of a position of trust, as defined by the Sexual Offences (Amendment) Act 2000

This act states that it is an offence for someone over the age of 18 to engage in sexual activity with someone under that age where they are in a position of trust. It gives specific conditions in which an adult is said to be in a position of trust in relation to a younger person.

These are limited to circumstances in which a child or young person is particularly vulnerable, or the relationship of trust is strong, and these circumstances include the child or young person:

▶ being in a care home, or in residential care or fostered

▶ being in full-time education in which the older person is involved in caring for them

▶ being in a hospital, children's home or residential establishment that cares for children with physical or learning disabilities, mental illness or behavioural problems.

It is important that all adults working with children and young people are aware of the fact that they are in a position of trust, and that they should not abuse it in any way.

How power and influence can be used and abused when working with children and young people

Adults who are in a position of trust are role models for children and young people, as well as people who have authority and influence over them. Children and young people may aspire to be like them and want to please them. It is important for this influence to be used in a positive way to support children and young people and build their confidence and self-esteem, and that adults show integrity through what they do and how they behave, as well as in their relationships with others. However, all of these things also mean that it is easier for an adult to do the things listed in the following table.

What they might do	How they might do it
Take advantage of an individual	Those in a position of trust may use their influence to exploit a child or young person for their own benefit.
Gain unauthorised access to private or sensitive information for their own or others' advantage	Adults may look at sensitive information, which they are not entitled to do, in order to find out more about the child or young person for their own advantage.
Manipulate an individual	Those in a position of power may try to manipulate a child or young person by controlling them and using their position to get what they want.
Use a position of trust to bully, humiliate or undermine	Adults may use their position to use verbal abuse in ways that make the child or young person feel humiliated or bullied.
Threaten punishment for non-compliance with unreasonable demands	Adults may threaten a child or young person by telling them that they will punish them if they do not do what they have asked them to.

▲ How adults may use power and influence to abuse children and young people

3.8 The range of indicators that an adult in a setting may have inappropriate relationships with children and young people

Although fortunately very rare, it is possible that an adult in your setting may develop an inappropriate relationship with a child or young person. You should be aware of the kinds of indicators that might suggest they are doing this, and act on this if necessary.

▶ **Being overly affectionate, giving gifts, or showing favouritism with a child or young person:** You may notice that an adult spends more time with or shows a preference for a particular child or young person, or seems keen to be with them.

▶ **Spending time alone with a child or young person:** You may notice that the adult is finding ways of spending time alone with the child or young person. This is never advisable, as both the child and the adult are vulnerable to allegations.

▶ **Making friends with a child's or young person's parents and/or visiting them at home:** Although it is important to have good relationships with parents, particularly when children are very young, it is important for practitioners to maintain professional boundaries. This means that they should not be friends outside the setting or on social media.

▶ **Using private texts or social media to communicate with a child/young person:** This is always inappropriate and most schools and early years settings will state it in their safeguarding policy.

How practitioners deal with suspected abuse in line with the educational setting's codes of conduct

In all cases, safeguarding concerns should be acted on immediately. Appropriate actions include those listed in the table below.

What practitioners should do	Explanation
Observing and recording as appropriate	Practitioners should immediately note down their concerns or what they have seen. They should include the date, where they were and what they were doing, and exactly what was observed or was said to them by the child or young person. This will help them to remember for reporting purposes. They should store this information confidentially – for example, in a password-protected file.
Following organisational policies and procedures for child protection	Within the organisation, it is important to make sure that practitioners use the safeguarding or child protection policy to ensure that each step has been followed correctly.
Following procedures set out by the local safeguarding partnership	The local safeguarding partnership will outline the steps to take if a school or early years setting has concerns about a child or young person. This will include what to do outside office hours.
Following accurate lines of reporting in a timely manner	Practitioners should always act on any safeguarding concerns at the earliest possible opportunity, by reporting to their DSL.
Maintaining professional boundaries	At all times, and especially when dealing with suspected or alleged abuse, practitioners will need to ensure that they remain professional.
Contacting the police if a child or young person is in immediate danger	In an emergency, or if they know a child or young person is in danger, adults should always call 999.

▲ Appropriate actions to take where there are safeguarding concerns

Case study

You are working in a secondary school as a language assistant and have noticed that a pupil is spending a lot of time in the department and is regularly hanging around waiting to speak to a particular teacher. You ask the pupil if you can help her but she is insistent on speaking to the teacher.
▶ Should you have any concerns in this instance?
▶ Would you do anything and, if so, what?

3.9 How abuse, neglect, bullying, persecution and violence may impact on children's and young people's development and behaviour

Research by a number of organisations has shown that these types of abuse will have an impact on a child's or young person's development if they are not addressed, particularly if they take place in infancy or early childhood. Depending on the type of abuse and how long it goes on, it can potentially affect all areas of development, and have long-lasting effects throughout an individual's life. In addition, those who suffer abuse and maltreatment may also be more likely to be exposed to other negative experiences such as parental substance abuse or poverty, which will also affect their development.

▲ How might a pupil be affected by bullying or abuse?

Area of impact	Effect
Educational attainment	If a child or young person is suffering some form of abuse or persecution, their brain development may be affected, which may cause low self-esteem and affect their cognitive development; this will have a direct impact on educational attainment. It is also likely to affect how much they are able to focus on what they are doing in the setting. They are likely to be distracted, unable to complete their work and may lack interest in what they are doing in school. They may also have more absences or lateness than others in the school or early years setting, which will again affect their attainment.
Attachments and relationships	In cases where children and young people have spent time in care and suffered abuse or maltreatment, they may suffer from attachment disorders. Those suffering abuse are likely to be anxious and upset, and may withdraw from their relationships with others, not wanting to talk to or spend time with them. They may distrust others and become isolated, which will affect their social and emotional development.
SEN	Children and young people who have special educational needs are likely to find it more difficult to make progress due to distractions and anxieties. They may be unwilling or unable to talk about what has happened, or, depending on their level of need, be unaware that they are suffering abuse.
Physical health	Children's and young people's physical health can be affected, particularly if they are physically abused or suffer from neglect. They may also lose their appetite, which may affect their growth and physical development. They are also at greater risk of developing health conditions such as type 2 diabetes, malnutrition, poor lung function, and vision and oral health problems.
Mental health	Abuse such as bullying or violence is likely to cause extreme anxiety, and loss of confidence and self-esteem for the victim. This will mean that, without support, the child or young person may have long-term psychological effects.
Unwanted behaviour: • self-harm, suicide • alcohol and/or drug misuse • aggression • risky or sexualised behaviour/promiscuity • criminality	The effects of abuse may cause different types of unwanted behaviour in children and young people, as listed here. This is because they are more likely to try to find ways of forgetting about what is happening to them, or try to get attention in another way, even if this is not positive attention. In some cases, they may carry out the abuse that has happened to them on someone else. In young children, an indicator of sexual abuse can be that they are using words or acting out situations that are not age appropriate.
Socio-economic status	Abuse, neglect and persecution may have long-term effects on a child's or young person's socio-economic status in the future. A study by the Public Health Research Consortium (PHRC) entitled 'Child Maltreatment and Adult Living Standards at 50 Years', using British data, found that of the 8,076 people studied, the level of maltreatment had a direct association with outcomes, and that this rose if there was more than one type of maltreatment.

▲ How a child or young person might be affected by abuse

Assessment practice

1. How does legislation influence what happens in schools and early years settings?
2. Name **three** pieces of legislation that have an impact on safeguarding practice.
3. What is the GDPR?
4. Give **two** examples of how schools and early years settings can support children's and young people's health and wellbeing.
5. Explain the difference between a child or young person defined as 'in need' and a child or young person considered 'at risk'.
6. Name **four** types of abuse.
7. Explain the steps you would take if you had cause for concern about a child or young person.
8. Define what is meant by an adult being in a position of trust.
9. Explain the purpose of the local safeguarding partnership.
10. How might abuse impact on a child's or young person's physical and mental health?

CORE Chapter 4:
Behaviour

One of the roles of adults when working with children and young people is to guide their behaviour. This is important so that they can not only learn to be with others and feel comfortable in a variety of different situations, but also attain and achieve well. This chapter looks at the many factors affecting behaviour, including a child's stage of development and their self-concept. We also look at the role of adults in supporting children and young people.

Learning outcomes

This chapter covers the following knowledge outcomes for Core Element 4:

4.1 How the stages of children's and young people's social, emotional and physical development may inform their behaviour, and how practitioners can use this information to meet children's/young people's needs

4.2 How a range of individual, environmental and educational factors can influence children's and young people's behaviour

4.3 The link between self-esteem, identity and unwanted behaviour

4.4 The development of self-concept and its impact on children's/young people's behaviour, cognition and social development

4.5 The importance of children and young people knowing how to adapt their behaviour to different social contexts

4.6 Why it is important to set and follow behaviour management policy and processes

4.7 How home, family circumstances and care history can affect children's and young people's behaviour

4.8 How children/young people may respond to both positive and negative verbal and non-verbal communication from adults

4.9 How and why practitioners provide positive approaches to motivate children's/young people's behaviour, attainment and achievement

4.10 Why practitioners use a range of strategies for setting clear expectations of behaviour

4.11 How and why practitioners use a range of strategies to support children and young people to develop self-regulation and resilience

4.12 Why practitioners use a range of strategies to deal with inappropriate behaviour

4.13 How and why practitioners use a range of strategies to motivate children and young people to test and stretch their skills and abilities

4.14 How practitioners assess risks to their own and others' safety when dealing with challenging behaviour

This chapter also includes eight knowledge outcomes from Assisting Teaching Performance Outcome 3. Text relating to Assisting Teaching is highlighted. Note that this content will not form part of the core assessments.

K3.9 Understand why stable adult and peer relationships are important

K3.14 Understand the approaches to the management of negative behaviours

K3.15 The strategies to help pupils understand, express and manage their feelings

K3.16 The positive effects of encouraging pupils to challenge and test their abilities

K3.18 How a range of factors can affect a pupil's self-concept

K3.19 Why it is important to give pupils independence and control

K3.20 Understand how a range of factors impact on pupils' behaviour

K3.21 Why it is important to recognise and reward positive behaviour with reference to behaviourist approaches

4.1 How the stages of children's and young people's social, emotional and physical development may inform their behaviour, and how practitioners can use this information to meet children's/ young people's needs

In Core Chapter 7, we look at the stages of social, emotional and physical development. Understanding and recognising the stages of development is important for practitioners because they often link to children's behaviour and overall needs.

By understanding children's and young people's development, practitioners are able to make sure that what they are expecting of children and young people is fair. A good example of this is taking turns. Developmentally, most three year olds can take turns, but two year olds will struggle with this. If a practitioner knows that a couple of children find it hard to share equipment, they may either provide additional equipment or guide the children so that they can develop the skill. In this section, we will look at the links between behaviour and stages of development.

> You should read this section alongside Core Chapter 7, pages 110–114.

How stages of social development inform behaviour

Social development is about the ability to be with others and to understand them.

> As you can see from Core Chapter 7, social development takes time.

Here are some links between behaviour and social development.

Understanding of social norms

Social norms are the invisible rules of behaviour that allow us to fit in with others. Most children from three years old will start to copy group behaviours. If they see that all the children around them are tidying up, they may start to do the same. Social norms can particularly affect older children's and young people's behaviour. This is because, developmentally, they have a strong need to fit in and be part of a group.

Case study

Patrick is 14 years old and loves music and singing. He would like to be a singer one day. When the music teacher announces that there will be a new choir, Patrick feels excited, but many of his classmates groan loudly. Patrick starts to join in with the groaning.

▶ What is the social norm in Patrick's class in relation to the choir?

▶ Why did Patrick join in with the groaning even though he likes singing?

▶ How might the social norms of his class affect Patrick's attainment?

Ability to relate to others and levels of empathy

Relating to others requires many skills. The ability to do this is linked to stage of development. While babies and toddlers have some ability to recognise the emotions of others, the ability to understand others' intentions takes longer. While most children have some level of this at around seven years, it continues to develop. In addition, to develop friendships with others, children and young people need to develop **empathy** – this is the ability to recognise and respond to the feelings of others. When there are problems with the ability to relate to others, children and young people may react to situations inappropriately.

Special educational needs and disabilities

Some children's and young people's social development and, therefore, behaviour can be affected by their special needs or disabilities. For example, a child who has social communication difficulties may want to play with a group of children, but not have the social skills to do so. The child may then become angry and hit one of them.

Stages of emotional development that may inform behaviour

Children's and young people's emotional development is linked to their behaviour. Here are some examples of how.

Ability to name and manage own emotions

The ability to manage emotions affects children's and young people's behaviour. This is known as self-regulation (see page 82). While, developmentally, young children find it hard to manage their emotions, typically, most older children and young people can control their impulses and emotions. This is partly because they learn to recognise how they are feeling and have the language to name emotions. This, in turn, can help them to use language to express how they are feeling rather than doing this through actions. Where children and young people find this difficult, we might see tantrums, anger and other outbursts.

Levels of maturity

In Core Chapter 7 we look at the typical ages and stages of social and emotional development. These can only be used as a guide as individual children and young people may show different levels of maturity.

Special educational needs and disabilities

Some children with special educational needs and disabilities (SEND) may not show typical emotional development. This might be because their special educational need or disability is causing them to be frustrated or affecting how easily they can manage their emotions. Some types of disability, such as hearing or sight loss, may also impact on children's and young people's social and emotional development. They may be frustrated because they cannot communicate as easily as their peers because they cannot fully understand or see them.

Stages of physical development that may inform behaviour

Throughout childhood and into adolescence children's bodies grow and develop. Physical development and growth can affect how some children and young people behave. Here are some examples of how physical development may affect behaviour.

Development of gross and fine motor skills

As discussed in Core Chapter 7, babies and young children develop skills that will help them to do more. These include gross motor skills that allow them to throw and kick, but also fine motor skills that allow them to feed themselves, pick things up and manipulate them. As fine and gross motor skills develop, children are able to explore more. They may, for example, start to climb on furniture or touch things that may not be safe. Sometimes, children may also want to touch, hold or do things, but have not yet mastered the necessary skills. This can sometimes lead to frustration.

Body changes as a result of puberty

During adolescence, young people's bodies change because of increased hormonal activity. Some types of hormonal activity are associated with moodiness as well as impulsiveness. In addition, sleep patterns can be disturbed, which can exacerbate swings in mood. A range of behaviours are associated with puberty, including anger, tearfulness, frustration and withdrawal.

Special educational needs and disabilities

Sometimes a child's or young person's physical development may stop them from doing something such as joining in with others or doing something well. An older child with limited fine motor skills difficulties may knock over a model that they were building, or a young person may not be able to join their friends who are sitting on a wall. This can cause frustration and anger, and may lead to a child or young person withdrawing or giving up an activity.

4.2 How a range of individual, environmental and educational factors can influence children's and young people's behaviour

There are many factors that influence children's and young people's behaviour. Some aspects of their behaviour relate heavily to their actual needs. By understanding some of the factors and, therefore, needs of children and young people, we can support their behaviour more easily.

Individual factors

Children and young people can show very different behaviours. This is because there are individual factors at work. Here are a few examples of individual factors.

Self-esteem

Self-esteem is about how you value yourself. How children and young people value themselves can make a difference to how they behave. We look at this further later in this chapter (Section 4.3).

Special educational needs and disabilities (SEND)

> We saw in Section 4.1 how some children and young people with SEND may, because of their stage of development, show some behaviours.

Age

> We look at how stages of development affect children's and young people's behaviour in Section 4.1 and also in Core Chapter 7.

Typically, children and young people find it easier to manage their impulses and behaviour as they become older. This is partly because they may have more advanced language skills as well as experience of how to manage their stress. Children and young people who have good language skills may find it easier to manage their impulses and behaviour. This is because they can use words to express how they are feeling.

Environmental factors

Where and how children and young people grow up can affect their behaviour.

Culture and religious beliefs

Culture, including religious beliefs, can affect children's and young people's behaviour. This is because it can affect the expectations that adults have of children and young people.

> There is more on this in Section 4.7.

Care history

Some children and young people do not live with their biological parents. They may be fostered or adopted. While this can be a positive experience, for some children and young people their care history may affect their emotional security and, therefore, their behaviour.

> We look at this in Section 4.7.

Family circumstances

Every family is different and so are their circumstances. Children and young people may live with many siblings or none. Their families may be wealthy or poor. Some may live in the countryside, others in the city. Some family circumstances can affect behaviour. Events such as bereavement, relationship breakdown or unexpected money worries can put pressures and stresses on parents or carers. As a result, they may not be able to provide emotional security, resources or time for their children. This in turn can lead children and young people to show negative behaviours.

Educational factors

In education settings, there are a number of factors that can affect behaviour.

Bullying and discrimination

Sadly, some children and young people experience bullying and/or discrimination. This can change their behaviour. They may withdraw, or they may become aggressive or uncooperative.

Peer relationships

When children and young people are with others who are supportive and friendly, we may see more positive behaviour. On the other hand, where a child or young person does not have friends or is not accepted by others, we may see a range of negative behaviours, including frustration and aggression.

Relationships between children/young people and practitioners

How well children and young people get on with adults can make a huge difference to behaviour. Where relationships are strong, children and young people are more likely to be cooperative and show positive behaviours. On the other hand, if relationships are poor, negative behaviours such as uncooperativeness, anger and lack of concentration are likely.

▲ How can you tell that this child has a good relationship with this practitioner?

AT K3.20 Understand how a range of factors impact on pupils' behaviour

We have already seen that there are various factors that can affect children's and young people's behaviour. Some additional factors are discussed below.

Lack of secure attachments

On page 118 we look at how attachments are made and also the different types of attachment. You should read that section alongside this one to understand the importance of attachments and what is meant by a secure attachment. Where pupils do not have secure attachments, they may have difficulty in trusting others, and also in understanding others' emotions and intentions. We may see a range of behaviours, including aggression and lack of consideration and care towards others.

Planned or unplanned transition

Where there are significant changes in pupils' lives, such as family breakdown or bereavement, we may see a range of behaviours. Examples of transitions and their effects are discussed on page 131–2.

Safeguarding needs

Some behaviours that pupils show may be linked to safeguarding needs. An example of this might be inappropriate sexualised behaviour.

> In Core Chapter 3 we looked at behaviours that may indicate pupils have safeguarding needs.

Short-term factors

Sometimes pupils will show unwanted or negative behaviours because their physical or emotional needs are temporarily not being met. Good examples of short-term factors include those described below.

Tiredness

When pupils are tired, they may find it hard to concentrate and also to control their behaviour.

This often means that there are more incidents of unwanted behaviour at the end of the day and towards the end of the week, when pupils are more tired.

Hunger

Being hungry is linked to difficulty in regulating emotions and impulses. Hunger can also be a barrier to concentration.

Stress

There are many reasons why pupils may feel short-term stress, such as exams, noisy environments or problems with their friendships. Stress can cause strong emotional responses that can be hard for some pupils to control.

Changes to routine

Knowing what to expect and having routines can give pupils a sense of security. Some find it very hard to cope when routines have to change. This can cause them to become overexcited and over-stimulated.

The link between the factors and the changes in behaviour a pupil may display

It is important that adults are able to look at pupils' behaviours and consider what is causing them. The following table lists how factors in pupils' lives may show in their behaviours. It is important to understand that pupils will vary in their responses.

Factor	Associated behaviours
Insecure attachment	Attention seeking, withdrawal, depression, anxiety, antisocial behaviour, self-damaging behaviour
Transitions	Distress, acting out of character, regression, attention seeking, depression and anxiety
Safeguarding needs	Distress
	Acting out of character
	Regression
	Withdrawal
	Attention seeking
	Antisocial behaviour
	Self-damaging behaviour
	Depression and anxiety
	Behaviours that mimic the type of abuse the pupil has experienced
Hunger and tiredness	Impulsiveness
	Lack of concentration
	Difficulty in controlling emotions
Stress – very short term	Impulsiveness
	Lack of concentration
	Anxiety
	Tearfulness
Change to routine	Impulsiveness
	Lack of concentration
	Anxiety
	Tearfulness

▲ How factors in pupils' lives may show in their behaviours

4.3 The link between self-esteem, identity and unwanted behaviour

The term **self-esteem** is often used to describe how we value ourselves overall. It is linked to our own identity or **self-concept** (how we see ourselves). Self-esteem can affect how we behave, how hard we try and also how we expect to be treated by others. Children and young people who have experienced bullying, for example, may develop low self-esteem. This, in turn, can affect their outlook on others. They may expect others to treat them badly and so may find it hard to trust others in the future. Self-esteem is not fixed. It develops over childhood and can change according to our life experiences.

Children's and young people's self-esteem can affect whether or not they show unwanted behaviours. Sadly, some children and young people come to the conclusion that they are not able to show expected behaviours. They may think that they are simply not capable of changing their behaviour. This, in turn, means they may continue to show unwanted behaviours and this, in turn, confirms their idea of themselves. Changing a child's or young person's self-esteem requires patience.

In the same way that children and young people can develop low self-esteem, some children and young people can develop feelings of superiority and overconfidence. This can lead to risk-taking behaviours and also a lack of empathy towards others. When children and young people are overconfident, they can sometimes become frustrated or angry when there is a gap between what they think they should achieve and reality. In some cases overconfidence can also mean that children and young people expect to be treated differently to their peers and, again, when this does not occur they may withdraw, show anger or be moody.

4.4 The three elements that inform children's/young people's self-concept

There are three elements to forming a self-concept:
1   self-image – how you see yourself
2   self-esteem – how you value yourself
3   ideal self – how you would like to be.

How self-esteem is influenced by the ideal self and self-image

It is thought that where an older child's or young person's ideal self nearly matches up to their **self-image**, they will have high self-esteem. On the other hand, if a child's or young person's ideal self differs a great deal from how they see themselves, they will have lower self-esteem.

Case study

Jantine is 14 years old. He has a few close friends and is doing well at school, although he is not top in any subject. He loves playing football although has not played in the first team, unlike his best friend. He is a little overweight and shorter than some of the other boys in his class. He thinks of himself as being 'sort of average'. His teachers and his parents think that he could do much better if he put in more effort. When asked who he admires most and why, he chooses a professional footballer. Jantine says that he thinks that this man is cool, good looking, clever, rich and has lots of friends. When asked if one day he could be like that, Jantine shakes his head and says 'no way'.
▶ How does Jantine see himself?
▶ What does Jantine's choice of the footballer tell you about his ideal self?
▶ How might Jantine's self-esteem affect how hard he works and tries to improve his school work and his football?

How children and young people develop self-concept

Self-concept develops over time. There are distinct stages in its development:
▶ **The existential self:** Very early on, babies become aware of themselves. They realise that they are separate to their parents or carers. They see that if they touch something, it might move. If they smile at an adult or another child, the other person may smile back. Babies also start to respond to their name, knowing that it is 'theirs'. We also see in early childhood that children often do things and then look to see what the reactions of others are. The development of self-awareness is thought to explain some classic toddler behaviours such as not wanting to share toys and saying things such as 'mine'.
▶ **The categorical self:** This is sometimes referred to as **self-definition**. It is about how children and young people define themselves. In early childhood, we will see that children often talk with certainty about their age, what they can do and their gender. Interestingly, as children and young people develop and compare themselves to others, the way they define themselves changes. They are often less certain in their statements and add in more qualifiers. They may say things such as 'I am quite good at …'.

The possible impact of positive and negative self-concept

It is useful to understand how self-concept can affect aspects of children's and young people's development.

Behaviour

Self-concept can influence how hard children and young people try to fit in to social norms. When children and young people identify themselves as being 'good' or 'sensible', they are more likely to show expected behaviour as they view themselves as being capable of it. On the other hand, when a child or young person categorises themselves as being 'difficult' or 'naughty', they will often display behaviours that reinforce this position. This can become a vicious cycle.

Cognition

We know that effort and practice can affect our learning. Where children and young people have a low self-concept in relation to their learning, they are less likely to concentrate and try. They may use strategies to avoid learning, such as attention seeking or disrupting others. On the other hand, children who have a positive self-concept may see themselves as capable and able, with practice and support, to learn.

Social and emotional development

Self-concept also affects our ability to regulate our emotions and our relationships with others. Children and young people who feel that they are good with other people are more likely to be warm and empathetic. This in turn means that they are more likely to attract more friends. On the other hand, children and young people who have low self-concept may withdraw, or show aggressive or frustrated behaviours. This in turn may limit the number and the quality of their friendships.

AT K3.18 How a range of factors can affect a pupil's self-concept

It is important to understand what makes a difference to pupils' self-concept. There are several factors.

The expectations and reactions of adults and peers

What others expect of you and their reactions to you are among the most important factors in the development of self-concept. Where adults and peers frequently show positive reactions and have high expectations, pupils are more likely to see themselves as being likeable and capable. On the other hand, where adults constantly look disappointed, angry or just bored, children and young people are likely to feel less important or valued.

Age

As children and young people grow and develop, their self-concept changes. This is because they not only become increasingly more self-aware, but also more aware of others. A good example of this is the way that, by three years, most young children are starting to explore what it means to be a boy or girl.

In Core Chapter 7 we look at the patterns of development in terms of self-concept.

Media

Social media, films and magazines can also play their part in the development of older children's and young people's self-concept, particularly in relation to self-concept and self-esteem. Pupils may start to feel that they are lacking in some way as they may be exposed to many images of slim, successful and apparently happy people.

Culture

How pupils value and see themselves can be linked to the culture in which they are being raised. In some cultures, for example, boys are valued more than others and so may have a more positive self-concept.

Abuse

Sadly, pupils who have experienced abuse are more likely to have a lower self-concept. This is because when pupils are badly treated, they may develop a self-image that assumes they deserve to be harmed.

Relationships

Friendships and the relationships pupils have with others, including parents and teachers, can make a difference to how they think about themselves. Positive relationships can help pupils feel emotionally secure and so help towards a positive self-concept.

Socio-economic background

Being from a poorer background can lower self-concept, especially for older pupils, who may be aware that they do not have the same clothes or phones as others. They may also be aware that they cannot go on holidays or join in with activities and hobbies. As comparison to others is a crucial way in which self-concept is formed, not being the same as others can be difficult.

How to support the development of a positive self-concept

There are many ways to support self-concept. The following are some examples.

Celebrating the diversity and individuality of all pupils

When pupils feel valued as individuals and cared about by key adults in their lives, they are more likely to develop a positive self-concept. There are many ways that we can enable this. First, we can listen and learn about the pupils that we work with. Taking an interest is a key way of celebrating diversity and individuality. You can also make sure that, when planning activities and resources, you reflect pupils' cultures.

Role modelling

Implementing the praise and reward strategies of the setting (e.g. star/helper of the day) can be useful.

Giving praise (see page 79) and using reward strategies (see pages 78 and 81) are useful strategies for behaviour, and they also develop self-concept.

Understand opportunities to support a pupil's self-efficacy

Pupils who are high in self-efficacy believe themselves to be capable and able to take control of their learning. This affects pupils' attitudes towards trying out new things. A pupil high in self-efficacy will believe that, with practice or help, over time they will be able to master a skill, task or experience. It is thought that self-efficacy begins in infancy and is linked to how adults encourage and support children.

There are several ways in which pupils develop self-efficacy. Being aware of them means that we can support pupils.

Mastery experiences

By giving opportunities for pupils to return to and master concepts, skills or tasks, pupils can learn that with effort and support they can achieve whatever they set their minds to.

Case study

Rahima hates maths and lots of other subjects. She often says that she can't do them. Usually, she is told that, as she has tried hard, she can just put her books away and finish. Today she has repeatedly failed at correctly answering some of the questions. Her new teacher is keen to help her. She begins by asking Rahima what she already knows and can do. She asks Rahima which question looks the easiest to tackle. She then asks Rahima which part of the question she will need help on. Together they work on the problem. The teacher then writes out another very similar question. She asks Rahima to point out the parts that she can do. Rahima can now do more than earlier. The teacher then asks Rahima where she needs help. They finish off together before the teacher writes out another very similar question. This time Rahima says 'I know how to do this' and smiles.

▶ Explain the dangers to pupils' self-concept and self-efficacy when they can stop an activity without successfully finishing it.
▶ Explain how the teacher's approach encourages Rahima to take control of her learning.
▶ How is Rahima also learning self-efficacy through mastery?

Vicarious/modelling experience

One of the ways that pupils can develop self-efficacy is through watching others and, from this, modelling attitudes and behaviours (**vicarious experience**). A pupil who sees another pupil who is struggling but who by persevering manages to master a skill or concept may then go on to copy this behaviour.

Key term

Vicarious experience: learning about behaviours and attitudes through observing others and imagining yourself in the same situation.

Emotional and physical experience

Another factor in self-efficacy is a pupil's state of mind and how relaxed or comfortable they are. Pupils who have low mood or who are stressed and anxious may find it hard to show self-efficacy. We need to consider these aspects when suggesting challenges or planning activities.

4.5 The importance of knowing how to adapt behaviour to different social contexts

When we look at behaviour, it is important to recognise that how we need to behave depends on who we are with and also where we are. We may joke and fool around when we are at a party with friends, but it would not be appropriate at a serious or sad event such as a funeral. This learning is part of our social development, although it is worth noting that children and young people who have social communication difficulties may not automatically be able to adapt their behaviour. This is why recognising children and young people who may need additional support is so important. Let's look at some of the key reasons why children and young people need to be able to adapt their behaviour.

Learning in educational settings

In order to learn, children and young people need to manage their behaviour. This is important for their own learning, but also so as not to disrupt others. Children and young people may need to be patient and persevere, but also to work cooperatively with others as part of their learning.

Developing impulse control

Impulse control is linked to the ability to self-regulate. It is important that children and young people can manage their immediate impulses as this can affect their learning. It may mean not giving up when frustrated or waiting one's turn to answer a question.

Conforming to social norms

In every situation, there are expectations and ways of behaving. These are called **social norms**. Recognising the social norms and adapting our behaviour helps us to fit in and be accepted by others. Children and young people sometimes need help to know what to do and how to behave in some situations.

Making friends and maintaining relationships

Children and young people who can adapt their behaviour are more likely to have friends and to have good relationships with others. This is because relationships require us to pick up cues about how to

▲ What are the social norms in this classroom?

behave based on others' actions, gestures and mood, and then to adjust our own behaviour. It is not a good idea to play a practical joke, for example, on someone when they are very stressed, or laugh when they are very upset. Children and young people also need to impulse-control in order to listen to others, take turns and not blurt out something that might offend someone.

4.6 The importance of setting and following behaviour management policy and processes

We know that children and young people find it easier to manage their own behaviour when they know what is expected of them. We also know that they can find it hard when adults are not consistent in these expectations. This means that all settings will have a behaviour policy. The policy will also include processes or procedures for adults to follow. When you start on placement or in employment in a new setting it is essential for you to find out about and follow the behaviour policy. Here are some benefits of having a behaviour policy:

▶ **Clarifying the expected standard of behaviour:** A behaviour policy helps not only adults, children and young people, but also parents, to understand the values and expected behaviours of a setting.

As we will see in Core Chapter 5, children and young people benefit when parents and adults work closely together.

▶ **Giving children a chance to have input, resulting in more ownership and buy-in:** A behaviour policy will include ways of involving children and young people in expected behaviour. This might include encouraging adults to explain the reasons for rules and also taking on board the comments of children and young people. Some school settings may have school councils or class representatives who can put forward their ideas for changes to aspects of behaviour policy.

▶ **Setting realistic expectations for behaviour:** We have seen that children's and young people's behaviour changes according to their development. A behaviour policy should set out expectations that are fair and realistic, and based upon age and stage of development. Stage of development is important when working with children who have special educational needs.

▶ **Safety for all children and young people:** One of the reasons why a behaviour policy is needed is to ensure safety. There may be rules, for example, about how many young children can be on the climbing frame at once, or rules for young people about how they move around school corridors or during a PE class. As well as physical safety, behaviour policies will also cover bullying and other aspects that might affect emotional wellbeing.

▶ **Consistent approach to behaviour management:** Where children and young people will spend time with more than one adult, it is important that all adults' expectations are the same. If children and young people find that different adults expect different things, they may become unsettled, and this may lead to some children and young people spending their time testing the system.

▶ **Fairness in how children or young people are rewarded and sanctioned:** It is essential that children and young people feel that they are being treated fairly. A behaviour policy that looks at both rewards and sanctions or consequences of unwanted behaviour can ensure that children and young people are treated fairly. Adults working in settings must make sure that they follow rewards and sanctions as set out in the behaviour policy, even if they do not always agree with it, as consistency is essential.

▶ **Opportunities to celebrate success:** Some behaviour policies, especially those in schools, also include ways to reward or celebrate the actions or efforts of either groups of children and young people or individuals. Examples of this include receiving a sticker in the classroom or a certificate in assembly.

Research

Find out your placement's behaviour policy.

What should happen if one young child bites another? Describe the steps staff should take in this situation.

4.7 How home, family circumstances and care history affect children's and young people's behaviour

Parental expectations

Parents play a significant part in shaping children's and young people's behaviours.

In Core Chapter 5, we discuss how parents may have different styles of bringing up their children.

Some parents may expect their children to show obedience, while others may focus on helping others. Some parents may not impose any boundaries or expectations of behaviour. Understanding parenting style can help us to understand how we can support children's and young people's behaviour.

History and consistency of care

Stability is important in children's and young people's development, particularly in terms of key adult relationships. Where family breakdown occurs and key people in children's lives are no longer present or available, this can cause emotional difficulties.

These in turn can cause children to show unwanted behaviours such as aggression.

> You can read more about attachment in Core Chapter 7.

Culture and community

How we behave is also linked to our family's culture and the community in which we live. In some cultures and communities, for example, children and young people are expected to show respect for adults by not questioning them or answering back. In some cultures and communities, boys are treated differently to girls and expectations of boys' behaviour may be lower. This can mean that some boys may find it hard to follow instructions, take turns or be patient.

Adult and child relationships and interactions

The warmth of relationships and interactions between adults, especially parents, can impact on behaviour. Where children and young people have been exposed to aggression, hostility or negativity, they may develop low self-esteem, and also model this behaviour. On the other hand, where there has been warmth and support, children and young people may feel more settled and emotionally secure. This can result in them showing more care and empathy for others.

How practitioners can use information about individuals' home, family and care circumstances to anticipate and deal effectively with unwanted behaviour

When it comes to supporting children and young people, this is essential. We need to find out from parents and carers the story of their children's lives and any changes to their circumstances. Information that is shared must always be kept confidential, but as professionals, we can use it in a variety of ways.

> In Core Chapter 5, we will look at the importance of working in partnership with parents.

Working with parents/carers to help them find support and advice

Sometimes, parents may let us know that their family circumstances are about to change or have changed.

They may also tell us about their child's behaviour at home. It is not uncommon for children and young people to show appropriate behaviour in settings, but to be very challenging at home. If we work with parents in ways that mean they feel they can tell us when they are struggling with behaviour, we can help them gain information and advice from a variety of sources. This might include parenting courses, bereavement and relationship counselling, or financial services.

Sharing information with relevant colleagues to support multi-agency work and early interventions

With permission from parents, unless there is a safeguarding issue, information can be shared with other professionals to support the child or young person.

> In Core Chapter 5 we look at the range of colleagues in multi-agency roles that work with the family or the child/young person.
>
> For more on safeguarding, see Core Chapter 3, page 47.

Supporting individuals through planned and unplanned transitions

The term **transition** is used to describe changes in children's and young people's lives. Some changes may be quite small and have few effects, but others, such as a bereavement or family breakdown, can be significant and may affect development, including behaviour. Knowing what is happening or about to happen in a child's or young person's life can help us to make the transition easier.

> See Core Chapter 7 for more about different types of transition and how to support children and young people in connection with these.

Informing a behaviour management plan

When children or young people show unwanted behaviour, we may draw up a plan to support them. This is sometimes referred to as a behaviour management plan or a behaviour support plan. In order for the plan to work, we need to know what might be causing the behaviour. Information about the child's or young person's family circumstances will help to influence it.

In some cases, children's and young people's behaviour is linked to a special educational need and it may not always be possible for them to modify their behaviour.

A good example of this might be a child who has autism who may not cope with sudden changes and may react by throwing an object or hiding away. If adults recognise when a child has special educational needs, they can adapt the environment and their interactions and so prevent behaviours that may cause problems for others. We look at special educational needs in Unit 11.

Setting and tracking individual behaviour targets

In some settings, such as schools, the behaviour management plan will also have some targets. These are likely to be shared with everyone involved but also with the older child or young person. To make these targets achievable, it is important to know as much as possible about what is happening in the child's or young person's life.

 K3.9 The importance of stable relationships and the impact of disruption, including placement disruption, on a pupil's development and behaviour

Stable relationships

Where children and young people care about an adult or have a strong attachment to them, they will find it hard when this person is not available to them. This might be a teacher who leaves for a new job or a step-parent who moves out because of relationship breakdown.

Repeated changing of adults can make children and young people very wary of trusting and caring about new adults. This in turn can affect their ability to care about other people's feelings. This can be a particular issue for children and young people who are in care. Children and young people may change foster placement, which may also involve moving area and school.

Significant disruption to children's and young people's lives can cause them to exhibit strong emotions, including aggression, jealousy and frustration, but also depression. The impact of disruption is one reason why, ideally, support during transition is important.

We look at this in Core Chapter 7.

The impact of disruption on a pupil's development and behaviour

Where there has been disruption in pupils' lives, we may see a range of behaviours:
▶ **Insecurity and withdrawn behaviour** are common behaviours where there has been disruption. We may also see attention seeking as part of insecurity.
▶ **Frustration and aggressive behaviours** may occur when pupils become overwhelmed by their feelings or when they are put under pressure.
▶ **Lack of self-esteem and confidence** may occur as pupils may not be getting attention and reassurance from the people they care most about.
▶ **Not meeting academic milestones** often happens because when pupils have disruption in their lives it can make it harder for them to concentrate and pay attention. School or course work may not feel like a priority.

4.8 How children/young people may respond to both positive and negative verbal and non-verbal communication

The way we communicate with children and young people makes a significant difference not only to their behaviour, but also to their learning. We have seen that the development of self-concept is significantly linked to how adults talk and respond to children and young people. Tone of voice and body language are often just as important as the words that people use. You may remember a time when someone said 'have a good day' while not looking at you and using a flat, bored voice!

How we communicate both **verbally** and **non-verbally** has significant impact on how children and young people respond.

> ### Key terms
>
> **Verbal:** the use of words as well as how the words are said.
>
> **Non-verbal:** communication that takes place without words being said.

Verbal communication

Talking to children and young people is a key way in which we can support behaviour and also learning. For verbal communication to be effective, it is important we think about the following factors.

Level of language

The length of our sentences and the words we use must be at the right language level for the child or young person. We need them to understand what is being said. If a message is very important, shorter sentences or even single words work best: 'Stop now!', 'Good work' or 'No!' Too much talking can stop children and young people from understanding the key messages.

Clarity

Some adults are not always very clear. They say things like 'Shall we put these away now?' when they really mean 'These are going away now.' They can then become cross when children or young people do not put the items away. Make sure you say what you mean.

Pause and response time

It is helpful to remember that there is a gap between something being said and the other person understanding what is meant. For babies, young children and young people with language needs, this gap can be quite long. It is helpful for all ages to leave pauses as this allows time for understanding. This is very important when explaining concepts or ideas. When using verbal communication for teaching, check children's or young people's understanding, and encourage them to ask questions or to comment.

> ### Practice points
>
> #### Giving instructions
> ▶ Make sure you have the child's or young person's attention first, e.g. say their name.
> ▶ Be clear whether you are giving an instruction or whether there is a choice.
> ▶ Keep instructions short but be positive in your body language and tone.
> ▶ For young children or young people with language needs, give one instruction at a time.
> ▶ Give praise or acknowledgement after each instruction has been carried out.

Non-verbal communication

Eye contact

Looking directly at the child or young person is useful as we can check that we have their full attention. Having a child's or young person's attention is not only important in learning, but also in supporting behaviour. We can also use eye contact and watch reactions to check that there has been understanding. Staring at a child or young person and holding their gaze is a good 'warning' strategy. On the other hand, during ordinary conversation, this can cause fear and be intimidating, making children and young people feel stressed.

Tone

The tone of our voice sends a message to children and young people. Enthusiastic tones are encouraging and can be persuasive. On the other hand, negative and sharp, angry tones can backfire. They can make children and young people feel stressed and increase aggression or fear. The volume of our voices can also influence the tone. Quiet, slow and calm speech can make children and young people stay or become calm because they can see that the adult is in control. Shouting, on the other hand, is ineffective in many situations. It creates stress and so can trigger angry or fearful responses in children or young people.

Proximity

How far away we are (our **proximity**) during communication can matter. Being close with warm tone and words can be encouraging and positive. Being very close when angry words and body language are being used can be intimidating, especially if the adult is higher than the child or young person. Occasionally, this can be useful to show a child or young person that we are not pleased or we mean what we say, but it is not a strategy to use frequently.

Gesture

The most common **gestures** are those we make with our hands and our heads. There are positive gestures like nodding, clapping or a thumbs-up; combined with a smile and warm words, they send positive messages. This in turn can encourage children or young people to show wanted behaviour or, when learning, to concentrate and persevere. Some gestures such as a 'no' with a head movement can be useful when combined with eye contact as a non-verbal signal to show a child or young person that they need to stop what they are doing.

Key terms

Proximity: the distance between the child or young person and the adult.

Gestures: actions involving fingers, hands or feet, used when communicating.

Pointing

Pointing is a gesture, but it has a special purpose in non-verbal communication. It draws a child's or young person's attention to a specific object or item. With babies, we use pointing and eye contact to show them something that will be the focus of our talk. This helps them link objects with words. With a young person, we may point to a chair where they are meant to sit or to a sign to remind them of the rules. How children and young people respond to pointing will be linked to eye contact, body language and also to how any words are said. 'Get here!' said as a command while pointing is very different to 'Look, it's over there', said with a smile to help a child find something.

Body language

Body language refers to how we use our bodies to communicate, and can also include facial expressions. Where adults are trying to be positive, they may use open body language. In open body language, the adult is relaxed, they smile and their arms are relaxed. When communication is negative or the adult is tense, we may see closed body language: arms might be folded and there is no smiling. Open body language is useful to send out relaxed, encouraging messages. This can help children and young people to feel good about what they are doing. Closed body language, sharp tone of voice, staring and stern words send out warning signals.

Practice points

Positive communication

▶ Positive communication strategies tend to work best with children and young people.
▶ Make sure that your non-verbal and verbal communication send out the same messages, e.g. do not smile if you are telling a toddler to stop hitting another child.
▶ Make sure that your voice has enthusiasm and is positive when encouraging children and young people.

4.9 Why practitioners provide positive approaches to motivate children's/young people's behaviour, attainment and achievement

We know that the amount of effort that we put in to anything can improve how well we do. To encourage children's learning, but also desired behaviour, practitioners use positive approaches. Many strategies work for both behaviour and supporting learning.

Reward systems

Many different types of reward system are used in settings. The simplest one, which is often used with young children, is to give a sticker at the time the behaviour is being shown. Other reward systems work by children or young people collecting tokens, points or stickers, with the view that doing so will lead to a reward. These systems include:

▶ **Star charts:** Star charts are often used for individuals, usually to tackle specific behaviours. Children and young people put a star or sticker on a chart when they show the wanted behaviour. When they have an agreed number of stickers, they then get a reward.

▶ **Marbles in a jar:** This approach is often used for groups of children or young people. They are given a marble that they put in a jar. Marbles are counted at the end of the week and rewards are decided. Rewards may include extra playtime or a game.

▶ **House points:** Children or young people are divided into groups, teams or houses. When they show wanted behaviour or have worked or achieved well, they are given points that are recorded. At the end of a half term or term, the house with the greatest number of points is given a certificate, trophy or extra treats.

Practice points

Using reward systems

▶ Children and young people know what they must do to get the reward.
▶ Expectations for behaviour or achievement must be realistic, otherwise, children and young people will quickly lose interest.
▶ Make sure that the reward is something of interest to the child or young person.
▶ Make sure that children and young people understand the reasons behind the expected behaviour or achievement goal.
▶ Review the system regularly to check that it is effective.

Tidying up star chart				
Name	Week 1	Week 2	Week 3	Week 4
Ayse	★ ★			
Sofia	★			
Ben	★ ★ ★ ★			
Max	★ ★			
Rufus	★ ★			

▲ How might having a tidy up reward chart change children's behaviour?

Establishing positive relationships and using appropriate praise

One of the greatest needs for children and young people is adult attention, respect and warmth. Sadly, where children and young people are not getting sufficient attention, they often show attention-seeking behaviours. By making sure that positive attention is given along with praise, we can often change behaviour. We can motivate children and young people and change their behaviour over time through getting to know them and showing that we care about and value them. It is worth finding out about children's and young people's interests – for example, their favourite programme or toy – so that we can have conversations about something other than their work or behaviour.

Practice points

Positive attention and praise

▶ Avoid giving attention when children and young people are showing unwanted behaviour to get attention. Instead, try distraction for younger children, or ignoring them.
▶ When wanted behaviour is being shown, give immediate positive attention and praise.
▶ Link the praise and attention to the wanted behaviour – for example, 'Well done! You are working hard.'
▶ Be sincere in your praise – for example, don't say 'That's amazing!' when the work is not. Children and young people know when adults are doing this and it loses its impact.
▶ Praise and positive attention will take time to work with children and young people who have low self-esteem or whose self-concept is based on being 'naughty'.

Formative feedback to help children/young people improve

Formative feedback is a way of giving children and young people information and guidance in order that they can improve their behaviour or attainment. For behaviour, this might mean talking through what a child or young person is doing well and what their next steps might be. This approach can also be used to improve attainment in schools, and may be done either in conversation or through written comments on work.

> ### Key term
>
> **Formative feedback:** verbal or written information that helps children or young people to work out how they can improve.

(AT) K3.21 Why it is important to recognise and reward positive behaviour, with reference to behaviourist approaches

In Core Chapter 2 we looked at different approaches to learning and behaviour. We saw that rewarding positive behaviour can be very effective.

> Look back at Core Chapter 2 and see if you can find the theorists who suggest that rewarding positive behaviour can influence future behaviours.

How to reward positive behaviour that is age and stage appropriate

We saw in Section 4.9 that there are various methods that can be used to improve children's and young people's behaviour, and their attainment and achievement. These include verbal praise, reward charts and house/class points. These methods work because they positively reinforce behaviours that we need to encourage in pupils. In addition, there are some other positive reinforcements that schools use:

▶ **Merit certificates:** These are given to pupils to reinforce effort or achievement. Having a physical piece of paper can encourage pupils because every time they look at it, they are reminded of their success. In addition, pupils may see other pupils receiving them and want to copy their success.

▶ **Assemblies:** Assemblies provide pupils with large-scale recognition. Pupils may be asked to stand or to talk about what they have done. This level of recognition is effective only if pupils enjoy having public attention. It can backfire with pupils who are less extrovert or confident.

▶ **Agreed enrichment activities:** Some schools offer pupils who work hard additional activities that are not available to the rest of the class. This can be a great incentive and motivator for some pupils. It can, on the other hand, be a source of resentment if other pupils feel that it is not fair. It can also be divisive with some parents.

▶ **Feeding back to pupils/parents/carers:** Have you ever heard comments such as 'Don't mess around'? Such comments with regard to behaviour are not very useful because they do not tell children or young people exactly what they do need to do. Feedback is different because it helps children and young people understand their next steps. Instead of 'Don't mess around', an example of formative feedback would be 'You can do this, but you need to wait your turn. What can you do while you are waiting?'

As well as feeding back to pupils, it is also important for parents/carers to know if their child needs help with their behaviour. By working together, we can agree consistent strategies and approaches. This means that the child receives consistent messages about expected behaviour. It also avoids situations where children or young people complain to their parents about being reprimanded and the parents are not aware of the policies and procedures that are in place and so complain to the setting.

Recognising and rewarding positive behaviour can make pupils feel good about themselves and act as encouragement. While, ideally, we need pupils to learn to manage their own behaviour for themselves, using a behaviourist approach can motivate some children and young people.

We have seen that reward systems and praise are used to encourage attainment. These strategies are the two main ways of rewarding positive behaviour according to behaviourist theory that we looked at in Core Chapter 2. The idea is that if pupils are recognised and rewarded for wanted behaviour, they are likely to maintain it.

There are some things to consider when using both reward systems and praise:

▶ A few words or even a thumbs-up can make a significant difference to managing and encouraging wanted behaviour.

▶ Avoid giving attention when pupils are showing unwanted behaviour to get attention – instead try distraction for younger children, or ignoring them.

▶ When wanted behaviour is being shown, give immediate positive attention and praise.

▶ Link the praise and attention to the wanted behaviour – for example, 'Well done! You are working hard.'

▶ Praise and positive attention will take time to work with pupils who have low self-esteem or whose self-concept is based on being 'naughty'.

4.10 How practitioners use a range of strategies to set clear expectations of behaviour

Children and young people find it easier when adults are clear about what they can and can't do. This is particularly important when they move setting or are in new situations such as going on an outing. A range of strategies can be used, as described below.

Establishing a structured approach

A structured approach is often about having routines. This means that children and young people get into habits of what to do and how to behave at certain times. A structured approach may include the start of the day, lunchtime and home time. Having a clear approach helps children and young people feel secure.

Setting age- and stage-appropriate ground rules and boundaries

Expectations for behaviour only work if children and young people can actually manage them. We saw earlier in the chapter how the age and stage of children and young people can affect their behaviour. Our starting point is always to think about what is fair before we set boundaries and ground rules. One of the changes as children and young people develop is that we should increasingly set the rules and boundaries with them. This allows them to understand the rationale of these and they are then more likely to respect them.

Alongside boundary setting, older children and young people need to know what the consequences of breaking boundaries might be. We might, for example, say to a group of seven year olds that they can play with a ball, but if they kick it towards the windows, the ball will be removed.

Acting fairly and consistently

We have seen several times in this chapter the importance of consistency. Children and young people find it hard when rules or expectations keep changing. This is why a behaviour policy is used in settings. Having said that, sometimes in order to act fairly, adults need to show a little flexibility. If this is the case, they need to tell children and young people why the rules have been changed or a child is being treated differently.

Modelling appropriate behaviour

One of the key ways in which adults help children and young people is by modelling the behaviour that is expected. If we want children and young people to talk quietly, we need to be quiet ourselves. We can encourage young children to tidy up by doing it alongside them or encourage young people to pick up litter or items from the floor by modelling this. Modelling behaviour combined with positive reinforcement (see below) can be highly effective.

Positive reinforcement

We have seen how by using positive reinforcement strategies such as praise or even rewards we can encourage expected behaviour as well as improve attainment. In new situations, when we see children or young people are doing something for the first time, we need to be quick to praise and acknowledge. This helps establish wanted behaviours quickly.

4.11 The range of strategies to develop self-regulation and resilience

Self-regulation is the ability to control our impulses and emotions. It is an important skill because it affects children's and young people's ability to cope when things are stressful, to concentrate and persevere, and also to maintain relationships. Children who have developed high levels of self-regulation are more likely to cope with new challenges in their lives and so develop resilience.

There are a number of ways in which we can help children and young people to develop self-regulation skills. When planning strategies, we need to consider a child's current level of self-regulation and tailor any strategies accordingly.

Playing games/interactive sessions that encourage turn-taking and impulse control

Many games, including those using technology, require children and young people to cope with strong emotions such as losing or winning. Adults can work with them to role-model and talk through ways of managing these strong emotions. It may be that children and young people learn to 'step back' when things are going badly, to calm down. Games and interactive sessions can be adapted to add to or reduce the amount of excitement/stress involved. Quick, short games that do not have prizes, for example, are easier to cope with than longer games with higher stakes.

Sharing stories that encourage reflection on own and others' emotions

The ability to use words to express complex feelings is important in the development of self-regulation. When children or young people are unable to express their feelings, they are more likely to show aggressive, frustrated and impatient behaviours. Working on language levels and vocabulary is, therefore, a key strategy. There are many ways of doing this, but using stories and books to discuss the feelings and motives of characters can make a difference. We can also use stories to help children and young people find connections between the characters' feelings and their own.

Modelling coping skills

Some children and young people are lucky. Their parents and the adults around them deal with stress well. This in turn allows them to copy the strategies that adults are using. When working with children and young people we need to show how to cope when things are stressful. Modelling coping skills as a strategy works best when adults explain what they are doing as well – for example, an adult might say 'I am counting to ten and taking deep breaths.'

▲ Why do games offer a way to help children and young people learn to control their emotions?

Encouraging physical exercise

Physical exercise can reduce the hormones that are linked to stress. Routine physical exercise is especially important when children's and young people's lives are stressful. In addition, during moments of stress, we can encourage children and young people to manage their emotions by doing things such as jumping up and down on the spot or going for a fast run around a playground until they feel a little calmer.

▲ How can physical exercise support these children's ability to self-regulate?

Supporting socialisation

Some children and young people may need adults to help them socialise, as their self-regulation skills are still developing. This is particularly important with young children, who may benefit from having an adult to guide them while they are still learning to manage their emotions. Older children and young people who, for a variety of reasons, find social skills such as turn-taking and sharing difficult may also need this support.

Encouraging problem solving and teaching how to reframe challenges in a positive light

Being able to reflect on why we are stressed and how to deal with it positively is a useful strategy for children and young people. It works better with children and young people who have developed good language and thinking skills. This approach requires adults at first to guide children and young people through it. A series of questions can be helpful. They can teach problem solving, and help children and young people to focus on next steps in a positive way.

Practice points

Here are examples of the types of question that might be used to encourage problem solving:
- ▶ What is happening that is making you feel stressed?
- ▶ What emotions are you feeling?
- ▶ Is the source of the stress very short term, temporary or longer term?
- ▶ Is the cause of the stress within your control? For example, 'I am behind with my work because I am watching too many films.'
- ▶ What can you do to eliminate or reduce the cause of the stress?
- ▶ If the stress is outside your control, what can you do to distance yourself from it or lower it? For example, use distraction techniques, exercise.
- ▶ Have you coped and survived similar stress before and, if so, what worked for you?
- ▶ What support might you need or use to help you cope with this stress?

Encouraging mindfulness

Mindfulness has been shown to be useful as a way of helping children and young people to reduce stress. There are several techniques, but they all work on the principle of encouraging children to 'step back', accept and focus on their feelings. To learn mindfulness, children and young people need to be guided but, over time, some older children and young adults will adopt it as a strategy without prompting.

Key term

Mindfulness: a technique of reducing stress that involves acknowledging emotions and sensations.

Creating opportunities for children and young people to take supported risks

Fear of failing or not doing well at something can hold back children and young people. They can develop resilience by trying out new things and challenging themselves. By overcoming challenges, children and young people can build resilience. The first step is often to encourage those children and young people who are low in resilience to 'have a go'. Ideally, we need to choose opportunities for children and young people that are challenging but not insurmountable, especially if we guide or support them.

K3.15 Understand the strategies to help pupils understand, express and manage their feelings

A significant component of self-regulation is the ability to understand, express and manage feelings. We have seen already that there are a range of strategies that may help pupils with their feelings, including modelling appropriate behaviour (see 'Modelling coping skills', page 82). There are some additional strategies to consider.

Creating an enabling environment

Some environments, especially those for young pupils, help them to manage their feelings because thought is given to the layout and also the resources on offer.

Teaching pupils strategies to manage their feelings

As well as mindfulness, which we looked at earlier (page 83), we can actively teach pupils strategies to manage their feelings. This might mean taking three deep breaths or stepping away from a situation that is making them feel stressed. When looking at strategies, it is important that they are age and stage appropriate.

Providing a safe place for pupils to talk

Talking about feelings is a key way in which we can support pupils. It is always helpful if there is a safe and quiet space away from others to do so. Some pupils may need time before they can start to open up about how they are feeling.

Developing an awareness of the 'language to express feelings'

We saw earlier that stories could be used to encourage reflection on feelings. Naming emotions is one key way in which we can help pupils learn to express their feelings. The most effective way is to do so at the point when we can see that pupils are experiencing strong emotions.

Using targeted activities and resources

It can be helpful to plan activities and use resources that help pupils express their emotions. There are a range of examples, such as using drama or role play, as well as sensory materials such as paint or sand. Some pupils can also find musical activities helpful in connecting them to their emotions.

The benefits of pupils being able to understand, express and manage their feelings

Managing feelings and emotions has many long-term benefits for pupils. These include:

▶ **Helping prepare them for adult life:** In adult life many things do not run smoothly. This means that dealing with stress and the emotions that come with it is good preparation for adult life.

▶ **Having fewer behavioural issues:** Many incidents of negative behaviour are linked to lack of self-regulation and the inability of pupils to cope with stress and emotion. Pupils who can identify their feelings and control them are less likely to have behavioural issues.

▶ **Having more positive and stable relationships:** Pupils who are emotionally aware are more likely to understand other people's feelings and also their intentions. This can help them develop friendships and also to work more easily as part of a team.

▶ **Having a positive self-concept:** A positive self-concept tends to be linked to how others view us and our own sense of worth. Where pupils can control their emotions, they are more likely to have friendships and positive feedback from others. This can help them to feel good about themselves.

▶ **Having good mental health and wellbeing:** Mental health and wellbeing are closely linked to a positive self-concept. Understanding emotions and also being able to talk about them can help pupils to have higher levels of resilience and so stronger levels of mental health.

▶ **Being able to contextualise experiences:** Most pupils will have periods of stress in their lives, such as exams, changing school or class, or falling out with a friend. Being able to understand emotions and cope with them will help pupils get things in proportion.

4.12 A range of strategies to deal with inappropriate behaviour

Adults can deal with inappropriate behaviour in children in various ways. Some of these strategies are actually about preventing inappropriate behaviours by understanding the needs of children and young people. A good example of this is attention-seeking behaviours. Attention seeking tells us that children and young people need more attention. The trick is not to respond to the behaviour itself at the time, but to increase the amount of attention given at other times.

Being fair and consistent

Throughout this chapter, we have looked at the importance of having fair expectations and also consistency. When dealing with inappropriate behaviour, it is important that it is dealt with consistently. This sometimes includes consistently ignoring it, as we have seen in the case of attention-seeking, as we need children and young people to learn that they do not gain attention through these behaviours.

Focusing on the behaviour, rather than the individual

We know that self-concept plays a part in behaviour. It is, therefore, good practice to talk about specific behaviours that need changing rather than about overall characteristics of a child or young person. For example, 'stop being silly' is a general statement. A child or young person may start to believe that they are simply silly. It would be better to say, 'You are making too much noise.' With older children and young people, it is also helpful to add in an explanation of how their behaviour is affecting others – for example, 'When you are noisy, it makes it hard for other people to concentrate.'

Using language that clarifies expectations

We can help children and young people move away from showing unwanted behaviour by clearly stating what they need to do instead: 'If you want to play with the large ball, you need to go outside.'

Following the positive behaviour policy and referring to it

Earlier in the chapter, we saw that adults must follow the behaviour policy of a setting. This provides consistency and also gives them a clear idea of how to handle different situations. With older children and young people, it can also be helpful to refer to the positive behaviour policy so that they understand that it is not you suddenly changing the rules – for example, 'You know you are not allowed to run in the corridors while you are in school. It is one of our rules.'

Implementing appropriate rewards and sanctions

Schools and some early years settings may have rewards and sanctions as part of their behaviour policies. Rewards may include being able to choose an activity, being given a sticker or certificate, or having a certain privilege. A sanction is the punishment or consequence of having broken a rule or boundary. For sanctions to work, children and young people need to know what will happen if they continue a certain behaviour – for example, 'If you keep throwing the balls around, you will be sent inside.' Children and young people also have to care about the sanctions. If the child or young person throwing balls around prefers to be inside, their behaviour is going to be unwittingly rewarded!

Practice points

Sanctions
- Make sure that you use sanctions according to any procedure laid out in a behaviour policy.
- Do not threaten a sanction unless you are willing to go through with it.
- Choose sanctions carefully, making sure they are proportional to the behaviour.
- Sanctions work best when they impact on what a child or young person enjoys doing, e.g. removing a computer game. Make sure that sanctions are fair and, if possible, link to the unwanted behaviour, e.g. washing a wall that has been scribbled on.

Removing the child/young person from the situation

Sometimes, children and young people cannot stop themselves from showing unwanted behaviours – they may be too tempting or the behaviour has become a habit. Removing a child or young person from the situation can sometimes be a good strategy. It can give the child or young person a chance to calm down or allow them to do something else that is positive.

Removing equipment

It is not always possible to remove a child or young person from a situation. Where objects or resources are the issue, these may be removed instead or put away. For young children, this should happen without too much being said. For older children and young people, a warning should be given and the removal becomes part of a sanction.

Distraction

Doing something else or changing the environment can work to distract children and young people. With babies and toddlers who have less impulse control, distraction is one of the main strategies used. A toddler who is banging a stair gate may be lured away by the sight of a puppet and this solves the problem.

(AT) K3.14 The possible impact of negative behaviours and approaches to the management of negative behaviours

The possible impact of negative behaviours

There are often consequences for pupils when they show negative behaviours, which over time can affect their progress and development. These consequences include:

▶ **Regression:** Adults and peers may become impatient and frustrated with the pupil. The pupil may lose out academically because they are not making progress.
▶ **Withdrawal:** Pupils may miss out on the support that peers can give them. They may not engage with lessons or participate in group activities, and so may miss out on learning.
▶ **Attention seeking:** Adults and peers may find attention-seeking behaviour frustrating and irritating. The pupil may start to lose confidence and self-esteem as a result of others' reactions to them.

Practice points

Managing attention-seeking behaviours

▶ Think about the cause of attention-seeking behaviour, e.g. boredom, insecurity.
▶ Avoid making eye contact during attention-seeking behaviour.
▶ If it is safe to do so, ignore the behaviour.
▶ Use distraction to take the other pupils' focus off the pupil who is attention seeking.
▶ Give the pupil plenty of personal attention and recognition when attention seeking is not taking place.

▶ **Antisocial behaviour:** Pupils may be excluded from lessons or separated from their peers. They may miss out on opportunities to learn, while also developing a negative self-concept (see page 72).
▶ **Self-damaging behaviour:** As a result of self-damaging behaviours such as smoking, pupils are likely to marginalise themselves from the education system and from some of their peers. This in turn may lower their self-concept.

Approaches to the management of negative behaviours

You will need to show that you understand various approaches to tackling negative behaviours. We have already looked at the following approaches to the management of unwanted or negative behaviours:

▶ Applying rules fairly and consistently in line with the setting's policies (page 73)
▶ Modelling and reinforcing positive behaviour (page 79)
▶ Praise, encouragement and use of incentives (page 78)
▶ Building positive relationships (page 79)
▶ Encouraging self-regulation (page 82).

In addition, here are some other approaches to consider:

▶ **Establishing the cause of the behaviours:** While it is possible to deal with unwanted behaviours at the time, it is always better to work out their cause. By doing this, it may be possible to prevent further incidents from occurring.
▶ **Involving pupils in setting rules and boundaries:** A good strategy for some pupils is to involve them in the setting of rules and boundaries, although it is important to do so

alongside the behaviour policy of the setting. Typically, the setting of rules and boundaries is done for things within the classroom, such as how it is to be decided which group of pupils gets to choose an activity. By involving pupils, they are more likely to respect and understand the rules.

Research

How does your work placement decide how pupils are involved in setting rules and boundaries?

Clarifying expectations on an ongoing basis

Some pupils need to be frequently reminded of what they need to do and the expectations for how they should behave. This is particularly helpful for pupils who may not be able to sustain certain behaviours without prompting.

Collaborative problem solving

Some negative behaviours can be managed by supporting pupils to find solutions for themselves. This approach works well because pupils who are involved are more likely to cooperate with the decisions. It may be that a pupil volunteers to sit away from their friend because they recognise that this will help their concentration.

4.13 How practitioners use a range of strategies to motivate children and young people to test and stretch their skills and abilities, including setting high expectations

Many children and young people are capable of a lot more than they realise. One of the challenges when working with children and especially young people is to help them realise this. There are several strategies that can work well and can help not just behaviour, but also academic progress and wellbeing.

Using age- and stage-appropriate praise and encouragement

We have seen that praise can be a positive reinforcement for behaviour. It can be powerful as a tool to help children and young people stretch themselves. To do this, practitioners need to praise children and young people when they are putting in effort or are showing high levels of perseverance and resilience. If praise is given when children and young people have not made much of an effort, there is a danger that they learn that even if they hardly try they can still get attention. For praise and encouragement to work, the expectations have to be fair while still challenging.

Involving parents/carers as part of a whole-school approach

Parents and carers play an important role in helping children and young people to work and try hard.

They need to know what their child's next steps might be in order to encourage them. This is why reports, parent–practitioner meetings and information sessions are important. Parents and carers can also share information about how their child is doing at home.

See Core Chapter 5 for further information about parent–practitioner partnerships.

Giving individuals a role/ responsibility

Being given responsibility, even at a young age, can help with self-concept and confidence. When giving responsibility it is important that it is age- and stage-appropriate, with a very high likelihood that the child or young person can manage it. If the responsibility is too much, it may backfire and they may learn that they are not capable. Responsibility for an eight year old might mean taking the register or a message to the office.

Encouraging self-reflection

While a key strategy with young children is to praise them, ideally, we need children and young people to do things for themselves rather than just to get praise from others. The transition to this requires that adults start asking questions such as, 'How did that feel?' or 'Are you pleased with yourself?' This can help children and young people learn to motivate themselves.

Rewarding success

Rewarding success is linked to positive reinforcement. There have, however, been some studies showing that adults should focus on rewarding effort rather than just achievement. While rewarding success can be useful in the short term and with young children, rewarding effort helps children and young people to learn the skills of perseverance.

Celebrating mistakes as learning opportunities

It is not possible to get everything right in life. For children and young people, this applies to both behaviour and learning. This means that if things do not work out for children and young people, we need to help them learn from their mistakes. For children with sufficient language and thinking skills,

we should encourage them to think about what they could have done differently and how they would approach a similar situation in the future. In terms of supporting behaviour, we might also ask why they think the behaviour occurred and the feelings behind it. By using mistakes as learning opportunities, children and young people can not only learn to modify their behaviour, but also to develop skills that are important to making progress in learning.

Encouraging children and young people to recognise one another's positive behaviour

Children and young people often find it easier to manage their behaviour when their peers are encouraging. This requires practitioners to create a culture where children and young people work together as a team. Practitioners can do this by praising children and young people who show care and support for others, and also by discouraging children from telling tales (snitching) on other children.

(AT) K3.16 Understand the positive effects of encouraging pupils to challenge and test their abilities

We have seen that there are a range of ways in which we can support children and young people to test and stretch their skills and abilities. It is also helpful to understand the positive effects of doing so.

Increasing motivation and interest

Most pupils find challenge motivating, provided it is within their grasp. By making sure that we plan challenging activities and experiences, pupils will enjoy and be more interested in what they are doing.

Experiencing regular success

Feelings of achievement and success are good for pupils' self-esteem. If activities and experiences are not sufficiently challenging, they are less likely to feel good about themselves.

Making effective progress

Everyone who is learning something likes to see that they are making progress. By creating opportunities for pupils to feel challenge and to test their abilities, they can see the progress they are making.

Developing emotional resilience

Something that is challenging may not always be easy or straightforward for pupils. Coping with frustration and setbacks and then going on to achieve or complete a task or activity can support emotional resilience. Pupils learn that they can cope with setbacks if they persevere.

Learning from mistakes

Part of learning something new or being given something that is really stretching is that it often involves setbacks and making mistakes. Pupils who understand that mistakes are part of the process tend to become more effective in how they approach learning.

Increasing confidence

Completing something that is challenging and succeeding gives pupils a huge sense of pride and achievement. This in turn supports their self-esteem and so can give them increasing confidence in their abilities.

(AT) K3.19 Why it is important to give pupils independence and control

Making sure that pupils have some level of independence and control supports many aspects of their development, behaviour and wellbeing. This means that when planning activities and routines and working with pupils, we should look for ways to give them some level of independence and control. Here are some of the ways in which this can help them.

▶ **Increases pupils' self-esteem/confidence:** Earlier in the chapter we looked at self-concept, self-esteem and also self-efficacy. When pupils are able to do things for themselves, they learn that they are capable. This in turn can give them confidence and so support a positive self-esteem and self-concept.

▶ **Prepares pupils to manage failure and disappointment:** In this chapter, we have seen the importance of resilience and self-regulation. By experiencing problems and overcoming them, pupils learn to cope with the emotions of failure and disappointment, but also develop resilience.

▶ **Gives pupils freedom to make informed choices/begin to assess risks:** When pupils have opportunities to make choices and be independent, they learn how to take and assess risks at the same time. This might be the risk of failure, if they do not succeed in the task that they have set themselves, or even the risk of

being laughed at by their peers. Learning to make informed choices and also assess risks helps pupils develop what will be significant life skills.

▶ **Helps pupils understand their own strengths and limitations:** Pupils can often see more clearly their own strengths and limitations when they have control over their own learning or behaviour. This in turn can help them understand when they need to ask for help, or it might encourage them to employ or learn new skills and strategies.

▶ **Encourages pupils to take responsibility for their own learning and improves academic performance:** One significant benefit of giving some control and independence is that it makes pupils more responsible for their learning. This can lead to higher levels of performance as pupils work harder to succeed. We also find as part of this that pupils' curiosity and motivation increases. Instead of doing the minimum to please an adult, they learn and work hard for themselves. This in turn can give pupils a strong sense of achievement.

▶ **Provides opportunities for challenge:** When pupils can set their own challenges, they often attain and achieve more. This, as we saw on page 86, has many benefits.

4.14 How practitioners assess risks to their own and others' safety when dealing with challenging behaviour

Sometimes, children and young people can show behaviour that might cause injury to themselves or others. A toddler, for example, might try to throw wooden bricks during a tantrum, or a 14 year old may throw a chair across a classroom. It is important that practitioners are able to quickly assess risks and find ways to deal safely with this type of behaviour.

Following the setting's policies and procedures

An important starting point is to know and follow the setting's behaviour policy and procedures. These should help you know when, how and if you should use physical restraint. The behaviour policy and procedures will also outline when, how and if you should move other children and young people away, and how and when to summon help.

Being aware of individuals' prior history

Knowing a child's or young person's prior history of challenging behaviour is useful. It means that we can plan ahead to prevent the behaviour from occurring in the first place. We can also think about how we might manage the behaviour if it occurs. While knowing about a child's or young person's history is useful, it is important for adults to always stay positive. Expectations of negative behaviour can actually provoke incidents.

Recognising triggers and early warning signs

Most challenging behaviours are caused by stress, boredom or frustration. Tiredness and hunger can also play a part. By recognising the triggers of challenging behaviour, we can also prevent incidents. This may mean giving additional attention and support to a pupil who you know will find a task difficult so that they do not have a chance to become frustrated. With a toddler, it might mean reading a story just before lunch. As well as recognising triggers, we also have to pick up on the early warning signs that an incident is about to happen. A few examples of early warning signs include:

▶ raised, angry voices
▶ excited, uncontrolled behaviour
▶ withdrawn, sulky behaviours.

Assessing the likelihood of harm to self and others

At the start of an incident, it is essential to stay calm and quickly assess what the potential risks are. If there is a lot of anger and frustration being shown, it is best to talk quietly and move slowly. This can help to calm down the situation. A risk assessment should be done to work out what may be the immediate dangers.

Removing or reducing unacceptable risk

As part of risk assessment, the behaviour policy and procedures should be followed to remove or reduce risk. This might involve instructing others to leave the area or removing objects that may cause injury. The focus is always on reducing the risk of harm.

Assessment practice

1 Give **two** reasons why children and young people need to adapt their behaviour to different social contexts.

2 Give **three** examples of factors that might influence a child's or young person's behaviour.

3 Explain how a positive self-concept may impact on a child's or young person's behaviour.

4 Why is it important that everyone in a setting follows the behaviour policy?

5 Give **one** example of a positive non-verbal communication, and explain how it might influence a child's or young person's behaviour.

6 Explain the role of praise in supporting children's and young people's positive behaviour.

7 Explain why self-regulation is important in children's and young people's ability to manage their behaviour.

8 Give **two** positive approaches to motivate children and young people.

CORE Chapter 5:
Parents, Families and Carers

When working within education and childcare, professional relationships with primary carers contribute to best practice and improved outcomes. In this chapter, we will consider the important role of parents, families and carers in the lives of babies, children and young people. We will explore strategies to build professional relationships with parents, the challenges and barriers to effective partnership working that may exist, and ways that these may be overcome. As a professional in education and childcare, parents may approach you for advice and guidance, and this chapter will consider where to find a range of reliable resources to support parents, carers and families.

Learning outcomes

This chapter covers the following knowledge outcomes for Core Element 5:
5.1   The advantages of working with parents, carers and wider families to support children and young people
5.2   The different contexts in which children may grow up and the importance of being sensitive to this
5.3   How to overcome possible barriers to effective partnerships with parents, carers and wider families
5.4   Where to find a range of reliable resources to support parents and carers and the wider family

5.1 The advantages of working with parents, carers and wider families to support children and young people

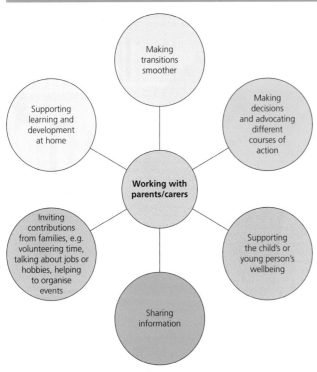

▲ There are several reasons why it is good to work in partnership with parents and carers

Parents, carers and families are sometimes referred to as the **primary carers** for their child/children. This means that they typically provide for their needs, have responsibility to ensure these are met and decide what is best for their child/children. Working collaboratively with professionals in education and childcare to develop professional partnerships with parents, carers and families can contribute significantly to the quality of the experience for all involved.

A shared level of expectation

Working in partnership with parents, carers and families creates a shared level of expectation. For example, exchanging information about the setting with the parent could be particularly useful. Parents and carers will need to be made aware of expectations for teaching and learning – for example, the approach to home learning, school uniform, code of conduct, and opportunities for parents and carers to be actively engaged. For babies and young children, this will include discussions around care needs, what to provide for children and what is provided at the setting. Policies also help parents and carers to understand the

level of expectation – for example, sharing expectations for behaviour may be helpful.

As we know, parents, carers and families want what is best for their children. There is a shared expectation that children will benefit from their experiences in education and care, both through educational attainment, but also, and significantly, that children will benefit holistically. Positive outcomes for children are, therefore, an acknowledged shared level of expectation. Parents and carers should expect high-quality education and care, provided by professional staff who are qualified, experienced and skilled to meet the children's individual needs within the legislative framework as required.

Making transitions smoother

Partnerships with parents, carers and families can be of particular benefit during transition.

> You will consider how transition may influence development in Core Chapter 7 (Section 7.6, page 131), which has useful information about the different types of transitions that typically exist in education and childcare.

There are many transitions that children will experience, such as changes to the family dynamic, and some of these will be unplanned. In this section, however, we will consider typical planned transitions in education and childcare. These include:

▶ starting nursery (or other early years setting)
▶ moving between carers in the early years setting (for example, from baby room to toddler room)
▶ starting primary school
▶ moving through classes and key stages in primary school
▶ starting secondary school
▶ moving through classes and key stages in secondary school
▶ starting at college (or sixth form)
▶ starting employment (apprenticeship).

Parents, carers and families know their child the best; they are very valuable sources of information for education and childcare staff, and education and childcare staff provide the same in return, offering advice and guidance, discussing any concerns and signposting to services as appropriate.

Professional partnerships rely on effective communication and trust. Building and maintaining effective professional partnerships supports smooth transition through effective communication, discussing any concerns and working collaboratively to prepare and support children before and during transition.

Let's consider how transition may impact children and young people, and how educational settings can support children and young people at these times.

- **Starting nursery (or other early years setting):** For babies, the stage of attachment and the role of the key person is fundamental in establishing a safe and secure transition. Preparation for starting nursery with young children should wherever possible not be rushed but a relaxed, gradual transition. Some young children may be very excited about starting nursery, but this does not detract from their emotional needs and the importance of the key person for building and maintaining secure relationships with children and their families.
- **Moving between carers in the early years setting (for example, from baby room to toddler room):** We often underestimate how moving from one room to another can be a huge transition for young children. The familiarity of a physical space offers emotional security and a level of independence to babies and young children. Moving between rooms gradually, mixing with children and staff from another room, can be helpful. Some early years settings will come together at specific times of the day, such as early morning and late afternoon as well as being able to enjoy mealtimes together. This social experience supports holistic development and wellbeing during this type of transition.
- **Starting primary school:** This is a huge milestone in a young child's life. The child is likely to feel a mixture of strong, powerful emotions, such as excitement, anxiety or fear. It is important to reassure children and for staff to prepare them. There are several approaches staff can take to support this transition. Staff from both settings can meet to allow for an exchange of relevant information. Visits and settling-in days are popular and prepare the child through gradual introductions. Making friendships is an important feature of this transition and when children feel secure in their personal and physical environment, they will be more likely to develop healthy dispositions for learning.

- **Moving through classes and key stages in primary school:** Again, the move between classrooms can bring strong feelings. Children may feel a little excited but are likely to have some concerns, too. As children get older and move through school, they are usually reassured by their strong friendship groups that they have established and moving class together with a friend can be far less scary. Children also begin to understand what the transition is, and it becomes an expected event that they can talk about more easily. This does not make the transition any less significant and staff should monitor how children are settling in and be mindful of their individual needs.
- **Starting secondary school:** This can, for some, be one of the biggest transitions in education. It brings together groups of children from different primary schools, so settling can be a difficult time. Children are also likely to be experiencing sensitive periods of time in their physical development, and with the onset of puberty there are many changes that children may experience. The changes in routine, the walk to school or the need to travel further, the different classroom layouts and the changes in teaching staff as well as lessons, expectations and even a change in uniform can all add to transition challenges for children. Settling-in days, taster days and activities to encourage friendship groups, through tutor classes and group activities for example, support this transition for children.
- **Moving through classes and key stages in secondary school:** As children progress through secondary school they often do so with strong friendship groups, but this is not always the case and staff should be mindful of interruptions to friendship groups and support a sense of belonging for all children. Expectations change as children progress through secondary school, exams, career choices and next steps planning in education.
- **Starting at college (or sixth form):** This can be another significant transition for young people. There may be a change in social groups as young people consider their career choices and options for further study. Making new friends, adjusting to new routines and new teaching and learning content can be challenging. Some areas of study, like education and childcare, require placement experience in a real work environment and this too brings challenges for students as they enter the world of work for the first time. Taster days, induction and

the skills of a mentor or personal tutor can really help students to settle into new routines and feel comfortable in their environment.

▶ **Starting employment:** Starting a job is very exciting but there will be feelings of apprehension, too. Students will be exposed to a world of work for potentially the first time and will very quickly be expected to meet expectations, follow new routines and work with colleagues. Induction, mentors and supervision opportunities will support a new member of staff, such as an apprentice, to feel confident in their new environment.

Transitions are not always planned and, even for planned transitions, children's holistic development and wellbeing may be impacted. Children with special educational needs or who are experiencing additional personal circumstances will need to be professionally supported through transitions to ensure consistency of education and care. Parents and carers should also be encouraged to be actively involved in transition. Unplanned transitions such as a sudden unexpected change in family dynamic may further impact on holistic health, development and wellbeing as well as potentially further impacting planned transitions and how well they may cope with challenging situations.

Supporting learning and development at home

Influences from the home environment are of tremendous importance for babies, children and young people. Home experiences also offer a great opportunity for learning to take place. Through positive partnership working with parents, carers and families, staff in education and childcare will be able to support this.

There are many examples of learning in the home environment – for example, younger children can learn a great deal from everyday routines. Children experience matching, sorting and counting quite incidentally when getting dressed, setting the table or going shopping, for example.

Young children enjoy stories; being read to and sharing books together not only provides opportunities for early literacy and a love of books, but can also just be the pleasure that children and parents/carers find in spending time together. Many early years settings will be able to share books for home reading, sometimes with props and activities that can be enjoyed together. Visits to the local library can also extend home school learning; there are often events for children and parents/carers to nurture a love of books and storytelling.

For older children, home learning may extend to topics and projects that they can work through at home. The key to supporting learning and development at home lies in communication and positive relationships between staff in education and childcare and parents, carers and families.

A child's love for music is often nurtured in the home environment. Musical instruments are very expensive and so some schools will lend children instruments to enable them to continue their learning in their home environment.

Developing a partnership with parents, carers and families that is strong enough to actively encourage learning and development at home is an important role for all staff across education and childcare.

Case study

Rubi is nine years old and enjoys being read to. However, despite her love of books, Rubi is not a keen independent reader. In class, the teacher has been using group reading strategies to engage Rubi and has observed her being interested and excited when reading in this way.

▶ How could a positive partnership with Rubi's parents support her learning and development at home?

▶ How could Rubi's teacher and other staff at the setting work with her parents to support Rubi with improving her independent reading interests and skills?

Research

Find out more about guided reading and how parents can be involved in supporting children with independent reading strategies at home.

Involving parents, carers and families in the setting

Actively involving parents, carers and families in a child's education and care is important. Settings can involve parents, carers and families in many ways, including:

▶ **Volunteering time in the setting:** Parents, carers and families may volunteer time in the setting, working alongside staff in education and childcare. This may include supporting off-site visits or listening to children read, or even specialist talks with older children around hobbies and interests – for example, cooking or sewing with the children. Such experiences strengthen the professional relationship between staff and parents, promoting a welcoming environment, as well as raising confidence in children while widening their experiences too.

▶ **Helping with events:** There are often opportunities when staff numbers need to be boosted, such as when taking children on organised events and celebrations. Parents, carers and families play a vital role here, often supporting planning stages as well as helping during an event. Parents, carers and families can be actively involved in their children's education, giving their time to support in any parent groups or organisations, for example. In some settings across education and childcare, there are parent teacher associations (PTAs). Regardless of the setting, parents, carers and families are much valued as key partners in education and childcare, and will often be called upon to support at events, open days and fundraising activities.

Sharing information and supporting the child's or young person's wellbeing

When parents, carers and families work in partnership with settings, trust develops between them. This encourages sharing important information about their children with staff, which means staff have a greater insight into the needs and personal circumstances of children. In the same way, parents can share photos of activities or events at home so staff can encourage some children to contribute during circle time, for example. It is not uncommon for early years settings and schools to use protected, secure online arrangements in line with policy and procedure, for sharing photographs and feedback which might share the child's achievements or participation as it happens.

When there is a trusting relationship between staff and parents, carers and families this helps the staff in all aspects of education and welfare. For example, parents and carers are much more likely to approach staff to share sensitive information about their child/children if there is a feeling of trust. When parents and carers do share important information about their child it can support staff to ensure that the child/children receive the best possible care. When staff are aware of a child's personal circumstances, such as a family bereavement,

ill health, mental health issue or a change in the family dynamic, they are much more able to support that child and monitor their progress.

Making decisions and advocating different courses of action

Advocacy involves listening to others, and providing accurate and relevant information and options to support an individual to make informed decisions. An effective advocate will always listen and never judge. When staff feel that they need to share information with parents, carers and families in the best interests of the child, they are advocating on behalf of the child. Parents, carers and families will also advocate on behalf of their child – for example, by discussing their child's needs and any specific provision that their child may need.

There are specific roles for parents and carers to get involved in decision making within education and childcare, such as parent governor or member of the PTA.

> **Research**
>
> Find out more about the role of parent governors and summarise the role they play in education and childcare. Contribute to a group discussion to share your findings. It may be useful to work in groups and look at the role of the governor in different types of settings, from early years to post-compulsory education.

5.2 The different contexts in which children may grow up and the importance of being sensitive to this

The characteristics of family structures

In order to work effectively with parents, carers and families, staff working in education and childcare must understand the characteristics of different family structures. In this section, we will look at some different types of family structure, including:

▶ **Nuclear families:** A nuclear family unit typically consists of two parents raising a child/children. This includes families where one or both parents may identify as lesbian, gay, bisexual or transgender (LGBT).

- **Single-parent families:** A single-parent family unit consists of a lone parent raising a child/children.
- **Extended families:** An extended family unit consists of multiple members of the same family living in the same home and possibly co-raising the child/children.
- **Foster families:** A foster family unit will consist of foster parents who care for children, typically, in the short term, who are not their own.
- **Adoptive families:** An adoptive family unit will consist of adoptive parents, and at least one child who has been adopted and lives with the adoptive family as part of the permanent family unit.
- **Blended/stepfamilies:** A blended or stepfamily unit consists of a combination of two separate families, with one or both parents having children from previous relationships.

▲ An adoptive family

The characteristics of parenting styles

The influence of parents, carers and families is significant for children's holistic development. There are different types of parenting style. To help us to understand the characteristics of parenting styles, let's consider some of them:

- **Authoritarian:** An authoritarian parenting style will place an emphasis on obedience and control. This style of parenting leaves little room for negotiation or compromise, and reasons for rules are not necessarily explained to children.
- **Permissive:** A permissive parenting style will typically have few rules or expectations. There may be a relaxed approach to behaviour, and children tend to have more choice and responsibility.

- **Authoritative:** An authoritative parenting style will set rules and expectations with clear boundaries. Parents will take time to explain these to their children, and to listen to and consider their views.
- **Instinctive:** An instinctive parenting style is, as its name suggests, strongly influenced by instinct. The style will be highly reactive to the parents' own upbringing.
- **Uninvolved:** An uninvolved parenting style is typically characterised by a lack of responsiveness, leaving children alone, and this may in extreme circumstances lead to neglect.
- **Helicopter:** A helicopter parenting style may mean that parents are heavily involved in every aspect of their children's lives, which may limit their independence and lead to frustration.

Why it is important to be sensitive to different parenting styles and different family contexts

Most parents, carers and families want what is best for their children. It is important to be sensitive to different parenting styles, and mindful of the important role parents, carers and families play as their child's first educators. This helps staff in education and childcare to:

- **Value and respect families:** This is critical to effective communication, making connections, and establishing and maintaining positive professional relationships based on trust. It also ensures fair and inclusive practice, with nobody shown preference or discrimination. This will also support the effective exchange of information between staff in the setting and parents, carers and families, which leads to better outcomes for children.
- **Contribute to inclusion in planning and provision:** Listening to parents, carers and families helps with planning effectively for children's needs and stage of development, and shows an appreciation of their individual circumstances.
- **Inform understanding of positive and negative behaviour:** Professional relationships with staff will support development of trust with parents, carers and families. This helps to promote ways of working together and modelling the same things, giving a consistency of expectation in relation to behaviour.
- **Inform understanding of developmental delay:** Parents and carers must be appreciated and valued as the child's first or primary educator. As such the parent or carer is often the first to notice any

concerns about their child's development. It is essential that staff in education and childcare settings listen attentively and sensitively to any concerns raised by parents and carers and act accordingly. Sometimes, staff in education and childcare will need to have conversations with parents and carers that are sensitive, such as discussing their child's development, raising any developmental concerns. All conversations are most effective when staff and parents, carers and families are aware of and sensitive to the individual family context and parenting approach, and are supportive rather than judgemental.

5.3 Understand the possible barriers to effective partnerships with parents, carers and wider families

When establishing effective partnerships with parents, carers and families there are many possible barriers that may exist. Some of these are as follows:

▶ **Time constraints:** Parents, carers and families will have commitments, including employment and responsibilities for other siblings or dependants. Finding time to hold a discussion beyond a few minutes can be challenging for some parents.

▶ **Work commitments:** Parents, carers and families will have a commitment to their employer or be self-employed. Some may also work irregular hours or shift patterns, so their availability may vary more than that of someone who works part-time or consistent weekday hours.

▶ **Limited resources:** Some settings will find it difficult to resource meetings. For example, there may be limited private areas for discussions to be held where parents, carers and families feel able to speak openly to staff, or if a meeting is planned at a time that requires additional travel, this puts an extra burden on the parent, carer or family, who may find the cost of travel a challenge.

▶ **Mistrust from families:** When professional relationships between staff in education and childcare and parents, carers and families have not been established it may be difficult to establish trust, making it less likely that parents, carers and families will approach staff and exchange information with them. Parents, carers and families

may also find it difficult to build a relationship with staff in education and childcare. This can be for many reasons. They may feel that by admitting they need support or by sharing personal circumstances they may be judged as parents and carers. Where barriers exist, it is the responsibility of staff in education and childcare to use strategies to actively engage them and break down any barriers in the best interests of the child or young person.

▶ **English as an additional language:** If English is not their first language or they have little or no ability to speak it, there may be a language barrier that exists between parents, carers and families and the staff in a setting. This brings challenges for all aspects of communication and working together.

▶ **Special educational needs or disabilities (SEND):** Parents, carers and families may have special educational needs themselves or care for an individual with SEND. Remember that not all SEND conditions are visible and it is important to be sensitive to the needs of all families.

▶ **Family members' own negative educational experiences:** Parents, carers and families may have had negative experiences themselves in their own education – for example, racism and/or bullying. Because of this, they may feel reluctant to engage with staff and may choose to hold back from information sharing.

How to overcome possible barriers

Staff in education and childcare settings should work in ways that overcome such barriers. Examples of useful strategies include:

▶ **The key person:** A key person is a member of staff who works in an early years setting; one of their main responsibilities will be to develop positive partnership working with the parents, carers and families of specific children. Older children and young people will benefit from the pastoral support of a class teacher or personal tutor, who will monitor and review the emotional welfare of the children and young people that they are involved with.

▶ **Offering an open-door policy:** Many settings across education and childcare will allow parents/carers to drop in and meet with staff at any time without requiring an appointment, with the aim of accommodating parents' varied lifestyles and commitments.

▶ **Encouraging home communication:** Settings will share information through a range of different media to enable consultation and improve communication, including secure family forums and apps, parent/carer questionnaires, and regular telephone or email contact. This must always be secure and access restricted only to those who are entitled to receive this information.

▶ **Ensuring the building is accessible:** Settings need to be accessible and inclusive for the benefit of all staff, families, children and visitors, who may have a variety of access needs – for example, adaptations in the physical environment to include hearing aid loops, Braille signs, wheelchair lifts, ramps and accessible toilets/ changing rooms.

▶ **Organising open days/evenings:** Many settings will organise open days or evening events to reach out to as many people as possible at a time that is convenient. This gives parents, carers and families time to exchange information and discuss their child/young person.

▶ **Using translators or child advocates:** Staff in education and childcare may use the specialist support of a translator or sign language interpreter, or they may work with other children and young people to support communication with parents, carers and family members. Newsletters should be presented in a way that all parents and carers can understand. The home language used by the child's or young person's parents and carers should always be valued; there is always a way of communicating effectively and staff must find an approach that works.

▶ **Offering home visits:** Staff in education and childcare may offer home visits at certain stages. This is a strategy that is often used during transition in the early years when young children are starting nursery for the first time, for example. Parents and carers will often feel more comfortable in their own home and this can remove any barriers that may exist for the parent or carer regarding time, access and travel costs. Home visits can also be beneficial for the teacher as they can begin to appreciate the holistic needs of the family.

Case studies

Read through the following case studies before responding to the questions. You may choose to work independently or with others.

Jayita is a single parent with two children, aged seven and ten years old. A childminder brings the children to school and collects them each day as Jayita has to work during this time.
▶ How can staff ensure that they communicate effectively with Jayita?
▶ Why is establishing that communication with Jayita so important?

Stefan is three years old and uses English as a second language. His parents do not speak English and manage to communicate with the support of Marianne, Stefan's older sister, who is aged eight.
▶ Why do you think it is important that staff are able to communicate with Stefan's parents?
▶ What might happen if Stefan's parents feel they are not included in conversations about their son's education and care?

Lucinda and Sam have two children, one in Key Stage 4 and one in the first year of a two-year Technical Qualification in Education and Childcare. Lucinda and Sam are both doctors; they work long and often unsociable hours, and often miss parents' evening.
▶ How can staff in education and childcare ensure that they are able to communicate with Lucinda and Sam?

5.4 Where to find a range of reliable resources to support parents, carers and wider families

From time to time, parents, carers and families may face challenges that will benefit from support from outside of the education and childcare setting – for example, an unexpected change to family circumstances that impacts on health, employment, income or housing.

There are a range of reliable resources provided by services to support parents, carers and families, including:

▶ charities
▶ the NHS and healthcare services
▶ community centres
▶ Citizens Advice.

▲ Citizens Advice

Professional staff in education and childcare should be prepared to signpost parents, carers and their wider families to different services that may be able to offer support at difficult and stressful times. Various sources of reliable support may be available, depending on the situation each family finds itself in.

Charities may organise self-help groups or advice sessions. Self-help groups will introduce individuals who are facing similar situations to one another, which can be reassuring for parents and carers, who can share their situation with others facing the same or similar concerns. Charities also often employ or train staff who can support parents, carers and families accessing their service by providing accurate, relevant and informed advice.

The NHS and healthcare services may provide a range of support services for parents, carers and families, not just related to physical health but also some support for mental health such as counselling services.

For more on this, see Core Chapter 1.

Community centres provide a neighbourhood space or hub for local residents to meet. There are often scheduled events planned at the community centre, such as youth clubs, sports events, Guides and Brownies,

Scouts and Cubs, and other groups may meet here too, such as the self-help groups already discussed.

Citizens Advice exists to provide advice and support to parents, carers and families – for example, with financial issues, as well as advice about benefits and other types of support.

Reflect

Work in groups to explore the different services identified above. Find examples from across the services listed and produce a factsheet to summarise the support available for parents, carers and families. This information could be collated as a resource file, or the information could be shared through a group discussion or peer group presentation with a question-and-answer session.

Assessment practice

1 Identify **three** benefits of parental engagement in education and childcare.
2 Suggest **two** ways in which parental engagement can be promoted in education and childcare.
3 Identify **one** barrier to effective partnership working with parents and explain how it may be overcome.
4 List **three** different parenting styles and explain each one.
5 Define the term blended/stepfamily unit.
6 Which type of family unit describes a family living with or close to relatives?
   a) nuclear
   b) extended
   c) adoptive
   d) stepfamily.
7 Starting nursery is an example of a transition. Analyse the role of effective partnerships with parents, carers and families during a transition.
8 A parent at your setting has confided in you that his family is struggling with large financial debt, and due to recent unemployment is feeling unable to cope. What support would it be appropriate to give?

Project practice

Read through the newsletter from a childminder to parents/carers below, then complete the tasks that follow.

Welcome to my summer newsletter, to keep parents informed about my childminding services and plans for the future, changes, holiday dates and general reminders. I would welcome your input! Should you have any ideas for subjects for my winter newsletter that you might find interesting, or any activities you want to share with me that I can do with your children, please let me know.

It has been lovely welcoming all the children back after a somewhat unusual time with the pandemic.

We missed all the children during lockdown, and they have all certainly missed each other! It has been lovely seeing them all restart their friendships with their buddies, and to watch the wonderful ideas and creative play they are getting involved in.

We have been spending more time in the garden for wellbeing, lots of fresh air and physical activity, and have been washing hands very frequently throughout the day.

The vegetables some of the children helped sow in mid-May and at the beginning of June are growing beautifully. We have harvested some carrots and

spring onions, which the children delighted in pulling out of the ground and eating!

Our watermelons are starting to form. It is amazing to see the two small mini-watermelons forming behind the flower!

All the children are involved in caring for the various fruits and vegetables, and have been watering them and watching them change almost on a daily basis.

We have been discussing how the watermelon flowers are pollinated by bees, wasps and other nectar-seeking insects who hop from flower to flower to distribute the pollen.

Since the children have shown a lot of interest in the plants, our summer project is called 'Plants that grow underground and plants that grow above ground'.

The children have created some lovely art work of sunflowers, pumpkins and watermelons. We also did an activity on healthy eating. Due to current restrictions, I will share the playroom enquiry wall with you by WhatsApp!

We have been sharing books on healthy foods and growing

vegetables, as well as nursery songs to support learning.

This week, we harvested our potatoes from the vegetable patch.

After collecting the potatoes, the children individually peeled and mixed their own ingredients to make tuna, potato and sweetcorn fishcakes using these freshly harvested potatoes. This brought the learning to life and children ate their fishcakes with lots of enthusiasm!

The sweetcorn is growing so fast. Although it is not ripe yet, the children have been watching the stalks grow. We will be measuring their length every day using a tape measure and recording the growth twice a week. The sunflowers are being measured too! I have been encouraging new words and more complex vocabulary around the activity where these can be introduced.

I hope you enjoyed seeing the pictures of your child harvesting from the veg patch and the cooking of the fishcakes on WhatsApp, along with other photos of your children engaged in activities this term!

General reminders

Plenty of wet weather changes of clothes – lots of water play is planned!

My holidays dates are:

Friday 14–21 Aug (incl.)

Thurs 24 Dec–1 Jan (incl.)

Task 1

▶ Identify the different ways the childminder is involving the parents/carers.
▶ Think about children in different settings across education and childcare, and how staff at these settings involve parents/carers and families. Make a list of as many different ways you can think of, and discuss with your peers the benefits to staff, parents, carers and families.

Task 2

Devise a leaflet for parents/carers that suggests a range of different ways to become involved in their children's education. You should identify the benefits of working in partnership with parents and carers.

Task 3

Describe how staff in education and childcare encourage home school learning.

CORE Chapter 6:
Working with Others

In this chapter, we will consider the range of diverse services that can be accessed by parents/carers, families, children and young people to offer support and guidance. When considering the range of services available we will take the opportunity to explore the roles of other professionals, and the significance of professional relationships and boundaries for effective partnership working. Collaborative ways of working for improved outcomes in the care and education of children and young people will be at the core of this chapter.

Learning outcomes

This chapter covers the following knowledge outcomes for Core Element 6:
6.1 How agencies and services support children, parents/carers and wider families
6.2 The roles of other professionals in supporting children, parents/carers and families
6.3 How to work collaboratively with other agencies and professionals
6.4 Why practitioners establish and maintain professional boundaries and relationships with children/young people, families and other professionals

6.1 How agencies and services support children, parents/carers and wider families

Charities and voluntary organisations

There are a range of charitable, voluntary or not-for-profit organisations that provide services for children, young people and their families. These are not-for-profit organisations that may also receive some funding from a local authority that values and requires the services that the organisation is able to provide within its region. Charitable organisations rely on donations to some extent, but are also able to provide services for children and young people as part of local authority provision. This involves a service-level agreement (a kind of contract) between a local authority and a charitable organisation, which allows the local authority to fund the voluntary setting in order that children and young people can benefit from the specialist support offered by the voluntary service.

There are many examples of such charitable and voluntary organisations and it may be useful to think about any such organisations that operate in your local area.

Good to know

Registered charities are part of the voluntary sector. Not all voluntary organisations are registered as charities (e.g. some community groups).

Some key organisations in this sector are:
▶ Family Action
▶ Family Rights Group
▶ Action for Children
▶ NSPCC
▶ Save the Children.

Some information is provided below on each of these organisations. As a member of staff it is useful to know about organisations that can support children, young people and families in particular circumstances. Staff in education and childcare may work as part of a professional team with staff from other organisations, including those listed above, in order to share information about the child, young person or family and work towards improved outcomes.

▶ **Family Action** aims to provide 'practical, emotional and financial support to families and to individuals who are experiencing poverty, disadvantage and social isolation'. **www.family-action.org.uk**

▶ **Family Rights Group** aims to support parents, carers and families by providing advice, guidance and advocacy, particularly regarding at-risk children and the care system. Family Rights Group will offer advice to individuals requiring support about their rights and any potential options that may be available to them in particular circumstances – for example, when social workers or courts make decisions about their child's or children's welfare. **www.frg.org.uk**

▶ **Action for Children** exists to provide support to children and young people through practical and emotional care, including advocacy services to ensure children's and young people's voices are heard, when they feel unable to do so themselves or if they find themselves in situations requiring specialist support. Action for Children will support children, young people and families in crisis – for example, children and families living in abusive situations, homelessness or in danger of eviction – and offers advice and practical help. **www.actionforchildren.org.uk**

▶ The **NSPCC** is a charity working to safeguard and protect children and young people from abuse. It provides many services, including national helplines, advice for children and families, therapeutic services, research and insight, as well as offering advice and training in schools and colleges. **www.nspcc.org.uk**

▶ **Save the Children** works in the UK and across the world to provide services to children, young people and their families, keeping them safe and healthy. The charity works with schools to support families with children's learning and literacy, helps low-income families with skills and resources to support their children in learning and development, and campaigns for fairer outcomes for children and young people. **www.savethechildren.org.uk**

Research

List as many charitable and voluntary organisations that work with children, young people and families as you can. Find out what services they provide and for whom. Create a resource file of the organisations that you find. Include information on which organisations operate within your own local area.

Public services

Public services can be broken down into two categories: **statutory** and **non-statutory** public services. Statutory public services are required to be provided by law, i.e. local or national government must ensure they exist and are funded. Statutory public services include the National Health Service (NHS), education and social services, local education authority service provision and Children's Services.

Non-statutory public services are not required by law, but are still needed by the public in practical situations and these services still provide crucial help. Examples include electricity, gas and water supplies. These are available but may not be publicly managed, but instead be provided by private companies, as is the case in the UK.

The National Health Service

The NHS was set up in 1948 to provide healthcare in the UK that is free at the point of use. This includes some mental health provision as well as services related to all aspects of physical health. Some services, such as prescription charges in England, ophthalmic services and dental services, are now charged for. However, they remain free of charge for children from birth to 16 years of age (or in full-time education), for those who are pregnant or with a baby under 12 months of age, as well as for families who are in receipt of certain benefits. Other exemptions may also apply. In Scotland, Northern Ireland and Wales no charges are made for prescriptions.

Good to know

In the same way that local authorities may develop service-level agreements with voluntary services to provide services for children, young people and families, the NHS also has links with private organisations. An example of this may be an individual accessing counselling through the NHS, where the counselling service may be provided by a private service.

Clinical commissioning groups (CCGs) are responsible for decision making involving the types of services that their local authorities will allocate funding to. This can lead to different levels of service provision and access in different local authorities. An example of this would be speech and language therapy.

Research

Work with your peers in a small group to list as many different types of services that are provided by the NHS as you can, and the type of support they offer for children, young people and their families.

Child and Adolescent Mental Health Services (CAMHS)

Mental health services provided by the NHS include dedicated services for children and young people. Specialist CAMHS are NHS mental health services that focus on the needs of children and young people.

Multidisciplinary teams that work within children's and young people's mental health services include one or more of the following specialist occupational roles:

▶ psychiatrist
▶ psychologist
▶ social worker
▶ nurse
▶ support worker
▶ occupational therapist
▶ psychological therapist (this may include child psychotherapists, family psychotherapists, play therapists and creative art therapists)
▶ primary mental health link workers
▶ specialist substance misuse workers.

Key term

Multidisciplinary team: a team that consists of professionals working together from across the sector who have different roles. For example, a health visitor and a social worker may work together with an early years practitioner to bring together their specialist expertise in order to support a child and their family at a particular time.

Research

Work together with your peers to explore the specialist roles listed above. Find out what each role involves when supporting children, young people and their families, and make notes.

Children's Services (education and social services for children)

Children's Services are provided by each local authority. The services offered within Children's Services include education and social services. Children's social services will provide specialist staff to support families with babies, children and young people in need of additional help, guidance and intervention as appropriate. The types of circumstances when social services may be accessed include:

▶ when there is a risk of harm or abuse to a baby, child or young person
▶ when a family is caring for a baby, child or young person with a disability
▶ when caring for **looked after children** and where fostering and adoption services are required.

> ### Key term
>
> *Looked after child (LAC):* a child who has been in the care of their local authority for more than 24 hours, sometimes also referred to as children in care. This can include children living with foster parents, in a residential children's home, hostel or secure accommodation.

Local education authorities

Children's education services are provided through local education authorities (LEAs, part of local government) and will include schools and colleges and their special educational needs provision. As you know, there are many different types of education and childcare provision. Education, health and care (EHC) plans are put in place by the local authority. The head teacher/manager will work with the SENDCo to make sure that these plans are reviewed as appropriate to ensure the strategies shared are being effective.

> For more on the different types of education and childcare provision, see Core Chapter 1.

Special educational needs review team

The EHC review team is responsible for statutory education, health and care needs assessments for children and young people aged from birth to 25 years, in line with the SEND Code of Practice.

When a child or young person has been identified as having a special educational need or disability, settings should make plans to:

▶ remove barriers to learning
▶ put in place effective special educational provision.

> See Core Chapter 11 for more on EHC and SEND in general.

SEND support is offered as part of the **graduated approach**. This is a four-part approach that works in a cycle. The four stages are:

1 Assess
2 Plan
3 Do
4 Review.

> ### Research
>
> Education, health and care (EHC) plans are developed, monitored and reviewed in line with the graduated approach. Find out more about the graduated approach as it applies to the role of staff in education and childcare.

6.2 Understand the roles of other professionals in supporting children, parents/carers and families

Children, young people and families may benefit from support from professionals who can offer specialist advice, guidance and intervention strategies as appropriate. Some of these specialist roles include:

▶ **Educational psychologist:** Educational psychologists are applied psychologists who work across the educational system and also in the community. They may also work with individuals and families.
▶ **General practitioner (GP):** GPs are qualified medical doctors working in health centres/surgeries within the local community. They work with others as part of multidisciplinary teams to support the **holistic** care needs of individuals. GPs work in health promotion and lifestyle change to prevent poor health across the lifespan. They also have a vital role in safeguarding and protection, working with other professionals to keep children, young people and families safe.

Key term

Holistic: overall or all round; the idea that the parts of something are interconnected so looking at the whole rather than each individual part. Here it means all-round care needs, with an appreciation of the contribution of each care need to overall wellbeing.

Other professionals working with the GP as part of a multidisciplinary team include nurses, midwives, health visitors (see below), physiotherapists and occupational therapists.

▶ **School nurse:** School nurses are typically responsible for an individual school or group of schools. The school nurse works with children, young people and families to promote holistic health, including the mental health and wellbeing of children and young people from five to nineteen years of age.

▶ **Health visitor:** A health visitor is a qualified nurse or midwife who has undertaken additional relevant training for this specialist role. The health visitor will work within the community and will support babies, young children and their families. Health visitors often hold clinics in a GP surgery or health centre but will also make home visits.

▶ **Social worker:** Social workers provide support for children, young people and families who need additional support. This additional support can be required to safeguard and protect babies, children and young people at times of need. They will also work with families and other professionals to ensure best outcomes for children and young people with disabilities, as well as those who are looked after children.

▶ **SENDCo:** The special educational needs and disabilities coordinator works with the nursery, school or college to ensure that the individual SEND needs of children and young people are met. They contribute to meetings and advocate in the best interests of the children. SENDCos will produce an EHC plan for children and young people aged up to 25 years of age. The SENDCo will offer advice, and work collaboratively with other professionals and families to ensure best practice is consistently applied. SENDCos in school settings will be qualified teachers. They will need to undertake further study to maintain their role.

See Core Chapter 11 for more on SEND.

▶ **Area SENDCOs:** Area SENDCOs are experienced teachers working with young children with special educational needs and/or disabilities (SEND) and their families. They work for the local authority and are able to offer advice as well as signpost to additional services and support.

▶ **Youth worker:** Youth workers work directly with children and young people, and typically work within the community. One important role of the youth worker is to develop healthy relationships with children and young people, often in the role of advocate, to make sure that children and young people are involved in decision making that affects them.

▶ **Counsellor:** Counselling is often available on the NHS and is accessed at a GP surgery. Counselling services may also be accessible via school or college. Counselling can help support children and young people to manage and cope with personal circumstances that impact their mental wellbeing.

Good to know

Mental health is a big issue for young people. According to statistics from Public Health England, approximately one in eight children and young people experience behavioural or emotional problems growing up.

www.nhs.uk/oneyou/every-mind-matters/childrens-mental-health

▶ **Occupational therapist (OT):** Occupational therapists develop care routines, and identify strengths and difficulties that children and young people experience in everyday life. For instance, a child with an identified need in fine and gross motor skills would see an OT; they work in education and childcare settings to support staff, other professionals, parents and carers in understanding these. Working together will allow for consistent practice that supports children and young people. Professional OTs have been trained in mental and physical health. They work to maximise children's development in all skills needed for play, learning and self-care activities (these are children's 'occupations'). An OT will consider personal, social and emotional, physical and environmental factors when working to promote participation and independence.

▶ **Speech and language therapist:** Speech and language therapists work to support the development of children's speech or language when speech and language needs have been identified.

This may include working alongside professionals to assess and offer supportive strategies for children experiencing swallowing difficulties. For example, the speech and language therapist may work with children with mild, moderate or severe learning difficulties, language delay and/or specific difficulties in producing sounds. The speech and language therapist may visit the nursery or school and support the staff working at different settings, providing strategies that have been developed to support children's speech and language, as well as person-centred strategies and approaches.

Research

Find out about integrated services for children, young people and their families in your local area, and the provision in place to support babies, children and young people and their families. A good place to start is by looking up Sure Start, Children's Centres and Family Hubs.

The benefits of working collaboratively with other agencies and professionals for improved outcomes for children/young people

When professionals work together towards shared goals, they promote a consistent approach towards best practice and improved outcomes for children and young people. For example, a child or young person with mental health concerns will benefit most from the advice of specialist professionals that is shared with all of those involved in their education and care.

It is much easier for children and young people and their families and professionals involved to access advice and support when there is good communication and collaboration between professionals involved. Communication should be clear and straightforward and value the contribution of all involved. The needs of children and young people should be reviewed regularly to make sure that any strategies and advice being followed remain effective. This is best achieved through regular communication and collaboration.

Collaborative working also enables the sharing of skills, knowledge and expertise to ensure best practice remains accurate and up to date.

Through collaboration, professionals will find referrals for expert intervention much more straightforward,

accurate and appropriate to meet the needs of children and young people. Staff in education and childcare will be skilled in child development and educational curricula and will be able to identify need in children and young people, simplifying the referral process. For example, with a child who is not reaching expected developmental stages, they will know that the child may benefit from the intervention of a healthcare specialist.

6.3 Work collaboratively with other agencies and professionals

▲ What sorts of information may be exchanged between the teacher and the parent/carer?

In this section, we will consider some key features involved in collaborative partnership working in education and childcare, which are important considerations when working with other agencies and professionals.

It is of course essential to build professional relationships with others in order to work collaboratively. For example, it is important to listen, to communicate effectively and to be reliable. Professional relationships are built on trust and respect: value one another's specialist expertise, and work towards shared goals in the best interests of the child, young person and their family.

Maintaining confidentiality and protecting sensitive data

Always remember the importance of confidentiality. Take this opportunity now to remind yourself of legislation relevant to confidentiality, data protection and how to store sensitive data securely. It is important to understand what we mean by sensitive data – for example, the personal information of children and young people, including their date of birth, home address, any personal circumstances and medical requirements as appropriate, will be protected through the Equality Act 2010. The General Data Protection Regulation (GDPR) 2018 is relevant to the data held about children, and the additional protection and safeguarding practices that must be followed. For example, children and young people may be less aware of the risks, consequences and safeguards involved in the processing of their personal data.

There are policies and procedures that staff legally must follow when working in education and childcare to ensure the confidentiality and storage of sensitive data is consistently upheld. Sensitive data includes any personal data that staff hold about babies, children, young people and families.

> For more discussion of legislation and policies surrounding confidentiality and sensitive data, see Core Chapter 10.

Research

- Look at the Department for Education's website to learn more about its publication *Keeping Children Safe in Education*.
- Look at the Early Years Alliance website to find out more about how sensitive data must be protected: **www.eyalliance.org.uk/preparing-your-early-years-setting-gdpr**
- Health and safety policies now include guidance around online security. Look at school, college and nursery policies to summarise how sensitive data is stored securely online. You may want to share your findings with your peers.

Gaining parental consent when appropriate

As discussed in Core Chapter 5 (page 91), it is essential to work closely with parents, carers and families. Staff working in education and childcare should always ensure they have gained parental consent as appropriate. For example, consent from those with parental responsibility for a child to go on trips and outings must be obtained before taking the child off the premises. Details about consent arrangements are usually discussed during registration periods when settling in to a setting. For example, parents/carers and families may give or refuse consent for photographs of their children to be used in newsletters or publicity, or for children to take part in short off-site visits that would enrich their experiences.

Reporting concerns and referrals

It is important that staff working in education and childcare are able, first of all, to recognise when intervention and collaborative partnership working is required and, second, that they are then able to identify the most appropriate service for intervention. Early intervention and referral to a specialist – for example, to a speech and language therapist if a speech, communication or language need is identified – can make a tremendous difference to the outcomes for the child's or young person's progress. Working closely with the child's or young person's family is often important during referrals, but be aware that child protection emergency situations may be an exception to this rule.

Following relevant policies/procedures

Policies and procedures are in place in education and childcare to keep everyone safe, to ensure legislation is being followed, and so that there is guidance and advice for staff as they follow any required action in any given situation. Unless there is a sound reason not to, staff should always discuss their concerns with their line manager or the most suitable person. For example, if there is a concern around a child's or young person's development, the special educational needs coordinator will need to be involved, and they will liaise with the head teacher/manager as appropriate.

6.4 Understand why practitioners establish and maintain professional boundaries and relationships with children/young people, families and other professionals

In Core Chapter 5 (page 91), we looked at the significance of establishing and maintaining professional partnerships with children, young people, parents, carers and their wider families. At the same time, professional boundaries are essential when working in education and childcare. When employed in this sector, the purposes of these boundaries are as follows.

Facilitating partnership working

Staff in education and childcare are responsible for collaborating with others in the best interests of the child, young person and their family. It is important that staff are able to identify needs accurately and recognise the benefits of working with relevant professionals when supporting children's and young people's needs. The setting within education and childcare may bring all of the professionals together, lead meetings and ensure everyone involved is kept up to date with outcomes, including reporting on the child's or young person's progress.

Protecting emotional wellbeing

Staff in education and childcare are educators in a holistic sense, and must be attentive to a child's or young person's all-round health, development and learning. Keeping children safe and responding to their emotional health will ultimately promote learning and their disposition to learning.

Respecting children's and young people's privacy

Children's and young people's rights must be valued at all times. Practice in education and childcare must ensure that children and young people are treated with dignity and that their right to privacy is maintained. For example, a child that requires support with personal care routines should be treated with respect, valuing their personal needs and respecting their privacy and dignity throughout.

Avoiding distraction from the practitioner's role

Staff in education and childcare must be aware of their job role, their responsibilities, and the boundaries and limits of their role. It is important to always understand what is expected and what action to take in different situations. It is also important to make sure that job descriptions are fully understood and followed by staff.

Providing structure and expectations

It is always important to set expectations clearly and ensure that everyone involved is aware of what is likely to happen, what their role is and what is expected of them.

Reducing conflict

Working in partnership with others can be complex. Everyone will have a view that is important to them. When working with others, effective communication is a key principle. It is important to listen to the views of everyone involved and always work towards shared goals that are in the best interests of the child or young person and their family.

Promoting safeguarding and preventing the misuse of power

Listening to others, respecting and valuing individuals, and making sure the voice of the child, young person and their family is heard is key to this. To do otherwise is to take advantage of trust and potentially allow the child's or young person's voice to be lost. Always remember that child-centred education and care is essential for best practice.

> It may be useful to reflect on the role of advocacy here (see Core Chapter 5, page 95).

Maintaining confidentiality

Staff working in education and childcare must always follow policy and procedures that are in place around confidentiality. As we have seen earlier in this chapter, maintaining confidentiality is essential in education and childcare.

> See also Core Chapter 10, page 160.

Practitioners' use of social media

In each childcare or educational setting, there will be policies around the use of social media, both in terms of staff's personal accounts and any official accounts for the setting. Misuse of social media is serious and can be detrimental to:

▶ professional boundaries
▶ effective partnership working
▶ confidentiality
▶ safeguarding.

Staff working in education and childcare must make themselves aware of all policies and procedures, including those involving social media, what is acceptable and what is not. These will set expectations for all staff and the use of social media. Having an appreciation of the seriousness of neglecting online policies and procedures is essential. For example, when working in education and childcare, staff may receive requests from children, young people and parents/carers who would like to connect with their personal accounts on online social media sites. It is important never to accept such requests.

Being connected to children, young people and their families through social media is not only unprofessional, but also places that member of staff at risk. These kinds of relationships with children and young people outside of the setting are inappropriate and unprofessional, and leave staff vulnerable to accusations of misuse of power in relation to safeguarding and protection.

Case study

Megan is a new member of staff at a school. She is keen to develop positive relationships with her students. At the end of Megan's first week, one of the students that she has been teaching finds her contact details on social media and sends her a friend request.
▶ What action should Megan take in this situation?
▶ Explain the importance of following a setting's policy.

Research

When working in partnership, professionals may collaborate together, developing a Team Around the Child or Family (TAC or TAF).

Find out about TACs and TAFs. Summarise the features of this collaborative partnership working, and the benefits to the child, young person and family of working in this way.

Case study

Alex is 13 years of age and attends his local secondary school. He has been living in foster care for the past two years. Alex struggles to develop friendships at school and is becoming increasingly withdrawn in group work. Alex does not contribute to class discussion and prefers to work independently. His tutor is also concerned about his wellbeing. The class teacher is concerned that Alex is becoming isolated among his peers and will struggle with the team project work planned for next term.
▶ Summarise the situation and how Alex may be feeling.
▶ Identify the professionals involved in Alex's education and care.
▶ Describe the role of the professionals involved and how collaboration could benefit Alex.

Case study

Hana lives with her two young children, Marianna aged six and Alfie aged three months. She has recently become a single parent, and has moved to a new area and is missing the additional support she had received from members of her extended family. The class teacher at the school Marianna recently started to attend has met with the head teacher to share their concerns about Marianna's emotional wellbeing. They have noticed that Marianna is not participating in class and is reluctant to communicate, even with adults. Hana is concerned about how she is coping with both of her children. During a visit to the GP surgery to register her family, the health visitor noticed Hana was upset in the waiting area. The health visitor made an appointment for a home visit to introduce herself to the family.
▶ Summarise the issue.
▶ Which professionals are already involved?
▶ Can you think of any other professional services that could become involved to support Hana and her children?
▶ Identify the support that you feel Hana and her family may benefit from, and give reasons for your response.

Assessment practice

1. Describe the role of the speech and language therapist.
2. Identify **two** benefits of working with other professionals in education and childcare.
3. Explain the importance of confidentiality when working in education and childcare.
4. A job description helps staff in education and childcare to know what is expected of them within the boundaries and limits of their occupational role. Is this (a) true or (b) false?
5. Describe what is understood by multidisciplinary working.
6. Name **four** professional roles that work with children and young people.
7. Explain why there are policies and procedures in place regarding the use of social media in education and childcare.
8. Using an example, analyse the benefits of early intervention for a child's or young person's speech, communication and language development.

CORE Chapter 7:
Child Development

All adults working with children and young people need to know how they grow and develop. This is needed in order to know how best to work with and plan for them. It is also needed in order to carry out observations and assessments, which we look at in Core Chapter 8. In this chapter, we look at the stages and patterns of expected development from infancy to adolescence. We look at attachment theories and how they affect healthy social and emotional development, as well as the development and importance of friendships. We also focus on the process by which babies and children acquire language and how adults can support language at all ages. We finish the chapter by thinking about how to support children and young people when there are changes in their lives. These are known as transitions.

Learning outcomes

This chapter covers the following knowledge outcomes for Core Element 7:

7.1   The expected patterns of children's/young people's development in infancy, early childhood, middle childhood and adolescence

7.2   Theories of attachment and their application to practice

7.3   How children/young people develop receptive and expressive language, and ways of supporting children

7.4   The role of adults in promoting language development at different ages

7.5   How children and young people develop friendships and the impact of these on wellbeing

7.6   How practitioners use a range of strategies to support children and young people through expected and unexpected transitions

This chapter also includes three knowledge outcomes from Assisting Teaching Performance Outcomes 3 and 4. Text relating to Assisting Teaching is highlighted. Note that this content will not form part of the core assessments.

K3.8   A range of transitions that a pupil will experience through school, and the possible positive and negative effects on pupils' wellbeing

K3.22   The expected levels of self-reliance and social behaviour at different ages and developmental stages

K4.1   Theories of language acquisition, and links to why communication and speech play such an important part in pupils' development

7.1 The expected patterns of children's/young people's development

Everyone working with children and young people needs to know what to expect in terms of their development. This information can then be used to identify children and young people who may need additional support, but also as a starting point to plan activities and manage behaviour. In this section, we look at cognitive development, physical development, and social and emotional development. Later in this chapter, we will look at expected development in relation to language.

Cognitive development

Cognitive development is about how we think, learn, remember and use information. It is sometimes known as intellectual development. There are many skills within cognitive development, such as the ability to problem solve, put things into categories and think about things such as number. Cognitive development also encompasses the way that we use our five senses. Sight, sound, smell, taste and touch all provide information to the brain that in turn helps us to coordinate our bodies and so adjust our responses to any given situation. The term **sensory perception** is sometimes used to describe the way the senses provide constant feedback to the brain.

A good example of a skill involving many aspects of cognitive development is doing a jigsaw puzzle. It requires thinking about the shape of the pieces and also being logical. When pieces do not fit, the eyes and hands provide information back to the brain which may prompt us to turn a piece slightly.

Cognitive development is closely linked to language development. This is because language plays an important role in how we process information and then retrieve it. The ability to look at things, name and categorise them seems to help us link pieces of information together. A good example of how language and cognition work together is the way in which, when you are stressed, you might say things out loud in order to organise yourself. The link between language and cognition is thought to be the reason why, although babies do have memories, we cannot retrieve our memories of being a baby.

▲ Why is memory important in this matching game?

Interestingly, cognitive development is one area in which we will find significant differences between individuals. These differences become very apparent during late childhood and adolescence. The reasons for the differences between children and young people are complex. They include the amount of time spent studying and reading, but also whether adults provide opportunities and support to do more challenging tasks requiring cognition.

Age	Cognitive skills
0–1 year	From three months: • Recognises familiar faces and voices From eight months: • Looks for an object that has been removed • Places an object in a container when asked • Finds an object that has been seen and then hidden
1–2 years	• Understands simple instructions, such as 'come' • Points to parts of the body • Points to a named picture
2–3 years	• Completes a three-piece puzzle • Copies a circle • Matches textures • Is able to point to little and big (e.g. 'Which is the big spoon?') • Matches three colours • Stacks beakers in order • Can find the odd one out in a group of objects (e.g. a large bead in a group of shells)

Age	Cognitive skills
3–4 years	• Tells if an object is light or heavy • Is able to repeat a simple story • Matches objects one-to-one (e.g. putting one plate on each placemat on the table) • Points to long and short objects • Is able to sort objects by shape and size • Knows the name of the primary colours • Names three shapes • Counts ten objects with support
4–5 years	• Recognises and writes own name • Picks up a number of objects (e.g. 'Find me four large beads') • Names eight or more colours • Is able to decide which object is the heavier by comparing objects • Is able to complete a 20-piece jigsaw
5–6 years	• Counts accurately to 20 or more • Can manage simple calculations using objects • Can play a board game involving simple rules • Can point to half and whole objects • Enjoys simple jokes • Is able to make connections between different experiences and articulate these easily
6–7 years	• Can read and write • Can play a board game that requires some logic • Can manage simple calculations without the use of concrete objects • Can predict what might happen next in a story • Understands and can make simple jokes • Can argue using some logic
7–11 years	• Able to read and write and, from around nine years, able to do so quite easily • Able to play board games and understands the need for rules • Learning how to tell the time and use money, and able to do so from nine years old • Can talk about hypothetical events (e.g. 'What would you do if you were given £50?') • Able to calculate without using objects (e.g. adding two numbers together) • Can make connections between what they already know and new information
11–16 years	• Ability in some situations to be systematic in order to solve problems (e.g. searching for a lost object carefully) • Developing ability to predict and speculate about complex abstract issues, e.g. 'Should everyone earn the same?' • Speed is increasing on some tasks as memory and processing skills develop (e.g. quicker to spot matching cards in a game) • Logic is developing and so games requiring strategy, such as chess and Monopoly, are enjoyed by some young people • Growing ability to analyse texts and abstract problems (e.g. 'How do you know that this character is lying?')
16+ years	• Significant differences between individuals at this age, partly dependent on their level of education and interests • Ability to think ahead in the short term, but not yet able to imagine the consequences of actions and decisions in the very long term; this is because the part of the brain that deals with decision making is still developing

▲ Cognitive skills at different ages

Physical development

Physical development is the range of movements and skills we use in everyday life, such as the ability to walk or to put on clothes. Physical development is important to overall development because being able to move, balance and use hands is linked to being independent, and to opportunities to learn and develop further skills. As you can see from the information in the table, the first four or five years are significant as many skills are gained in this time. Babies move from having survival reflexes to being able to consciously control some of their movements. After early childhood changes are less rapid, although as you will see there are some changes during puberty.

One of the key differences between the skill levels of older children and young people is the opportunity to develop and practise skills. This means that a young person who is interested in gymnastics will develop strength and balance, whereas a young person who enjoys running will develop increased levels of stamina.

Physical development is often divided into two broad areas: fine motor movements and gross motor movements (see table).

Fine motor movements are small, precise movements of the hand or sometimes the foot. They include movements such as turning a page in a book. **Gross motor movements** are larger movements that require whole-limb or whole-body movements, such as lifting a box or walking.

Reflect

Observe for 5 minutes a child or young person engaged in an activity.
- Record how they are using their fine and/or gross motor movements.
- How easily could they manage the activity without these skills?

Age	Fine motor movements	Gross motor movements
Birth	• Babies are born with a range of survival reflexes, such as the palmar reflex, where they grasp anything that touches their palm • Reflexes are not conscious movements • Over time, many reflexes are lost and replaced by controlled movements	
3 months	• Clasps and unclasps hands	• Moves head to watch things
6 months	• Can pass a toy from one hand to the other • Can reach and grasp toys	• Can sit up with support • Can roll from front to back
9 months	• Can hold and bite bread crust • Can put hand around cup or bottle • Can use rattle or shaker • Can play with simple toys (e.g. rattles, cups)	• Can sit up without help • May be crawling or attempting to move • Stands while holding on to something
12 months	• Points to objects using index finger • Can pass a toy to an adult and release it	• Stands and can walk holding on to furniture
1–2 years	• Picks up objects between thumb and finger (**pincer grasp**) • Can use spoon to feed • Can hold a cup and drink from it • Can build a tower of three bricks	• From eighteen months is walking well • Enjoys climbing into low chairs • Pushes or pulls toys on floor • Walks down steps one at a time, using two feet to each step • Towards two years, can run and stop without knocking into objects
2–3 years	• Can use a spoon to feed independently • Develops a preferred hand for holding pencils and other objects • Can build a tower of seven or more cubes • Can make circular marks and also horizontal and vertical lines with pencil or paints	• Walks upstairs one foot joining the other • Climbs climbing frame • Can throw ball • Can ride a tricycle and steer it • Can kick a ball gently • At three years, can stand and walk on tiptoe
3–4 years	• Can build a tower of nine cubes • Threads large wooden beads • Holds pencil in preferred hand • Can cut with scissors	• Jumps from low step two feet together • Walks up and down stairs using alternate feet for each stair • Can steer tricycle and manage corners • Can balance briefly on one foot at four years
4–5 years	• Can use a spoon and fork well to eat • Can dress and undress, but can't do laces, button or zips • Can cut along a line with scissors • Can thread small beads • Can use jigsaws and toys with small parts • Can copy name	• Can sit with knees crossed • Can stand and run on tiptoe • Can bounce and catch a large ball • Can kick a ball with some accuracy

Age	Fine motor movements	Gross motor movements
5–7 years	• Can thread a large needle and sew large stitches • Can colour within the lines of a picture or shape • Forms letters correctly and, from six years, finds handwriting easier • Can colour in shapes and, from six years, with increased accuracy • Can use scissors to cut along line and, from six years, can cut out circles	• Can walk on a narrow line • Can stand on one foot and hop easily • Can skip and move rhythmically to music • Can hop on each foot • Can throw, catch and kick well • Uses coordinated movements for climbing, swimming and riding a bike • Can walk backwards quickly
7–11 years	• Increased skill and accuracy across all fine motor movements • Drawings increasingly detailed and skilled • Handwriting may be joined-up • Easily making fine movements required to use technology	• Increased coordination allowing for skill in sports (e.g. football, gymnastics, swimming) • The level of mastery is time dependent
11–16 years	• Puberty may temporarily affect fluency of movements after a growth spurt; changes in body shape may affect spatial awareness • During adolescence, some young people may become short-sighted; this may affect their ability to see clearly, which might in turn affect their movements • During puberty, the heart and lungs grow and there is potential for increased stamina • Changes during puberty also increase overall strength – especially in boys, whose muscles increase	
16+	• High level of skill in both fine and gross motor development, but skill level on any task is dependent on how much time is spent on the activity; this in turn links to interest levels	

▲ Fine and gross motor movements

Social and emotional development

Social and emotional development encompasses two areas of development that are closely linked, which is why they are often grouped together. Social development is about the relationships we have with others and also how we adjust our behaviour to fit in with others. Emotional development is about our feelings and also our identity.

The diagram shows how social and emotional development is made up of many different elements.

> In Core Chapter 4, we looked at self-concept and also self-regulation. You may wish to revisit these sections as they cover elements of emotional development.

Social and emotional development is closely linked to the relationships that children and young people have with adults, especially their close family.

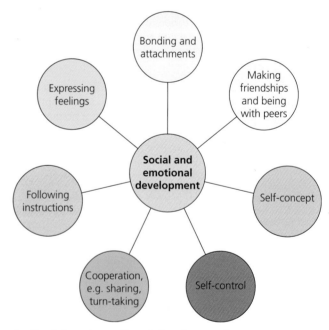

▲ Social and emotional development

Age	Social development	Emotional development
0–3 months	• Watches parent's face • Smiles and coos	• Cries to show distress • Will calm down when hears voice of parent
6 months	• Responds to faces and tones of voice	• Screams with annoyance • Enjoys being with parents and family members • May self-soothe by sucking fingers
9 months	• Laughs and enjoys being played with	• Is unsure about strangers • Shows preference to be with parents or main caregivers
12 months	• Enjoys playing simple games such as peek-a-boo	• Cries if cannot see parent or main caregiver
15 months	• Enjoys playing simple games with adult (e.g. building up and knocking down stacking beakers)	• Confident to explore environment if parent or main caregiver is present • Shows affection to familiar family members and friends
18 months–2 years	• Will bring toys and objects to share and show adults • Interested in other children of same age but cannot play with them cooperatively • May try to make adults laugh (e.g. put cup on head)	• Shows strong emotions including anger as well as pleasure • Can be determined • Tantrums when frustrated • May show jealousy if attention given to another child • Changes emotions quickly • Will become distressed if cannot see parent or familiar adult • Beginning to empathise with another person's distress by showing own distress
2–3 years	• Interested in being with other children • **Parallel play** is seen • Shows concern when others are crying • Is not yet sharing or turn-taking unless supported by an adult • Shows kindness and compassion spontaneously towards others	• Begins to be aware of their gender • Has quickly changing emotions • Likelihood of tantrums when frustrated • Has feelings of jealousy and anger towards other children • Will want to be close to a parent or a familiar adult • Will become distressed if cannot see parent or familiar adult • Shows increasing independence (self-care skills and play)
3–5 years	• Will enjoy playing with other children • Can play cooperatively and take turns, unless tired • Enjoys pretend play and will take on different roles (play becomes more complex from four years)	• Will find it easier to separate from parents, especially if with familiar adults or friends • Will still show strong emotions but will cope with upsets more easily • Can explain their feelings • Express likes and dislikes
5–7 years	• Preferred friendships often same sex • Can cooperate in deciding rules for games • Ability to communicate with others freely and without prompting from adults	• Starting to be more self-conscious and embarrassed; also reflecting on how they are doing in comparison to others (e.g. noticing when others get a sticker) • May occasionally have tantrums but mainly showing cooperative behaviour
7–11 years	• Friendships are stable and important, and usually same sex • Some girls' friendships can be intense • Understand rules and consequences • Play may become elaborate, with turn-taking	• Increasingly aware of their achievements in comparison to others • Able to manage their immediate impulses and so rarely have outbursts • Still need reassurance and support from parents and family members • Have a sense of right and wrong, which can be quite black and white • Self-esteem is usually positive in this period

Age	Social development	Emotional development
11–16 years	• Increasing amount of time spent with friends rather than family members • Friendship groups become larger • Influence of friends and peers becomes stronger	• Increasing levels of insecurity as a result of changes to body shape, peer pressure and developing sense of the ideal self For more on this, see Core Chapter 4. • Behaviours associated with self-esteem may occur (e.g. eating disorders, self-harming) • Hormonal swings, which can result in tantrums, outbursts and lack of cooperation • Exploration of own identity and a distancing from family • Higher levels of risk taking and experimentation that peak at around 16
16+	• Friendships are more selective and not necessarily same sex • Romantic relationships may be forming	• Risk-taking behaviours and experimentation starting to reduce • Increased levels of independence and also, in some people, confidence

▲ How social and emotional development links to children's and young people's relationships with adults

▲ At what age can children share resources?

Key term

Parallel play: two or more children engaged in their own individual play but in close proximity to each other.

Test yourself

1 Give two features of social and emotional development for children aged two to three years.
2 Give two features of social and emotional development for children aged seven to eleven years.
3 At what age would you expect a child to be able to thread some large beads?
4 At what age might you expect a baby to be sitting up alone?
5 At what age might you expect children to start to play board games?

7.2 Attachment theory and how early attachments influence adult relationships

Children's and young people's development is significantly influenced by the quality of the relationships they have, particularly with their parents and other key people in their lives. These special relationships are called **attachments** or **bonds**. For this outcome, we look at the theories behind attachment and their importance.

There are several theories of attachment it is worth knowing about. They tend to build on one another rather than compete.

Bowlby

The importance of attachment to children's and young people's later lives was studied by John Bowlby. His work has been very influential and has been used as a starting point for other theorists.

Innate attachment to one figure

Bowlby suggested that babies were born primed to develop an attachment to one key person in their lives. He focused particularly on that attachment being the mother. He suggested that this was a survival instinct for a baby because by attaching to one person, the baby could be protected and have its needs met.

Maternal deprivation

In his research, Bowlby looked at the family circumstances of young people who were in an offenders' institution. He found that nearly all of them had had a separation from their mothers. He concluded that being deprived of a mother in the early years of a child's life would affect their later social and emotional development. He called this maternal **deprivation**. In his work, he found that even a short separation of just a week in the first two years of life could affect later behaviour and the quality of the mother–child relationship.

Separation anxiety

As part of his work on maternal deprivation, Bowlby also noted that young children became very distressed when they were separated from their mothers. He looked at what happened when mothers and children were separated because of hospital admission. He noted that, when this occurred, there were clear stages:

▶ **Protest:** In the early stages of not being with their mothers, young children cry, scream and are very distressed.

▶ **Despair:** Children become withdrawn and very quiet, as if they have given up hope.

▶ **Detachment:** After a period of separation, children 'give up' on their attachment and, when reunited, will avoid contact with their parent.

Internal working model

Bowlby was one of the first to recognise that the quality of the first bond or attachment a child makes will be a template for later relationships, and also for the child's or young person's view of others. Bowlby called this an 'internal working model'. In Core Chapter 4, we looked at how attachment can impact on behaviour. We saw that where attachment is not secure, children and young people may show more aggression or have a lower self-concept.

Revisit Core Chapter 4 if you need to remind yourself of this.

▲ What is this baby learning about relationships?

The importance of Bowlby's work

There have been some criticisms of Bowlby's work, some of which he accepted. First, he focused only on mothers providing the attachment and having caring responsibilities, rather than any other caregivers. He also suggested that babies would make a bond only with one person. He called this **monotropy**. Subsequent research has shown that babies can make strong attachments to more than one person, including fathers. Bowlby was also criticised for suggesting that mothers should stay with their babies for the first two years of their lives. This has now been challenged by other researchers (e.g. Schaffer and Emerson).

Here are some of the ways that Bowlby's work has changed many practices.

▶ **Policies in hospitals and early years settings:** The understanding of separation anxiety means that when children are in hospital, parents can stay with and/or visit them. It also means that early years settings have settling-in policies to ensure that babies and children do not become distressed due to missing their parent(s). Later work from a married couple called the Robertsons showed that the impact of separation can be reduced if children have become attached to another adult before separation takes place. This work is the basis for the **key person system** that is used in early years settings (see page 94).

▶ **Continued contact for absent parents:** Bowlby's work also shows the importance of children having continued contact with absent parents – for example, in the case of family breakdown. It also explains why, when contact between the absent parent and the child breaks down, children are reluctant to spend time with the absent parent because of detachment.

Ainsworth

Susan Ainsworth worked with John Bowlby and developed his work further. While Bowlby focused on the physical presence of the mother, Ainsworth looked at the quality of the attachment to the mother. She considered how sensitive mothers were to their babies' and toddlers' needs. She then came up with an experiment to test the quality of attachment that babies and toddlers had with their mothers. The experiment is known as the 'Strange Situation'.

Strange Situation experiment

The experiment took place with babies and toddlers aged between nine and eighteen months. It took around 20 minutes and is in two parts.

Part 1:
▶ Child and mother are put in a room. Mother is asked not to participate as the baby or toddler explores.
▶ A stranger enters and talks to the parent. The parent then leaves the room.
▶ The stranger engages with the child, following their cues.
▶ The parent comes back in and the stranger leaves.

Part 2:
▶ Parent leaves the room and the child is alone.
▶ Stranger comes in and engages with the child, following their cues.
▶ Parent enters and the stranger leaves.

Susan Ainsworth looked at many aspects of the child's reactions during this experiment, including the reaction of the child when the parent left and then came in again. Ainsworth also considered how much the child explored and interacted with the stranger. Based on the reactions of the babies and toddlers, three types of attachment style were noted, as described below, although a fourth has since been added following research by Mary Main and Judith Solomon in 1986.

1   **Secure attachment:** Babies and toddlers who have parents who are sensitive to their needs are more likely to be securely attached. Secure attachment behaviours mean that babies and toddlers are able to explore when their parent is present as they use them as a safe base. They are relaxed when the stranger is present alongside the parent, but show distress when the parent leaves. They are pleased to see their parent return and are quick to calm down and recover.

2   **Insecure avoidant attachment:** Babies and toddlers who show this style of attachment tend to ignore the parent and do not react when the parent leaves. They do not explore very much and show no fear of the stranger. Their reactions to the mother and the stranger are similar. It is thought that children with insecure avoidant attachment have parents who routinely ignore the needs of their child.

3   **Insecure ambivalent/resistant attachment:** Babies and toddlers who showed this attachment style were clingy to the parent even before the experiment started. They were intensely fearful of the stranger. When the parent was reunited with the baby or child, they were hard to comfort and settle down. Babies and toddlers showed anger or helplessness. It is thought that this type of attachment style is linked to inconsistent parenting, where the child's needs are met at some times but not at others.

4   **Disorganised-disoriented attachment:** This fourth attachment style was added after it was noted that some children did not fit neatly into the other three categories. While babies and toddlers in the other categories followed a pattern in how they behaved, babies and toddlers with this style showed

a range of emotions, including fear and freezing. While some wanted to be close to the parent, others did not.

Influence

This piece of work has helped influence advice to parents. It is now understood that tuning in to children and being sensitive to their needs can affect later development. Classes such as baby massage are often used to increase the amount of responsiveness between parent and child. The research also identified that parents who had experienced trauma, including bereavement and depression, were more likely to have children with disorganised-disoriented attachment styles. The link between attachment and depression is now increasingly recognised and more support is provided to parents.

Criticisms

There are some criticisms of the experiment. First, it is thought that babies' and toddlers' experiences of being left with others may affect their responses. There is also some thought that parents are responding to their babies' temperament. We know, for example, that some babies at birth are easier to settle than others.

Rutter

As with Susan Ainsworth, Michael Rutter used Bowlby's work as a starting point for his own research. He concluded that Bowlby had failed to see the difference between a baby who has never formed a relationship with a mother and one who did have a relationship and then experienced separation. He used the term **privation** for babies who had never formed an attachment, and **deprivation** for those babies and toddlers who had been separated from their mothers.

The different effects of privation and deprivation

Rutter looked at case histories of children who had experienced either privation or deprivation. He saw that children who had never formed an attachment fared worse than those who had started off with an attachment. They were more likely in childhood to show attention-seeking behaviours and to be dependent, as well as being ready to form relationships and friendships with anyone. The effects in later life included antisocial behaviour and lack of empathy.

Case study

Amy is four years old. She was taken into foster care when she was six months old because social workers were concerned about her health and wellbeing. Her mother was unable to care for or bond with her due to an alcohol addiction. After her mother started a rehabilitation programme, Amy was briefly placed with her, but her mother began drinking again. The social workers were concerned and she was placed in care once more but with a new foster carer. After a few months, the foster carer was taken seriously ill and the placement ended. Amy has since been in five other short-term placements. At school, her teachers find her behaviour challenging. She has lower levels of language than the other children, and finds it hard to share and care for others.

▶ Using Rutter's theory of attachment, explain whether Amy is likely to have experienced privation or deprivation.

▶ How might Amy's behaviour and development be linked to her early life?

Cognitive and language development

Rutter also noted that there was a link between attachment and cognitive and language development. He saw that, as well as providing an emotional template, attachment has a role in supporting cognition and language.

Influence

Rutter's work has helped early years settings to recognise the role of attachment in children's education, and in emotional and social development. This work has helped professionals focus on the quality of attachment.

Recognition of the different outcomes for children stemming from privation and deprivation has also meant that young babies who are removed into care are usually put with a foster family so that they can develop an attachment. This is because the experience of having an attachment is recognised as being protective.

Criticisms

There are some criticisms of Rutter's work based on his choice of case histories, as the numbers involved are relatively small.

Schaffer and Emerson's work

Rudolf Schaffer and Peggy Emerson looked at babies for the first 18 months of their lives. They visited them monthly in their homes and asked parents to keep a diary. When visiting the parents, the researchers noted the adults' sensitivity to the children as well as their interactions.

Babies attach to adults who are responsive

By noting how adults responded to their babies and looking at the babies' reactions, they observed that the quality of responses mattered more than the length of time that an adult spent with them.

Development of attachments

Schaffer and Emerson's work also established that there was a sequence by which babies developed attachments (see table).

Stage	Age	Features
Asocial stage	0–6 weeks	Babies are happy to be with anyone. They stare at human faces or representations of faces (e.g. a smiling sun).
Indiscriminate attachment	6 weeks–7 months	Babies are happy to be with anyone but from around three months smile more at familiar faces and are likely to be soothed more easily by a familiar adult. They have no fear of strangers and can be left without showing separation anxiety.
Specific attachment	7 months onwards	Babies will develop one 'special person' for whom they have a clear preference. They show separation anxiety when this adult is not available. They also show stranger anxiety.
Multiple attachments	10 months	Where babies regularly see other adults, including grandparents, childminders or early years practitioners, they can develop attachments to them. The quality of these attachments will depend on the responsiveness of the adult, not the amount of time spent with them.

▲ Schaffer and Emerson's sequence of attachments

Schaffer and Emerson also picked out some particular features of this development:

▶ Stranger anxiety – when babies start to be fearful or wary of unfamiliar adults, even when they are with their parents.
▶ Separation anxiety – when babies start to cry when their parent leaves the room.
▶ **Social referencing** – when babies look at their parents to help them respond, e.g. they hear a loud bang and if the parent does not seem bothered, they do not cry.

> **Key term**
>
> *Social referencing:* how babies and young children look at adults' responses as a guide to how they should themselves react.

Influence of Schaffer's and Emerson's work

Schaffer and Emerson were able to show that Bowlby's theory that babies attach to just one caregiver was not accurate. They were also able to show that the quality of adult response matters more than time. This has proved reassuring for working parents, who now know that, provided they spend 'quality time' with their baby, an attachment can still be formed. The work of Schaffer and Emerson about the sequence of attachment has been used by some settings to influence their settling-in policies.

Criticisms

Concerns have been raised that Schaffer and Emerson's sample size was too small and reliant on parent observation. In addition, the study was not carried out in several different geographical areas, so there may be cultural bias.

▲ From what age can children form multiple attachments?

7.3 How children develop receptive and expressive language

Language development is linked to many areas of development. Language helps us to understand and communicate with others. This means that it is closely linked to children's and young people's social and emotional development, including their ability to show appropriate behaviour. Once children are talking fairly well at around three years, we can see that the way they play with others changes. They are likely to take turns and be more cooperative. Language development is also linked to children's and young people's ability to learn and think in complex ways. Language is usually divided into two broad areas:

1 **Receptive language:** Receptive language is about listening to and understanding what is said. This is an important component of communication. For babies, and later on for children and young people, learning a new language, this tends to be the first step.

For more on children and young people learning a new language, see Core Chapter 12.

2 **Expressive language:** Expressive language is about using vocabulary or words and sentences to express meaning. In babies and toddlers, expressive language may consist of just single words combined with gesture or facial expression.

It is useful to know how babies and young children develop language. It is also interesting to see how over time children and young people use language. The table below describes expected development of language.

Age	Expressive language	Receptive language	Ways to support development
6 weeks	Coos	Recognises parent's voice and calms down if crying Turns to look at speaker's face	Responding to baby during vocalisations, smiling and making eye contact Plenty of cuddles and smiles
3 months	Makes happy sounds when spoken to	Can be soothed quickly when adult talks and holds baby	Talking to the baby and responding immediately to vocalisations
6 months	Babbles with repeated sounds (dah-dah) Laughs and chuckles when happy	Turns to look at parent if hears voice across the room	Using routines with repeated phrases and words Talking to the baby but leaving pauses so baby can respond Using exaggerated facial expressions that mimic what the baby is feeling (e.g. smiling)
9 months	Makes sounds to gain attention Babbling becomes longer and baby will babble when alone	Understands two or three phrases used frequently by adults (e.g. 'no', 'bye-bye')	Continuing to talk during routines using repeated phrases and words Gaining baby's attention, pointing to objects and naming them Waiting for baby to respond and showing pleasure when baby vocalises
12 months	Babbling is tuneful and in long strings Raises voice to gain attention	Can follow simple instructions when adult is giving visual cues such as pointing (e.g. 'Find your shoes') Understands words used frequently in routines (e.g. 'cup', 'spoon', 'go for a walk')	Talking about what the baby is doing using a commentary style (e.g. 'You are banging the bricks!') Continued use of talk during routines Allowing time for baby to respond Pointing to objects that baby is interested in and naming them

Age	Expressive language	Receptive language	Ways to support development
15 months	Continues to babble Uses two to six words	Understands many words Can follow a simple instruction of three or four words (e.g. 'Give me the ball')	Talking in the 'here and now' about what the toddler is doing Sharing books and following the toddler's interest Giving one simple instruction at a time Allowing time for toddlers to respond to questions or instructions
18 months	Talks using babbling and different sounds when alone Uses 6–20 words When adults talk, toddlers will often echo back last word	Enjoys looking at books and pointing to pictures Understands instructions and simple conversations Enjoys hearing and tries to join in nursery rhymes	
2 years	Uses 50 or more words Puts two words together to make simple sentences Refers to self by name Talks to self Echoes back words when adults are talking	Carries out a simple instruction, which may have many words (e.g. 'Tell Mandy that lunch is ready') Can point to several parts of the body Understands a wide range of words Speech may be difficult to understand	Modelling simple sentences (e.g. 'You have eaten everything up!') Avoiding asking too many questions Making eye contact and getting down to children's height Making sure you have their attention before talking, even if this means waiting for them to finish what they are doing Listening carefully to what children are trying to say, even when speech is unclear
2.5 years	Uses 200-plus words Knows full name Constantly asking simple questions such as 'what' and 'where' May stammer if in a rush or when trying to say a complex sentence Says and knows a few rhymes	Enjoys simple books Knows and recognises a few rhymes Understands most of what adults say to them Is starting to follow an instruction with two parts (e.g. 'Get your toothbrush and bring it here') Speech is becoming clearer	Avoiding asking series of questions and always allowing plenty of time for children to respond Not telling children who are stammering to slow down – instead slow down your own speech Showing children that you are listening to them by getting down to their level
3 years	Asks many questions beginning with 'what', 'why' and 'who' Speech is tuneful and children can whisper, for example Large vocabulary Uses 'I', 'me', 'he' and 'him' Most of what is said can be understood by others	Listens to stories and enjoys sharing books Can follow instructions in two parts (e.g. 'Find Teddy's hat and put it on him') Speech can usually be understood by adults	Talking about what children are doing and following their lead in what they want to talk about Keeping background noise down so as to be able to hear what children are saying when their speech is unclear Not correcting children's speech, but instead repeating back to them what they are trying to say, using correct pronunciation and grammar
4 years	Can be understood easily by others Most of what they say is grammatically correct Loves asking questions Enjoys telling stories	Enjoys hearing jokes, especially ones with sounds Knows several nursery rhymes Can pick out rhymes Loves hearing stories and sharing books	Encouraging children to tell you about events that have happened or to retell a story in a book Using questions to help children think and explain (e.g. 'I wonder why you like those shoes') Using opportunities to model new vocabulary (e.g. 'That is a lovely shade of blue. It's called royal blue')

Age	Expressive language	Receptive language	Ways to support development
5–7 years	Often asks the meanings of words or the word for an object Loves using words accurately and will correct others (e.g. 'That's not a shoe, that's a boot!') Argues and squabbles using language	Loves hearing and making up jokes Can pick out individual sounds in words (important for learning to read) Can listen to instructions or a story as part of a group without interruption	Encouraging children to settle disputes using language Planning experiences and activities to introduce new vocabulary (e.g. hatching chicks, cooking) When reading to children, explaining the meaning of unfamiliar phrases or words
7–11 years	Can use language to help solve problems and to organise their thoughts Uses language to express their feelings to others Can use language to explain their thinking to others	Can follow a complex story or instructions Vocabulary continues to develop as a result of reading, experiences and conversations with adults	Encouraging the use of language for explanation and problem solving by making comments or questions (e.g. 'I wonder why that won't stay in place') Modelling and encouraging children to use language to help them learn and remember (e.g. 'How do you think you can remember that?')
11–16 years	Can use language to present an argument or to talk hypothetically Can use language to rationalise their concerns or anxieties Able to consciously moderate their language according to who they are with	Able to listen to others and retain information	Modelling and talking to young people about how language changes according to who you are with (e.g. formal and informal) Encouraging young people to debate and question, and supporting them in this Using newspapers and media to help them analyse how words and phrases can have impact
16+ years	May be skilled communicators depending on their self-esteem and experiences	As above	As above

▲ The development of receptive and expressive language

Test yourself

1 At what age is a child likely to be able to use 200 words?
2 From what age do children enjoy hearing and using jokes?
3 Explain the difference between a seven year old's use of language and that of a sixteen year old.

Theories relating to children's/young people's language development

Over a number of years, several theories looking at the development of language have been put forward.

Some of these link back to the learning theories we looked at in Core Chapter 2.

Noam Chomsky

Chomsky suggested that babies were born with the potential to learn language. He proposed that this was innate or instinctive. He looked at the way in which babies and young children appear to follow a pattern in terms of how they learn language and are able to detect grammar. He used the term **language acquisition device (LAD)** to talk about the structures in the brain that made this possible.

Since Chomsky's work in the 1960s, further knowledge about how babies and children develop language has been acquired. It is now thought that Chomsky's belief that learning language is instinctive is correct, but also that there might be a critical period in which this needs to take place.

Jean Piaget

> In Core Chapter 2, we looked at Piaget's work in relation to how children and young people think. You will need to review this in order to look at the four stages of the development of thinking that he outlined.

Piaget suggested that there were four stages in the development of children's and young people's thinking. His view of language was that it is a tool to support thinking, and so reflects their level of understanding at the time. He used the term **egocentric** speech to describe when talk is not aimed at anyone else. Young children will often talk out loud to themselves when they play. The other form of language use is **socialised**. This is when children use language as a tool for communication.

Piaget's work focused on children being active in their learning and using their experiences as a basis for their thinking. It has been criticised for underestimating children's thinking and language.

Stage of cognitive development	Use of language at this stage
Sensorimotor	Language use is egocentric Crying is to meet babies' own needs
Preoperational	Children continue to use egocentric language (e.g. talk as they play) One feature of this stage is **animism** and their use of language reflects this (e.g. giving a cuddly toy a voice or drawing a smile on a moon) In this period, children start to use language symbolically and talk about things that are not present
Concrete operations	Children's language changes in line with their ability to think logically
Formal operations	In this period, they use 'socialised' language that reflects their ability to 'decentre', recognising that others may have different perspectives

▲ Use of language at each stage of cognitive development

Key term

Animism: ascribing feelings and personality to inanimate objects, e.g. 'my car is happy'.

Jerome Bruner

While Chomsky recognised that babies and young children come primed to learn language, he did not particularly focus on the role of the adult. Bruner's work suggests that adults also have a role in helping babies and children develop language. He used the term **language acquisition support system (LASS)**, suggesting that adults have the ability to, step by step, support babies' and children's language through, for example, everyday routines. An adult might say 'all gone' when a baby finishes a feed, but then later on, when the child has more language, add complexity by saying 'Look, it's all gone.' In this way, Bruner suggested that adults were scaffolding babies' and young children's language. Interestingly, research that looks at how adults, especially parents, interact with babies and young children appears to confirm this. Bruner's theory explains why there can be significant differences between the language learning of children of the same age – some may be better supported by adults than others.

▲ Explain how sharing a book with an adult may develop this child's language.

Lev Vygotsky

> We have already looked at Vygotsky's theory of learning in Core Chapter 2. It would be helpful for you to reread this section.

In terms of language, Vygotsky viewed it as central to learning. The interactions that children have with their parents, family members and others help to develop their cognition. Unlike Piaget, Vygotsky believed that it was language that drove thought.

Vygotsky suggested that thought and language begin by being two different activities – for example, when a baby babbles it is not using babbling as a way of thinking. At around the age of two or three years, the activities merge and at this point the child uses language to help them think.

Vygotsky also differentiated between two types of speech: inner speech, which helps us to think, and external speech, which we use to communicate with others. An example of inner speech would be when we say either aloud or inwardly, 'Then, I am going to …' as a way of directing ourselves. Vygotsky believed that until children are about seven, they are not able to use these types of speech in distinct ways, which means their speech is often a blend of the two, with young children often providing a running commentary on themselves as they play.

▲ How is the adult helping to develop this child's language?

Vygotsky's approach is significant because it suggests that, without interactions, children's ability to think will be limited. His approach is why adults may pose questions to children and young people as a way of extending their learning. The role of interaction in learning also means that the quality of the relationships we have with children and young people is significant.

B.F. Skinner

> In Core Chapter 2, we looked at the theory of operant conditioning (page 25) so refer back to that now.

Skinner applied his theory to how children develop language. He thought that the responses of adults following vocalisations such as babbling were responsible for the development of language. While it is true that babies and young children do need adults to respond to them, operant conditioning theory does not explain the steps behind how children learn language. If children were learning only through imitation and praise, they would not make grammatical mistakes such as 'me swimmed' as adults are unlikely to have said that. Overall, Skinner's theory of language development is not seen as being helpful.

Test yourself

1 What do the terms 'LAD' and 'LASS' refer to?
2 Which theorists suggested them?
3 Outline why Vygotsky's approach to language differed from that of Piaget.

K4.1 Theories of language acquisition, and why communication and speech play such an important part in pupils' development

For this outcome, you will not only need to know the theories of language development, but also how speech and language affect pupils.

Theories of language acquisition

Speech and language play a significant role in learning and development.

For this outcome, you need to understand a range of theories of language acquisition. We have already considered these theories in this chapter and it will be useful to look back on the relevant earlier sections in order to answer these questions.

Cognition and learning

Language is linked to cognition and so to learning. This is because language plays a significant role in memory. Words tend to trigger memories, which in turn helps to connect different pieces of information. Pupils who have strong levels of vocabulary find it easier to make and retrieve memories when they can encode them in more detail. A pupil who sees a large white and black bird, but only knows the word 'bird', is less likely to have a detailed memory of it than a pupil who is able to identify it as a magpie.

> **Case study**
>
> A Year 4 class went on a nature walk in the woods. One of the pupils said, 'Look at those trees. They look like skyscrapers from a film.' Another pupil responded that they were like the pine trees in her grandfather's garden. She added that pine cones come from pine trees. Another pupil said, 'My mother always uses pine cones to make Christmas decorations.'
>
> ▶ Explain how the pupils were drawing on their memories by using language.
> ▶ Identify some specific vocabulary that these pupils were using.
> ▶ Why is it important to develop vocabulary to aid learning?

Ability to verbalise and express thoughts

Language also helps pupils to express their ideas and thoughts. Those who can do this well often have good levels of vocabulary. They will also have had adults who have role-modelled how to express ideas and thoughts.

Ability to reason and discuss

Good levels of language are also needed to argue, negotiate and discuss. Pupils who have strong language can use these skills in their writing.

Ability to socialise and interact with adults and peers

Speech and language play an important role in helping pupils to communicate with others, make friends and also cope in group situations. Where speech and language are delayed, pupils may show atypical behaviours for their age, which are often linked to isolation and frustration. On the other hand, pupils who are good communicators often have more friends, and good relationships with adults and peers.

The range of factors that may affect communication and speech development

The development of language is linked to a range of factors. The table below describes some of the factors that may affect communication and speech development.

Factor	How it affects communication and speech development
Environment	How many opportunities pupils have for interaction, both at home and at school, can make a difference to their language development.
	Sometimes the physical environment can also be a barrier – a good example of this is a noisy classroom where pupils cannot hear one another, or when there are too many pupils trying to talk to an adult at once.
Sensory and physical impairments	Some pupils may have hearing loss, which may affect how easily they acquire language and also their ability to speak clearly; it can also make it harder for pupils to understand what is being said.
	Sometimes physical impairments may be a barrier to language because pupils are not able to do the same things as others and so miss out on the language that is associated with the activity (e.g. sports).
English as an additional language (EAL) See also Core Chapter 12.	Some pupils who are new to English may temporarily not be able to understand or use English; they may still be able to communicate, but may not be able to understand everything that is said or to join in discussions.
Long-term medical conditions	Long-term medical conditions may affect pupils' attendance – if, due to illness, they cannot attend a school or early years setting, they may miss out on the education activities and teaching that the other children and young people are having; this can affect the opportunities to learn new vocabulary associated with the activity.
	They may also miss out on opportunities to use language in specific ways, such to discuss, negotiate and analyse.

Factor	How it affects communication and speech development
Communication and language delays and disorders	Some pupils have difficulty in acquiring or using language for a range of reasons.
	Pupils may need additional support and interventions from speech and language therapists.
Autism spectrum disorder (ASD)	Some pupils who have ASD may find it hard to express themselves using language or may use language in unusual ways, for example through using monologues, or repeating others' final words or phrases.
	Others may find it hard to use language for social interaction – they may take things literally or not pick up on the body language of others. A feature of natural conversation is to take turns, but this aspect may be difficult for some pupils with ASD. This is why ASD is considered to be a social communication disorder.
Selective mutism	Pupils with selective mutism may have good levels of language, but due to anxiety find it hard to speak in front of others. Selective mutism is situational in nature, meaning that a pupil may talk at home or to certain people or other pupils but not in other situations. If any pressure is placed on a pupil to talk, this will have an adverse effect, as the pupil is not able to choose when and to whom they will speak.

▲ Factors that may affect communication and speech development

7.4 How adults can promote language development at different ages

It takes four years for children to develop fluent language. In these years, it is important that they have plenty of sustained and warm interactions with the adults in their lives. While children may be fluent at four years, older children and young adults need to learn to use their language to solve problems, express their feelings and to interact with others. The role of the adult in this period is to develop further vocabulary and thinking skills. There are many strategies and activities that can be used to support the development of language, as outlined in the table below.

Age	Strategies and activities	Notes
0–2 years	Sharing nursery rhymes	Nursery rhymes help babies and toddlers to bond with adults and also to hear the sounds of the language
	Using repetitive language	Babies and toddlers need simplified and repetitive language
	Giving simple instructions	Toddlers are able to follow a single instruction, but adults can help them by pointing or showing what needs to happen
	Maintaining appropriate eye contact	Gaining babies' and toddlers' attention with eye contact helps them to focus and learn language
	Using visual aids (toys and puppets) Using simple picture books Using gesture Talking about what is happening ('the here and now')	Babies and toddlers need to link the words that we are saying to actions and objects – adults can do this by using gesture, but also by talking about things as they are happening Visual aids and story books can be helpful
2–4 years	Sharing books (story sacks and props)	Looking at books can encourage children to talk and develop vocabulary
	Engaging in child-initiated conversation	Listening and responding to what children want to talk about is a key way in which we can develop language
	Facilitating circle time	Circle time, if it is fun and carried out in small groups, can help three year olds take turns; it is not advised for two year olds
	Providing a range of role-play activities	Older two and three year olds enjoy role play; the props can provide opportunities for children to use new vocabulary Role play also encourages children to talk to one another

Age	Strategies and activities	Notes
4–7 years	Modelling correct use of language, tone and expression	Throughout childhood, modelling language is important; this means using accurate vocabulary and being grammatically correct
	Engaging in paired reading activity	Paired reading is a strategy used in Key Stages 1 and 2; it can help improve confidence and fluency
	Encouraging descriptive language	We can promote vocabulary by modelling words used for description
	Planning literacy activities and word games	As children's language develops, they enjoy playing word games such as 'I spy' and, for older children, Scrabble and word search games
7–11 years	Introducing a wide range of texts	Children's vocabulary and understanding of grammatical structures is helped when they read widely, but also when they are read to; this means that a variety of stories, books and poems are important
	Providing opportunities for creative writing	Creative writing can help children use the vocabulary that they are developing
	Facilitating group discussion	Group discussions can help children learn to express themselves, although they may need adults to role-model turn-taking and also to give them confidence
	Introducing new vocabulary through spelling and definitions	Children enjoy learning new words; some words can later be remembered more easily if children understand the roots of them
11–19 years	Involving children and young people in discussions and debates	In small and large groups, we can help children and young people learn to use language to present arguments and debate; this use of language means listening carefully to others and using language as a tool to analyse
	Facilitating individual and group presentations	Presenting information to others can help young people to develop skills involved in explanation It can also build confidence provided that support is given to those young people who find it hard to talk in front of others
	Encouraging sophisticated vocabulary through wider research and reading	Reading a wide range of texts, including poetry, can increase vocabulary and knowledge By encouraging research on topics of interest, we can support young people to develop high-level as well as specialist vocabulary, such as professional vocabulary that is used in particular career pathways

▲ Strategies and activities that can be used to support the development of language

Reflect

Create a leaflet for parents of children aged from birth to five years that will give them practical tips and strategies to support their child's language development.

7.5 How children and young people develop friendships from infancy through to adolescence

In the 1930s, Mildred Parten looked at how babies and young children play together. She suggested there were stages in social play, with toddlers playing next to each other and three year olds being able to play cooperatively.

In the 1980s, Robert Selman proposed a framework that outlined the different developmental stages of friendship. His work was based on interviews with children and young people. He noted that there are significant differences between children's and young people's understanding of friendship. This is reflected in the wide and overlapping age bands. The following table describes Selman's five stages of friendship.

Level	Stage	Age	Features
Level 0	Momentary physical interaction	3–6 years	Children will play with others according to circumstance and convenience rather than because of deeper feelings
Level 1	One-way assistance	5–9 years	An understanding that a friend does nice things for you but not understanding that friendship works two ways The desire to have friends at this age can mean that some children will stay friends with another child who is not particularly kind to them
Level 2	Two-way fair-weather cooperation	7–12 years	Expectation that friends will repay a favour, gift or action Friendship may end if one child feels that they are not getting anything in return
Level 3	Intimate mutual sharing	8–15 years	Acts of kindness and generosity occur without an expectation of a reciprocal action High levels of trust and loyalty, but may feel that another is betraying them if they have separate friendships or take part in activities in which they are not included
Level 4	Mature friendship (autonomous interdependence)	12+ years	Ability to accept others and be accepted Ability to recognise the differences between their friends Understanding that their friends will have other friends they do not have in common

▲ Robert Selman's five-level framework of friendships

Reflect

Ask children and young people of different ages about their friendships:
1   Ask whether they have friends and why they are friends.
2   Find out what they think makes a good friend.
3   Compare their answers to Robert Selman's framework of friendships.
4   To what extent do you feel that Selman's framework of friendships relates to your own conversations with children and young people of different ages?

Henri Tajfel's and John Turner's social identity theory

In-group vs. out-group

At break time in schools, we will often see distinct groups of older children and young people. In secondary schools, for example, it is common to find a 'sporty' group, a 'popular' group and a 'brainy' group. Each group has a clear identity. We see the division of people into groups in all walks of life, such as football fans and supporters of political parties. Sometimes, these divisions cause conflict and violence. Tajfel's and Turner's social identity theory looks at why and also how people do this.

Tajfel and Turner suggest that being part of a group (the **in-group**) and feeling in some way superior to another group (the **out-group**) raises an individual's self-esteem. Being part of the in-group can provide a sense of purpose and belonging, and so can become part of someone's identity.

The three stages of social identity

Tajfel and Turner suggest that the three stages in the development of a social identity are as follows.
1   **Categorisation:** Very early on in childhood, we learn to put things into categories. A Labrador is a dog. Dogs have fur. Dogs are animals. Categorising is a normal part of cognitive development. It allows for short cuts in our thinking. As well as objects and other things such as animals, we also categorise people. We categorise by size and age, but also by the jobs people do. The process of categorisation also helps us to understand our own identity by recognising what we are like in comparison to others. A three year old out of nappies may say, 'I am not a baby' as a result of recognising that babies wear nappies and cannot walk like they can.
2   **Social identification:** Once a child or young person has identified with a group, their reactions and behaviours increasingly reflect those of a group. A young person who is part of a highly competitive swimming team might train more often

or buy a certain brand of swimming goggles. It is worth noting at this point that children and young people, as well as adults, will identify with and be a member of several groups.

3 **Social comparison:** Once children or young people have identified themselves with a group, they need to draw favourable comparisons with other groups. This is how they maintain high self-esteem. An individual in the 'brainy' group at school will notice the test scores of other children and be pleased that their group has higher grades.

▲ What effect might their friendship have on these boys' resilience?

How friendships can positively impact on children and young people

Friendships often help children and young people to feel valued. They can provide many benefits, including the following.

Mental health

Humans are social beings. This is one reason why, by the time a child reaches six or seven, having friends becomes so important. When children or young people have difficulties in making friends or have friendship groups that are not supportive, this can affect their mental health negatively.

Resilience

The ability to cope with setbacks and problems is partly linked to how much support a child and young person has available to them. Friends, especially in adolescence, can provide understanding and support. They may also be able to help a young person reflect or seek further help.

Social skills

Throughout childhood and adolescence, children and young people learn social skills and also boundaries through friendships and being with others.

Self-concept

We have seen that Tajfel's and Turner's theory of social identity says that being part of a friendship group is linked to identity. A positive self-concept is more likely if a friendship is supportive. It is worth noting that sometimes children and young people may have friendships that are not supportive, and this may be harmful in terms of self-concept.

Self-esteem/confidence

As we saw in Core Chapter 4, there is a link between self-esteem, confidence and self-concept.

> Revisit Core Chapter 4 if you need to remind yourself of this.

Where children and young people have friendships that are supportive, they are more likely to have higher levels of self-esteem. On the other hand, where a child or young person does not have friends, their self-esteem may be lower.

Children and young people with special educational needs and disabilities

For children and young people with special educational needs and disabilities, friendships are particularly important. They provide the benefits that we have seen, but they may also in some cases provide mutual support if the other child or young person has similar needs.

K3.22 The expected levels of self-reliance and social behaviour at different ages and developmental stages

In a school where there are many different ages of children and young people, it is important to know what you can expect from different ages of pupils. The table below gives some examples of self-reliance and social behaviour at different ages. It is important to recognise that this can only be a guide because, as we saw in Core Chapter 4, there are many factors that can affect individual pupils' responses and behaviours.

> Revisit Core Chapter 4 if you need to remind yourself of these.

Age	Expected levels of self-reliance and social behaviour at this stage
5–7 years	Start to understand what it means to be embarrassed
	Have preferred friends
	Take turns and share
	Understand the purpose of rules
	Seek approval from adults
	Respond well to being given responsibilities
7–12 years	Be more settled and predictable
	Have a wider circle of friends
	Form close friendships with same-sex peers
	Have greater empathy
12–16 years	Experience a range of emotional changes with puberty
	Enjoy the feeling of maturity
	Still require adult support and guidance
	Value friends' and others' opinions more
	May question rules and challenge boundaries
16–19 years	Develop in emotional maturity, but still need guidance

▲ Some examples of self-reliance and social behaviour at different ages

7.6 The difference between expected and unexpected transitions, and how these may affect children in positive or negative ways

A transition is an interruption or change to a child's or young person's life. Some transitions are small and have little impact on children and young people, but others can affect their learning, behaviour and development. Some transitions are expected and so can be planned for. Others can occur suddenly, so there is no time to prepare children and young people.

Expected transitions

Expected transitions are often easier because adults and parents can prepare children and young people in advance. The table below gives some examples of transitions that can be planned for. We also looked at transitions in Core Chapter 5 (page 91).

Transition	Description
Transition from home to childcare	For babies and young children, being with new carers is an important transition; this might mean starting at a childminder, nursery or pre-school
	Some children may also move from one early years setting to another
Movement between school years or between school and FE or HE	Starting school, moving school years or changing establishments are significant transitions because children and young people have to adapt to new routines, new adults and a new peer group
Adolescent transition and body changes	While growing up is normal, the physical changes in moving from being a child to an adult can provoke anxiety
	As well as physical changes, there are also emotional and social changes that take place
Gender transition	Sometimes, children and young people feel that their biological gender does not match with how they feel about themselves; under medical and psychological supervision, they may start the process of changing gender
Changes in relationships	Changes in relationships, such as a parent's boyfriend moving in, can be planned for
	Changes in relationships may also include a friend who is moving away or a change of teacher
Post-school decisions	When young people leave school, they need to make a decision about their next steps; moving to a job, apprenticeship or further study can feel daunting

▲ Examples of expected transitions

> **Key term**
>
> **Gender transition:** when a child or young person wants to change from their biological gender to the one that they identify with.

Unexpected transitions

These are changes in children's and young people's lives that were not planned. They can be stressful because adults and parents may not have had the time to prepare children and young people. The table below gives some examples of unexpected transitions.

Transition	Description
Moving house or location	Some children and young people live in rental accommodation and may change home every six months or year
	Parents may not know whether or not they can stay in their home
Illness	The illness of a parent or of a child or young person can cause significant disruption – a child or young person may need time off school and in some cases may need to go to hospital
	Where a parent or family member is ill, a child or young person may find that their home life is disrupted; they may even need to become a carer
Change of employment	Any changes in family life can be disruptive – a change of employment might mean that a parent needs to work at night or may not be as available to help with homework or to play
Change to family structure	Changes to family structure may include family breakdown where one parent leaves, but also the formation of a new stepfamily
	A change of family structure may also occur if a grandparent or other family member moves in
	The arrival of a new baby can also change a family's usual routines and structure
Pregnancy	An unplanned pregnancy is a significant life change for a young person – they may need to make decisions about continuing the pregnancy or how they will manage with a baby
Bereavement	The death of a parent, family member or friend is likely to have a significant impact on a child or young person, especially where it is sudden or unexpected

▲ Examples of unexpected transitions

How practitioners use a range of strategies to prepare and support children/young people through transitions

We have seen that there are a number of circumstances where children or young people will face a transition. Sensitive adults can reduce the emotional and social impact of these transitions. There are a number of ways in which we can support children and young people.

Providing accurate and current information to the child or young person

Knowing what is happening or what is going to happen can reduce anxiety in children and young people. It is important that any information shared with children and young people is accurate and also links to what parents or colleagues have said. If there are differences or inaccuracies, children and young people may become confused or find it hard to trust in future. As part of giving information, adults must also be careful to be realistic and honest, to avoid false hopes or raised expectations.

Giving opportunities to discuss feelings and ask questions

As well as having information, children and young people need time to talk about the transition. Older children and young people may need to think through and talk about their feelings. All ages of children are likely to have questions. Sometimes, these questions may seem trivial, such as 'Will my hamster be able to come?', but they should all be taken seriously. Sometimes, children and young people will ask one question to see whether they can trust the adult before asking another question.

Interestingly, some children and young people may need time to discuss their feelings or ask questions. This is because they may need time to process the information, especially if they have had a shock. It is, therefore, important to expect that children and young people may raise questions or want to talk about the changes in their lives several times. Young children may also ask the same question repeatedly.

Involving individuals in their own transition planning

One of the ways that we can reduce stress during and after transition is to give children and young people some control and help them make some decisions. It is important, though, that any transition planning that we involve them in is age and stage appropriate. A good example of this might be the way that an older child might choose a piece of work to show to their next teacher or a young child has a box into which they pack their favourite toys when they move home.

Using school-readiness strategies

For young children about to start reception class, it is important that we help them to prepare. School readiness is the collection of skills that children need to make this transition. These include language, self-care skills and their ability to self-regulate. Children also have to be able to do some self-care tasks, such as being able to dress and feed themselves.

▲ How can self-care skills help children to feel more confident when starting school?

Following settling-in policies and procedures

Early years settings and reception classes usually have policies and procedures in place to help babies and children make the transition from home. These **settling-in policies** can reduce separation anxiety for babies and children, especially those who have never been cared for by anyone but their parents. The aim of settling-in policies and procedures is to make sure that babies and young children have developed a relationship with an adult from the setting or school so that they can cope when their parents are not there. Good settling-in policies and procedures also involve parents as they need to feel confident that their children will be happy and can cope.

Implementing support through a buddy system, counsellor, mentor or learning support assistant

In school settings, children and young people can be supported through a buddy system. This is a system where children or young people can talk to another child or young person. This works very well when a pupil is new to a school or class. In cases where a child or young person has experienced family breakdown or bereavement, the other child or young person may have had a similar experience. As well as a buddy system, trained adults can also support children. This might include a counsellor, mentor or a learning support assistant. Adults can provide support to individual children and young people or to small groups where appropriate. As well as discussion, they may also use resources such as books and stories or provide play opportunities that will allow children to express their emotions.

Liaising with parents/carers and other professionals

When preparing for transition and supporting children and young people, we need to talk to others involved, including parents and any professionals who work with the child or young person. This is because we need to agree strategies and also make sure that the messages children and young people receive from adults are the same. This can prevent confusion and also anxiety.

▲ How can sharing information with parents help with transitions?

Referring individuals for specialist support as appropriate

Some transitions, such as a parent with a diagnosis of terminal illness, are so significant that specialist support needs to be sought. Referrals to specialist services and organisations, including bereavement charities and child psychiatrists, can happen only with parental consent. In some cases, it may be appropriate to signpost organisations to parents. In addition, many organisations that deal with family breakdown, mental health issues and bereavement have online pages or packs that are designed for early years practitioners and school staff.

K3.8 The range of transitions that a pupil will experience through school

Pupils will have a range of transitions during their time in education. These will include starting and leaving schools, but also transitions while in school, such as moving from one key stage to another. Older children also have to cope with the onset of puberty, while young people may face the pressure of taking significant tests or assessments.

Possible positive and negative effects of transition on pupils' wellbeing

It can be hard to predict pupils' reactions to changes in their lives. While some will embrace the opportunities that a new school or change of key stage might bring, others might be fearful. We have seen how supporting transitions can make a difference to how well children and young people cope. The following tables give examples of the possible positive and negative effects of transition on pupils' wellbeing.

Positive effects	Explanation
Changes in motivation or confidence	Going to a new school or class or changing key stage can be very motivating for some pupils. They have a chance to start afresh to build new relationships with their peers and also with teachers. In some cases, such as going to secondary school, they may also be motivated because of the opportunity to study new subjects.
Development of independence	Pupils may find that in their new environment they are expected to work more independently than they have been used to, which is positive as it will give them more opportunities. However, it may take some time to adjust to the changes in expectation.
Development of maturity	Some transitions require that pupils take more responsibility; this in turn can make them feel more mature.
Excitement about the new experience or challenge	Some transitions are seen by pupils as positive – it may be that they know they will like the adults or that there are interesting learning opportunities available.

▲ Positive effects of transition on pupils' wellbeing

Negative effects	Explanation
Changes in motivation or confidence	Where pupils are missing their friends or a favourite adult, they may show lower levels of motivation or confidence. For some, change may seem frightening and they may lose confidence if they are not adequately supported. How change affects individual pupils can be linked to their personality, but also to their previous experience of change.
Change in levels of resilience and self-reliance	Some situations will result in pupils losing confidence and so they will show lower levels of resilience and self-reliance – an example of this would be where a pupil is not happy with their exam results and so gives up.
Anxiety	Where pupils are not prepared for transition, they are likely to show anxiety as a result of stress.
Uncharacteristic behaviour	As a result of unhappiness or anxiety, some pupils may show uncharacteristic behaviours. These can range from angry outbursts and withdrawal to self-harm behaviours such as cutting or hair pulling.
Disengagement in education or activities; lack of concentration	A pupil who is disengaged or lacks concentration may be anxious and feel preoccupied about a change that is happening in their home or social life. They may start to show some of these feelings before the transition happens.
Problems eating or sleeping; lack of self-care	Where pupils are anxious, they may find it hard to eat or sleep. In some cases, they may overeat or stay in bed to compensate for their unhappiness. Older pupils who may be responsible for their personal hygiene may lose the motivation to take care of themselves as a result of depression triggered by the transition.

▲ Negative effects of transition on pupils' wellbeing

Assessment practice

1 Give **one** example of a gross motor skill that would be expected in a child aged four years.

2 At what age might you expect a child to be able to thread large beads?

3 Outline the main criticisms of Bowlby's work in relation to attachment.

4 Explain what is meant by the term 'attachment'.

5 What are the signs of separation anxiety?

6 At what age might you expect a child to have around 200 words?

7 Give **one** example of an unexpected transition and describe how it might affect a child aged eight years.

8 Give **one** strategy that can be used to support the transition of a four-year-old into school.

CORE Chapter 8:
Observation and Assessment

Whatever type of educational setting you are going to work in, you will need to know about and use observation and assessment. This is because as educators we need to be able to look at what children and young people know so that we can plan for them and take forward their learning and development. Because assessment is an ongoing process, schools and early years settings will use different types of observation and assessment in different situations, and it will serve a range of purposes.

Learning outcomes

This chapter covers the following knowledge outcomes for Core Element 8:
8.1   The purpose of national assessments and benchmarks
8.2   The different purposes of formative and summative assessment
8.3   The purpose of accurately observing, recording and reporting on children's and young people's participation, conceptual understanding and progress
8.4   The different roles that practitioners play in assessment processes and requirements

This chapter also includes one knowledge outcome from Assisting Teaching Performance Outcome 2. Text relating to Assisting Teaching is highlighted. Note that this content will not form part of the core assessments.
K2.2   Different types of assessment and their purpose
The knowledge from this chapter also corresponds with Core Skill 3: Use formative and summative assessment to track children's and students' progress to plan and shape educational opportunities.

8.1 The purpose of national assessments and benchmarks

National assessments and **benchmarks** are one of the ways in which schools and early years settings monitor children's and young people's progress. All registered early years and educational settings have a **statutory** obligation to do this and to report their results. Standardised assessment, where results are checked against a standard, also provides a consistent way of reporting to parents and local authorities about how children and young people are progressing at specific ages and stages. This process is **regulated** by Ofqual, which states in the Apprenticeship, Skills, Children and Learning Act 2009 that its objectives are to ensure that national assessments are reliable, consistent and comparable, and that the public can have confidence in this.

> For more information on Ofqual, see Core Chapter 1.

> **Key terms**
>
> **Benchmark:** a point of reference for checking standards.
>
> **Statutory:** something that is required by law.
>
> **Regulation:** control of a process by a set of rules.

Tracking and recording children's and young people's achievement

The key purpose of national assessments and benchmarks is to track and record children's and young people's achievement against that of others of the same age and stage. It also helps us to look at individuals over time. This is helpful in several ways:

▶ It builds a national picture of how children and young people are progressing in different areas and across different subjects.

▶ It informs professionals and helps them to plan for children's and young people's individual needs.

▶ It informs parents about their child's progress.

Depending on your role and the age group with which you work, you will need to know about and support this type of formal assessment at different stages as prescribed by national guidelines. You may also be asked to record pupils' progress in different formats.

Differentiating between individuals' performance

National assessments also give us an opportunity to look at how children and young people vary in their achievements at different stages. It is important to remember that all children and young people are unique and will learn and develop at their own rates as well as having strengths and weaknesses in different areas. It is helpful to look at individuals' performances and to see how they are progressing over time. Early years managers and head teachers will also look regularly at pupils' assessment data to see how individuals are moving forward, and to notice if progress is not being made so that steps can be put in place to support them.

Promoting standards and confidence in the National Curriculum, and supporting the regulation of state-funded provision

Where the government, and therefore the taxpayer, funds educational settings (known as **state-funded** provision) – for example, in the case of state schools and some elements of early years provision – they need to be seen to give value for money. Because of this, it is important that they are **accountable** for the way in which they work. They will also need to be registered and inspected by Ofsted to ensure that they are working to a high standard. Along with checks on pupil progress through assessment, these measures ensure that there is regulation in the way in which educational settings work. This is then fed back to parents and local authorities.

> **Key terms**
>
> **State funded:** money that the government provides for something.
>
> **Accountable:** required or expected to justify actions or decisions.

National assessment is also a way of promoting standards and confidence in the National Curriculum. This means that it is a way of ensuring that children and young people are working towards a similar level of achievement nationally in key areas, particularly literacy, numeracy and science. Formal assessment will take place at specific times during a child's or young person's progression through the education system, starting with the Early Years Foundation Stage (EYFS).

> For more on types of national assessment see Section 8.1, and for more on formal assessment throughout the education system, see Core Chapter 1.

8.2 The different purposes of formative and summative assessment

AT K2.2 Different types of assessment and their purpose

These include:
- Diagnostic
- **Formative**
- Benchmark (interim)
- **Summative**
- Statutory.

Key terms

Formative assessment: frequent, often informal, assessment that is designed to generate ongoing evidence of children's and young people's progress and attainment, and is used to inform the next steps.

Summative assessment: a final assessment, usually occurring at the end of a period of study, which is used to sum up children's and young people's overall level of attainment, and to provide data for stakeholders.

We will use different types of assessment for different purposes during a child's or young person's educational journey. Some of these will be written down and formal, while others may simply involve looking at how a child or young person approaches a task or interacts with others, and forming a picture of them. Each approach is valuable and all give us information about pupils' levels of understanding and achievement, while formal assessments enable managers to track and monitor children's and young people's progress over time by providing data.

Assessments can also highlight if a child or young person needs extra help in a specific area of development or learning. However, it should be remembered that assessment is only one aspect of the educational process and it is also about practitioners knowing the whole child or young person, and what they know and are able to do. Educators should ensure that they are always assessing for a reason and be clear on what this is.

Formative assessment

Formative assessment is sometimes called **assessment for learning (AfL)**. It is ongoing, which means it takes place on a day-to-day basis when teachers, teaching assistants and early years practitioners are talking to children and young people, observing them and listening to the ways in which they respond to learning activities. We also use it to consolidate or go over pupils' previous learning and check how much they can remember. It can be used at the end of the day and assessment will then feed in to planning so that teachers and early years practitioners can use it to inform the next steps of children's learning. Formative assessment helps us to set specific targets for children and young people as it gives an up-to-date indication of what they know and how they are learning.

Examples of formative assessment are shown in this diagram.

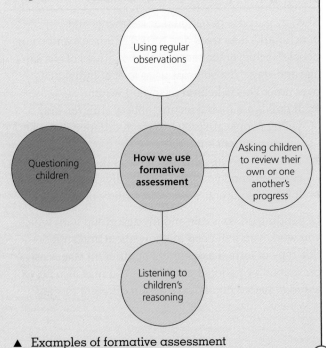

▲ Examples of formative assessment

Using regular observations of children and young people

We may use **formal** or **informal** observations of children so that we can look more closely at what they are doing and plan for their individual needs. In the EYFS, practitioners carry out observations and note down aspects of children's learning and development as an integral part of the curriculum. This helps them to track children's knowledge, skills and development towards the early learning goals. This progress is continually saved to a child's individual profile or **learning journal**. In schools, formal observations will follow a set format and you may be given a template to use when carrying them out so that you can note down particular points – for example, how long the child is able to stay focused on a task.

> For more on the EYFS and the early learning goals, see Core Chapter 2, page 16.

They may also be used when working with children and young people who have special educational needs, to help us to look at specific areas (see Sections 8.3 and 8.4). Observations may also include quotes or photographs of children and young people, which can also be used as evidence of their achievement.

> For more detail on the purpose of observations, see Section 8.3, page 143.

Key terms

Formal observations: structured observations taking place within a set time in which the observer has specific criteria to look for.

Informal observations: simple observations that take place during the course of the day, which may look at behaviour, relationships or confidence.

Learning journal: in the EYFS, individual learning journals may be used as a record of a child's progress and achievements during the year. They may include observations, photos and quotes from the child.

Sometimes you also might make observations of children and young people that assess behaviour, wellbeing or relationships with others, or look at how they approach a task. You may also note down observations during breaks or extracurricular activities, which may still be relevant to the child or young person as a whole, and their progress or development.

For example, it may be that you become aware of something that is not related to a learning activity, such as a safeguarding or wellbeing issue, or an incidence of bullying. You should make a note of this and feed back to colleagues later, so that they are aware of it.

Case study

Sophie is on playground duty with Years 1 and 2. She notices that two Year 2 pupils, Amira and Della, have been walking round the playground deep in conversation for a long time. When they pass her, she asks if they are OK and Amira starts to cry. Della tells her that Amira's parents have split up and that she is upset about it.
▶ What would you do first?
▶ Why is it important for staff working with Amira to know about this?

▲ How do you make a note of children's and young people's learning when you are working with them?

Questioning children and young people to check their knowledge and understanding of a particular topic or concept

When working with small or large groups, or with individuals, careful questioning enables us to find out exactly what they know and to assess their learning. We can target our questions in a way that encourages children or young people to expand on their answers and tell us more. We call this **open questioning**. A closed question, on the other hand, will usually require only a one-word answer and will not give us much information about what children and young people know.

> For more on questioning pupils during learning activities, see Assisting Teaching Performance Outcome 2.

Key term

Open question: a question that cannot be answered with a yes or no response.

Reflect

▶ Reflect on these two versions of a question that might be asked at the start of a topic:
  1 Adult: Today we are going to be looking at producers and predators. Is a bird a predator, Sophie?
  2 Adult: Today we are going to be looking at producers and predators. What can you tell me about what this means?
▶ Looking at the questions above, which would you say is an example of an open question?
▶ How will the pupil's answer give us more information about what they know?

Listening to pupils' reasoning when they are talking about their learning

When we are working with pupils, it can be a helpful method of formative assessment to talk to them about what they are doing and why they are doing it. In this way we can build a picture of their thought processes. It also gives us an opportunity to guide them in their learning if this is needed.

Asking pupils to review their own or one another's progress

Another method of formative assessment is known as **self-assessment** or **peer assessment**. This involves asking children and young people about how close they think they are to meeting learning objectives at the end of a session. It helps them to evaluate their own learning and think about what they need to do next.

With younger children, thumbs-up or traffic light systems may be used at the end of a lesson or activity so that teaching staff can gain a quick snapshot of their level of understanding.

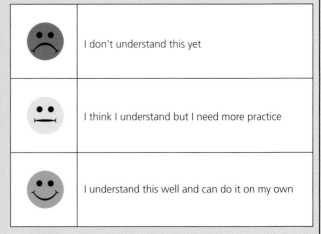

😞	I don't understand this yet
😐	I think I understand but I need more practice
🙂	I understand this well and can do it on my own

▲ What type of self-assessment have you seen used in classrooms and early years settings?

With older children, teachers may ask them to write their own assessment under their work in exercise books, or ask them to show how they feel about their learning at the end of the session by talking about specific success criteria.

Peer assessment, or assessing one another's work, is also often used with older children and young people. They will need to develop experience over time so that they can use this approach effectively; this will also help them to learn to assess their own work and to self-reflect on their learning.

The kinds of questions peers could be asked might be:
▶ Have they met the learning objective? How can you tell?
▶ Can you find a place where they have done well and explain why they have done well?
▶ Can you find an area in which they can improve and explain how they could do this?

Core Chapter 2 has more on how to review children's and young people's learning, and how to give feedback to them during learning activities.

For more detail on supporting pupils during learning activities, see Assisting Teaching Performance Outcome 2.

Practice points

▶ Make sure you know the learning objective of each session when working with children and young people so that you know what you are assessing them against.
▶ Use mainly open questioning to help assess children's learning.
▶ Check on learning towards the objective by talking to children about what they are doing.
▶ Ask children and young people to regularly self- and peer-review their own and one another's work.

Summative assessment

Summative assessment, or assessment of learning, will take place at the end of a scheme of work, stage or academic year. This is so that teaching staff are able to report to parents and senior managers about the progress of children and young people in their class or year group. In early years settings and primary schools, this will include the more formal assessments prescribed by the Department for Education that provide data to schools and, at a national level, to Ofsted. In secondary schools up to GCSE, teachers will regularly assess pupils and set their own tests and exams, although this may vary between schools.

The kinds of summative assessment that will take place include the following.

Early Years Foundation Stage Profile

The EYFS Profile is an assessment that is carried out at the end of the summer term in reception, before children move in to Year 1. It is a report for parents and teachers about children's development and learning at the end of the EYFS. This form of summative assessment requires teachers to report children as Expected or Emerging against each of the 17 Early Learning Goals.

Teachers will also need to report on their characteristics of learning, or the different ways in which children learn. These are:

▶ Playing and exploring – investigation, experiencing and 'having a go'
▶ Active learning – concentration, perseverance if they find something difficult, and enjoying their achievements
▶ Creating and thinking critically – developing their own ideas, making links between ideas and developing their own strategies for working things out.

The EYFS Profile also helps to support transition to Year 1 and helps teachers plan for children's needs at the start of Key Stage 1.

Research

If you work in a primary school, find out more about the EYFS Profile and how it is carried out. Speak to teachers and teaching assistants in reception classes about what they do with children to assess their learning.

End of Key Stage 1 teacher assessments

Teachers must report pupil levels in English reading, English writing, mathematics and science at the end of Key Stage 1, or when children are seven. Teacher assessment means that teachers must make their own professional judgements using a range of evidence from their observations and knowledge of pupils across the curriculum. They must also manage formal assessments to support their judgement: National Curriculum assessments in reading and mathematics are sent to schools and carried out by teaching staff in order to support teacher assessment. In addition, teachers may choose to carry out an optional English grammar, punctuation and spelling test to support their teacher assessment. At the time of writing in 2020 these are due to be discontinued from 2022/23, and Reception Baseline Assessment (RBA, see below) will be used as a starting point for measuring progress in primary schools.

Reflect

You are working as a teaching assistant in a Year 4 class at the start of the autumn term. A new pupil has just arrived from another school and their achievement records have been sent to the school. The teacher has asked you to look at their records with them so that you can both get to know the pupil.
▶ How will this exercise help you and the teacher?
▶ How else might you gather information about the pupil?

▲ Do you think it is important to have a baseline assessment when children start school?

Key Stage 2 Statutory Assessment Tests (SATs)

These externally marked tests are carried out in the summer term of Year 6, before pupils move to secondary school. They are in English reading and grammar, punctuation and spelling, and maths. In addition, every two years a sample of pupils from around 1900 schools also take a science test, which is marked externally. These results will then be passed to secondary schools so that they have an up-to-date picture of each child's academic achievement. However, in many cases, schools will also carry out their own assessments, and base GCSE predications on these. Key Stage 2 SATs are also used to form part of school league tables, which are published nationally.

Key Stage 3

From Key Stage 3 onwards, schools are no longer required to carry out national assessments. However, teachers are expected to assess pupils' progress in key areas on a regular basis and feed back to head teachers so that they can monitor pupils and add this to their data. It is a statutory requirement that they report end of key stage outcomes as well as report to parents. Assessment will usually take the form of end-of-year exams, but schools may vary in their approaches. Secondary schools will usually carry out diagnostic assessments at the start of the September term in Year 7 (sometimes known as **CATs** or **Cognitive Abilities Tests**) as this will give them a snapshot of pupils' abilities and understanding in key areas and demonstrate how they learn best. These results may then be used to group pupils by ability, and in some cases they are used to predict GCSE outcomes.

The following qualifications, which are provided by recognised awarding bodies and organisations, are not part of national assessment as they are designed and carried out differently, but they are still national benchmarks and are still regulated by Ofqual.

Key Stage 4: GCSEs/International GCSEs

GCSEs or International GCSEs (sometimes known as iGCSEs) in a range of subjects are taken by all pupils in secondary schools in England, Wales and Northern Ireland at the age of 16. The results of GCSEs give pupils a stepping stone to the next stage in their education if they go on to take A-levels or T Levels or consider an apprenticeship. They also provide schools with data on pupils' level of achievement. It is a requirement that schools publish their Key Stage 4 results.

Diagnostic assessment

This form of assessment gives us a picture of a child's or young person's level of achievement at any stage. This can be a useful means of assessing their existing knowledge at the beginning of a new topic or scheme of work. It is also helpful to carry out a diagnostic assessment if a new pupil starts at a setting before their records arrive from a previous school or setting. An example of diagnostic assessment is the **Reception Baseline Assessment (RBA)** – so called as it takes place when children enter primary school.

Reception Baseline Assessment (RBA)

This takes place during the autumn term in reception classes. It is carried out within the first six weeks of a child starting school, will be overseen by the class teacher or early years coordinator, and looks at what children know and are able to do when they come in to school. It is an oral (spoken) assessment in which children are given a series of simple tasks to do while working one to one with an adult, such as describing pictures or counting objects. This assessment then gives schools a starting point from which to measure pupils' progress while they are in primary school. The RBA will be starting in September 2021.

In practice

In early years settings, children will also have a progress check at age two. Parents, healthcare workers, early years staff and any other professionals working with the child are invited to contribute. Find out more about it and how it is put together.

▶ Why do you think this check is carried out at such a young age?
▶ How does the progress check at age two help professionals to plan for next steps?

Reflect

Reflect

A Year 5 teacher carries out a 'knowledge harvest' with their pupils at the start of each new topic. The teacher asks them to write down specific questions about what they want to find out during the topic. At the end of the topic, they have to answer their own and others' questions based on what they have found out.

▶ What type of assessment is a 'knowledge harvest'?

▶ How will this exercise help pupils and the teacher?

Benchmark assessment

Benchmarks are standards that have been set for learning. In other words, they are the expectations for children's and young people's learning and development when they get to the end of a stage or key stage. For example, at the end of Key Stage 1, most children may be at Level 2 in English, maths and science. Benchmarks also allow schools and colleges to measure where they are against others in a similar situation using their assessment data.

Statutory assessments

Statutory assessments are those that have to be carried out by law. Schools and early years settings need to carry out a range of statutory assessments as children and young people go through school:

▶ In the early years, the statutory requirements are the EYFS Profile before the child goes in to Year 1, and the RBA as outlined above.

▶ In primary school, until 2022/23 these are the end of Key Stage 1 teacher assessments. In Year 6, they are SATs.

▶ In secondary school, the statutory requirements are as described above at Key Stage 3 and Key Stage 4.

8.3 The purpose of accurately observing, recording and reporting on children's and young people's participation, conceptual understanding and progress

As we have already mentioned, observations are a way of gathering information on children and young people. We make observations of children and young people all the time, as we work with them and get to know their personalities and their likes and abilities. However, more formal observations and assessments of children and young people help us to find out more about their learning and progress. These in turn give us a way of meeting individual needs and planning for next steps. These are all very important parts of the **planning, learning and assessment cycle**. It is known as a cycle because as educators it is something that we are doing all the time and because each aspect is reliant on the others. It is also important to record this information accurately and in a timely way so that it can be shared with colleagues and parents.

START HERE
Observation – Looking at what children and young people can already do in a variety of situations. Noticing when they need more support, but also if they are not showing expected learning and development.

Plan – Using this information, practitioners plan resources, activities and ways of working to support children's and young people's interests, and their learning and development.

The child or young person

Assessment – Looking at what the observations are telling us about the child's or young person's learning and developmental needs, but also any interests or areas where they need additional support.

▲ The planning cycle

Key term

Planning, learning and assessment cycle: the process through which children's needs and abilities are identified, which enables teachers to plan for next steps.

Observations can take different forms and you may be asked to complete and record them in a range of formats. It is helpful to know about why we refer to different forms of observation as they will be suitable to use in different situations. Your setting may provide a template for some of these, but others, such as free description, will be noted down as they happen.

Common formats for observations

▶ **Checklists:** These are simply observations that check off what a child or young person is able to do; the focus in this situation will be on whether or not they are able to do it rather than on the process. For example, checklists may be used as part of the RBA to say that a child is able to count to ten.

▶ **Snapshots:** These are often used in early years settings through quickly writing down or taking a photograph to capture something a child has done. They will usually have a short description to put them in context.

For more on snapshots, see Section 8.4.

▶ **Free descriptions:** These allow us to write down everything that a child or group is doing, usually during a timed period. They will provide more information than a snapshot, and will be detailed, which means they will usually last only 5 to 10 minutes. They can be tricky to carry out as it can be difficult to write everything down quickly.

▶ **Event/time samples:** These are used to check on how regularly a child or young person carries out a particular activity or behaviour over a period of time. The observer needs to stand away from the child so that they do not interrupt or influence their behaviour. This type of observation is sometimes used for children and young people who have special educational needs as it helps us to identify specific areas for development.

Practice points

Observations

▶ Make sure you are clear on what you have been asked to observe.
▶ Always ensure that your observations are as accurate as possible.
▶ Sit back from the child or young person so that you are not a distraction.
▶ Become involved with what is happening only if the teacher has asked you to do so.
▶ Include only the level of detail that is needed.

Identifying developmental progress

Our records and regular observations of children and young people will also help us to track their

developmental progress. We need to have a good understanding of child development to be able to do this. (Refer to Core Chapter 7 for more on this.) It is particularly useful with younger children, as their development progresses relatively quickly during the early years, which is why observation is a key part of the EYFS.

The EYFS *Development Matters* document also helps us to look at children's progress against expected age-related milestones by setting them out in detail. We should also look at the way in which children and young people approach different activities, their level of confidence and how they work with others, as this forms part of their social and emotional development. Through watching them and recording what we have seen, we are able to document different stages of development.

Key term

EYFS Development Matters: non-statutory guidance to support early years practitioners with observation, assessment and planning.

Informing planning and feedback

Observing children's and young people's learning and development, and feeding back to colleagues, is a key aspect of your role, whether in early years settings or schools. Feedback from individual learning activities will need to include information about children's and young people's participation and what happened during the session. It may also include what they said, their approach to learning and how they worked with others. Feedback may be recorded on the lesson plan, or on an evaluation or feedback sheet. In this way, we will be able to monitor children's and young people's progress and will have evidence of how they have responded in different situations and when working in groups or individually.

When working with children and young people it helps to write things down as they happen as it is difficult to remember everything afterwards, particularly if you are working with a group. Observations also allow us to identify whether children and young people are responding positively to particular topics or learning activities, which helps us to review our approach to teaching.

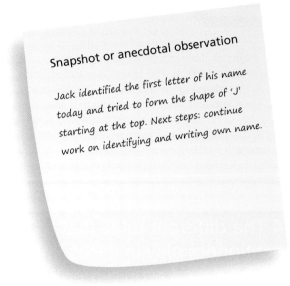

Snapshot or anecdotal observation

Jack identified the first letter of his name today and tried to form the shape of 'J' starting at the top. Next steps: continue work on identifying and writing own name.

▲ Example of a feedback to teacher sheet

▲ How do you feed back to colleagues after carrying out learning activities with children?

Adhering to policies and procedures relevant to recording information, maintaining validity and reliability

Core Skill 3: Use a variety of media to track and record children's and young people's progress, providing the appropriate level of detail to reflect the audience and purpose (English Skill GEC3).

Use appropriate technology and media to track children's/young people's progress (Digital Skill GDC1).

Information about children's and young people's learning may be recorded through formal observation sheets, in photographs, on feedback sheets to colleagues or through lesson evaluations. It may

then be transferred to digital spreadsheets or other commercially available computer assessment programs. When recording and reporting information, it is important that all educational practitioners use the methods set out in their school's or early years setting's assessment, recording and reporting policy. Another important aspect of recording is to ensure that it is done accurately and that the information that is recorded is necessary. You should also make sure that you only record what is seen at the time, to ensure that the observation is **valid** and **reliable**.

Key terms

Valid: worth consideration; should be recorded.

Reliable: able to be trusted.

When recording and reporting information about children and young people, you should also be aware of legal requirements regarding confidentiality and the storage of records, whether these are paper-based or on a computer or tablet. Information and data on children and young people should be held in line with GDPR (General Data Protection Regulation) legislation and data protection laws. Remember that, for safeguarding reasons, photographic records of children and young people should be taken only using equipment that belongs to the setting.

Practice points

Recording and reporting information

▶ Ensure information is valid and reliable.
▶ Remember confidentiality and keep records secure.
▶ Store any passwords securely.
▶ Ensure that pupil records are updated regularly.

In practice

Ask if you can see a copy of your school or early years assessment, recording and reporting policy. What does it say about the following?
▶ The types of assessment used in your setting
▶ How assessment outcomes are recorded
▶ Confidentiality
▶ Reporting to parents

Enabling interventions

Observing will help us to gather evidence about a child's or young person's current level of learning or development in a particular area. This will in turn enable us to plan for the right type of **intervention** from adults where required. For example, children and young people who over time show that they are having problems with literacy or mathematical concepts may need to have extra support through targeted interventions. Interventions may also be introduced for other areas, such as speech and language, problem solving, social skills or behaviour. They will provide individual or small-group support for areas that children and young people find more challenging, and should enable them to develop confidence and make progress.

Key term

Intervention: an activity or strategy which is used in addition to those which have already been carried out in the classroom, designed to support children who are working below national expectations but who should reach them with the right support.

In practice

Find out about some of the interventions that are offered in your school.
▶ Are they available to all year groups?
▶ How and when are they delivered?

Sharing information with relevant colleagues, the family and other agencies

Keeping accurate observations and records on children's and young people's participation and progress will also ensure that we have evidence we can share with parents and colleagues. At any time, we should have access to up-to-date information about their progress in different areas. This is important so that we can write reports and give information to parents and other agencies if needed.

Test yourself

As part of its RBA, a primary school carries out assessments of children's communication and language development. The teaching assistant who is trained in delivering the assessment feeds back to the teacher about all of the children so that specific interventions can be put in place for those who need it.
▶ How does this process support teaching and learning?
▶ Why is this area of development important?

8.4 The different roles that practitioners play in assessment processes and requirements

Depending on your role, the age of the children and young people you work with, and the setting in which you work, your involvement is likely to be slightly different. However, all practitioners will be involved in assessment and should understand its importance.

Early years practitioners

All staff in early years settings will work closely to assess and monitor young children in line with the requirements of the EYFS curriculum:

Ongoing assessment (also known as formative assessment) is an integral part of the learning and development process. It involves practitioners knowing children's level of achievement and interests, and then to shape teaching and learning experiences for each child reflecting that knowledge.

(Source: Statutory Framework for the Early Years Foundation Stage, 2021)

Observe, record and review children's progress

The EYFS requires that practitioners carry out regular observations throughout this stage. Practitioners in both early years settings and school reception classes will be doing this all the time. Key persons in particular will need to ensure that they monitor the learning and development of their key children closely, and work with parents to encourage them to share developments at home.

Observations may take the form of photographs of children with a brief sentence to explain what the child was doing or saying, and should include the area of learning and development; this is why such observations are sometimes known as snapshots (see page 151). In some settings, they may be stored on tablets or computers, while in others they are printed out and put in a child's learning journey document or journal, which should be accessible to all relevant adults in the setting.

Other observations may be noted down without photos as notes, particularly in the case of something significant that has happened quickly, so that it is not missed – for example, 'Tania was able to put on and zip up her coat independently.'

▲ Which area of development and caption do you think you might find on this photo?

It is also important that the child's learning journal contains observations from all of these areas, so it is helpful to check regularly for gaps. If a child is particularly able in one area, or regularly goes to work on activities that interest them, there may be lots of observations and photographs of this, but it is important to ensure that all areas of a child's learning and development are being tracked and covered through observations.

Assess children's individual needs

Throughout the EYFS, early years practitioners will be using observations every day to look at children's learning and development. This also helps to assess their individual needs going forward. For example, observations may highlight that they have a particular interest that regularly engages them, or when their behaviour is different from usual. Knowing about children's individual needs will help us to plan activities that will interest them and be enjoyable as well as providing challenges.

Plan activities and support statutory assessments

Based on what they know about children through observation and assessment, early years practitioners will then plan next steps and future learning for children. This should be based on their 'individual needs, interests and stage of development', according to the EYFS statutory framework, which includes the different ways in which children learn. Practitioners will need to show that they are planning activities that challenge children and take their learning forward. These should be a mix of adult-led and child-initiated activities.

In the case of statutory assessments such as the RBA and the EYFS Profile, the role of early years practitioners will be to ensure that they are assessing, tracking and monitoring children's progress regularly so that they have an up-to-date picture of their level of development when it comes to the statutory assessment.

Teachers, lecturers and teaching assistants

Teachers, lecturers and teaching assistants work in the following ways to assess and monitor children's and young people's progress.

Track children's and young people's understanding and progress

Schools and colleges need to have assessment procedures that allow them to track the way in which children and young people are progressing. While the role of both teachers and lecturers is to ensure that they are constantly monitoring individual pupil progress and levels, teaching assistants are more likely to take a supporting role in the process. This means that they will feed back to teachers or lecturers on lessons they have carried out with pupils so that this information can be recorded centrally. Alternatively, they may be asked to enter the results of summative assessments on to computer systems.

As the tracking of pupil progress is likely to be done through online records, teaching staff may need specific training in the use of computer software. In addition to being a template for assessment, most commercially available computer programs will work out specific data – for example, checking on the achievements of boys and girls, or looking at pupil achievement year on year and subject by subject. This helps management teams to look at strengths and weaknesses, and provides a wider picture of achievement.

Provide targeted feedback to enable children and young people to improve

Through ongoing assessment, teaching staff are able to provide targeted feedback to children and young people. This means that they will use assessment to be specific about what aspects of their learning should be targeted through teaching in order to help pupils to make progress. Teachers and lecturers will set learning targets for pupils – usually once every few weeks – so that they have something to work towards. Teaching assistants working with specific pupils should be aware of these targets and pupils should be reminded of them regularly while they carry out learning activities.

> **Case study**
>
> Brian is working in a Year 3 class and regularly takes out a small group of children to support them with their writing. They have three literacy targets, which are stuck on to the inside covers of their literacy books. While working with the group, Brian notices that two of his group need to go back over their work to check their spelling and punctuation, and this happens to be one of their targets.
> - Why is it important for Brian to say something about this?
> - How will this targeted approach enable the children to improve?

Prepare children and young people for national assessments

Teachers, lecturers and teaching assistants will all need to be able to prepare pupils for national assessments such as the SATs at the end of Key Stage 2. They will need to ensure that the curriculum requirements of the assessments have been covered through teaching and learning, and that they have prepared the pupils as to what to expect. Through careful regular assessment and monitoring, they will be able to tell which pupils may need more support as they work towards the requirements of the test.

Assessors

Assessors will usually work with older students in sixth form and FE colleges. Some of their roles in relation to assessment are described below.

Assess individuals' performance/relevant knowledge

The role of an assessor is to regularly check students' progress against a set of knowledge and skills in a technical qualification, such as an apprenticeship. As a result, they will need to have experience, or what is known as occupational competence, in carrying out the role themselves. Assessors will need to regularly visit students in their workplace to observe them, assess what they are able to do, provide them with feedback and make plans for next steps towards their qualification. They will also mark assignments and look at students' portfolios of work, which may be paper-based or online.

▲ Why is it important for work-based learners to be observed in the workplace?

Ensure that the standards and requirements of the specification are met

Technical qualifications will set out exactly what students need to know and be able to do in order to meet the requirements of the specification. Assessors will need to check students' progress against the knowledge and skills that are set out in their chosen subject. If the requirements are not yet met, this will be fed back to the student and reassessed at a later date. If students are unable to meet the criteria, they will not pass the qualification.

Coaches and mentors

The roles of coaches and mentors are slightly different in that a mentor's role is more long term and informal, whereas that of a coach has a structure and is more likely to focus on individual goals. A key aspect of the role of a coach or mentor is to support another person's learning and development, and to provide pastoral advice and guidance. However, each of them aims to help and support pupils to achieve their full potential.

Set and review key performance indicators

Key performance indicators are a way of showing that something is on target to be achieved or met. **Mentors** help pupils to make changes in their thinking or learning so that they can progress. They should

be a role model for the mentee (the person they are mentoring) and able to advise them about what they need to do next. A **coach** supports learning and development, and helps pupils to review and improve their work through challenging their ideas and encouraging them to reflect on what they are doing.

In each case, coaches and mentors will need to set targets and assess individuals' progress towards these. They will then look at ways in which pupils can continue to move forward with their learning.

Provide support that is relevant to individual needs and advise on how to improve individual performance

Coaches and mentors will get to know pupils so that they are in the best position to work with them and identify barriers to their progress and achievement, which may be connected to special educational needs, self-esteem, issues in their personal life or motivation. They may need specific support or special considerations – for example, in exam situations, particularly if they have had any issues that affect their learning, such as a family bereavement or an illness.

Coaches and mentors may be able to advise children and young people as to how they can improve their individual performance – for example, through discussing their mind-set or looking at other aspects of their learning. Coaches and mentors may also need to share information with colleagues, particularly if there are any safeguarding issues.

CORE Chapter 9:
Reflective Practice

Whatever your role, whether you work in a school or an early years setting, you will need to be able to engage in reflective practice. This calls for you to regularly step back and think about your own practice and evaluate what you are doing. The process is called continuing professional development (CPD), and you will be supported in doing this with your line manager. In this chapter, we will look at why reflective practice is important and how it will help you to develop in your role when working with children and young people.

Learning outcomes

This chapter covers the following knowledge outcomes for Core Element 9:

9.1   The key concepts of specific models of reflection and how they can be applied in practice

9.2   The current priorities and debates in education

9.3   Why practitioners must engage in feedback and continuous professional development

9.4   How practitioners can meet their own developmental needs

9.1 The key concepts of specific models of reflection

Models of reflection give us as individuals the tools to think about and act on our practice. Management teams in schools and early years settings are also encouraged to reflect and self-evaluate on a regular basis, as it helps them to set annual targets for the organisation, and to see the best way forward for the setting and the children and young people within it.

Several theorists have outlined what they consider to be important aspects of learning and reflecting on experience. These models are designed to help those who use them by giving the exercise of reflection a structure. They encourage the individual to step back and look at the past so that they can learn from their experiences and plan for the future. You need to know the key concepts of each of them so that you can consider how they can be applied in practice, and use the aspects that are helpful to you.

Kolb's experiential learning cycle

David A. Kolb, an American theorist, published his **experiential learning theory (ELT)** in 1984. Experiential learning means learning from experience, and is based on the learner having some form of reflection in the process. In his model (shown in the diagram), Kolb assumes that learning involves four different stages, and that we learn effectively only when we have passed through each of these. The cycle can be started at any point, however, the sequence of passing through it should remain the same.

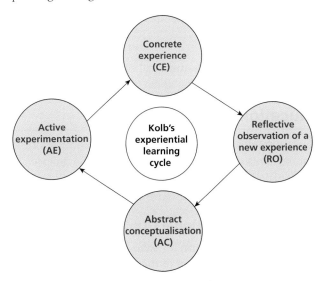

▲ Kolb's experiential learning cycle

> **Key terms**
>
> **Experiential learning theory (ELT):** the theory that knowledge is created through experience.
>
> **Abstract conceptualisation (AC):** this is when the learner has a new idea or has changed their thinking due to their experience.
>
> **Active experimentation (AE):** the learner applies their new way of thinking to a future experience.
>
> **Concrete experience (CE):** this is when the learner encounters an activity or experience for themselves.
>
> **Reflective observation of a new experience (RO):** this stage is when the learner thinks back, or reflects, on their experience.

At each stage in the cycle, it is very important for the learner to be supported effectively, whether by a teacher, trainer or mentor. This is because they need to be shown how to think critically as they pass through the different stages.

Gibbs' reflective cycle

Another model of reflection is known as **Gibbs' reflective cycle** and was developed in 1988 by Graham Gibbs. This model is said to be **iterative**, which means you learn through repetition and improve each time.

Gibbs states that there are six stages of reflecting on experience, under the following headings:

1 **Description:** What happened? This should include all details about who was there, what happened, and what you and others did. What was the result?
2 **Feelings:** What were you and others thinking or feeling before/during/after the situation? How do you and others feel now?
3 **Evaluation:** What was good or bad about the situation? What did you or others do that made these positives or negatives happen?
4 **Analysis:** What sense can you make of the situation?
5 **Conclusion:** What could you have done differently? What did you learn?
6 **Action plan:** Do you need to develop new skills so that you could handle this type of situation better in the future? Can you plan to make some changes? Make sure you include a date for review.

Boud, Keogh and Walker's model

David Boud, Rosemary Keogh and David Walker's model was developed in 1985 and contains three stages of reflecting on practice. This model has a focus on feelings and emotions, and encourages the individual to separate them into those that are positive and those that are negative.

The three stages are as follows.
1   **Experience:** In the first stage, the experience takes place, and the learner will have feelings, ideas and behaviour related to this.
2   **Reflective process:** The second stage involves thinking about what has happened, using positive feelings and removing those that might be obstructive (get in the way), then re-evaluating.
3   **Outcomes:** The third stage is about looking at the experience again in light of what has been learned and using this new perspective to change behaviour.

As part of this chapter, you will need to be able to consider how reflective models can be applied in practice. In each of these theories, the learner needs to revisit an experience or learning activity, think carefully about what happened, and then consider how they might change or develop from the experience. If we think about our job role, or activities carried out within it, this process can be very helpful.

9.2 Current priorities and debates in education

When you are working in education, you will need to have some idea of the kinds of current discussions, priorities and debates that are going on in this area. You can keep up to date with these through making sure that you are aware of current news stories, looking at websites and magazines aimed at the teaching and childcare sectors, and making sure that you know about any current news stories and debates that are taking place. Distance and online self-directed learning have also become more accessible to those who are unable to attend college or university, and it is now possible to undertake qualifications in your own time.

See page 156 at the end of this section for some useful resources.

For the purpose of this qualification, you will need to know about the following areas.

Education reform

Education reform means the way in which education requirements change over time. This may be due to new legislation or government innovations, and has changed many of the following areas.

The impact of National Curriculum reforms

The National Curriculum for schools was first introduced in 1988 as part of the Education Reform Act. Up until that time, schools were able to decide what was taught and when. From 1988 onwards, the curriculum for pupils aged five to sixteen was divided into twelve subject areas, each of which was prescribed in detail through programmes of study. In 2014, however, new National Curriculum reforms considerably 'slimmed down' the National Curriculum in many areas. This has meant that schools have more freedom in making decisions about what and how to teach, although **core subjects** in primary school remain prescriptive – in other words, much of what must be taught is outlined.

> **Key term**
>
> **Core subjects:** English, maths and science.

The pros and cons of selective education

A selective, or grammar, school is one that allows children to enter only on the basis of an examination – that is, the child will sit the exam and the school will then decide whether or not they should be admitted. These schools usually provide secondary education. The idea of selective education is very **divisive**, which means that some people are strongly for or against it.

Those who are in favour of selective schools say that they encourage **social mobility**, meaning that children of less **affluent** parents can have access to an education with those of a similar ability, which is not based on social background.

> **Key terms**
>
> **Social mobility:** movement of individuals or groups between different social classes or levels.
>
> **Affluent:** being wealthy, having a relatively large amount of money and/or material possessions.

Those who are against selective education say that children whose parents can afford to have tutors and additional support may be more likely to pass the tests. In addition, selective schools are likely to contain more children from affluent and/or professional backgrounds than children from disadvantaged families.

High-stakes accountability, via Ofsted, and its effect on staff and children

Ofsted, the Office for Standards in Education, is a body that regularly inspects schools, colleges and early years settings with the aim of ensuring that standards in education are consistent. It will then publish a report on its website that is accessible to anyone. The inspection process can cause anxiety and stress among staff in schools, colleges and early years settings because Ofsted is looking at outcomes for children and young people, and making a formal judgement about how well settings are managed and run. Ofsted will also inform settings about what they do well and what they need to do better. Ofsted is important, however, as it looks independently at different aspects of what organisations do and holds them to account by reporting to parents and the government.

> **Key term**
>
> **Ofsted:** stands for the Office for Standards in Education, Children's Services and Skills. Ofsted inspects and regulates services providing education and skills for learners of all ages, including those that care for babies, children and young people.

> **Research**
>
> Find the most recent Ofsted report of a school or college that you know here: www.gov.uk/government/organisations/ofsted

> **Reflect**
>
> What do you think about Ofsted and the process of inspection?
>
> Do you think that it is necessary? Give reasons for your answer.

How education is funded in England: schools, further education (FE) and higher education (HE)

As mentioned in Core Chapter 1, the following types of school, FE and HE setting are currently funded in the ways described in the following table.

Type of setting	Funding
State or 'maintained' schools	Funded by government and run by local authorities
	There are different types of maintained school, including community schools, foundation schools, voluntary aided or controlled schools, and special schools
Academies and free schools	Entirely government funded but not run by local authorities
	Academies and free schools have control over their budgeting, and greater flexibility over their curriculum, finances and teachers' pay
Independent/private schools	Paid for by fees from parents/carers
	No government or state funding, although some places may be funded by local authority if pupils are placed there for a specific reason, such as SEND
	Some specialist independent schools may be funded through donations if they have charitable status, for example, those run by the National Autistic Society or Royal National Institute of Blind People
Further education Sixth form colleges	Funding is provided through the Education and Skills Funding Agency (ESFA)
Higher education	Universities provide higher education in England
	They are funded in different ways: • through tuition fees paid by students • through government funding • through endowments from (money donated by) previous students

▲ How different settings are funded

National assessments

National assessments are those which take place at different stages during a pupil's schooling. Their purpose is to provide a picture of pupils' levels at specific stages. This can be helpful when looking at the national picture.

The arguments for and against National Curriculum tests

There have been many discussions for and against the use of National Curriculum tests (SATs). These have always taken place at the end of Years 2 and 6 in England, and are used to track and measure progress during the primary years. However, this is due to change in 2022/23 when the Key Stage 1 tests are removed and a formal baseline assessment (the RBA) will take place at the start of reception in England from 2021. Critics say that children and young people have too many tests and assessments, and that this encourages teachers to 'teach to the test' rather than offer a broad and balanced curriculum.

> For more on national assessments, see Core Chapter 8.

> **Good to know**
>
> In Wales, pupils are also assessed in reception in the first six weeks of school. This is known as the Compact Profile. Pupils in Wales also sit assessment tests in reading and numeracy at the end of each school year from Year 2 to Year 9.

The advantages and disadvantages of GCSEs versus iGCSEs

GCSE (General Certificate of Secondary Education) exams have been taken at age 16 in England, Wales and Northern Ireland since 1988. Some students choose to take **International GCSEs**, sometimes known as **iGCSEs**, which are qualifications for English speakers overseas (GCSEs are designed for students in the UK). International GCSEs are recognised by many other countries and many of them are accredited, which means that they are regulated by Ofqual.

> **Key term**
>
> *International GCSE (sometimes iGCSE):* International General Certificate for Secondary Education. The iGCSE is available internationally.

International GCSEs are at the same level (Level 2) as GCSEs, although there may be some differences in course content and the amount of coursework required for different subjects. Apart from practical subjects such as art and drama, both GCSEs and iGCSEs now tend to be tested mainly through exams at the end of two years of study, although until recently GCSEs included more coursework. Some iGCSEs are still graded A–E, whereas others are awarded using the GCSE 9–1 grading scale. iGCSEs tend to be offered by private and international schools, as UK state schools do not offer them, and those studying them may go on to study the **International Baccalaureate** between the ages of 16 and 18. Some say that iGCSEs are easier than GCSEs, even though both are accepted by universities and held in similar esteem.

Key term

International Baccalaureate: two-year international programme leading to an internationally recognised diploma, which prepares students for higher education.

Case study

Luke, who lives in Prague and studies at an international school, will be taking iGCSEs next summer. His mother is Czech and his father English, and he is bilingual. Luke's school offers iGCSEs, so that he will have a recognised qualification in the UK if he chooses to go to university there.
▶ Why are iGCSEs a good way of measuring attainment for English speakers at international schools?
▶ Would iGCSEs still be a good option if Luke decided to stay in the Czech Republic for university?

Technology and education

Twenty years ago, technology in the classroom was usually limited to one PC in the corner of the room. Nowadays, most classrooms have interactive whiteboards and laptops, and teachers and pupils use a range of technology to support teaching and learning. As technology has been developed and improved, its impact has been widely felt, particularly when supporting pupils with SEND.

The pros and cons of technology

Many people feel that the use of information and communications technology (ICT) in the classroom is part of the teaching and learning process, as children and young people need to be able to use it and it is part of the National Curriculum's computing aims. It can also be used very creatively across different subject and curriculum areas. Others, however, say that it can limit social interactions, and that many children and young people already spend enough time looking at screens. Technology can also quickly become outdated, has a tendency to cause issues and is an expensive outlay for educational settings.

> For more on the use of technology, see Core Chapter 2, Section 2.6.

▲ What types of ICT do you use with children and young people in your setting?

The opportunities offered by blended learning

Blended learning offers students a combination of classroom-based and online learning. It gives students the opportunity to access teaching and learning materials online at any time, as well as supporting each individual's needs. On the negative side, it may add to the workload of teachers and relies on the technology working successfully.

Key term

Blended learning: a style of teaching that uses a blend of online and face-to-face teaching.

Children's health and wellbeing

Children's health and wellbeing can be affected by several factors in the classroom.

The impact of exam stress on children's/young people's health and wellbeing

Children's and young people's health and wellbeing can be affected by exam stress, in particular their mental health. It can be difficult for adults to pick up on signs of stress when it is more prolonged and is affecting children's and young people's health and wellbeing. Mental health is a priority and all adults in educational settings should be mindful of the additional stress on children and young people at exam times, and should look out for any signs of stress such as mood changes, lack of appetite or health problems.

> For more on the importance of children's and young people's emotional health and wellbeing, see Core Chapter 3, Section 3.4.

The quality of support for children with SEND

There are often discussions in the media about the quality of support for children and young people with special educational needs and disabilities. Funding and provision may vary depending on locality, and accessing appropriate provision can be challenging for some pupils, depending on the funding that is available. A report from the National Audit Office in September 2019 stated that 'whilst some children with special educational needs and disabilities are receiving high quality support, many others are not getting the help they should'. It also made a series of recommendations, including an investigation into the reasons for local variations.

> For more on SEND, see Core Chapter 11.

You may find some of the websites listed in the 'Research' box helpful for keeping up to date with aspects of education. Teaching and public services unions are also a helpful source of information, and there are online blogs and social media pages specific to your role.

Research

Using the websites listed below, or others, find out more about a current aspect of education that interests you.
- ▶ Times Educational Supplement (TES): **www.tes.com**
- ▶ Nursery World: **www.nurseryworld.co.uk**
- ▶ Professional Association for Childcare and Early Years (PACEY): **www.pacey.org.uk**
- ▶ Early Years Educator (EYE): **www.earlyyearseducator.co.uk**
- ▶ Education Today: **www.education-today.co.uk**
- ▶ BBC: **www.bbc.co.uk**
- ▶ Teach Primary: **www.teachprimary.com**

It is also worth finding out about different trade unions and whether you might join one when you start your employment with a school or early years setting. Unions offer support, advice and legal representation if you have any issues in your role. Members also have access to training, and unions may **lobby** parliament on a range of topics on behalf of their members.

The first three listed below are public service and education specific.
- ▶ Unison: **www.unison.org.uk**
- ▶ National Education Union (NEU): **www.neu.org.uk**
- ▶ Voice: **www.voicetheunion.org.uk**
- ▶ GMB: **www.gmb.org.uk**
- ▶ Unite: **www.unitetheunion.org**

Key term

Lobby: when an individual or organisation sets out to influence governmental decisions.

9.3 The importance of receiving ongoing developmental feedback

As part of your role in a school or early years setting, you are likely to receive some kind of ongoing developmental feedback, or **continuing professional development (CPD)** with your line manager. This may also be known as performance management or appraisal, and may involve being observed in your practice. It is important because it encourages you to reflect on what has happened, and to proactively and regularly examine your role and how it relates to the role of others in your team. CPD usually takes place on a yearly cycle, and you will be asked to review what you have done and think about what you would like to achieve in your role in the future.

> ## Key term
>
> ***Continuing professional development (CPD):*** ongoing professional training and development to keep up to date.

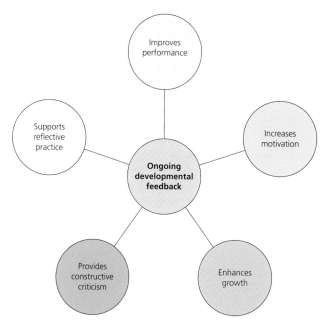

▲ Have you been able to meet with your line manager to set professional targets?

It is important to receive ongoing developmental feedback for the following reasons.

▶ **Improves performance:** Ongoing feedback will help you to reflect on your performance and think about

how you can develop. If you are observed working with children or young people, your feedback may suggest the use of strategies or teaching points that can be used to improve your work with them and better support their learning and development.

▶ **Increases motivation:** Talking to another person about your role and setting targets that are time limited should help to develop your motivation and give you renewed enthusiasm for your role.

▶ **Enhances both personal and professional growth:** Feedback enhances our personal and professional growth as it allows us to see our situation from another point of view. A change of perspective can often help draw our attention to things that we may not have seen before.

▶ **Provides constructive criticism:** We often say that the person giving feedback is acting as 'a critical friend'. This means that they are showing us how we might improve our practice by working with us to develop positive steps forward.

▶ **Supports reflective practice to identify developmental needs:** Ongoing feedback is designed to encourage you to reflect on your practice and enable you to start to think about developmental needs through a structured process.

Before a CPD or performance management meeting with your line manager, you are likely to be asked to complete a self-evaluation or self-assessment of your role, which might include questions such as these:

▶ Is my job description still accurate? Are there any changes that need to be made, and if so what are they?

▶ What do I think are my greatest strengths and which are the areas I need to improve?

▶ What areas of my job satisfy me the most?

▶ Do I have gaps in my knowledge? What skills or training would help me improve my performance?

▶ What goals or targets would I like to work towards over the next 12 months?

These questions are helpful to consider as they will encourage you to reflect on what you have done in your role and what you would like to do going forward. They will also focus you on your experiences and give you some ideas to take with you to the meeting.

> **Case study**
>
> Becca is working as a teaching assistant in a primary school and has been asked to prepare for her first appraisal with her line manager. She has been given a list of questions to think about, including any additional training she feels she might need. However, she has a busy week before the meeting and runs out of time to prepare for it.
> ▶ Should Becca still go to the meeting?
> ▶ What should she say to her line manager?

In addition, working with others to have a more active role in your own professional development has other advantages, which include:

▶ **Maintaining up-to-date knowledge and skills:** Taking time to reflect on your role with others may draw attention to additional training needs and enable you to develop your knowledge and skills.

▶ **Improving provision and outcomes for children and young people:** Staying alert to changes and improvements that can affect your practice is likely to improve educational outcomes.

▶ **Adhering to regulatory requirements and keeping up to date with legislative changes:** Working with others will help you to keep up to date and implement any new statutory requirements as they come in, as schools and early years settings will be required to do this.

▶ **Ensuring understanding of current priorities, debates and approaches in education:** Ongoing CPD will help to draw your attention to these and make sure you have appropriate training.

> See Section 9.2 for more on keeping up to date with current issues through websites and journals.

▶ **Making meaningful contributions to a team:** All those who work in educational settings will be working as part of a team. It is important to think regularly about how what you do impacts on others, and how you can best support them. In doing this you will be supporting the aims of the team as a whole, as well as the children and young people in the setting.

▶ **Improving opportunities for progression and promotion in own role:** Ongoing CPD will mean that you have a record of how you have been proactive in reflecting on your role and moving forwards. It will improve opportunities as it will bring your hopes and expectations to the attention of managers, while also enabling them to be aware of your strengths and interests.

9.4 How practitioners can meet their own developmental needs

Your own professional development should be ongoing, and personal reflection should help you to regularly think about ways in which you can change and improve your practice. You should also be able to meet your professional development needs and keep up to date in other ways, through:

▶ **Self-directed learning, reading and research.**

> For details of this, see Section 9.2.

▶ **Shadowing and visits to other settings:** An easy way of accessing information, gaining ideas and thinking about your own practice is through watching or shadowing others. You may be able to observe an experienced practitioner working with the same age group in your setting. If not, ask if you can go and visit another setting to do this. Seeing how others work will be invaluable in helping you to develop your confidence.

▶ **External training, workshops, conferences:** Throughout your career you will have access to external training. This will keep you up to date with current practice, and will enable you to explore areas of interest or gain further qualifications to enhance your role. As soon as you start working in your first role, make sure you keep a record of any additional training or CPD you undertake. As well as external training, this should include any whole-staff development training sessions that might take place at meetings or **INSET days**, such as ongoing safeguarding or health and safety training. Include the date of the training and a brief outline of what it entailed. Keep this record throughout your career and refer to it when you apply for jobs as it will contain useful information.

▶ **Appraisal, peer observation, feedback, and setting and reviewing professional goals:** Although you will set and review goals as part of your ongoing performance management with your line manager, you can also think independently about your practice and should regularly reassess goals. Peer observation also enables you and a colleague to observe each other's practice and give feedback. This process also helps you to reflect on and examine what you do as part of your role.

Key term

INSET day: in-service training day, or day when teaching staff meet in term time, without pupils, for additional training.

In practice

Find out whether you can go in to another setting to observe other professionals at work. This may be for whatever length of time is convenient, whether this is an hour or a whole morning. Before you go, think about one or two things that you are going to look at (e.g. behaviour management, displays, staff relationships with children and young people, organisation and routines), but don't try to pack in too much.

▶ Write down anything that is helpful to you in your chosen area.
▶ See if you can implement in your own practice some of what you have seen.
▶ Reflect on what has happened.

Assessment practice

1 What does reflective practice mean?
2 Why are theories of reflection helpful in practice?
3 Give **two** examples of current debates and priorities in education.
4 What are some of the pros and cons of using technology when working with children and young people?
5 What do we mean by blended learning?
6 In addition to having regular feedback, how else can you keep up to date with different aspects of educational practice?
7 Explain the importance of receiving professional feedback from others.
8 How can you work independently in meeting your own development needs?

CORE Chapter 10:
Equality and Diversity

As part of their role in any school or early years setting, adults will need to promote equality, diversity and inclusion. This is important so that all children and young people are involved, respected and given full access to the curriculum as well as the wider life of the school, college or early years setting, and they learn these values for life. Promoting equality and diversity means that the differences between individuals are recognised and respected. Your organisation will have policies on equal opportunities and inclusion for all, and these will set out its aims for ensuring that these practices are part of the life of the setting and the wider community.

Learning outcomes

This chapter covers the following knowledge outcomes for Core Element 10:

10.1 The basic principles of laws, regulations and codes of practice that underpin equality, diversity and human rights

10.2 The links between legal requirements and organisational policies and procedures relating to equality, diversity, discrimination, confidentiality and the rights of children and young people

10.3 Why it is important to promote equality, diversity and inclusion

10.4 The consequences of labelling children and young people, and the importance of having high and realistic expectations

10.5 The possible barriers to children's and young people's participation, and how practitioners can use strategies to overcome these

This chapter also includes one knowledge outcome from Assisting Teaching Performance Outcome 4. Text relating to Assisting Teaching is highlighted. Note that this content will not form part of the core assessments.

K4.7 The potential barriers pupils may face in the learning environment and how to overcome them

10.1 The basic principles of laws, regulations and codes of practice in relation to equality, diversity and human rights

United Nations Convention on the Rights of the Child 1989

UNICEF (the United Nations charity supporting children worldwide) describes the United Nations Convention on the Rights of the Child, or UNCRC, as 'the most complete statement of children's rights ever produced'. The United Kingdom, along with 195 other states, signed and **ratified** this legally binding agreement in 1989. It states that all children and young people – whatever their ethnicity, gender, religion, language or ability – should be treated equally and without discrimination. The UNCRC acknowledges the rights and freedoms that all children and young people under the age of 18 should be given through a series of 54 articles or entitlements. All of these rights are linked and there is none that is more important than the others. The nations that have ratified the treaty must fulfil it by international law and it is the most widely ratified human rights treaty in the world.

The UNCRC has four general principles (as described in the table). These help us to interpret the other remaining articles and are key to ensuring the rights for all children.

> **Key term**
>
> **Ratify:** to vote on or sign a written agreement to make it official.

> **Research**
>
> ▶ Read through the summary of these articles, which you can find on the UNICEF UK website: **www.unicef.org.uk**
> ▶ As well as those listed above, what other articles should you know about if you are working in a school or early years setting?

The Equality Act 2010

The Equality Act 2010 is the key legislation for **equality** and **diversity** in the UK. It replaced and updated nine previous equality laws in England, Scotland and Wales in order to protect the rights of individuals and ensure that they are protected from unfair treatment. Under the terms of the Equality Act 2010, all individuals should be given the same rights and opportunities so that they are able to reach their full potential. There are nine 'protected characteristics' under the act that everyone in the UK is protected against **discrimination** on the grounds of (see the next page).

> **Key terms**
>
> **Equality:** being equal in status, rights and opportunities.
>
> **Diversity:** recognising our individual differences.
>
> **Discrimination:** unfair treatment of a group of people due to **prejudice**.
>
> **Prejudice:** a set of preconceived negative ideas about a particular group of people.

Article 2: Non-discrimination	The UNCRC applies to every child without discrimination, whatever their ethnicity, sex, religion, language, abilities or any other status, whatever they think or say, whatever their family background
Article 3: Best interest of the child	The best interests of the child must be a top priority in all decisions and actions that affect children
Article 6: Right to life, survival and development	Every child has the right to life; governments must do all they can to ensure that children survive and develop to their full potential
Article 12: Right to be heard	Every child has the right to express their views, feelings and wishes in all matters affecting them, and to have their views considered and taken seriously; this right applies at all times – for example, during immigration proceedings, housing decisions or the child's day-to-day home life

▲ The four general principles of the UN Convention on the Rights of the Child

It is important to understand that discrimination can be categorised as either direct or indirect.

▶ **Direct discrimination** means treating an individual worse than another owing to a protected characteristic. This can be easy to identify – for example, not allowing a child with diabetes to come to the setting as there is no one trained to support them.

▶ **Indirect discrimination** is discrimination in which a rule is applied to all and affects some in a more negative way than others. It can be less easy to identify but still amounts to the same thing – for example, a building that has been chosen for an event that is not accessible to those with a disability.

Protected characteristics

There are nine protected characteristics under the Equality Act. This means that everyone in the UK is protected against discrimination on the grounds of any of these. For example, pregnancy and maternity are a protected characteristic, which means it is illegal for someone to lose their job because they are pregnant or have a child.

▲ Why is it important that individuals are not discriminated against on the basis of these characteristics?

Special Educational Needs and Disability Code of Practice: 0 to 25 years 2015

The SEND Code of Practice 2015 sets out the statutory guidance for early education providers, schools, colleges, health and social services professionals, and

local authorities for children and young people from birth up to 25 years of age. Its basic principles are that children and young people with all areas of need should have access to a family-centred system for their care and education so that they can achieve the best possible outcomes, thus ensuring they are treated equally.

There should be collaboration between different services, which should work together with families, who should be able to participate in any decisions that are made and to express their views. Where children and young people are not making adequate progress in their early years setting, school or college, the setting should be able to request an education, health and care (EHC) needs assessment from the local authority so that they can develop an **EHC plan**. This can then lead to additional funding for the setting to provide more support for the child or young person.

See page 179 for more on EHC plans.

> **Key term**
>
> ***Education, health and care (EHC) plan:*** an EHC plan is for children and young people aged up to 25 who need more support than is available through special educational needs support; it is drawn up to outline provision for a child or young person following an assessment of special educational needs. EHC plans identify educational, health and social needs, and set out the additional support to meet those needs. Find out more here: **www.gov.uk/children-with-special-educational-needs/extra-SEN-help**
>
> For more on assessment of special educational needs, see Core Chapter 11, page 178.

Under the SEND Code of Practice there are four broad areas of need. However, a child or young person may be affected by more than one of these needs.

1 **Communication and interaction:** This means that the child or young person has difficulties in the area of speech, language and communication. This may make it harder for them to be able to understand or make sense of what others are saying, or to be able to express what they want to say in the appropriate way. An example of this might be a child or young person who is on the autism spectrum, as they are likely to have difficulties in this area.

2 **Cognition and learning:** This means that the child or young person may find learning more of a challenge than others of the same age. This may

mean that they have a specific learning difficulty, such as dyslexia, which affects a particular aspect of their learning, or have difficulty in understanding some or all aspects of the curriculum. Learning difficulties may be wide ranging, and in some cases are categorised as either moderate, severe or profound and multiple. They may also affect organisation and memory.

3 **Social, emotional and mental health:** This means that the child or young person may have difficulty managing their relationships and emotions. This is also likely to affect their behaviour and learning, and can affect others' learning. An example of this might be a child or young person who has a condition such as ADHD, but it could also be unwanted behaviour due to the child's or young person's experiences. Children with social and emotional difficulties may also be affected by mental health conditions that are likely to affect their wellbeing.

4 **Sensory and/or physical:** This means that the child or young person may have a physical need, condition or disability, or a sensory impairment that may affect their vision or hearing. This includes sensory processing difficulties, which can also relate to behaviour. In these situations, they may need to have additional support, resources or materials in order to access the curriculum.

> For more on the SEND Code of Practice, see Core Chapter 11.

General Data Protection Regulation (GDPR) legislation

All adults working in early years settings and schools need to be aware of legislation surrounding confidentiality, particularly the General Data Protection Regulation legislation, or GDPR. This EU legislation replaced much of the previous data protection legislation. As schools and early years settings will collect and store data on both staff and children and young people, they should ensure that this is kept and disposed of securely. Your setting's confidentiality policy will set out your responsibilities under this legislation, which has six key privacy principles:

1 Data must only be collected for a valid reason and be processed fairly and transparently.
2 Data must only be used for the purpose for which it was originally obtained.
3 Only the necessary amount of data should be collected.
4 Data should be kept up to date and accurate.

5 Data should not be stored for any longer than is needed.
6 Data should be protected and secure – for example, using passwords or locked away.

In addition, data may be shared where this is necessary, such as in cases of safeguarding or children's and young people's welfare. Where possible, data should be shared with consent; however, where safeguarding is an issue it can be shared with relevant authorities without consent.

10.2 The links between legal requirements and organisational policies and procedures relating to equality, diversity, discrimination, confidentiality and the rights of children and young people

In order to comply with legal requirements, your school or early years setting should have a range of policies and procedures in place around equality, diversity, discrimination and confidentiality. This is to ensure that children and young people, parents, staff, visitors and all those who have contact with the organisation are aware of the way in which it operates and the agreed way of working. It also ensures that staff have a reference point so that they know how to respond in different situations and are proactive in ensuring that all children and young people have equal opportunities. Equality and diversity policies should ensure that all staff and children and young people know how to:

▶ treat others
▶ challenge negative attitudes in others
▶ ensure that facilities and activities are accessible and inclusive for all
▶ plan for and promote multiculturalism and diversity in lessons
▶ ensure learning resources are inclusive and do not discriminate
▶ ensure that teaching is inclusive and uses a variety of methods.

Inclusion policy

This may be a standalone policy but could also be part of the SEND or equality and diversity policy. It should set out how the school or early years setting will value, respect and celebrate individuality, and enable all children and young people to achieve their best outcomes through breaking down barriers to learning.

The following articles of the UNCRC are also relevant here:

- Article 24: Every child has the right to the best possible health, including healthcare, water and food, and a clean environment and education on health and wellbeing.
- Article 28: Every child has the right to an education.
- Article 30: Every child has the right to learn and use the language, customs and religion of their family.

Confidentiality policy

This policy will outline how the setting will keep to its obligations under GDPR, and protect and store the personal information of children and young people and staff. It should also include details of how the setting will share information, where needed, with other professionals when this is in the best interests of the child or young person.

Accessibility policy

See Core Chapter 11, Section 11.1.

Partnership working – sharing information

Safe partnership working may form part of the confidentiality policy and explain the need to share information with others only on a need-to-know basis. Partnership working is also linked to the SEND Code of Practice, as this highlights the importance of parents, children and young people and professionals working together to share information safely and improve outcomes.

Admissions policy

Schools and early years settings should have an admissions policy, which should set out their criteria for allowing entry. Under the SEN Code of Practice, in cases of children and young people who already have an EHC plan, parents are able to name and gain a place for their child at their preferred school.

Special educational needs policy

All schools and early years settings are required to have a policy for SEND under the 2015 SEND Code of Practice (see Core Chapter 11, Section 11.1).

Safeguarding policy

This policy will need to refer to various DfE guidance documents. See Core Chapter 3 for details.

Research

- ▶ Find out the location of policies and procedures in your setting.
- ▶ Make sure you know who is responsible for equality and inclusion.
- ▶ Check your responsibilities under your confidentiality policy.

10.3 Why it is important to promote equality, diversity and inclusion

As well as knowing about legislation and policies, all adults in the setting will need to promote equality, diversity and inclusion when working with children and young people. It is important for you to be a good **role model** and to demonstrate this through your actions, what you say and how you treat others, so that everyone feels valued and welcome. Schools and early years settings should also use other methods to promote positive images and messages around diversity, and use teaching and learning experiences that reflect the wider community, so that all children, young people and adults feel included and differences are celebrated.

You should remember that it is also possible to unintentionally discriminate against some pupils. One example is reward systems, although these may be a useful way of recognising achievement.

Key term

Role model: someone who is looked to by others as an example.

Some common ways to do this include the following:

- ▶ A range of books and stories should be available in schools and early years settings, which reflect different countries, cultures, languages and backgrounds, as well as images and stories about children and young people who may look different, so that everyone is represented.
- ▶ Resources that are used by the school or early years setting should reflect cultural diversity – for example, in early years role-play areas or in subject areas such as history or geography.
- ▶ The setting should show through learning experiences and events that it is inclusive and promotes inclusion and diversity. These kinds

of opportunities may include activities such as themed weeks, celebrations of different festivals, crafts, cooking, dancing or listening to music from different cultures and backgrounds.

▶ Your school or early years setting should promote equality, multiculturalism and diversity through the way in which lessons are taught.

▶ Your setting should have a range of displays and information boards that reflect different cultures, age groups, languages and religions.

▶ Older children and young people should be given opportunities to talk about prejudice and stereotyping so that they can recognise what is meant by these and explore their own views.

▶ All families should be welcomed and events that are held at the setting should reflect different cultures.

Good to know

Always check and make a note of the correct pronunciation and spelling of children's and young people's and parents' names, and ensure that you remember them correctly.

Reflect

Look at the following scenarios and, for each one, consider whether it is an example of discrimination. If so, is it direct or indirect?

▶ A pupil with a physical disability, who is a talented musician, cannot gain access to the main part of the school's music department as it is upstairs.

▶ A parent has to come in to school every lunchtime to administer medication to her five year old who has diabetes as there are no members of staff who are trained or prepared to do this.

▶ A refugee family who don't speak English are not able to access an open morning for new parents.

▶ A three-year-old partially sighted child has been refused access to a local nursery.

Responsibility of adults	Why this is important
Complying with legal responsibilities (Equality Act 2010)	All those working in schools and early years settings are obliged by law to comply with their legal responsibilities under the Equality Act 2010 see Section 10.1.
Preventing discrimination	There should be clear policies and guidelines for equality and diversity in the setting, and if discrimination occurs it should be challenged and/or reported. You should remember that discrimination may also be unintentional, for example, giving rewards for attendance to pupils, some of whom may never be able to achieve this.
Ensuring equality of opportunity	All individuals are entitled to the same opportunities regarding participation, and access to activities and experiences
Meeting individual needs/ensuring accessibility	Each child or young person has unique needs and aspirations, and should be given support by adults to meet those needs so that they can access the curriculum and wider life of the school. Adults should also look carefully at the ways in which achievements and behaviour are recognised, so that all pupils' needs and preferences are taken into account.
Appreciating and celebrating differences/valuing diversity	Schools and early years settings should show how they celebrate and appreciate differences and value diversity in different ways, so that all children and young people develop a positive sense of identity
Recognising and valuing different family circumstances and cultures	Schools and early years settings should have an awareness of the different backgrounds and circumstances of children and young people so that they can acknowledge and value these differences See Core Chapter 5 for more on different family structures.
Ensuring dignity and respect for all	All children and young people and their families are entitled to respect from the setting so that they also learn to respect others

▲ Promoting equality, diversity and inclusion in early years settings

▲ How does your setting ensure that it is a welcoming and inclusive environment?

10.4 The consequences of labelling children and young people

When we work with children and young people, we may hear about the term **labelling**. Labels are sometimes used by adults to categorise children's and young people's circumstances or needs – for example, medical needs, areas of SEND, looked after children, Traveller children, those with mental health issues, or those who are 'at risk' of offending.

Although in some cases, the purpose of labelling allows professionals to successfully apply strategies to support children with additional needs, for example, it can also have negative connotations and it is important to get to know each individual rather than make assumptions.

We should always think about and challenge our own perceptions of others and try to avoid labelling where possible as this can lead to negative and discriminatory attitudes. Using labels may also have a direct impact on children and young people, particularly if we have low expectations of their abilities as a result. Remember that there is no one word to describe any person, and nobody should be defined by a label.

Causing the individual to feel stigmatised, which can lead to social, emotional and mental health issues

Labelling may cause the child or young person to feel **stigmatised**, which means that they may feel labelled with a sense of disapproval by others. This in turn can cause the person not to feel valued, and to have low self-esteem or feel that others are not interested in them.

Changing how others view the individual, particularly if they have a negative or limited understanding of a need or disability

If a child or young person has been given a label, or it has been applied in a negative way, this may cause others to see them differently. It is important that we meet and get to know each person on an individual basis and base our views on this. We can also try to change others' perceptions of a child or young person by highlighting their strengths or sharing their positive achievements.

Establishing a set of limits associated with that label, which may lead to practitioners offering the individual limited opportunities

Labelling can also cause some people to see the label rather than the person, and to think that they are restricted in their abilities. This may mean that they are not given equal opportunities or a chance to access the same activities as others.

Placing a burden of guilt or 'blame' on the individual's parents

Parents may feel that they have failed or that they are inadequate due to negative labels. For example, labelling may highlight any guilt they may feel because of the circumstances that have had an impact on their child. This will also increase any negativity they feel around their child and make it harder for them to be positive themselves.

Case study

Jeanette works as a teaching assistant and has just been told that Aidan, who is a looked after child, will be starting at her primary school on Monday in the Year 4 class she supports. She knows nothing else about him as they have no other information at present. Jeanette says to the class teacher, 'Oh, it looks like we are going to have another one working on my table.'
▶ Why are Jeanette's comments unacceptable?
▶ What should her attitude be towards Aidan?

It is important to have high and realistic expectations for children and young people. This is because a 'can do' attitude and mind-set will encourage them to feel motivated, and so aim higher and achieve more. This will empower them, raise their self-esteem and encourage their development. If expectations are low, or they and others feel that something is missing or they won't be able to achieve, it will be harder for the child or young person to motivate themselves and as a result their achievements may be lower.

Positive expectations	Result
Encouraging independence	If adults encourage children and young people to do things for themselves rather than doing things for them, this will develop their confidence and belief in themselves and their own abilities
Increasing motivation and confidence	A positive outlook and belief in their own ability will improve children's and young people's motivation and help to develop their confidence in their work
	We can support them by giving plenty of positive praise, as well as by the use of rewards, house points and other age-appropriate motivational tools, depending on the setting's policies
Improving academic outcomes	Having high yet realistic expectations encourages children and young people to develop and improve learning
Creating a culture of achievement	Schools and early years settings should create and celebrate a culture of achievement so that children and young people feel that they can set their own personal best and feel rewarded for effort, regardless of ability

▲ The importance of having positive expectations for children and young people

10.5 The possible barriers to children's and young people's participation, and how practitioners can use strategies to overcome these

As we have seen, barriers to children's and young people's participation may not just be physical. They can be due to a range of issues, attitudes and expectations from those around them, which may all affect their self-esteem and influence how they can access the curriculum and the wider life of the setting. The impact of these barriers will be that the child or young person who is affected will not feel included or part of the group, and this in turn can have wider and longer-ranging effects.

Physical accessibility

Physical barriers to participation may occur if the learning environment has not been designed to suit the ages of the children and young people who are using it, or if provision has not been made for pupils who have SEND, where this is needed. This needs to be addressed so that they are not excluded from any aspect of the learning environment.

Mental health issues

Mental health issues may prevent children and young people from participating if they feel unable to do so, or are depressed, withdrawn or anxious. If adults are not aware, and appropriate support and treatment is not sought, this may have long-term effects on their learning and participation in education.

Attitudes and expectations

See Section 10.4.

Curriculum

The early years setting or school should ensure that it has an inclusive curriculum that meets the needs of all individuals. This means learning experiences that take in to account all abilities, needs, backgrounds and ethnic backgrounds, and that teach children and young people about different religions and cultures. Diversity should be shown to be valued, and differences should be recognised and celebrated.

Family background

Children and young people will come from a range of family backgrounds, which may or may not be supportive and take an interest in and support what they are doing at the setting. They may also have challenging personal circumstances, such as being a young carer, or come from a background of abuse or neglect. All of these factors will affect how they feel about themselves and whether they are motivated and feel able to participate in teaching and learning activities.

> See Core Chapter 2, Section 2.7, for more about family backgrounds.

Socio-economic barriers

This means the circumstances of different groups of people. If the child's or young person's background means that they have poor living conditions or limited resources, this may affect how much they are able to engage with learning activities. For example, those from lower-income families will find it more difficult to pay towards educational visits or extracurricular activities.

How practitioners can use strategies to overcome barriers to children's and young people's participation

Strategies for overcoming barriers to participation, and how they can be used, are given in the chart below.

Strategies to overcome barriers to participation	How to do this
Training to understand inclusion	All members of staff should be aware of the setting's policies for equality and inclusion If they are working with an individual, they should have training where necessary, and as much information as possible about the individual's needs, condition or disability
Partnership working, including supporting children's and young people's psychological wellbeing	Working closely with parents and other professionals will enable practitioners to find out as much as possible about the child or young person and share professional knowledge about their background; it will also give them opportunities to ask for ways in which they can best support them, as well as to find out about available resources For more on psychological wellbeing, see Core 5 and 6.
Adaptations to the physical environment	Adaptations may need to be made to the environment, particularly if a child or young person has sensory needs or a disability There should also be additional resources where these are needed; this may mean installing a hearing loop, for example, or making sure there is enough space for wheelchairs
Providing accessible curriculum and assessment	The curriculum should be accessible to all children and young people so that they have the resources they need to fully participate in teaching and learning activities in line with their needs They should also be given appropriate assessment and feedback so that they can make progress and understand their future learning needs
Reviewing equality, diversity and inclusion policies	All equality and inclusion policies should be reviewed on a regular basis to ensure that they are up to date and that staff have read and understood their responsibilities
Providing information about financial support	In cases where children and young people and their families need financial support and help, schools and early years settings should be able to give them further information about how to access this – for example, through local education authorities or Citizens Advice
Supporting children and young people through transitions	See Core Chapter 7, Section 7.6

▲ Strategies to overcome barriers to participation, and how to use them in your practice

Research

In 1968, Jane Elliott, a teacher in Iowa, USA, carried out an exercise with her class to explore the effects of racial discrimination. A very powerful documentary about this, A Class Divided, showed the effects of treating people differently according to their physical characteristics. The recording is available on video-streaming sites. Watch the first 16 minutes of the documentary and answer the following questions.

▶ What do you think about this lesson and how it affected the children?
▶ What barriers were created by treating the class in this way?
▶ What do you think would be the long-term effects on the group if this were permanent?

(AT) K4.7 The potential barriers pupils may face in the learning environment and how to overcome them

Environment

Staff should ensure that the learning environment is appropriate for the needs of all pupils. It should be the correct temperature so that they can concentrate, and lighting and noise levels should not prevent them from being able to do their work. All pupils, whatever their needs, should be able to access the resources and materials required without any distractions.

Ensuring that lighting and noise levels are appropriate

Although you may be prepared for the activity, and have checked that the space will be available, there may be last-minute disruption, such as workmen outside or another group making a noise close by, that disrupts what you are doing. Light levels are also important, and pupils should have an appropriate amount – check blinds are available, for example, if the area is in full sun. Adverse weather such as snow or thunderstorms will also cause disruption and mean children and young people are unlikely to be able to concentrate on their work. In this situation it may be better to move if possible, or to postpone what you are doing.

Making adjustments to the physical space to accommodate disabilities

See Section 10.5.

Ensuring availability of appropriate resources

There should be sufficient resources available so that the group has enough to work with. If the resources are shared with other groups or classes, or you need batteries or instructions on how to make them work, make sure you have tried this out before starting the activity so that it does not interrupt teaching and learning.

▲ How do you ensure that the physical environment is accessible to all pupils?

Teaching and learning

The quality of teaching and learning will clearly be important in terms of how easily pupils are able to access the curriculum. If this is of poor quality, with poorly planned or organised teaching that is not differentiated, or if pupils are not supported in achieving learning objectives, this will make learning more difficult for them.

The following table describes some routine ways in which we as adults involved in education ensure that all pupils are given the best possible opportunities to achieve.

Strategies to overcome barriers to learning	How to do this
Clarifying learning objectives	At the start of any learning activity, all pupils should be aware of learning objectives. Adults should make sure that they are displayed or written at the top of the page so that pupils can refer to them if needed during the activity and remind themselves what they should be able to do by the end of each session.
Adapting learning activities to pupils' individual needs	Depending on the individual needs of the pupils you are working with, you may need to adapt learning activities for them. This may mean talking them through what they need to do, or providing additional materials or support so that they are able to carry out the activity as independently as possible. In addition, pupils with communication needs may be supported using AAC (augmentative and alternative communication). This refers to systems, devices or strategies to enable them to communicate, and may range from gestures or simple pictorial representation to more complex computer programmes. For more information on augmentative and alternative communication (AAC), see Core Chapter 11, Section 11.11.
Providing bilingual resources to pupils with English as an additional language (EAL)	Pupils who speak English as an additional language may need to be provided with bilingual resources to help them access the curriculum. If you are not sure of their level of understanding, you should always check that they have understood the learning objectives to ensure that they have everything they need when carrying out activities. If you do not know what additional resources are available for EAL pupils, you should check with teachers. See also Core Chapter 12, Section 12.5.
Ensuring resources are understood and prepared in advance	Before starting work with pupils on any learning activity, you must make sure that you are clear on exactly what they need to do and the resources they will need to do it. Check that what you need is available and that you understand how to use it. In addition, you should make sure that you have access to power if it is needed, or have enough batteries where necessary. If resources need to be prepared, try to do this before the time that you need them – for example, by doing any photocopying or gathering additional materials – as this may take longer than you think. If you can, ask teachers for plans in advance so that you have enough time to prepare and think about what you need to do.
Providing appropriate feedback to support progression	When working with children and young people, you will need to provide them with feedback and encouragement to support their progression. This means asking them to check their progress against learning objectives and giving them support where needed, which may be in the form of appropriate questioning to direct their thinking, or scaffolding their learning so that they can make progress. See also Core Chapter 2, Section 2.5 for more on how feedback supports learning.
Include all pupils in the activity	You should always make sure that all pupils are included in learning activities. Due to differences in personality, there will always be those who are more keen to put their ideas forward and be involved, particularly when working as part of a group. However, make sure you involve quieter and less confident pupils, and question them about their progress and ideas. You can also use what you know about pupils – for example, if they have a particular interest or skill – to involve them further. Involving all pupils is important, both in terms of making them feel part of the activity and also in allowing you to find out about their learning. See also the section titled 'The pupil', below.

▲ Strategies to overcome barriers to learning, and how to use them in your practice

The pupil

Barriers to learning may come from pupils themselves – for example, if they find learning challenging due to low ability or self-esteem, or if they have learning or behavioural difficulties that make it harder for them to focus on the activity. They may also be affected by home circumstances if these are difficult – for example, if they are distracted by something that is happening at home, or if they are anxious or hungry. Peer pressure may also make it harder for them to concentrate – for example, if they want to do what others are doing and be seen to act in the same way.

> For more on factors affecting learning and development, see Assisting Teaching K2.3.

As a teaching assistant, you may be better placed to notice when a pupil is not 'themselves', or they may confide in you if something is worrying them. However, if their behaviour or what they are doing is interfering with their learning or that of others, you should always take action. This may take different forms:

▶ **Intervening to manage disruptive behaviour:** This is important and you should intervene straight away so that the behaviour does not interrupt teaching and learning. Remind pupils about the agreed expectations for behaviour in the class or school. If the disruptive behaviour continues, act in line with your school's policy and use the sanctions that have been agreed.

▶ **Keeping pupils focused on tasks:** It can be easy for pupils to be distracted or for the conversation to move away from learning, particularly if you are working in a small group. Always be mindful of this and refocus pupils where necessary.

▶ **Encouraging pupils to participate:** Children and young people may need encouragement to participate in activities, particularly if they are finding them difficult. Make sure you note which pupils are not taking part so that you can do this.

▶ **Breaking down learning into smaller steps as needed:** If pupils find tasks difficult, they may need adults to break them down into smaller steps so that they can work on them in stages.

▶ **Following a pupil's EHC plan where appropriate:** If you are working with pupils who have an EHC plan, you should know about and understand their needs, and be aware of their targets and areas for development so that you can support them effectively.

▶ **Referring any concerns to appropriate colleagues or professionals:** Make sure you note down any concerns about pupils' learning or behaviour so that you can pass these on to teachers or the SENDCo where needed.

▶ **Developing confidence and self-esteem:** All pupils will need praise and encouragement when working on learning activities, particularly if they are finding a task challenging. Noticing what they have done and building on their successes will develop their confidence and encourage them to keep going.

Assessment practice

1 What is the purpose of the Equality Act 2010?
2 Name **five** of the protected characteristics identified in the Equality Act 2010.
3 Why is it important to know about the GDPR when working in schools and early years settings?
4 Give **four** reasons why it is important to promote equality, diversity and inclusion.
5 Outline the consequences of labelling children and young people.
6 How does having high and realistic expectations support the development of children and young people?
7 What kinds of barriers to learning might exist in an educational setting?
8 Explain **three** ways in which practitioners can use strategies to support children's and young people's participation. Include reasons why each is effective.

CORE Chapter 11: Special Educational Needs and Disability

Part of your role, whether you are working in a school or early years setting, will be to support children and young people who have special educational needs and disabilities (SEND). The number of children with SEND is increasing: in January 2019, 14.9 per cent of all those in schools in England had special educational needs (source: School Census, DfE). In this chapter, we will look at the legislation that is in place to support them, and consider how their overall development can be affected, and the kinds of strategies you might use as an early years practitioner or teaching assistant.

Learning outcomes

This chapter covers the following knowledge outcomes for Core Element 11:

11.1 The laws, codes of practice and policies affecting provision for children and young people with disabilities and those with special educational needs and disabilities

11.2 How professionals and organisations support children/young people with special educational needs and disabilities

11.3 The principles of integration and inclusion, and the differences between them

11.4 Why practitioners must use appropriate terminology when discussing the needs of children and young people with SEND

11.5 The differences between the medical and social models of disability

11.6 How a primary disability might affect children's/young people's social, emotional and physical development

11.7 A range of cognitive skills necessary for effective educational development, and how single or multiple disabilities might affect these

11.8 How cognitive difficulties may impact upon language, communication and educational development

11.9 How a chronic condition may affect children's/young people's emotions, education, behaviour and quality of life

11.10 How adults remove barriers in order to empower and value individuals, depending on their specific learning difficulty, medical condition or disability

11.11 When and how speech can be supplemented or replaced by augmentative and alternative communication

11.1 The laws, codes of practice and policies affecting provision for children and young people with special educational needs and disabilities (SEND)

As an early years practitioner or teaching assistant, you will need to be aware of your own statutory duties and responsibilities when working with children and young people who have **SEND (sometimes called SEN)**. Although the main statutory document is the Special Educational Needs and Disability Code of Practice 2015, there are also three separate guidance documents that break down the statutory duties and responsibilities of practitioners within each age range. These are set out in broadly the same way but focus on relevant areas.

> **Key term**
>
> **SEND (sometimes called SEN):** 'A child or young person has SEN if they have a learning difficulty or disability which calls for special educational provision to be made for him or her' (SEND Code of Practice, 2015).

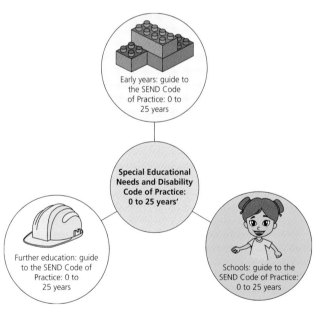

▲ Special Educational Needs and Disability Code of Practice: 0 to 25 years

Each of the three documents starts with the same headings, with a short explanation in each of these areas.
- ▶ **The context:** The Children and Families Act 2014 and its new statutory obligations (see page 176).

- ▶ **Principles underlying the code:** These are the seven principles that must be observed by all professionals who work with children and young people who have SEND – for example, enabling children and young people and their parents to participate in decision making.
- ▶ **Working together across education, health and care for joint outcomes:** Under this part of the Children and Families Act 2014, local authorities have a duty to ensure that services work together to improve the quality of provision for children and young people with SEND.
- ▶ **The Local Offer:** All local authorities must publish a Local Offer, which outlines in a clear way what is available in the local area for children and young people who have SEND.

> **Research**
>
> Using the document that is most relevant to your occupational specialism, look up the four headings above, which start around page 5.
> - ▶ What are the seven principles underlying the code?
> - ▶ Where can you find out more information about each of these four headings?

Early years: guide to the SEND Code of Practice: 0 to 25 years

According to the Early Years Foundation Stage (EYFS) Statutory Guidance, all maintained nurseries and other providers who have funding from local authorities in England must have regard to the SEND Code of Practice 2015, to meet the needs of children with SEND in schools and early years settings. The guide to the SEND Code of Practice for early years settings was published in September 2014 and highlights the main duties and responsibilities for early years providers. As practitioners working with this age group will see them at the earliest stages, they are also well placed to notice and act upon any concerns around their development.

> See page 178 of this chapter for details of the support available for those working with children from birth to five years.

The focus of the guide is on a number of areas, some of which are outlined below:

▶ **Improving outcomes for children with SEND through high aspirations and expectations, including the EYFS statutory requirements:** All providers must follow this framework, in particular with regard to the safeguarding and welfare requirements. They must ensure that they follow their duty under the Equality Act 2010 and prevent those who have SEND from being placed at a disadvantage.

▶ **Progress check at age two:** All children should have a progress check between the ages of two and three, and parents should be provided with a short report on their child's learning and development. This should identify strengths and also any areas of concern, so that plans can be put in place to provide additional support.

> See also page 178, under the heading 'The support available in childcare, schools and colleges for young people with special educational needs and disabilities'.

▶ **SEND in the early years:** Identifying and supporting. Providers must have systems in place in order to identify and support children with SEND. The document states that children's progress can be assessed using the Early Years Outcomes document; from 2021 the non-statutory *Development Matters* can be used. Where there is a cause for concern it is important that this is acted upon without delay. Where needs are identified providers must work with parents to act upon the four stages of action, also known as the **graduated approach**: assess, plan, do and review. This should involve parents as well as specialists where needed.

▶ **The role of the SENDCo (sometimes known as the SENCo) and area SENDCo in early years provision:** There must be a qualified teacher who acts as the SENDCo in a maintained nursery; other early years providers may be part of a network of settings that share a SENDCo – for example, childminders who are part of an agency. Local authorities may also provide area SENDCos to give advice and guidance to early years providers in the area. The SENDCo must ensure that everyone in the setting understands their role with regard to supporting children with SEND, works closely with parents and professionals, and provides advice and support to colleagues.

▶ **Requesting an EHC (education, health and care) needs assessment:** If a child has not made expected progress, despite steps towards assessing and meeting their needs by the early years provider, the setting may need to request an EHC needs assessment through the local authority. Parents can also request one, as can young people over the age of 16.

> For more on EHC plans, see page 179 of this chapter.

▲ What should you do if you are asked to support a child with SEND?

Schools: guide to the SEND Code of Practice: 0 to 25 years

Schools and **alternative provision settings** also have statutory duties and responsibilities under the Children and Families Act 2014 and the SEND Code of Practice 2015. The schools guide to the SEND Code of Practice: 0 to 25 years was published in September 2014 and highlights the main duties and responsibilities for schools.

> See page 178 for details of the support available for those working with children and young people from five to fifteen years.

Key term

Alternative provision settings: education providers for pupils who are unable to go to a mainstream school. This may be, for example, due to exclusion or illness.

The guide's focus is on a number of areas, some of which are outlined below.

▶ **Improving outcomes for children with SEND through high aspirations and expectations:** As with early years children, pupils with SEND in schools as well as those with medical conditions are entitled to the best possible provision. Mainstream schools must provide support and an inclusive environment to enable them to receive this alongside their peers.

▶ **Identifying SEND in schools:** A school should have a SEND policy that outlines its approach to identifying and responding to SEND at the earliest point. This should be done with the full knowledge and involvement of parents, so that they can reinforce this at home.

▶ **Deciding whether to make special educational provision and defining desired outcomes:** Where a pupil does not make expected progress despite intervention by the school, specialists may be involved, with parental approval, to continue to support the pupil's needs using appropriate strategies and interventions.

▶ **Requesting an EHC needs assessment:** If a child has not made expected progress, despite steps towards assessing and meeting their needs by the school, the setting may need to request an EHC needs assessment through the local authority.

For more on EHC plans, see page 179.

Research

Choose one of the following to research:
▶ Early years: guide to the SEND Code of Practice: 0 to 25 years
▶ Schools: guide to the SEND Code of Practice: 0 to 25 years
▶ Further education: guide to the SEND Code of Practice: 0 to 25 years.

1 What can you find out about your own responsibilities through the guidance?
2 How would you ensure that you were able to access any training needs?

Further education: guide to the SEND Code of Practice: 0 to 25 years

This guidance is for further education colleges, sixth-form colleges, 16 to 19 academies and independent colleges. These institutions all have statutory duties and responsibilities under the Children and Families Act 2014 and the SEND Code of Practice 2015. The further education guide to the SEND Code of Practice: 0 to 25 years was published in September 2014 and highlights the main duties and responsibilities for colleges. Its focus is on a number of areas, some of which are outlined below.

▶ **Statutory duties of post-16 institutions:** Colleges must work with the local authority on arrangements for children and young people with SEND. They must admit a young person if they are named on an EHC plan, and fulfil their duties to those who have SEND and who may not have an EHC. They must not discriminate in any way against young people with a disability and must make reasonable adjustments to ensure that they have what they need to prevent disadvantage.

▶ **Identifying and supporting children and young people in college:** The college must put in place whatever is needed to support children and young people who have SEND, and keep this under review. They should work with students and their parents to assess, plan, do and review, and ensure that all staff are trained where needed. Colleges need to have a named person on-site to oversee SEND provision, similar to the role of the SENDCo in schools and early years settings.

▶ **Preparing for adulthood:** All those who work with children and young people with SEND should encourage and support them as they prepare for adult life, and support them to achieve the best outcomes in employment, health, independence and community participation.

▶ **Young people's right to make their own decisions:** After the end of the academic year in which they turn 16, young people can make requests and decisions under the Children and Families Act 2014, although their parents can still support them in doing this.

▶ **Planning the transition into post-16 education, and training and careers advice:** Young people with SEND may need specialist provision post-16, and schools and colleges should work in partnership to allow them to attend taster days. They should also ensure that students have access to careers advice that allows them to consider the widest range of career options, through activities such as work experience and taster sessions.

▶ **Pathways to employment:** Children and young people with SEND should have the support they need to achieve the skills, experience and qualifications they require. Colleges should provide courses that offer pathways to employment and prepare students with SEND for work. They should do this through helping them to develop the skills employers need and value, often through work-based training such as apprenticeships and internships.

The link between these guidance documents, the Children and Families Act 2014 and the Special Educational Needs and Disability Code of Practice: 0 to 25 years 2015

These guidance documents link to the SEND Code of Practice 2015 as they are specific to the age groups concerned. The SEND Code of Practice 2015 is a long document and so this guidance enables providers to look at those aspects that are relevant to them. The Code of Practice sets out the duties, policies and procedures that all organisations working with children and young people from birth to the age of 25 must take into account in relation to their care and education. This is a statutory requirement.

The Children and Families Act 2014 influenced the SEND Code of Practice as it brought in wide-ranging reforms in the areas of special educational needs, adoption, family courts and social care. These reforms highlighted a need for better cooperation between professionals when working with SEND children and young people, and these were incorporated into the code. For example:

▶ the requirement for a Local Offer (see page 179)
▶ joined-up services across education, health and care
▶ the requirement for education, health and care (EHC) plans
▶ statutory rights for young people in further education
▶ a focus on preparing for adulthood and planning for the transition to paid employment.

Test yourself

1 What is the purpose of the three documents?
2 What are the responsibilities of a SENDCo?
3 What is meant by a Local Offer?
4 What legislation do the guidance documents bring together?

▲ Local Offer

The purpose of a range of organisational policies and procedures that support children and young people with SEND

A number of policies and procedures will be in place in your setting to support children and young people with SEND. In many cases, these policies link to legal requirements and should be read alongside the SEND policy. All staff will need to be aware of them to ensure both consistency and transparency when working with these pupils.

SEND policy

All schools and early years settings will need to have a SEND policy to show how they support children and young people who have special educational needs and disabilities. The policy should set out the setting's aims and objectives, and outline the procedures that should be followed when identifying, assessing and providing for those with SEND. The policy should provide clear guidance to parents, staff and children and young people, particularly around the following:

▶ **Identification:** Schools and early years settings must have a clear policy for the way in which they identify and respond to SEND. The SEND Code of Practice highlights the importance of early identification so that effective provision can be made to support the child or young person.

▶ **Assessment:** If a child or young person is identified as having SEND, schools and early years settings will have carried out an initial assessment, working alongside parents. This should be reviewed on a regular basis so that progress or any lack of improvement can be monitored. Where the child or young person is making little or no progress over time, the policy is likely to ask for more specialist assessment from other agencies outside the setting through the SENDCo.

▶ **Provision:** When SEND support has been agreed alongside parents, the policy should outline how agreed interventions and targets will be put in place, and the success criteria for meeting these outcomes, as well as a review date. The views of the child or young person must also be taken into account, as well as input from teachers, the SENDCo and other professionals. This cycle is known as the **graduated approach** (assess, plan, do, review).

Equality policy

An equality or equal opportunities policy should set out the commitment of schools and early years settings to equality and anti-discriminatory practice, and meet the requirements of the Equality Act 2010. It should state how **inclusion** is a key part of the environment, curriculum and community.

> ### Key term
>
> *Inclusion:* the process of identifying, understanding and breaking down barriers to participation and belonging.

Accessibility or access policy/plan

It is a legal requirement of the Equality Act 2010 that schools should have an accessibility or access policy or plan. This should complement the SEND and equality policies of the setting, and should set out access arrangements for children with disabilities, staff and visitors. As well as physical access to buildings and facilities, the access policy should state how the setting makes provision for equal access to the curriculum and wider context of the school for all pupils.

Alternative provision policy

The policy for alternative provision sets out what a mainstream (usually secondary) school will do in cases where pupils cannot attend due to emotional, behaviour or health reasons. This may be linked to SEND where pupils have these specific needs but are unable to attend school. It does not apply to early years settings.

Anti-bullying policy

In schools and early years settings, this may form part of the behaviour policy. It will set out what the provider has in place to prevent all types of bullying among children and young people, and the roles of staff and parents in acting on any incidents that may occur.

Behaviour policy

All schools and early years settings will have a policy for behaviour that gives clear guidelines on the expectations of the setting. Staff and children and young people should be aware of sanctions that will be put in place if the rules are broken, as well as the kinds of positive reinforcement that can be put in place when expectations are met. It is important for all children and young people, and particularly those with special educational needs in this area, to be clear on boundaries and expectations for behaviour.

Medical needs policy

This policy may also be part of a first aid or health and safety policy. It will set out the setting's requirements for children and young people with health and medical needs and conditions – for example, procedures for administering medicines and who is able to do this. In the case of early years children, the EYFS states that settings should have a policy for administering medicines, which should be read alongside the EYFS guidance.

Teaching and learning policy

This policy sets out the way in which a school or early years setting provides activities and opportunities that meet the individual learning needs of each child and young person through a differentiated curriculum. This should encourage independence and creativity, and enable them to work collaboratively when needed.

Complaints policy

All educational provision should have a complaints policy so that parents are able to raise concerns and make complaints. It should set out a clear procedure to be followed and show the different stages complaints will go through. There should also be information on what the complainant should do if they are not satisfied with the way in which a complaint has been dealt with.

> ### Research
>
> Using your setting's SEND policy, and looking in particular at the areas of identification, assessment and provision, outline the steps which are taken when a pupil is a cause for concern and may have an area of special educational need.

The support available in childcare, schools and colleges for young people with special educational needs and disabilities

The SEND Code of Practice sets out what early years settings, schools, colleges and other educational institutions should do to support SEND children and young people. It is a framework to help all educational professionals as well as those from health and care settings and youth offending teams.

> For more on the SEND Code of Practice and the four areas of need, see Core Chapter 10, Section 10.1.

In addition to what is set out in the Code of Practice, children and young people who have SEND will also be entitled to the following support.

0–5 years

▶ **A written progress check when a child is two years old:** Between the ages of two and three, all early years practitioners must carry out a progress review and provide a written summary to parents of the three prime areas of children's development: communication and language, physical

development, and personal, social and emotional development. This review must outline the areas in which the child is making good progress, and also those in which they may need some additional support or a further assessment. If there is any cause for concern – for example, that they may have a developmental delay – this must be highlighted so that action can be taken.

▶ **A child's health visitor carrying out a health check for a child when they are aged two to three:** This check looks at a child's physical development milestones, as well as their health and wellbeing, to ensure that they are making expected progress. It also enables intervention where progress is not as expected, so that appropriate steps can be put in place to support the child.

▶ **Reception Baseline Assessment (RBA) (from autumn 2021):** This is an on-entry assessment of mathematics and language, communication and literacy in the first few weeks of primary school. Its purpose is to measure each child's progress to the end of Key Stage 2 when they leave primary school. It is not intended as a diagnostic assessment (see page 142) although it can be used to inform teaching in the first term.

> See also pages 16 and 148.

▶ **A written assessment in the summer term of a child's first year of primary school:** This assessment takes place at the end of reception, and should form part of the Early Years Profile, which takes place at the end of the Foundation Stage.

> For more on this, see Core Chapter 8, page 147.

▶ **Reasonable adjustments for children with disabilities:** A reasonable adjustment is something that settings must do under the Equality Act 2010 to ensure that a person with disabilities is not placed at a disadvantage when compared to those without disabilities. This, therefore, applies to staff and visitors as well as children and young people. Reasonable adjustments may be, for example, providing training for staff where needed, ensuring there is enough equipment for children with disabilities, and promoting inclusion in all areas of learning and development.

Case study

You are working in a secondary school and are employed as a learning support assistant for Fabiola, who has disabilities and learning difficulties. She has an EHC plan and works with you on academic targets, much of the time out of class. At a review meeting after half a term in Year 7, her parents comment on the fact that although Fabiola is out of the class receiving interventions and one-to-one work with you, this is not helping her to be included with her peers, and she feels isolated.

- ▶ Has the school made a reasonable adjustment in Fabiola's case?
- ▶ Can you suggest any ways in which Fabiola could feel more part of the class?

5–15 years

- ▶ **A special learning programme:** Where schools identify that additional support is needed they should, after discussion with parents, put into practice a programme of support that targets the pupil's area of weakness. This will then be monitored so that progress can be checked regularly.
- ▶ **Extra help from a teacher, teaching assistant or mental health lead:** This support programme means that the pupil will receive regular support from a school-based professional in line with their needs.
- ▶ **Opportunities to work in smaller groups or other areas of the school:** The additional support may be provided in small groups or individually, within the class or in other areas in the school.
- ▶ **Observation in class or at break:** School staff may carry out observations of pupils in class or at break time to help them assess their level of need.
- ▶ **Help taking part in class activities:** Pupils with SEND may need extra help during class activities to help them to access the curriculum.
- ▶ **Extra encouragement in their learning – for example, to ask questions or to try something they find difficult:** Pupils may need encouragement or specific questioning techniques, such as scaffolding their learning and giving effective feedback, to enable them to manage their own learning.

See also Core Chapter 2, Section 2.2.

- ▶ **Help communicating with other children or young people:** If children and young people have communication needs, they may need help when speaking to their peers or to adults using **augmentative and alternative communication (AAC).**

See also Section 11.11.

- ▶ **Support with physical or personal care difficulties, such as eating, getting around school safely or using the toilet:** Specially trained staff may need to support pupils with physical or personal care needs, according to school policies.

The education, health and care (EHC) plan

Where early years settings, schools and colleges cannot meet the needs of children and young people through normal provision, they may put them forward for an assessment for an EHC plan. EHC plans are intended to support children and young people from birth to 25 years with needs that fall outside of the SEND provision offered by childcare settings, schools or colleges. This can take place only after schools or early years settings have taken steps to meet the needs of children and young people, but they have not made expected progress. These steps would need to be evidenced through using and recording the graduated approach (assess, do, plan, review) so that it is clear what measures have been taken so far.

An EHC assessment will take place when requested by the school or early years setting, a parent if they feel it is appropriate, or it can be requested by the young person themselves if they are between the ages of 16 and 25.

After the child or young person has been assessed by the local authority, the EHC plan will be drawn up. It will need to specify their needs and the support that is required for their SEND, health or social care. It should set out the anticipated outcomes as a result of the support, and include the reports that have been provided by all professionals who work with them. Once in place, it should be reviewed at least once each year. It will stay in place until the child or young person leaves education, or they no longer need it.

In practice

Ask in your setting if you can see an example of an EHC plan for a child or young person.
- ▶ How does it set out the responsibilities of the setting for supporting them?
- ▶ What does it say about how the plan will be reviewed?

11.2 How professionals and organisations support children and young people with special educational needs and disabilities

A range of professionals and organisations support children and young people with special educational needs and disabilities, as described below.

Teachers

Teachers and early years practitioners will support the individual needs of all children and young people for whom they are responsible. Each child is unique and, although children and young people will be of broadly a similar age, they may be at different stages in their development. This means that there will be children and young people with a range of needs in each class or age group, some of whom will need to have additional support to access the curriculum. There are two aspects to this strategy:

1 If a child or young person has an identified special educational need, they will have specific targets and provision in place that will need to be coordinated by the teacher, along with the special educational needs and disabilities coordinator (SENDCo) or early years SENDCo. The child's or young person's parents and other healthcare or education professionals may also be involved. There should be regular reviews so that their progress can be checked and targets reviewed to ensure that the measures that have been put in place are effective.

2 If a child or young person does not have an identified special educational need, but parents and practitioners have a cause for concern, they will need to ensure that they are documenting what this is, speaking to parents, and differentiating work and educational experiences appropriately to allow for this. They will also need to raise the awareness of the SENDCo or early years SENDCo and involve them in setting up assessments with other professionals if necessary.

Educational psychologists

An educational psychologist is a professional who is trained in psychology and child development. Educational psychologists can assess the educational needs of children and young people, and provide support and advice to parents, teachers and early years practitioners. They may also provide curriculum materials, teaching approaches or behavioural strategies to help support the child's or young person's needs more effectively.

Medical practitioners

Medical practitioners such as doctors and nurses may be involved in supporting children and young people where they have health and medical needs. For example, a child with spina bifida who is in a mainstream school is likely to have an EHC plan and medical practitioners will meet regularly with and advise the school on how to support their medical care needs. They may also be asked to provide reports for annual reviews of the child's or young person's progress so that all those working with the child or young person have up-to-date knowledge of their condition.

The role of a multi-agency team in providing integrated support for children and young people with special educational needs and disabilities

There are many benefits to working in a multi-agency team to support children and young people with SEND, particularly where they have serious health issues, safeguarding issues or severe needs. Different agencies may include health professionals, youth workers, social workers and mental health services, as well as teachers or early years workers.

The role of the multi-agency team is to ensure that children and young people who have multiple needs can receive coordinated support more quickly. Information sharing is of key importance, and is required by legislation so that provision for children and young people with SEND is more effective.

The views of the child or young person and their parents should also be sought regarding issues that concern them, and these should be included in meetings and annual reviews.

11.3 The principles of integration and inclusion, and the differences between them

Over the years, there have been many developments in the way in which children and young people with SEND have been educated. The principles of integration and inclusion differ in the way that this should be approached. The principle of integration looks at meeting the needs of SEND pupils in a way that still thinks of them as being separate or apart from others. The principle of inclusion encompasses the needs of all children and young people, including those who have SEND, in a way which anticipates and allows for their needs. The differences between these two principles are explained in the table below.

Examples of reasonable adjustments for children and young people with SEND

▶ A child has a congenital heart condition and is just starting nursery. The nursery, along with the child's parents, gives training to all staff on how to monitor and manage the condition and how they will manage any periods of absence due to hospital stays.

▶ A pupil who has sensory processing difficulties may be given ear defenders to keep out the noise rather than be taken away from his peers to a quiet area to work.

▶ A pupil who has come back to school with hearing loss following meningitis is provided with a hearing induction loop and sits at the front in all lessons.

▶ A pupil who has severe dyslexia is provided with a scribe (amanuensis) during some lessons.

▶ A pupil who is temporarily in a wheelchair due to a broken leg is given a peer 'buddy' to ensure they are able to move around the school and to use the lift with them when needed.

Principles of integration	Principles of inclusion
Children and young people with SEND require separate support and extra resources to access the curriculum	A curriculum should offer all students equal rights, access and choices. This means making reasonable adjustments in advance to enable all children and young people to participate wherever possible.
The success of children and young people depends on their ability to adapt to the learning environment	The learning environment should be adapted to support the success of each child and young person in the setting
Extra adaptations and support within the learning environment should only benefit those with SEND	Extra adaptations and support within the learning environment can benefit everyone

▲ How the principles of integration and inclusion differ

Reflect

Looking at the following examples, consider how the setting can approach each situation in an inclusive way.

▶ A Year 2 pupil who has Asperger's Syndrome who is socially isolated from his peers and wants to use the computer whenever he finishes his work.

▶ A child in nursery who has food allergies so is excluded from cooking activities.

▶ A Year 9 pupil whose behaviour has recently become a cause for concern.

▶ A disabled pupil in Year 11 who would like to audition for the school play.

▶ A diabetic pupil in reception whose mother has to come into school each day to test his blood sugar and administer insulin.

11.4 Appropriate terminology to use when discussing the needs of children and young people with special educational needs and disabilities

All those working with children and young people who have special educational needs and disabilities should use appropriate language when working with them and describing their needs. In the past, negative terminology has been used, which can be offensive and highlight the **disability** or need rather than the individual. This can in turn be hurtful and damaging to the confidence and self-esteem of the child or young person, and can also be hurtful to their family. We should try to avoid labelling people or emphasising their needs. For example:

▶ You should refer to 'a person with a disability', rather than 'a disabled person'. This places the emphasis on the individual, rather than on the disability.

▶ It is important to avoid phrases such as 'suffers from', which implies discomfort, pain or despair. This type of language makes the assumption that a person who has SEND has something wrong with them or is to be pitied.

▶ You should also avoid language which implies that individuals are victims – for example, 'confined to a wheelchair' should be 'wheelchair user'. Many people who use a wheelchair view them as liberating rather than something that is confining.

▶ Avoid colloquial language to describe a disability or medical condition – 'fits' or 'spells' should be 'seizures'. Medical terms should be used in each case.

It is important that you use the correct terminology when discussing the needs of children and young people who have SEND, particularly as your setting is likely to have policies and requirements in place to do this. These requirements are summarised in the following table.

> ### Key term
>
> **Disability:** 'A physical or mental impairment which has a substantial or long-term negative effect on your ability to do normal activities' (DfE, 2010).

Requirement	Why this is important
Complying with organisational policies	All staff in your setting will need to use appropriate terminology when referring to children and young people with SEND. This will be in line with the requirements of the organisation's policies, such as the SEND policy.
Avoiding stereotyping or labelling	When working with or talking about children and young people with SEND, practitioners should avoid making assumptions about what they can or can't do. Stereotyping and labelling are damaging and can be barriers to the achievements of children and young people who have special educational needs and disabilities.
Valuing and respecting individuals	Using appropriate language is an important part of valuing and respecting others and protecting their rights. In the same way, we should not use any other discriminatory language – for example, racist, sexist or homophobic – to describe other people.
Maintaining professionalism	Practitioners should use the correct terms so that they maintain professionalism when working with pupils with SEND and their families.

▲ When and why it is important to use the correct terminology

Case study

Alix is about to bring her daughter, Sasha, to the nursery for the first time. Sasha is two and has epilepsy, which is mainly controlled but she has to wear a padded helmet to stop her from hurting her head if she has a seizure. You have a meeting with Alix and her husband to discuss Sasha's needs and what to do in the case of a seizure, but the staff team have not talked about this in advance. One member of staff repeatedly refers to her seizures as 'fits' during the meeting.

▶ How might this make Sasha's parents feel?
▶ Why is it important to be well prepared for this type of meeting?

11.5 The difference between the medical and social models of disability

Historically, children and young people with disabilities were segregated and educated away from other pupils, in separate environments. This was primarily because a disability was seen as a problem that belonged to the individual. In the 1980s, the **social model of disability** was developed and this highlighted how disability was caused by society and how it was organised, rather than the person's impairment. The social model is inclusive and encourages society to think about how people with disabilities can participate with others rather than being segregated.

The table below describes the medical and social models of disability. The differences are similar to those between the principles of integration and inclusion, in that the child or young person with SEND should not be the one who needs to make changes.

Along with the Disability Discrimination Act in 1995 and later the Equality Act 2010, the social model of disability has changed access and participation for people with disabilities as it has challenged society to remove barriers. Barriers may occur owing to negative attitudes, such as assuming that people with disabilities will be unable to do things, or that there is something 'wrong' with them. Barriers may also be physical, such as inaccessible buildings or a lack of equipment.

Medical model	Social model
Child is faulty	Child is valued
Diagnosis	Strengths and needs defined by self and others
Labelling	Identifies barriers and develops solutions
Impairment becomes focus of attention	Outcome-based programme designed
Assessment, monitoring, programmes of therapy imposed	Resources are made available to ordinary services
Segregation and alternative services	Training for parents and professionals
Ordinary needs put on hold	Relationships nurtured
Re-entry if 'normal' enough or permanent exclusion	Diversity welcomed, child is included
Society remains unchanged	Society evolves

(Source: Mason, M. and Rieser, R. (1994) *Altogether Better (From 'Special Needs' to Equality in Education)*. Charity Projects/Comic Relief)

▲ The medical and social models of disability

11.6 How a primary disability may affect children's and young people's development

According to the Disabled Living Foundation (Family Resources Survey, 2015/2016), there are around 13.3 million people in the UK with a disability and, of these, 800,000 are children under 16.

A **primary disability** refers to the disability that affects the person the most, and may be related to physical mobility or impairments, learning or cognitive impairments, or social or behavioural impairments. The impact of these may be different in different children, even if they have the same condition or disability.

Disabilities may also be caused by long- or short-term health conditions, and can be permanent or temporary – for example, in the case of accidents or illness. Some people with disabilities may have more than one impairment or restriction on their daily life.

For more on cognitive difficulties, including explanations, refer to Section 11.8 and Assisting Teaching K4.2.

If a child or young person has a disability it is likely that this will also affect their development in other ways. This is because they are still growing and developing, and also because development is **holistic** and a disability in one area of development will impact on others. You should also remember that a primary disability may not always be visible to other people – for example, in the case of ADHD (attention deficit hyperactivity disorder) or dyslexia.

The tables below describe how a primary disability may affect both social and emotional development, and physical development.

Key terms

Primary disability: a physical or mental impairment that has a negative effect on a person's ability to carry out normal activities.

Holistic: overall or all round; the idea that the parts of something are interconnected so looking at the whole rather than each individual part. Here, it means all-round care needs, with an appreciation of the contribution of each care need to overall wellbeing.

Area of effect	Result
Impulse control	Some disabilities – for example, Tourette's syndrome – will affect a person's ability to control their impulses. This may mean that they have 'tics' or difficulty controlling their behaviour or physical movements. In some cases, this can be controlled with medication, although this is not always the case. A primary disability may also affect impulse control if a child or young person has social and emotional needs and is unable to control their emotions.
Language development	A primary disability may affect social, emotional and language development if a child or young person becomes easily frustrated and finds it hard to communicate. They may be unable to express their emotions if they have less developed language skills than others, or if their emotions due to their condition affect the way in which they come across.
Mood and emotions	Depending on their type or level of disability, a child or young person may find it overwhelming at times and need support in managing their emotions. Younger children may not understand why they are not able to do some of the same things as other children. There may also be frustration or anxiety that comes out as anger.

▲ How a primary disability may affect social and emotional development

Area of effect	Result
Attention, concentration and memory	A primary disability can affect physical development if it causes a child or young person physical pain or discomfort. They may, therefore, find it harder to concentrate and keep their attention on a task for as long as others. They may also be on medication to control pain or other symptoms of their condition, which could lead to tiredness and distraction. A cognitive or learning disability is likely to affect memory as it may take longer for a child or young person to learn new skills and to consolidate them. See also Section 11.7.
Sensory processing	Sensory processing refers to difficulties that children and young people have with receiving and processing information which is received through the senses. Sensory processing systems absorb and filter information around the five senses of sight, taste, smell, hearing and touch, but also around proprioception, or spatial awareness, and vestibular, which is our balance and how we move against gravity. We all need to be able to process this sensory information and filter out things we should either respond to or ignore. Difficulties in sensory processing are often a feature of children and young people on the autistic spectrum, for example, they may be hypersensitive (sensory avoiding) or hyposensitive (sensory seeking). Difficulties with sensory processing may have a significant impact on the way in which a child or young person experiences and interacts with their environment if they are unable to use these filters. For example, they may become overloaded by what they can see or hear in the learning environment, which may cause them to react in a specific way.
Motor control	Motor control is the ability to control and coordinate physical movement. If the disability or condition is in the area of physical development, this may affect how the person controls their movements or speech, for example, in the case of cerebral palsy. Motor control may also be affected if the child or young person has a cognitive difficulty that impacts on their processing skills. It may take longer for them to send the information to various parts of the body and, therefore, to practise these skills.

▲ How a primary disability may affect physical development

Research

What can you find out about sensory processing and the types of behaviour which may indicate that a child or young person has sensory processing needs? How might this need affect them in the classroom?

11.7 The range of cognitive skills necessary for effective educational development, and how single or multiple disabilities might affect these

Cognitive skills enable a person to focus their attention, remember information and process it, and to apply what they have learned in different situations. They are, therefore, a key aspect of educational development.

The development of cognitive skills may be particularly challenging for children and young people who have **neurological** disabilities and disorders. Although all individuals are different and their level of cognitive skills may vary, children and young people who have single or multiple disabilities may be affected in the areas described below, depending on their type and level of need.

Key term

Neurological: relating to or affecting the brain and nervous system.

Attention

When we are learning something new, we need to be able to concentrate on what we are doing or listening to over time. Depending on their type and level of disability, children and young people may not be able to sustain their attention on what they are doing for as long as others of the same age.

Short- and long-term memory

Our memories are important when learning, as they enable us to remember language, information and experiences, whether these occurred a short or long time ago. Often when we are teaching, we start by asking children what they already know about a subject, or what they remember from last time. Children and young people who have single or multiple disabilities may find this challenging and need to have support to help them to remember.

Perception

Perception is the ability to work something out using a range of information that is presented to us. This may not always be obvious to others and can be more abstract – for example, when interpreting why a character in a book has behaved in a particular way. Those with certain disabilities may find this more difficult to work out.

Logic and reasoning

Logic and reasoning, or being able to make connections, will help us when learning as they enable us to process and interpret information. Logic and reasoning are important for being able to solve problems and think about why things happen, which is a key part of learning. Children and young people who have single or multiple disabilities may find it harder to make these types of connection.

Auditory and visual processing

Auditory and visual processing skills involve the interpretation of information through sounds and images. When we are learning, we use all of our senses, including vision and hearing, and then process this information.

Children and young people who have auditory and visual processing disorders will not have an auditory

or visual impairment but will have problems making sense of the information they receive. Children and young people with auditory processing disorders (APD) may find it difficult to understand speech and respond appropriately, particularly if it takes place in a noisy environment. Those with visual processing disorders (VPDs) may have a range of difficulties, including having trouble judging distances, spatial processing, or the way in which they see shapes and symbols. They may also have difficulties with fine and gross motor skills. These can all have an effect on their confidence and the way in which they respond in the classroom.

11.8 How cognitive difficulties may have an impact on language, communication and educational development

Depending on their nature and severity, cognitive difficulties are likely to impact in some way on the development of language and communication, and, therefore, educational development in other areas. This is because a child or young person will need to have a good developing memory in order to remember language and vocabulary, as well as having the processing skills needed for understanding and using language and organising their thoughts. The process of learning is also dependent on language and the two skills support each other, so cognitive difficulties will make it harder for these children and young people to develop their communication and language skills; the effects of this may be wide ranging.

> See Core Chapter 7 for more on language and cognitive development, and receptive and expressive language.

Area of skill	Area and impact of cognitive difficulty
Language and communication	Children who have cognitive difficulties may also find it difficult to use both **receptive** and expressive language, and take longer to process information. Language may be slower to develop, as may the specific vocabulary they need to access the curriculum. As discussed in Section 11.6, it may be harder for them to express their feelings, which can lead to frustration and misunderstanding or upset. As language and communication are so crucial to our relationships with friends, family and others, these are also likely to be affected unless we are able to take the children's needs into consideration.
Reading, writing and comprehension skills	Children and young people who are having difficulties with their cognitive skills may also find language skills such as reading, writing and comprehension more challenging. They may find more difficult comprehension questions even harder as they will have problems picking up inferences or looking beyond the obvious. They may take longer to learn and refine skills in this area.

Area of skill	Area and impact of cognitive difficulty
Mathematical skills and concepts	Children and young people with cognitive difficulties may also find mathematical skills and concepts challenging, as they are built on logical and abstract thought. The individual needs to be able to think carefully in steps and apply their knowledge in different situations. Children and young people may need support in talking through what they are being asked to do and how they can apply their existing knowledge. This includes children or young people with dyscalculia, a cognitive difficulty with understanding numbers and making calculations.
Vocabulary and communication skills	A child or young person will need to have a good developing memory in order to remember language and vocabulary, and to organise their thoughts. Cognitive difficulties are likely to affect this and make it more difficult for them. They will have less ability to process their thoughts and articulate them to others. This is difficult not only in learning situations, but children's and young people's communication with their peers may also be affected.
Attention span	Children and young people with cognitive difficulties may find it harder to concentrate and hold their attention than others. They may find it hard to focus on what they are doing and to apply new knowledge in different situations, so it will be harder for them to be motivated, organise their learning and access the curriculum. This includes children or young people with ADHD, a behavioural disorder that includes symptoms such as inattentiveness, hyperactivity and impulsiveness.
Coordination skills	A cognitive difficulty may also impact on a child's or young person's coordination skills. Problems with coordination will also impact on their fine and gross motor development, so handwriting, tying laces and games may all be difficult for these children and young people. This includes dyspraxia, a neurological condition that affects physical coordination, making children and young people seem clumsy, as well as affecting their organisational skills and ability to organise their thoughts.
Logical reasoning	See Section 11.7.
Memory and building on prior knowledge	See Section 11.7.

▲ The impact of cognitive difficulties on different aspects of learning

Key term

Receptive language: the ability to understand what is being said through language.

See Assisting Teaching K4.2 for more details on these cognitive difficulties, and their effects on learning and development.

11.9 How a chronic condition may affect children's or young people's emotions, education, behaviour and quality of life

Chronic health conditions are those that are long-standing, often lifelong, and will, therefore, have both physical and psychological effects on a person. At different times they are likely to cause a child or young person anxiety, pain and often fatigue, so are likely to affect their behaviour and emotions. As some of these conditions may be controlled with medication, the child or young person may also have to deal with side effects, including feeling more tired or depressed.

All those who work with children and young people who have chronic conditions should be aware of who they are and what their conditions involve, so that they are prepared for what to do if support is needed. This kind of information will be held by the SENDCo and there should be regular contact with parents and families as well as healthcare workers to keep up to date with each child's or young person's needs.

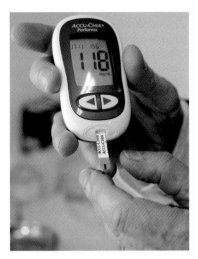

▲ You may need additional training if you are working with a child or young person who has a chronic health condition

Muscular dystrophy

Muscular dystrophy is a progressive muscle-wasting condition that can take different forms. It can mean that a child's or young person's life expectancy is significantly reduced. An awareness of this, alongside the fact that they are finding it more and more difficult to control their movements, the side effects of medication and anxiety about the future may well have an effect on their emotions and quality of life. They may also find it difficult to concentrate on day-to-day tasks.

Epilepsy

Epilepsy is a neurological condition; it can usually be controlled with medication, although this can cause side effects in some people. Epilepsy causes seizures, which can be severe, but equally you may be unaware that a child or young person has a diagnosis if the epilepsy is controlled. Its effects can, therefore, vary depending on how severe it is. The child or young person may have anxiety about having seizures or be wary about taking part in some activities. If you know that a child or young person you work with has epilepsy, you should be clear on what you should do if they have a seizure, and this information should be on their EHC plan or in their records.

Severe allergies

These may be worse at different times of year (e.g. in the case of hay fever) or they may be triggered by specific foods such as nuts. Severe allergies can be very dangerous to those who have them, and can be life-threatening if they are not treated immediately. A child or young person in a school or early years setting who has a severe allergy should have access to specific medication, which should be kept on-site at all times so that it can be administered immediately by trained staff. Having a severe allergy may cause a child or young person to have anxiety about what can happen if they have an episode. We can reassure them by ensuring that we have plans in place so that all staff know what to do in the event of this happening.

Cystic fibrosis

This is a genetic condition, and one in twenty-five people in the UK carry the faulty gene, often without knowing. If both parents carry it, there is a chance that their baby may be born with the condition (source: Cystic Fibrosis Trust). It is usually diagnosed as part of newborn screening using the **heel prick test**. Cystic fibrosis affects how salt and water move both into and out of cells in the body, and affects the lungs and digestive system even though the individual may look healthy. They are likely to need a range of different treatments, including medication, physiotherapy and being careful about their diet. People with cystic fibrosis may also have organ transplants if their symptoms are severe.

If you are working with a child or young person who has this condition, they may find it overwhelming to deal with and need emotional support from their family and adults in school, as well as from their peers. They may get tired very quickly and it may be hard for them to focus on the life of the setting.

> ### Key term
>
> **Heel prick test:** this is a blood test that is carried out on all babies when they are a few days old to test for serious conditions.

Depression

Depression and mental health issues are now at the forefront of public awareness, and occur in around 1–3 per cent of children and young people (source: Royal College of Psychiatrists). Although these issues clearly affect the emotions, they may also cause problems in behaviour and relationships as well as academic work. Depression can also cause eating disorders, self-harm, drug or alcohol misuse, and withdrawal from others.

Adults may not be aware of any of these issues, and it is important to have positive relationships with children and young people so that it is easier to detect when something is wrong, and so that they are more likely to trust and confide in you.

Fragile X syndrome

Fragile X is an inherited genetic condition that causes learning disabilities. It can cause a range of problems with learning and behaviour, which can be mild to severe, and is detected only through a genetic test. As well as having learning disabilities, children and young people with Fragile X may have a short attention span and be overactive and impulsive, as well as having social, emotional and communication problems. They may share features of autism, such as social anxiety and difficulties relating to others, a preference for routines, as well as repetitive body movements such as spinning or flapping. The condition may affect quality of life in some more than others, depending on its severity.

Sickle cell disease

This is the name given to a group of inherited disorders that affect the shape of red blood cells and cause painful episodes called sickle cell crises, as well as tiredness, shortness of breath and **anaemia**. Sickle cell disease predominantly affects people who are from an African or Caribbean background, and can also cause a delay in growth and a greater risk of serious infections.

Those who have sickle cell disease will need ongoing and lifelong specialist treatment. If they have an episode, they may be absent from the setting for several days at a time on a regular basis. They will need support from their family as well as the setting, and although symptoms may not always be obvious, those with this condition are likely to need help in managing their feelings.

> **Key term**
>
> **Anaemia:** a health condition in which there are not enough red blood cells in your body, which means that your body may not get enough oxygen.

Diabetes

Diabetes is a chronic condition in which sugar levels build up in the blood and become too high because the body is unable to make insulin. There are two main types of diabetes: Type 1 and Type 2. Type 1 may be genetic, which means that it often runs in families and is a lifelong condition; it can be present from birth or can arise later It is the type most likely to be seen in children. Type 2 can come on later in life and be caused by poor diet and lack of exercise. In each case, they are managed by injecting insulin with meals so that glucose can be kept at a safe level, although with Type 2 oral medication may be used initially.

Diabetes may cause a child or young person to feel unwell, or to be anxious about managing their levels. They may sometimes find it hard to focus on schoolwork, and it can cause problems with memory and processing skills if it is not managed effectively. They may also have more time off due to hospital appointments.

> **Research**
>
> Find out more about two of the chronic conditions above and prepare a presentation or factsheet to share the information with others.

11.10 How adults can remove barriers in order to empower and value children and young people

Adults must support children and young people with SEND by promoting their independence and removing any **barriers to their learning**. This is because we need to ensure that they have full access to the curriculum and wider aspects of learning in the school or early years setting. We also need to encourage them to do as much as they can for themselves so that they do not become reliant on adults doing things for them – this is very important.

The way that adults do this will depend on the specific needs of the child or young person and will vary between them, but may include the actions listed in the table below.

> **Key term**
>
> **Barrier to learning:** anything that prevents a child or young person from taking part fully in the activities or experiences that are offered by the school or early years setting.

See Assisting Teaching K4.7 (page 293) for more on potential barriers.

What adults can do	How they can do this
Create an accessible and secure environment	The learning environment must be accessible to all those with SEND in the setting. In other words, they should have access to any specific materials or resources they may need. Staff should also have access to equipment to support them (e.g. if a hearing loop is needed) and training to ensure that they are supported effectively. The environment should be adapted if necessary, and there should be an inclusive ethos which ensures that there are equal opportunities for everyone. In addition, the environment should be secure and safe, in line with health and safety requirements, and checked for any hazards that may be specific to children and young people with SEND.
Promote value and respect	Your school or early years setting should have an ethos of promoting value and respect for all. This should be part of the equality policy, and means that everyone who comes in to the setting should be treated fairly and with respect. When you are working with children and young people with SEND, ensure that you model this behaviour as children and young people will take their lead from the adults around them.
Involve the individual in planning their own learning	From an early age, children and young people of all abilities should be involved in making self-assessments of their learning and thinking about next steps. For those with SEND who are involved with meetings and talking to adults about their learning targets, this is particularly important and will support them in developing their independence and confidence. See also Core Chapter 8.
Provide context and relevance to learning	Any adult working with children and young people will need to be able to do this. It is much harder to take on new knowledge and skills, particularly those that are more challenging, if we are unable to see their relevance to our lives. In some cases, children and young people with SEND may find it harder to make these types of connections, and so we may need to make sure that they have understood the relevance of what they are doing.
Use enabling language	Adults must ensure that they use enabling language at all times when speaking to children and young people, particularly those who have SEND. This means ensuring that the way in which they speak to them is positive and inclusive. This is because they may feel that they are unable to carry out tasks and activities, or have low self-esteem.
Work with the family and other professionals	All educators will need to work with parents and families, and with other professionals when supporting children and young people who have SEND. This is because it is the best way to gain knowledge and understanding of the needs of each individual. By sharing background information, both formally and informally, and meeting regularly with others to discuss the child's or young person's progress, you will ensure that channels of communication are kept open and relationships are positive.
Implement the setting's policies and procedures	All adults must ensure that they comply with the policies and procedures of the setting, as these will be dictated by government legislation and guidance. You should have read and understood the policies listed in Section 11.1 that are relevant to SEND so that you can support all children and young people effectively and know about how the school or early years setting aims to remove barriers.

▲ How adults can support children and young people with SEND

Case study

You are working as a teaching assistant in a primary school and have just been told that a boy called Thusan will be joining Year 2 in your class from September. Thusan has a visual impairment called nystagmus and his vision is very poor, so some adaptations will need to be made in the classroom and around the school. The SENDCo has told you and the teacher that Thusan does not need to have a learning support assistant, but that for the first few weeks he may need some extra support to get settled. You have been told that he takes some medication and has involuntary head movements, but you know little else about his needs or condition. His parents are coming to school for a meeting with you, the class teacher and the SENDCo to discuss his needs, but he will be unable to come for a transition visit himself before starting as he has recently had an operation.

▶ What should you do before the meeting?
▶ Why is it important for as many people as possible to be involved in supporting Thusan's first few weeks at your school?

11.11 When and how speech can be supplemented or replaced by augmentative and alternative communication (AAC)

We all use many ways of communicating, and it is something many of us do without thinking. Communication enables us to share information with other people and to interpret what they are saying to us. For those who have special educational needs and who cannot communicate without support, the following systems will enable them to develop their independence and participate more fully in all areas of their life. They will give them the opportunity to develop their relationships with others, express themselves more easily and live more independently as they grow older.

Augmentative and alternative communication (AAC) may be used to support children and young people who have a condition or impairment that makes it difficult for them to communicate effectively with others. This may be due to a learning difficulty, a speech or physical difficulty, a brain injury or autism spectrum condition. The term AAC covers all types of communication and strategies that support the creation of speech and communication, and may be used as a temporary measure (e.g. in the case of an accident or illness) or a permanent one. These measures may or may not involve technology, but all are designed to help those who face challenges with spoken communication and those who are communicating with them. Children and young people who need support in this area will need adults in schools and early years settings to work together with speech therapists to help them to find the type of AAC that works best for them.

No-tech communication

No-tech, or unaided, communication involves the use of gestures and body language, pointing, signing and facial expression to support communication. Children and young people who have limited vocalisations or no speech may find it easier to use these forms of communication, as well as talk partners, in order to ensure that their intended meaning is passed to another person.

▲ How does AAC support children and young people in schools and early years settings?

Low-tech communication systems

Low-tech, or aided, communication usually involves AAC that does not need any form of power such as a battery. It may involve pen and paper, **picture exchange communication systems (PECS)**, photographs or symbols to support communication. These will give the child or young person a starting point when communicating and also when receiving information so that it is easier to process and understand.

> **Key term**
>
> **Picture exchange communication systems (PECS):** a method of communication that uses simple pictures.

High-tech communication systems

These may include mobile devices, laptops, tablets, speech synthesis or eye-tracking devices. High-tech communication systems will usually need batteries or mains power. They may be recommended after an assessment by a speech therapist or AAC specialist. High-tech communication systems should be used to fit the needs and requirements of each individual and what suits them best, using the physical movements they are able to control – for example, their head or eyes. High-tech systems may also involve the use of voice output communication aids (VOCAs), which produce the sound of a voice.

For more information on communication aids and examples of their use, visit the website of The Communication Trust: **www.thecommunicationtrust.org.uk**

▲ How can alternative methods of communication enhance our work with children who have speech, communication and language needs?

Assessment practice

1 What is the main legislation affecting SEND in England?
2 Explain the purpose of the progress check at age two.
3 How is the SEND Code of Practice linked to the Children and Families Act 2014?
4 Name **four** policies or procedures in your school or early years setting that support the needs of children and young people with SEND.
5 What support is available for children with SEND between the ages of five and fifteen years?
6 What is the purpose of an EHC plan and when is it used?

7 Explain the importance of a multi-agency team when working with children and young people who have SEND.
8 Give **three** reasons why it is important to use the right terminology when talking about the needs of children and young people with SEND.
9 Name four ways in which adults can support children and young people by removing barriers to participation.
10 Discuss the link between cognitive ability and the development of language. Your response should give three examples of the different skills it may impact and how you might support the child or young person in each case.

CORE Chapter 12:
English as an Additional Language

Increasing numbers of children and young people in education settings are able to use more than one language. While this may seem a new development for some parts of England, the reality is that the use of more than one language is normal in other countries, such as Wales. This chapter looks at the process by which a new language is learned, the factors affecting how easily children and young people can pick up a new language and also how practitioners can support children. We also look at the social and emotional needs of children and young people who are learning to use more than one language.

Learning outcomes

This chapter covers the following knowledge outcomes for Core Element 12:

12.1 The characteristics of the five stages of acquiring an additional language

12.2 How a range of factors might affect language acquisition

12.3 How a child's/young person's home language affects their education and development

12.4 The communication, social and emotional needs of children/young people being taught English as an additional language

12.5 How practitioners can use a range of strategies to support children/young people being taught English as an additional language

12.1 The characteristics of the five stages of acquiring an additional language

The term **English as an additional language** is sometimes abbreviated to **EAL**. While this term is applied to everyone who speaks a language other than English at home, children and young people with EAL may acquire English in two broad ways and so have slightly different needs.

1 **Simultaneous language learning**: Some children and young people come in to settings already knowing English as they have been exposed to it since early childhood. Simultaneous language learning occurs when, for example, a child has one parent that uses English and another that speaks Urdu, or they may have spent time playing with English-speaking children. In some cases, adults may not even realise that the children and young people use another language or languages at home.

2 **Sequential language learning**: This occurs when children and young people learn English after they have already developed their home language. They may come in to settings and not be able to understand or communicate in English.

Key terms

Simultaneous language learning: where children are exposed to two or more languages in their first three years.

Sequential language learning: where a language is learned after a home language has been established.

The five stages of acquiring an additional language

Sequential language learners who are new to English when they first arrive in a setting usually develop English following a broad pattern that has five stages.

1 Silent/receptive stage

Children and young people attempt at first to use their home language. When this does not work as a strategy, they move into a silent or receptive stage. While the term 'silent' stage is sometimes used, it is important to remember that children and young people can still communicate. They may, for example, point to objects or find ways of attracting adults' attention. The main feature of this stage is that they are not yet attempting to try out English. Instead, they are learning to tune in or listen to the sounds of the new language. Over time, children and young people start to recognise frequently used words and their meaning. The first words that children and young people understand are often linked to routines such as 'snack time' or 'line up', as well as things that have particular importance for them. It is important that pressure is not put on children and young people to talk in this period.

2 Early production

Once children and young people have begun to understand more of what is being said, they may start to use the odd phrase or word spontaneously. They may, for example, copy other children by saying 'thank you' or defend their possessions by saying 'that's mine!' This is known as **early production**.

Some first words are also said during group or whole-class routines such as 'good morning everyone' or in early years settings during songs and rhymes.

Key term

Early production: being able to say or repeat some words.

3 Speech emergence

In this stage, children and young people are no longer using 'set phrases' but instead are having a go at talking. Sentences are often quite short and limited (e.g. 'that's blue', 'I don't like it'). This is, however, a great breakthrough. For some children and young people early production and speech emergence happen at about the same time.

Practice points

Supporting the early stages of language acquisition

▶ Children and young people will need a lot of reassurance and one-to-one support.
▶ Use visual timetables and photos to prepare children and young people for transitions, e.g. moving to the canteen for lunch or going to the hall for PE.
▶ Expect that children and young people may lose concentration easily until they have intermediate fluency.
▶ Use routines as a way of helping children and young people recognise key words and phrases.

4 Intermediate fluency

In this stage, children and young people are increasingly able to express themselves. They may not always be able to talk in long sentences or use language to explain fully what they know or are feeling. Younger children are more likely in this stage to use a word from their home language if they do not know it in English. This is sometimes known as **code switching**. It does not mean that the child has become confused or is mixing up their languages. It just means that they do not yet have the equivalent word or phrase in English. Older children and young people in this stage might point to an object or picture and ask how to say it in English.

5 Continued language development/ advanced fluency

In this stage, children and young people increase their knowledge of and **fluency** in English. They increase their vocabulary, and this helps them to express more complex ideas and thoughts. Children and young people of school age may still need additional support to develop skill and confidence in literacy.

> **Key terms**
>
> *Code switching:* using a word or phrase from one language when speaking another.
>
> *Fluency:* being able to use a language easily and to an advanced level.

12.2 Factors affecting language acquisition

How long will it take for a child or young person who is new to English to pick it up? This is one of the questions most frequently asked by both parents and adults working with children and young people. Unfortunately, the answer is complex as there are many factors at work.

Age and stage of development

The age of a child or young person is one of the most important factors. Older children and young people usually acquire the language more quickly than children aged under four. They have an advantage in that their brains have already mastered a language and so connections in the brain have been made. Older teenagers can also use other strategies, such as online tools, and know how to ask questions in order to make progress.

Personality

The level of children's extroversion and openness to new experiences can make a difference to their progress. Children who are sociable and not afraid of trying out new things will find it easier to pick up another language.

Cognition

Children's and young people's brains have to process and learn a new language. Some children and young people are able to remember the sounds and meanings of new words and phrases faster than others. They may also be able to quickly understand and remember the grammatical rules of the new language they are learning.

Bilingualism

Children and young people who have already mastered two languages (**bilingualism**) may be quicker to pick up a third than those who have not.

> **Key term**
>
> *Bilingualism:* the ability to use two languages.

Cultural background

The support that children and young people have at home, and also whether their parents have some English, can make a difference to language acquisition. Where education and learning English are seen as being positive, there may be better progress.

Special educational needs or disabilities

While not all children and young people with special educational needs or disabilities (SEND) will have difficulty in acquiring English, social and communication difficulties may cause their progress to be slower. Some children and young people who have medical conditions may have fewer opportunities and less exposure to English because of repeated absence from the setting and so need longer. We have seen that language learning also requires processing of information, and children who have learning difficulties may need additional support with this.

Learning environment and available support

How much support children and young people have from adults and their peers has a significant impact on language learning. At first, children and young people need a lot of adult help, both practically but also emotionally. Where this is provided in combination with opportunities to listen to and eventually practise English, progress tends to be much faster. Slower progress is made when children and young people are left to 'naturally' (passively) pick up English, and where no attempt is made to help them link sounds and phrases to meanings of words.

12.3 How home language affects education and development

The impact of having a home language alongside English is quite complex. The research on this shows that for many children and young people there are positive benefits.

Understanding of language overall

One of the main factors in acquiring and using English is the strength of the home language. Children and young people who have not fully mastered the language used at home, or who are exposed to a mixture of incomplete or ungrammatical languages, find it hard to make good progress in their education unless they have more support. This is one reason why parents of young children who have a home language are encouraged to use it rather than switch to English.

Self-concept, family connections, social interactions and relationships

Self-concept is a term we looked at in Core Chapter 4.

> Revisit Core Chapter 4 if you need to remind yourself of this.

It is used to describe the way that we think about ourselves. It is the 'who am I?' question. Languages play a part in self-concept because they link with a family's history, culture and traditions. As part of children's and young people's developing self-concept, the languages they speak and how well they have acquired them can make a difference to a range of social relationships and interactions.

Firstly, where children and young people have not mastered their home language, they may lose out on opportunities to make relationships and understand the culture of their wider family. This can be disorientating since knowing about your family's culture and traditions and being able to use the family's language is important. In some cases, children and young people master English and, while retaining the understanding of their home language, lose the ability to express themselves in it. In such cases, this can affect the quality of relationships within the immediate family unit. The importance of home language acquisition, but also maintenance of it, is one reason why parents are encouraged not to switch to English in the home.

As well as potential difficulties in family connections, children and young people who have not yet mastered English may also find it hard to socialise outside of the home. They may find it harder to make friends or not feel confident to join in extracurricular activities.

Children and young people may have family members who live in another country and/or who do not speak English. Without the home language, they would not be able to make relationships and so would lose touch with their family's history and traditions. Where children and young people do not master their family's home language, they often report that they feel like an outsider. The emotional impact on development is one of the reasons why, wherever possible, families are encouraged to maintain their home language.

How children and young people learn a curriculum

When children and young people learn about a subject in one language, they are likely to acquire the concepts and vocabulary in that language. For children and young people who started their education in their home language, this can mean that they may not be able to show the equivalent competence in English. A good example of this is mathematics. Most bilingual adults, even if they are fluent in the other language, will do calculations in the language in which they were taught.

Acquisition of additional languages

Languages are effectively codes. Children and young people who have mastered their home language and English, either simultaneously or sequentially, are likely to find learning new languages easier as their brains have developed to handle using more than one code.

12.4 Understanding communication and social/emotional needs

In order to support children and young people, it is important to understand both their communication and their social and emotional needs.

Communication needs

Some common challenges connected with communication include the following.

Unequal proficiency

It is quite common for children and young people to have areas of strength as well as weakness in English. They may be able to talk and understand quite well, but not be able to read or write, or in the case of young children, know that books in English are read from left to right and from top to bottom. Similarly, some children and young people who started their education in their home language may have had English lessons that focused only on listening and reading. It is, therefore, important not to make any assumptions about children's and young people's competence until you have worked with them for a while.

Difficulty understanding the curriculum

Some children and young people may not have the vocabulary or technical words that allow them to understand or fully take part in activities or lessons. They may not have come across the term 'times', as in 'two times four', or 'sentence' when asked to read a sentence out loud. Where children and young people have started their education in their home language, they are likely to have followed a different curriculum and so may have gained knowledge in some areas, but not others. It is particularly important to think about this when helping children and young people with subjects such as mathematics and science.

Children/young people may have difficulty accessing resources in English

Both sequential and simultaneous language learners typically have some missing vocabulary. This means that when trying to read English they may not know the meanings of certain words or may be mistaken about their meaning. This can make studying frustrating or difficult for them. It is, therefore, important when supporting children and young people to check whether they understand the meanings of words and also to think about the vocabulary they will need in order to access the activity. For instance, if a child is about to complete an activity about shapes, it will be important to teach the names of shapes first.

Difficulty responding to questions in English

Until children and young people have mastered English, they may need more time to respond to questions. This is because their brains will take longer to process a question and then to retrieve and formulate an answer. When questions are asked to a group of children or young people, they may not be able to respond quickly and so may appear not to have understood or to know the answer. Repeated experience of not being able to answer quickly may stop them from trying to contribute.

> **Practice points**
>
> ▶ Consider asking a question to an individual child rather than to the group.
> ▶ Prevent other children or young people from interrupting or shouting out.
> ▶ Allow plenty of time for a response and show that you are happy to wait.

Social and emotional needs

As well as communication needs, children's and young people's progress can be affected by how they are feeling.

Negative attitudes towards their culture, language, ethnicity or religion

While there are many benefits to being able to speak more than one language, including higher levels of cognition, these benefits disappear if children and young people are faced with discrimination or simply negative attitudes. Unfortunately, sometimes when children and young people have arrived in settings not speaking English, they have been considered to be a 'problem'. As language is linked to culture, ethnicity and in some cases religion, where there are negative attitudes, children and young people can feel that their own identity is being rejected in some way. Negative attitudes are conveyed through gesture, facial expression and overall body language. Children and young people can see very quickly whether or not adults and their peers are welcoming.

Isolation from their peers

It can be hard for children and young people to start out in a setting and realise that they cannot communicate easily with others. For children and young people who have always had friends, the early period of language learning can be very tough. Some children and young people can become withdrawn and even depressed in this period. This is one reason why, in the silent/receptive period, it is important to encourage non-verbal interactions and to find some activities that do not rely on language that they can do with their peers. A good example of this for older children and young people is sport, and for younger children playing with sensory materials.

> ### Practice points
>
> Always acknowledge non-verbal ways of communication that a child or young person uses.
> - Find practical tasks or play activities that require little or no language, which children and young people can join in with.
> - Make sure that in breaks and at mealtimes, children and young people have a friendly, kind peer who can sit or play with them.
> - Observe carefully signs that a child or young person may be becoming withdrawn or depressed. Talk to parents about the child's or young person's mood at home.

▲ Reflect on how this activity is meeting these children's social and emotional needs

Language support available at home

Think about how it might feel to be the only one in a class not to have learned your spellings or not to have been able to complete a homework project because your parent can't help you. Sometimes, there is a mismatch between tasks that are set for home and the ability of parents to support them. This can lead to children and young people feeling that they are missing out in some way. Best practice in this situation is to make sure that children and young people have additional support in settings to complete tasks or to select tasks that can be done without home language support.

12.5 Strategies to support children/young people being taught EAL

There are many strategies that can be used to help children and young people as they are learning English. Different strategies work with different ages and also at different stages of learning a language.

Using EAL specialist support

It is important to get as much specialist EAL support as possible. Support can vary between settings and also local authorities or cities. Here are some examples of specialist support:
- **EAL teachers or tutors:** These may work directly with the child or young person, or they may provide advice or resources.
- **Translators and interpreters:** Some settings have access to people who can translate documents into a home language or interpret. These services are very important when working with parents in order to share information. They may also be needed to assess children or young people.
- **Bilingual support:** Some settings help children and young people when they first join by using an adult who has the language, if available, to help them settle and to ensure that they can access the curriculum.

Peer and group support

For the first few days in a setting, children and young people benefit from having a friend or mentor who can play with them, show them things and prevent them from feeling isolated. It is also important to create a welcoming atmosphere where the culture is to help one another. Any unkind comments, unfriendly actions or bullying need to be dealt with firmly. The culture of the group is significantly influenced by adults. Competitive environments that focus more on individual achievement rather than on group effort or group achievement tend to make it harder for children and young people to get group support.

Making the verbal curriculum more visual

During the silent/receptive period (see page 194), it is important for children and young people to make connections between what they can see and the words that are being used. This means also using props, posters, photos and visual timetables. It also means using body language or facial expressions to communicate. Children and young people also find it helpful to have books that have plenty of pictures or diagrams in them. This strategy also benefits other children and young people who may have language difficulties.

▲ Explain how this game will help these children learn about body parts

Providing opportunities to talk before writing

For older children and young people, research has shown that talking before writing can be very helpful. Words or phrases that children or young people want to use can be written down for them. This is a strategy that often improves the written work of the whole group.

Using drama and role play

Drama and role play can be outlets for children's and young people's feelings. While young children will often use their home language in role play, older children and young people can use drama and role play as a way of learning the language of emotions, and also vocabulary and phrases linked to context. Drama and role play is also visual, which may mean that children and young people can understand more of what is happening.

Scaffolding learning

The term scaffolding is discussed in Core Chapter 2.

> Revisit Core Chapter 2 if you need to remind yourself about this.

In terms of language learning, it means thinking step by step about what a child or young person already knows and what they need to learn next. This might mean making a list of vocabulary that a young person will need to know before a lesson takes place or choosing a simpler text that introduces the young person to the concept. For young children, scaffolding learning is linked closely to planning play and activities. Adults, for example, may join children as they play or during activities and draw their attention to English words to describe what they are doing or what they are using – for example, if a child is digging in the sand tray with a spoon, the adult may point to the spoon and say 'Spoon. You have a spoon.' Look again at scaffolding learning in Core Chapter 2.

Creating language-rich environments

There are many ways of creating a language-rich environment, depending on the age and stage of development of children and young people. The key is to focus on the following questions.

Will there be opportunities to listen to language at the right level?

This means thinking about background noise, how activities are planned and the vocabulary level being used.

How will links be made between words and the meanings of words?

This is about using visual cues and props, as well as thinking about showing and demonstrating to aid understanding.

Will there be opportunities for verbal and non-verbal interactions?

This is about making sure that children and young people can express themselves without any pressure.

Are there appropriate opportunities for literacy?

This is about helping children and young people learn to read and write. For young children, this might mean sharing very simple picture books. For older children and young people, this might mean that adults help them to write words or check that they understand what they are reading.

Providing bilingual resources

Thanks to technological advances, a wide range of bilingual resources are now available. These are very useful for older children and young people, who can, for instance, use online dictionaries, which often include features that allow them to hear how words in English are pronounced. It is worth noting that online translation of sentences or whole texts can be very unreliable, so should be used with caution. In addition, older children and young people may be helped to acquire mathematical and scientific concepts and vocabulary in their home language through the use of online lessons and materials.

For younger children, a range of bilingual picture books are available, some accompanied by audio. These often come with a 'pen' that when put on to the text or the picture allows the child to hear the text either in their home language or in English. This feature is important as it allows children to hear a book in English as well as in their home language. A text-only bilingual book is of limited use for pre-school children unless an adult who is fluent in the home language is available to read it.

Working in partnership with parents/carers

A shared understanding between families and settings is important.

> This is discussed in Core Chapter 5.

We need to know about how the child or young person is feeling, and also whether the family has any questions or concerns. We also need to find out more about children's and young people's previous experiences. By working in partnership, we can provide more targeted support and also reduce the emotional impact. To achieve this we need to make sure that families feel welcome and also that barriers to communication are removed. We might need, for example, to find an interpreter to make this easier. Where this is not possible, you may need to ask an adult to help, although you will need to explain

the importance of confidentiality. When sharing information about progress and concerns, it is not good practice to involve children and young people in interpreting for their own families.

Practice points

Partnership with parents

- ► Find out about the language(s) that are used at home. Who speaks what and when?
- ► Ask about whether the child or young person has had any exposure to English.
- ► Find out about what the child's or young person's level of home language is and, if they have attended school, how they were getting along.
- ► Talk to parents about their child's personality.
- ► Find out about the interests and hobbies of the child or young person.
- ► Share with parents information about the setting and also details of how they can contact you.

Celebrating an individual's culture

We have seen that language and culture go together. We have also looked at the way that children and young people make better progress where their culture is valued and respected. In settings, this means creating an environment and activities where many cultures, religions and ways of family life are celebrated. This might mean playing a range of music, showing and using fabrics and artefacts from different cultures, and providing a wide range of foods. It also means helping children and young people to realise that every family is unique and we all have different traditions, festivals that are celebrated and priorities.

Creating an environment that celebrates the rich differences that exist even when people share the same language and culture makes it easier to show that we celebrate individual children's and young people's culture. It is worth noting that some older children and young people may not always want attention drawn to them, because they are trying to fit in. This means that, before asking a direct question that puts them on the spot or singling them out, you should check beforehand if they are happy about this.

Case study

Ahmed is an outgoing, confident eight-year-old boy. However, he is new to English. Before he started at school, his teacher found out from Ahmed's family that he had a favourite football team. He paired Ahmed with a kind, friendly child who also supported the same club. The teacher used a visual timetable and lots of photos to help Ahmed understand what was about to happen next. The teacher also used Ahmed's interest in sport as a starting point for teaching some simple English words. Ahmed now has some single words such as 'goal', 'ball' and 'striker' that he can say when he sees photos. His teacher is planning to build his vocabulary further using this interest. The teacher has also given Ahmed some practical responsibility in the classroom to maintain his confidence. This week, Ahmed has started spontaneously to use some phrases such as 'No, it's my turn!' and has also joined in with a few of the words of a class poem.

▶ What stage of language acquisition is Ahmed showing?

▶ What strategies has the teacher used to support Ahmed's progress?

▶ How have Ahmed's social and emotional needs been met?

Assessment practice

1 What are the features of the silent/receptive stage of language acquisition?

2 Explain how age might be a factor in the acquisition of language.

3 Give **two** other factors that might influence the language acquisition of English.

4 How might having a strong home language support the acquisition of English?

5 Give an example of one communication need and one social and emotional need when a child or young person is acquiring English.

6 Explain how specialist EAL support can be used to support children and young people.

7 How can peer or group support be used to help children and young people?

8 Give an example of a bilingual resource that might help a young person to learn some new English words.

CORE Skills

As part of the Employer-set Project, you will be assessed on the following four Core Skills. This chapter looks at the skills themselves, and gives guidance as to what they mean and how they can be demonstrated.

Core Skills

Core Skill 1 Communicate information clearly to engage children and young people, for example, to stimulate discussion and to secure understanding

Core Skill 2 Work with others to plan and provide activities to meet children's and young people's needs

Core Skill 3 Use formative and summative assessment to track children's and students' progress to plan and shape educational opportunities

Core Skill 4 How to assess and manage risks to your own and others' safety when planning activities

Core Skill 1: Communicate information clearly to engage children and young people

> You should read this section alongside Core Chapter 2 around communication and providing effective feedback, as well as Core Chapter 4 on the use of positive language and motivation.

To pass the Employer-set Project and gain this qualification, you must demonstrate that you are able to communicate information clearly to engage children and young people.

Below we look at some ways to do this.

Ensure that communication is age-appropriate

This means that you should use language and communicate information that is appropriate for the age and stage of development of the children and young people you are working with.

Young children

You may need to use more simple language and vocabulary with young children and check on their understanding, particularly when giving instructions. They will also enjoy rhymes, songs and repetition, which can help them to remember key information, particularly if these are part of a daily routine. An example of this might be a particular song that they sing at lunchtime or home time, or a lullaby at nap time.

Older children/young people

Older children may need adults to provide them with concrete examples when communicating with them. At times, they may respond well to humour as this will gain their attention. They will need illustrative stories to demonstrate meaning, and examples that encourage them to test their own values and critical thinking skills. An example of this might be a fictional story or play with a moral, such as a fable.

Explaining technical information to a non-technical audience

You may need to explain vocabulary and information that is new to the topic or area you are learning about, to ensure that all children and young people are clear on what it means.

Using verbal and non-verbal cues

Verbal and **non-verbal cues** are important when communicating with children and young people.

This includes the body language you show them while communicating. For example, with very young children it is important that you get down to their level when speaking to them, as standing over them is intimidating and may not encourage them to respond. Verbal cues are prompts that are given through speech, such as direct questions or instructions. However, they may also be more indirect through the clues given by our tone of voice, whether we speak slowly or place emphasis on particular words.

> **Key terms**
>
> **Verbal cues:** prompts that help the listener to answer, e.g. speaking more slowly or emphasising particular words.
>
> **Non-verbal cues:** prompts using body language, e.g. facial expression, eye contact or gestures.

Encouraging and modelling interaction

Communication and interaction are key elements of teaching and learning, and all those who work with children and young people will need to be able to model and encourage good communication skills through demonstrating these themselves. You may also need to adapt the way you do this depending on the needs of the person you are communicating with.

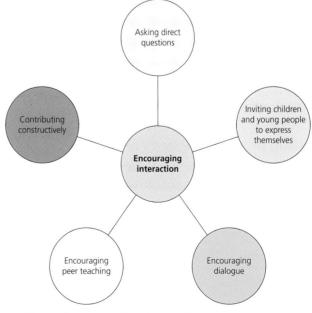

▲ Ways of encouraging interaction

Asking direct questions

You should make sure that you are clear when questioning children and young people, so that you know they understand what you are asking. Make sure that you ask only what you need to know, and ensure that you give them time to think and respond. You should also show that you value what they say by acknowledging their responses, particularly if they are finding the subject matter difficult. For example, 'Yes that's a good answer Matt, can you think of any other reasons?'

Inviting children/young people to express their own ideas through discussion, interactive activities or creative tasks

Make sure you involve all children and young people in discussions or activities, particularly if they are not confident in putting forward their ideas. Sometimes, it may also help to use creative or interactive tasks to enhance or encourage communication where children and young people have difficulty in expressing themselves verbally.

Encouraging a dialogue through oral and written formative feedback

See Core Chapter 2, Section 2.5, page 40.

Encouraging children/young people to teach one another

Encouraging children and young people to work together on projects and group activities will give them opportunities to share ideas and listen to one another, rather than just put forward their own ideas.

Providing active and constructive contributions

For more on effective feedback, see Core Chapter 2, Section 2.5, page 40.

Using positive language

In your work with children and young people, you should always try to use positive language so that you recognise their contributions and respond to what they say in a way that values them. This will help to build their confidence and self-esteem so that they feel able to progress in their learning.

For more on this, see Core Chapters 2 and 4.

▲ What makes effective communication an important part of your work with children and young people?

Helping children and young people to focus on strengths, rather than disadvantages

Make sure you build on what children and young people know and are able to do, so that they start from a place of knowledge. This will develop their confidence rather than focus on what they don't know or are unfamiliar with.

Using praise and constructive feedback to build confidence as well as competence

You should praise children and young people for their contributions and show that you are listening to them by giving effective feedback.

Modelling language that celebrates diversity

You should make sure that you use language that is inclusive and that celebrates the differences and individuality of children and young people.

See Core Chapter 10 for more on this.

Adapting contributions to meet the needs of the children and young people

Think about the communication needs of the children and young people you are working with – for example, their age, whether they have special educational needs, or if they speak English as an additional language. These may all impact on the way in which you communicate with them.

See Core Chapter 12 for more on English as an additional language.

Read through the UNICEF document 'Communicating with Children: Principles and Practices to Nurture, Inspire, Excite, Educate and Heal', which is available on the UNICEF website: **www.unicef.org**

Find out more about communicating with the age group you work with. What key points do you find useful? How might they influence the way in which you communicate with children and young people?

Practice points

Effective communication

▶ Use body language that shows you are open and approachable.

▶ Be positive in your communication with children and young people – smile and be interested in what they have to say.

▶ Remember you are a role model for the way in which they communicate with others.

▶ Speak clearly and give eye contact.

▶ Do not interrupt children or young people, or say things for them; give them an opportunity to speak.

▶ Give children and young people 'thinking time' when you ask them a question.

Core Skill 2: Work with others to plan and provide activities to meet children's and young people's needs

You should read this section alongside Core Chapter 5: Parents, Families and Carers, and Core Chapter 6: Working with Others, as well as Core Chapter 11 Special Educational Needs and Disability, and the Occupational Specialism unit on planning: Performance Outcome 2.

This Core Skill involves the following aspects.

Communicating openly and effectively with other professionals, speaking clearly and confidently

Establishing professional relationships with relevant colleagues and parents/carers – see Core Chapters 5 and 6.

Determining a child's or young person's specific needs – see Core Chapter 11.

Passing on information that could impact on other teams/professionals – see Core Chapters 6 and 11.

Sharing ideas and best practice – see Core Chapter 6.

Planning collaboratively

Liaising with colleagues to plan appropriate activities for children/young people – see Core Chapter 6.

Discussing how best to support children and young people in meeting objectives, taking into account their individual needs or learning targets. This or may not be related to an area of SEND – for example, a child or young person who needs support with staying focused, or someone who works best with a partner – see Core Chapter 11.

Contributing to long-, medium- and short-term planning – see Core Chapter 8 and Performance Outcome 2.

Sharing resources – see Performance Outcome 2.

Presenting information in an organised and logical way – see Core Chapter 8 and Performance Outcome 2.

Supporting education in the setting

Using high expectations and encouragement to create a positive learning environment – see Core Chapter 4.

Managing behaviour effectively and in line with the setting's policies and procedures – see Core Chapter 4.

Monitoring education activities through observation and assessment – see Core Chapter 8.

Contributing to effective record keeping, using precise terminology, and correct grammar, spelling and punctuation – see Core Chapter 3 and Performance Outcome 3.

Good to know

As part of Task 2 in the Employer-set Project, you will be required to make a presentation to your peers. When doing this, you should take into account the requirements of Core Skill 1 around effective communication and clear language, and Core Skill 2 around presenting information. You will also need to listen to the presentations of others, and show that you can listen actively to them and make constructive contributions to discussions.

Core Skill 3: Use formative and summative assessment to track children's and students' progress to plan and shape educational opportunities

> You should read this section alongside Core Chapter 8: Observation and Assessment.

You must be able to use formative and summative assessment to track children's/young people's progress to plan and shape educational opportunities. This includes but is not limited to:

▶ Establishing learning goals for/with the child/young person
▶ Observing the child/young person and recording data on their progress, as appropriate
▶ Using questions and answers or formal tasks to check the child's/young person's understanding
▶ Analysing assessment data to determine the next steps in supporting the child/young person to meet their goals.

As part of Core Skill 3, you will need to know how to use formative and summative assessment in order to track children's progress in the early years.

> For more about the purpose of assessment, and definitions of formative and summative assessment, see Core Chapter 8, Section 8.2.

Establishing learning goals for/with the child or young person

Learning goals and targets will help a child or young person to have something to aim for and to self-assess their learning. In the case of pupils in school settings, you will need to be able to work with teachers to set regular targets based on your most recent assessments. Many schools will do this once every half-term, and regularly support children and young people in assessing their progress towards the targets as they do their work.

Observing the child or young person and recording data on their progress, as appropriate

> For more on this, see Core Chapter 8, Section 8.3.

Using questions and answers or formal tests to check the child/young person's understanding

> For more on this, see Core Chapter 8, Section 8.2, on summative assessment and questioning.

Analysing assessment data to determine the next steps in supporting the child or young person to meet their goals

You are likely to work alongside colleagues to analyse data from national assessments so that you can work out the child's next steps for learning. In the EYFS, as you are regularly observing and assessing pupils' progress; you will use this information alongside what you know about children's development. You can use the current *Development Matters* statements to help you with this process.

> For more on analysing data from national assessments, see Core Chapter 8, Section 8.1.

In practice

Pupil A and pupil B in Year 3 underwent teacher assessments at the end of Key Stage 1. They can be assessed as 'working towards expected standard', 'working at expected standard' or 'working at greater depth'.

Consider the data presented below for these two pupils.

	English reading	English writing	Mathematics	Science
Pupil A	Working towards expected standard	Working towards expected standard	Working at greater depth	Working at expected standard
Pupil B	Working at expected standard	Working at expected standard	Working towards expected standard	Working at expected standard

▶ Would you be able to use this data to inform these children's targets for the start of Year 3? Explain your answer.

Core Skill 4: How to assess and manage risks to your own and others' safety when planning activities

As part of Core Skill 4, you will need to know how to assess and manage **risk** to your own and others' safety. This means both in the learning environment and when you are outside the school or early years setting on trips.

Assess and manage risks to your own and others' safety when planning activities, using the Health and Safety Executive's 'Five steps to risk assessment'

You should know about and understand the different kinds of risks that may occur when planning learning activities. The **Health and Safety Executive (HSE)** has published a list of five steps to support this.

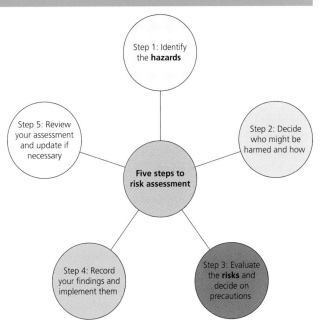

▲ The Health and Safety Executive's 'Five steps to risk assessment'

Key terms

Risk: the chance, whether high or low, that someone could be harmed by a hazard.

Health and Safety Executive (HSE): an independent regulator for the prevention of work-related death, injury and ill health.

The HSE's 'Five steps to **risk assessment**' are as follows:

Step 1: Identify the hazards

According to the HSE, you should look at the whole activity you are going to carry out, from beginning to end, so that you can identify each **hazard**. When you are doing this, take in to consideration the fact that these are likely to include different types of hazard:

▶ physical
▶ security
▶ fire
▶ food safety
▶ personal safety.

Physical hazards

These will be the ones you might come across in the general environment, such as coats being left on the floor and causing a trip hazard, broken glass around a litter bin, or damage and mess caused in outdoor areas overnight by foxes. Materials and equipment should be checked, as should the immediate area you will be working in before carrying out learning activities. You should remember to check both the indoor and outdoor learning environment regularly, particularly if you are working in an early years setting.

▲ Identifying a physical hazard

Security hazards

These may occur when unidentified people gain access to the site or young children or older pupils are able to leave it without permission. If you are working outside, gates should be checked to ensure they are not left open, and hedges to ensure there are no gaps. Security hazards may also occur with younger pupils if a different adult arrives to collect them at the end of the day or session without being given permission by parents. You should ensure that you know the school's policy for collection and for ensuring that children are kept safe and secure at all times.

For more on this, see the information on safeguarding in Core Chapter 3.

Fire hazards

In the case of cooking or science activities, safety equipment such as fire blankets should be available for use if needed during the activity. Fire extinguishers and electrical items will need to be checked regularly to ensure that they are not faulty, and the dates of these checks should be displayed on the equipment.

Food safety

Adults should be good role models when cooking and working in kitchens, pointing out hazards to children and young people where they occur and making sure that equipment is used correctly. Hazards may include hot surfaces and flames, and sharp knives. Food preparation should always be carried out hygienically and in line with food handling and safety requirements. All children and young people should inform the setting of any allergies or specific dietary requirements.

Personal safety

Safety equipment and **PPE** should always be used where needed, and staff should be aware of the correct procedures when carrying out activities that have a higher level of risk. If you are to be using any specialised equipment with children and young people, such as glue guns or sewing machines, always ensure that they have been given clear instructions and are supervised at all times.

Step 2: Decide who might be harmed and how

When carrying out a risk assessment, you will need to think about who has the potential to be harmed so that you can record this. When working with children and young people, you should consider whether they are more at risk, and the kinds of steps you can put in place to reduce the risk. If children or young people have special educational needs or a disability, or other specific requirements, how will this affect the level of risk? How might they be harmed?

See Performance Outcome 3, K3.6 and K3.17, for more on risk assessments.

Step 3: Evaluate the risks and decide on precautions

If a hazard has been identified, the next stage is to consider the level of risk and how likely it is to happen (high, medium or low risk of occurrence). The kind of precaution or action you take should take this into account. For example, if you are working outside in an early years setting on a hot day, the children should wear sun hats and sun cream, or stay in the shade if possible.

When going on off-site visits, risk assessments will need to be carried out by the member of staff who is organising the trip. This should take account of issues such as:

▶ adult/child ratio
▶ transport (e.g. insurance, seat belts, or check the route if walking)
▶ child allergies, medical needs or SEND of children and young people so that any medication can be taken
▶ first aid requirements
▶ on-site risk assessment at the location.

In practice

Ask your school or early years setting if you can look at a risk assessment for an off-site visit. There is likely to be a member of staff who manages this – for example, a school may have an **educational visits coordinator (EVC)** whose role is to go through risk assessments with the staff members who are managing the trip.

Step 4: Record your findings and implement them

You should record your findings on a risk assessment form so that you can refer to it if needed. If further action needs to be taken following the assessment, you should ensure that this happens. You may need to also share this with other staff.

Step 5: Review your risk assessment and update if necessary

A risk assessment should be reviewed annually and updated as necessary if circumstances are different or anything changes. This may need to happen sooner if there is an incident or a significant change at the setting.

In practice

Carry out a risk assessment in an area of your setting, taking into account the five steps outlined on the previous two pages. You may be able to use a template that is used regularly by your setting. If not, there are others available, such as the HSE risk assessment template provided below.

Health and Safety Executive

Risk assessment template

Company name:

Date of next review:

Assessment carried out by:

Date assessment was carried out:

What are the hazards?	Who might be harmed and how?	What are you already doing to control the risks?	What further action do you need to take to control the risks ?	Who needs to carry out the action?	When is the action needed by?	Done

More information on managing risk: www.hse.gov.uk/simple-health-safety/risk/

Published by the Health and Safety Executive 09/20

▲ A risk assessment template from the HSE

For more information on managing risk, visit **www.hse.gov.uk/simple-health-safety/risk/**

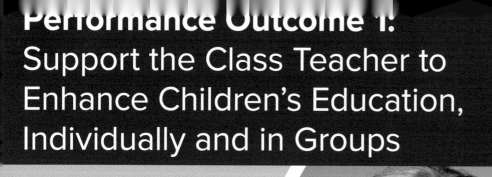

Performance Outcome 1:
Support the Class Teacher to Enhance Children's Education, Individually and in Groups

A key aspect of your role when working in schools will be to support class or subject teachers. Part of this support will be to work with individuals and groups, and this will vary depending on the requirements of the lesson and pupils' needs.

You will need to work closely with teachers to ensure that you are clear on your own role as well as how to manage behaviour. This unit looks at the kinds of strategies you could use when working with pupils, and considers different types of resources.

You should also know about the importance of giving pupils regular feedback to support their learning, and also giving teachers feedback on pupil participation and progress. Finally, this unit looks at the benefits of learning outside the classroom and the distinctive qualities which it offers as an educational environment.

Learning outcomes

This chapter covers the following knowledge outcomes for Performance Outcome 1.

K1.1   The requirements of each key stage of the school curriculum:
  – Primary (Key Stages 1 and 2)
  – Secondary (Key Stages 3 and 4)
  – Post-16 provision

K1.2   A range of teacher- and student-led pedagogical strategies and how they are used within a lesson

K1.3   The benefits of individual work and group work, and the strategies that support this

K1.4   How ongoing feedback to pupils supports and facilitates independent learning

K1.5   How to select appropriate resources in order to identify and help address weakness, consolidate strengths and develop individualised expectations

K1.6   How learning outside the classroom, including outdoor education, positively enhances children's education and development

K1.7   What distinctive qualities are offered by the outdoors as an educational environment compared to traditional classroom environments

K1.1 The requirements of each key stage of the school curriculum

This knowledge outcome is included in Core Chapter 2. You will find this on page 20.

K1.2 A range of teacher- and student-led pedagogical strategies and how they are used within a lesson

When you are supporting teaching and learning in different learning environments, you will need to use a range of **pedagogical** strategies to meet the needs of pupils. In Core Chapter 2, we looked at teacher-led and student-led learning (see page 38). The table below gives examples of teacher-led and student-led strategies and how they can be used in lessons.

Pedagogical strategies

Teacher-led strategies

For teacher- or adult-led pedagogical strategies, adults are at the centre of the learning process. They take on a traditional role which relies on:
▶ instruction
▶ a closely controlled environment and curriculum.

Student-led strategies

Student-led (also known as pupil-led) pedagogical strategies encourage children and young people to lead the learning through their own interests and to listen to the views and opinions of others.

In student-led learning, the role of the adult is to:
▶ facilitate
▶ coach
▶ encourage learners.

> **Key term**
>
> **Pedagogical:** educational, or related to teaching.

Strategy	How it is used within a lesson
Lecture/presentation	The adult presents information to pupils about a given topic.
	Pupils listen and then usually carry out their work based on what they have listened to.
Rote learning	**Rote learning** requires pupils to learn something by heart through repetition.
	An example of this might be learning times tables through saying them many times.
Call-and-response questioning	This strategy is used when the teacher requires a specific response from pupils to get their attention or to ask them for a particular answer.
	An example of this strategy to gain younger children's attention: • The teacher says '1, 2, 3' (call). • The children reply with 'Eyes on me' (response).
	An example of call-and-response questioning with older children: • The teacher asks a question of the whole class. • The children have to respond with the correct answer, either through raising their hands individually or speaking together (such as when learning times tables).
Teacher-led feedback	Teacher- or adult-led feedback can be used to: • praise and encourage • ask further questions • scaffold children's learning in order to deepen it or direct it in a particular way.
	For more on feedback to pupils, see K1.4 in this chapter.

Strategy	How it is used within a lesson
Collaborative learning	Pupils might be asked to work together and collaborate on a task. They will need to: • listen to one another's ideas and opinions • think about the best way to reach the learning objective. Collaborative learning helps learners to: • work with others towards a common goal • think about views other than their own.
Inquiry-based learning	Inquiry-based learning is a way of engaging pupils in the process from the start, as it is based on what they would like to find out. It may be used at the start of a new topic or programme of study, to find out exactly what they would like to know about it. This helps to direct their learning and engage them in the process.
Discussions/debates	Discussions and debates enable pupils to: • put forward their own ideas • think about how to present an argument to others • listen to others • think about other people's points of view • balance advantages and disadvantages.
Practical tasks	Practical tasks allow pupils to find out more about something through hands-on experience. Tasks are regularly used in subjects such as technology or art and design. When working on practical tasks, pupils are encouraged to plan and evaluate what they have done by writing about it.
Self-assessment	This is a form of assessment where pupils assess or review their own work. • First they look at the learning objectives. • Then they go back over their work to check whether they have met them.
Peer assessment	This is similar to self-assessment but pupils assess or review *each other's* work and check that they have met the learning objectives. They might also make suggestions as to how the work could be improved.
Sustained shared thinking	This is when pupils work together over a certain time to solve a problem or develop and extend their learning. This term is often used in the early years curriculum as it is a good way for children to: • develop their communication skills • understand how to make connections in their learning.
Digital learning communities	These are online private groups which facilitate pupils' learning through technology. They can be useful for: • peer-to-peer learning • collaborating on projects • meeting specific learning objectives.
Massive open online courses (MOOCs)	MOOCs are courses of study which have unlimited students. They are accessed online, but they are context-based which means that they are more open-ended than online courses. The difference between a MOOC and an online course is that a MOOC changes to reflect the participation and collaboration of its students, rather than having a set structure.
Virtual reality aids	These are virtual environments created by a computer. Pupils may wear headsets or 3D goggles. They offer pupils a means of experiencing different situations, such as: • visiting aspects of history • looking at aspects of the world such as natural disasters • visualising 3D designs.

Strategy	How it is used within a lesson
Discussion forums	These are electronic message boards which pupils use to have discussions and conversations through messaging others. Access might be limited to members of a class, or be open to a wider audience.
Social networks	Social networks include online social media sites, apps and other forums accessed via the internet. These offer pupils the opportunity to post messages and photos online to individuals or groups, potentially around the world, and can be formal or informal. They might be set up for a specific topic or to enable students to access specific resources.
Video-sharing websites	Video-sharing websites enable individuals to post their own films online. These can be used for and by students to support and enhance learning.

For more on self and peer assessment, see Core Chapter 8.2.

▲ How might virtual reality aids support pupils' learning?

The advantages and disadvantages of teacher- and student-led pedagogical strategies

Teacher- and student-led strategies will be more appropriate in different situations, and there may be advantages and disadvantages to both approaches. For example:

▶ For teaching some aspects of science and maths, pupils will need to have teacher-led sessions to be taught different processes and specific methods of working.

▶ Student-led sessions might lend themselves better to investigations and collaborative work. Lessons might become noisy as pupils will need to talk and discuss while they work.

Some pupils prefer one way of learning over another. For this reason, a mixture of approaches is often used.

Type of activity	Advantages	Disadvantages
Teacher-led	• The teacher is able to direct learning and is 'in control' of learners. • Pupils work through tasks independently and teachers find out through marking their work what they understand and how they have applied it. • Pupils are given more structure to their learning and some may prefer this method of working.	• Pupils are not proactive and are waiting for the teacher to direct their learning. • Pupils could become disengaged or 'switch off'. • Strategies such as rote learning do not allow for a deeper understanding. • This might be less meaningful for pupils. • Pupils are not encouraged to express themselves and have less time to ask questions.
Student-led	• Pupils are responsible for their own learning and progress. • They are encouraged to support and collaborate with others rather than compete with them. • This develops their communication skills. • All pupils are involved and actively participating. • It encourages pupils to self-reflect on their learning. • This approach gives some pupils greater motivation.	• This might lead to a noisier classroom environment. • It is more difficult to manage from the teacher's point of view. • Teachers might not be able to monitor what individual pupils have learned. • This approach sometimes has to rely on technology. • Some less socially confident pupils may be less confident/comfortable with this way of working.

How theoretical approaches underpin teacher- and student-led pedagogical strategies

Most teaching strategies incorporate several underpinning theories. It is now recognised as best practice to use a mixture of theoretical approaches to learning, so a range of approaches might be used during a lesson.

Some of these theories are identified and outlined below, and there is more detail on each of them in Core Chapter 2.

In practice

The next time you are with a teacher in class, look at the way in which the teacher has structured the lesson and led the responses of the pupils.
► Is the lesson teacher- or student-led, or a combination of both?
► How does it support pupils' learning and motivate them?
► What theoretical approaches can you see being used as part of the lesson?

Theory	How this theory underpins pedagogical approaches
Behaviourist	This is based on the idea that learning can be encouraged by the use of: • praise and rewards • adults role-modelling, or showing pupils how to do something. Examples of this are: • adults demonstrating practical tasks such as the use of technology • using a reward system such as house points, to encourage concentration and effort.
Cognitivist	The cognitivist theory focuses on the processes involved in learning and puts the emphasis on the learner, or pupil, rather than the teacher. An example of this approach is: • inquiry-based learning, where pupils think about what they already know and set themselves goals as to what they might like to learn.
Constructivist	This theory is based on the idea that learning is linked to experience and builds on what learners know. According to this approach, pupils should be given opportunities to engage in guided tasks which are scaffolded by adults.
Humanist	The humanist theory is another learner-centred approach which is based on the whole person. Examples of humanist principles might be: • group work and collaborative projects, which help pupils to develop social skills and set goals for their own learning.
Connectivist	This approach is based on technologies, the resulting information and connection with others. Examples of this are: • digital learning communities • MOOCs. Both of these enable pupils to connect with one another and use technology to gather information.

K1.3 The benefits of individual work and group work, and the strategies that support this

There are benefits for pupils in both individual and group work when carrying out learning activities, and different strategies for adults to support their work. Broadly speaking:
► individual work is likely to be more teacher-led
► group work is likely to be pupil-led.

In both situations, you need to be aware of the needs of the pupils you are supporting, and of any specific resources they need to support their learning.

Individual work

Individual work usually takes place following whole class teaching input, and pupils will be asked to work on activities which are based on this. The role of the adult is to:
► work one-to-one with individuals if they need support
► move around the room to ensure that pupils are staying on task and working towards learning objectives.

The benefits of individual work

▶ **It is easier for pupils to concentrate**: If pupils have difficulty in concentrating when they are in a larger group, or if others are affecting their behaviour, working independently can enable them to focus on what they are doing. They can think about their own learning and what they need to do next, and use their time effectively. However, the classroom will need to be quieter to allow all pupils to concentrate.

▶ **Learning can be differentiated**: Teachers can ensure that tasks are differentiated so that individual pupils are given work which is accessible to them. These should be set so that pupils' learning can be extended and they can continue to move forward.

Key term

Differentiation: setting work which is at an accessible level for each pupil and their needs within a class.

▶ **Pupils are empowered to take control of their own learning and learn at their own pace**: Pupils should be encouraged to be as independent as possible, and take control and responsibility over their own learning. There should be opportunities for them to find things out for themselves and develop their independence rather than asking an adult for help.

You can support less confident individuals by giving them strategies for managing their learning, such as thinking about how to approach it if they don't know what to do.

Always give pupils a checklist of approaches when they don't know what to do; for example:
- Check that they have done everything they can.
- Look for clues in the learning environment.
- Ask a friend.

▶ **It is easier to assess individual work**: When assessing individual pupils, you can be very clear on exactly what they know and understand about the task or topic, and assess whether they have met learning objectives.

What to do when I am stuck in my learning

1. Make sure you know the learning objective and take some time to think about what you are aiming to do.
2. Make sure you read any questions carefully and look around for working walls or displays in the room that might help you.
3. Quietly ask a partner to explain what you need to do.
4. If you have tried everything you can, ask an adult for help.
5. Have a go! Don't let a lack of confidence hold you back.

Getting stuck can lead to learning more...

▲ Do learners in your class know how to proceed when they don't know what to do?

Strategies for individual work

The kind of strategies which adults use with individuals will vary, depending on the pupil and the situation as described in Section K1.2. These are summarised in this chart.

Strategy	How this might be used
Lecture/ presentation	The adult teaches to all pupils, who then carry out a learning activity based on what they have been taught. Usually, the teacher presents the knowledge part of the session and then adults will move around the class and check on learning.
Rote learning	Pupils learn facts through repetition. Adults might teach specific strategies, such as **mnemonics**, to help with: • spelling • learning dates or important facts.
Call-and-response questioning	This can be another helpful strategy if pupils are memorising facts. For example, another child or an adult says a familiar phrase or statement, and the pupil knows the response. This strategy can be used to review or reinforce learning.

Key term

Mnemonic: a system for improving and helping memory.

Group work

Pupils might work in groups if they are required to:
▶ collaborate on a task, or
▶ carry out an activity which requires the input of several pupils.

Groups working together are likely to need some kind of adult intervention to keep them on task and working towards the learning objectives. Younger pupils in particular will need support, as they might find it more difficult to listen to the views of others and stay on task.

The benefits of group work

These include:
▶ **Being able to share knowledge**: Pupils can talk to the rest of the group about what they know, so that they can 'pool' their knowledge. This will help them to make progress in their learning.
▶ **Developing social and communication skills**: Any kind of situation where pupils are working together, listening to one another, talking and sharing information will develop their social and communication skills. They need to think carefully about how they put their ideas across, and make sure that they listen to what others have to say.
▶ **Sharing diverse perspectives**: Depending on their views and experiences, pupils will be able to share different perspectives on a topic or subject. This will expose them to opinions other than their own, and give them opportunities to consider and discuss them.
▶ **Giving one another peer support**: Pupils working together as part of a group should be able to give each other support and encouragement to achieve the learning objective.

Strategies for group work

Strategy	How this might be used
Collaborative learning	Pupils might be asked to collaborate on a project or piece of work which will take place over several sessions. • They might need to plan, carry out and evaluate the task together. • They could be asked to work on a one-off activity as a group, which means that they need to discuss and carry out the task together.
Inquiry-based learning	Groups might work together on an activity, based on what they would like to find out about a subject area or topic. They will then need to: • share resources • talk about how they are going to present their information.
Discussions and debates	Pupils might need to work in a group to discuss or debate a specific subject. This means that: • they should all be involved • everyone should be able to put their ideas forward.

Teaching assistants might be asked to work with both individuals and groups.

Working with an individual

Teaching assistants might work regularly with pupils who have special educational needs and disabilities (SEND) on a one-to-one basis. In this situation it is important to consider:
▶ the child's background and learning needs
▶ their targets
▶ their education, health and care (EHC) plan, if they have one.

Working one-to-one with an individual has many benefits:

1   You can feed back to pupils about their progress towards their own personal targets and the learning objectives.
2   It is easier to adapt the pace and content of what pupils are doing to suit their individual needs, such as:
    –   breaking the task down into smaller steps, or
    –   using specific resources or equipment to work towards learning objectives.

> For more on resources, see Section K1.5.

3   You might be asked to work with an individual pupil if there is something specific that they have not understood during a lesson or topic that they need to **consolidate** and work on further.
4   The pupil might lack confidence in their own abilities, and need more practice in the topic as well as reassurance from you.
5   Working one-to-one with an adult gives pupils opportunities to work more slowly on a task or learning objective if this is needed.

Key term

Consolidate: to review or reinforce learning.

Good to know

A potential disadvantage of working one-to-one with an adult is that pupils might become too reliant on having support. For this reason, make sure that you don't try to do tasks for them or give them the answers or solutions. Instead, you should help to develop their independent learning skills.

The ultimate goal is to give pupils the strategies that they need to work independently and manage their own learning.

Working with a group

If you are working with a group, you will need to balance your attention to make sure that:
▶   they are all involved and on task
▶   their individual needs are being met during the session.

Children with more confident personalities can sometimes 'take over', making the less confident children reluctant to answer or put forward ideas. You will need to move around the group, checking to make sure that they are all listening to one another and sharing ideas.

On a practical level, when supporting individuals or groups of pupils:
▶   Before the session you should be familiar with the learning objectives and what pupils need to do, so that you are able to support them effectively.
▶   At the start of the session, it is helpful to always outline ground rules and expectations for behaviour so that pupils are clear on what is expected.
▶   Use praise when learners are doing the right thing and making positive choices, so that appropriate behaviour is recognised.
▶   If there is something you need to double-check on how to approach the task, do this by researching or asking the teacher to explain it to you in advance, so that you can refresh your own practice if necessary.

Case study

Marianne is supporting a Year 6 class every morning. She has been asked to work with Bhumika during the maths lesson, who has been finding the fractions and percentages topic difficult.

Bhumika has a series of activities to do based on what the class have been doing over the past two weeks, and the class teacher has sent Marianne the plans in advance at the weekend.

However, Marianne is not confident in the area of fractions, was not in class on the day the main teaching input was given and has not had time to go over it. As a result, she is concerned that she is not going to be able to support Bhumika effectively.
▶   What should Marianne do in this situation?
▶   Should she continue with the lesson?

Practice points

Preparing to support individuals and groups

▶ Make sure you are clear on the learning objective and what you need to do.

▶ Set boundaries and expectations for behaviour at the start of the session.

▶ Think about the types of strategies you are going to use.

▶ Take time to prepare for the activity and familiarise yourself with any resources.

▶ Make sure the learning environment is comfortable for learners and conducive to learning.

▶ Ensure you know the names of all pupils and as much as you can about their needs and any learning targets.

K1.4 How ongoing feedback to pupils supports and facilitates independent learning

Effective feedback is a very important part of the teaching and learning process.

Whether you are working with individuals or groups of pupils, you should always provide them with feedback on their progress. This must be specific so that it is clear, and it should take place both during and just after the learning activity.

When providing feedback, it is important that pupils are involved in the process and have opportunities to act on it, so that they can develop the skills of self-reflection which will help them to become independent learners.

Types of feedback

There are different ways of providing effective feedback, and these may be verbal or written:

▶ **Verbal feedback**: You can do this through effective questioning, scaffolding pupils' work, praise and encouragement.

▶ **Written feedback**: You can do this through marking and annotating pupils' work.

Verbal feedback

For all pupils, but particularly the youngest in school, give verbal feedback during the activity or as soon as possible afterwards, so that they can link it to their learning. It will be more difficult for pupils to make this link if the feedback is given too long after the activity.

▶ Make sure you use vocabulary which is appropriate for the pupils' age and stage of development, and check that they understand your meaning.

▶ After giving verbal feedback, you might be required to annotate the pupil's work, if appropriate, to show that this has taken place.

You can give verbal feedback to older pupils during or just after the activity.

Feedback should:

▶ encourage pupils to think for themselves about solutions to any problems, and also to consider the strengths and weaknesses of their work

▶ be very clear so that pupils know exactly what they are doing correctly.

▲ How do you provide feedback to pupils during or after learning activities?

Written feedback

You might give pupils feedback after an activity in a written format through marking, but this depends on their age and how much they will be able to use what has been written.

Teaching assistants might be asked to mark the work of the pupils they are supporting. If you are asked to do this:

▶ Make sure that you are familiar with the marking policy of your school to ensure that you are consistent with other staff.

▶ The policy might be very detailed and might even include the colour of the pen you should use.

▶ If you need help, ask teachers for support and clarification.

Marking usually includes a comment about the pupil's work and a challenge for them to take the learning further.

If pupils are carrying out peer- or self-assessment, they will probably follow a set format.

> For more on assessment and how it is used, see Core Chapter 8.

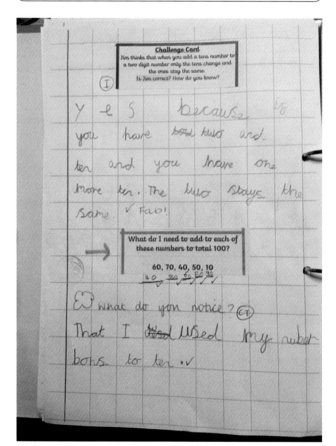

▲ How has the pupil's learning been extended here?'

Purpose of feedback

When you are providing written or verbal feedback, make sure that it:

▶ encourages self-reflection

▶ gives pupils appropriate information to improve

▶ clarifies their achievement of learning aims and objectives.

Encourages self-reflection

Feedback can encourage self-reflection, enabling pupils to think about their learning and how they are going about it. This is important as it helps them to become more independent learners and to think about what they need to do next.

If pupils regularly think about their learning and how they meet learning objectives, self-reflection will become part of their learning process. This type of ongoing feedback and assessment is sometimes called **assessment for learning**, or AfL.

> ### Key term
>
> **Assessment for learning:** information from assessment is used to raise the achievement of pupils in finding out what they need to do to improve.

Gives pupils appropriate information to improve

Providing ongoing feedback to pupils:

▶ gives them information about precisely what they need to do to make progress with their learning

▶ encourages them to think about their progress towards the success criteria, so that they can assess and evaluate their own work, and take their learning forward.

Clarifies their achievement of learning aims and objectives

Effective feedback ensures that pupils have understood their progress towards achieving learning aims and objectives.

▶ Learning objectives should be clearly displayed during the lesson, and also written on pupils' work as a heading so that they can refer to it.

▶ When pupils have achieved or are working towards the learning objective, this should be clear to them during and after the session.

▶ Sometimes, marking will show this through highlighting the learning objective in a specific colour to show that it has been achieved.

▶ In other cases, pupils might mark each others' work and underline the objective – this will depend on school policy.

Feedback strategies to use with individuals and groupwork

You can use the following feedback strategies with individuals and groups of pupils.

Effective questioning

This is a very important aspect of feedback. It will enable you to support learners and take their learning forward by using open questions to provoke them to think further about a task.

▶ For example, if you ask 'Does anyone know which is the adjective and which is the noun?' – this is a closed question, as it only requires a one-word answer.

▶ Effective questions open up learning. In this situation, it might be better to ask, 'Can someone give me some examples of other adjectives which could be used here?'

Scaffolding learning

Scaffolding is based on Lev Vygotsky's theory about the zone of proximal development and was developed by Wood, Bruner and Ross in the 1970s.

▶ The principle of scaffolding is for learners to be supported to reach the next stage in their learning through guidance and encouragement.

▶ It is important not to change the task itself, but to break it down into smaller steps and to observe learners carefully as they complete each one.

The purpose of scaffolding is to create opportunities to develop learner independence. You should intervene only if pupils cannot work through any difficulties on their own.

The scaffolding framework pictured here has been developed by Paula Bosanquet, Julie Radford and Rob Webster to support learners with SEND so that they avoid what is known as 'learned helplessness' – in other words, becoming over-reliant on adults.

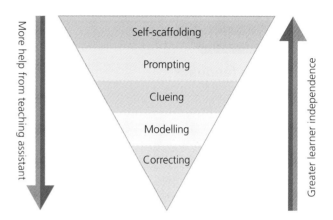

▲ 'How can you ensure that you encourage maximum learner independence during learning activities?'

Source: Bosanquet, Radford and Webster, *The Teaching Assistant's Guide to Effective Interaction: How to Maximise your Practice.* Routledge, 2016

▶ **Self-scaffolding**: This involves observing the learner and allowing them time to consider and tackle the task themselves.

▶ **Prompting**: This stage involves giving encouragement or questioning learners with prompts, such as 'What is the first thing you need to do?'

▶ **Clueing**: This might involve giving a small clue to learners so that they are able to move forward in their learning.

▶ **Modelling**: If pupils are learning a new skill, you might need to model it for them. They can then watch and attempt to do it themselves.

▶ **Correcting**: This is where adults give pupils the answer. It should be avoided as it does not require any independent thinking.

> For more on scaffolding learning, see Performance Outcome 2, in Section K2.5.

Praise and encouragement

All of us need our efforts to be rewarded, and of course this is the same with children. Pupils might need additional motivation or encouragement, particularly if the task is difficult for them.

However, rather than just saying 'Well done' during an activity, be specific in your feedback: 'Well done, you have really listened and are thinking carefully about each stage when creating your graph.'

> **Practice points**
>
> ### Providing feedback
> ▶ Use AfL where possible to help pupils evaluate their own progress.
> ▶ Give feedback during or as soon as possible after the activity.
> ▶ Question pupils effectively and scaffold their learning where needed.
> ▶ Make sure all pupils are involved and given feedback, whether verbal or written.
> ▶ Use praise, and acknowledge what pupils have attempted or achieved.
> ▶ Make sure that after receiving feedback, pupils know what they might do next and are motivated to do it.

For more on strategies to promote learning, see Performance Outcome 2.

Providing feedback to teachers

Teaching assistants should also provide feedback to teachers on pupil participation and progress, during and after learning activities. You will need to do this using the method which is preferred by the school. This might be verbal feedback or recorded on specific feedback sheets.

▶ Comment in particular on any pupils who have found the activity very straightforward and have completed it quickly, as well as those who have found it challenging, and reasons for this.

▶ Think about the learners' levels of engagement in the activity – perhaps they haven't met the objectives but they have been enthusiastic and tried hard throughout, so record or feed this information back in some way.

▶ If planning has been done well and the activity is pitched at the correct level, most pupils should have been able to complete the task successfully.

▶ In some cases, there might be a space for you to record your observations on planning sheets, and this can then be handed back to teachers following the activity. The level of detail you can give might vary, but the most important thing is to say whether pupils found an activity difficult and were unable to meet the objective, or whether they completed it very quickly.

The lesson plan for religious education below shows how information has been added after the lesson in the column on the right. In this case, the teaching assistant fed back to the teacher verbally after the session, and this was subsequently added to the planning sheet.

You might also be asked to complete more structured observations by teachers or external professionals if there are specific things which need to be checked or assessed. Observations are a tool which we use to find out more about pupils, in relation to their behaviour or learning.

For more about carrying out observations, see Core Chapter 8.

Year 5 Religious Education lesson plan	
LO: To understand why it is important for Jews to read the Torah.	**TA:** Work with small groups to support, question and help generate ideas.
Week 3 of Judaism	**Observation/information for next steps**
• Discuss the language of the Torah and recap what they know. What language do Jews read it in? They read it regularly and treat the scroll with great respect. Why? Because of the teaching it contains, Jews believe it can teach them how God wants them to live.	Owen remembered it was Hebrew and that it teaches us how God wants us to live.
• Read the story of 'Rebekah at the well'. Discuss what happens in the story. Why was Rebekah chosen to be Isaac's wife? What does this story teach? What can we learn from Rebekah's example?	Melissa said that the story said that Rebekah did the right thing.
• Children to brainstorm in pairs other people they have heard of, past or present, who have set an example by their behaviour – can be anyone they think – famous person, sports person, celebrity.	
• **Activity**: Draw a picture of this person and write down who they have chosen, explaining why this person is a good role model for others.	Sam – wrote about Mother Teresa. Joe C – Prince William for always doing his duty – but then didn't write it. Luke – the Stig for being cool. Rachel was not clear, named the doctor who cured her of her spots. Jack said the Pope. Lots of them chose members of their family despite being encouraged to think of others who are well known.
• **Plenary**: Discuss who they have chosen and why. Recap what the Torah shows Jews and why they read it regularly.	At end of session, pupils had met the objective although Rachel, Emma and Biram not able to say why the Torah is important to Jews.

▲ What do you use to feed back to teachers following learning activities?

K1.5 How to select appropriate resources in order to identify and help address weakness, consolidate strengths and develop individualised expectations

Your lesson plan or discussion with teachers before the lesson should inform you about the appropriate resources that you need so that you can support learning activities effectively, whether this is with an individual or a group.

▶ If additional resources other than books and stationery are needed, you should make sure you know in advance where to find them within the school. If you wait until the day itself, others may be using them or they may not have been returned, and you will not have time to track them down.

▶ There is likely to be a specific resources area for different subjects if you are in a primary school, and within secondary schools and colleges they should be located by department.

▶ When you first look at plans or work on them with teaching staff, you might identify unfamiliar resources or requirements, so you will need to find out about them.

▶ You might also have your own ideas about additional resources which could be helpful to pupils, or have something which you could bring into school to support teaching and learning.

Always ask teachers as soon as possible if you need more information so that you can plan more effectively to meet the needs of the learners and help them to meet learning objectives.

This table shows factors to consider when using resources.

Considerations when using resources	Why this is important
Pupils' age, and their emotional and social development	If you are working with younger pupils, you will need to think about whether they have used the resources before and might need help. Where possible, you should encourage: • all pupils to get any resources they need from the immediate learning environment (for example, dictionaries or maths equipment) • older pupils to bring what they need to lessons, as this will help to develop their independence. If resources are unusual or pupils have not used them before, this might affect their behaviour at the start of the session. Be ready for this and have strategies prepared to manage it.
Different metacognitive strategies	Metacognition means the way in which pupils think about their own needs and how they learn best so that they can direct their own learning. They reflect on their learning and know what they need to support it. Children and young people might therefore need to bring additional resources with them to do this. For example: • A pupil with dyslexia might know that they need to rehearse what they are going to write before they put in on paper, and bring a small whiteboard to do this. However, you might need to remind them to do this. For more on metacognition and learning, see Core Chapter 2 on page 39.
Pupils' individual ability levels	Some pupils might need specific resources or equipment to support their learning which are related to their ability levels. • You might need support from teachers or the school's SENDCo so that you are prepared for what they need to do. • You might need to make the resources yourself, such as a visual timetable or other means of support to access the curriculum.
Stretch and challenge	All pupils should be challenged during learning activities so that they can make progress. However, you might be working with an individual whose ability means that they need to be stretched more than the rest of the group. If you know the needs of the learners you are working with, think about this and bring appropriate resources to enable them to make progress.
Curriculum needs	Always check the lesson plan for curriculum-specific resources before you start the session, so that you have them in advance and can concentrate on the learning. For example: • in a PE lesson you might need bats and balls.
Adaptability for a variety of pupils (SEND/EAL)	You might need to adapt or add to the resources to suit the specific needs of pupils who have SEND or English as an additional language (EAL). For example, this could mean: • ensuring that resources are accessible to pupils who have a visual impairment • checking that they will not be put at a disadvantage by a particular resource. See Core Chapters 11 and 12. Where necessary, you might need to adapt or make your own resources in order to meet pupils' needs, for example: • creating and laminating cards which can be reused.
Diversity	Make sure that the resources you use give a wide representation of diversity, in terms of race, culture, disability and various aspects of identity. These should be available within your school and represent a variety of identities from all elements of society.
Pupils' interests	It can sometimes help to gain pupils' attention at the start of an activity if you start with a 'hook', or something which is linked to an area of interest for them. Teachers might also have ideas about pupils' areas of interest, or something which is familiar and puts the learning in context for them.

K1.6 How learning outside the classroom, including outdoor education, positively enhances children's education and development

Learning outside the classroom is valuable for pupils for a range of reasons:
▶ Children and young people benefit from being in a different environment.
▶ The outdoors offers them an opportunity to take supported risks and develop their confidence.
▶ It supports all areas of development, including physical, social, emotional and cognitive skills.
▶ For all pupils, and particularly those who have SEND, the outdoor environment allows them to explore learning in a different context, free from the walls of the classroom.

'I don't have ADHD when I am out in the woods.'

David, aged 14

Source: Forest Schools Association website

▲ How can working in an outdoor environment develop pupils' social skills?

Aspect of outdoor learning	Benefit for pupils
Physical exercise	Physical exercise and fresh air contribute to children's overall physical and mental wellbeing.
Scientific development	The outdoor environment supports pupils' scientific knowledge by: • encouraging a respect for the environment and the natural world • increasing their knowledge of animals, plants and lifecycles.
Improved life skills	Life skills are developed by: • enhancing children's and young people's awareness of safety, hazards, risk and challenge • developing their cognitive, social and emotional skills • encouraging them to work collaboratively.
Independence	The outdoor environment gives children and young people opportunities to develop their independence, self-confidence and perseverance by overcoming challenges and fears.

Where learning outside the classroom may take place

Learning outside the classroom might be in a range of different spaces and support different areas of the curriculum.

▶ It might take place within the school or grounds themselves, or can also be on a local walk or school trip.
▶ Some of these trips might take place in a day, while others are residential trips where pupils spend one or more nights away from home.

As well as supporting the curriculum, spending time outside the school is beneficial as it gives children and young people the chance to experience learning in different environments and develop their confidence through practical experiences.

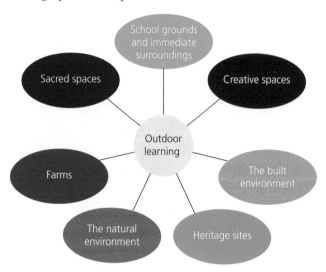

▲ Spaces for outdoor learning

▶ **School grounds and immediate surroundings**: Depending on where the school is located, you might have areas within the school grounds or close by which you can use for teaching and learning. These areas might:
- be plant- or animal-related, such as a pond or nature area
- support subjects such as maths, science or geography through the use of investigations
- encourage art activities.

The school grounds are also likely to be used for outdoor PE and games sessions.

▶ **Creative spaces**: Schools sometimes arrange cultural trips with pupils to theatres, cinemas or art galleries to reinforce areas of the curriculum such as literacy or art.

▶ **The built environment**: It may be useful for different aspects of the curriculum to explore the built environment if schools are located in towns or cities. This can:
- support subjects such as geography or maths
- allow pupils to collect data or look at features of the environment such as street furniture.

▶ **Heritage sites**: These could include:
- cultural heritage sites, for example historic buildings such as castles, stately homes or monuments
- natural heritage sites such as the Lake District, the Jurassic Coast, or rivers, lakes and mountains.

These areas can support work in history, geography, or science.

▶ **The natural environment**: This could include areas outside the town or city if children do not spend time in more open areas such as parks, woods, the beach or the countryside. This will reinforce areas of the curriculum such as science or geography.

▶ **Farms**: For children and young people, visiting farms can:
- provide opportunities to discover where their food comes from
- develop their understanding of farming and the countryside.

Most schools visit farms with the youngest year groups, although older children will also benefit from learning more about farming and spending time with the animals.

▶ **Sacred spaces**: Visiting sacred spaces such as churches, mosques, temples and other places of worship:
- supports religious education
- gives children and young people a greater understanding of other faiths
- contributes to their spiritual, moral, social and cultural development.

Good to know

▶ Detailed **risk assessments** must be completed when taking pupils out of school for any reason, and parental consent is always required.
▶ You will need to ensure that pupils with allergies, SEND and medical needs have the equipment or medicines they need with them, and can access the outdoor learning environment.
▶ Adult-to-pupil ratios will need to be considered in planning and practised during outdoor learning opportunities.

Key term

Risk assessment: a check for potential risks so that measures may be put in place to control them.

For more on risk assessments, see Core Skill 4 on page 207.

Key aspects of different theoretical and philosophical approaches that relate to outdoor education

Forest School

The concept of Forest School initially came from Scandinavia, and they were first set up in the UK in the 1990s. The UK definition of Forest School is:

'An inspirational process that offers children, young people and adults regular opportunities to achieve, develop confidence and self-esteem through hands-on learning experiences in a local woodland environment.'

Source: Forest School, 2002

Forest School has six principles and criteria for good practice:

> **Principle 1** Forest School is a long-term process of frequent and regular sessions in a woodland or natural environment, rather than a one-off visit. Planning, adaptation, observations and reviewing are integral elements of Forest School.
>
> **Principle 2** Forest School takes place in a woodland or natural wooded environment to support the development of a relationship between the learner and the natural world.
>
> **Principle 3** Forest School aims to promote the holistic development of all those involved, fostering resilient, confident, independent and creative learners.
>
> **Principle 4** Forest School offers learners the opportunity to take supported risks appropriate to the environment and to their age group.
>
> **Principle 5** Forest School is run by qualified Forest School practitioners who continuously maintain and develop their professional practice.
>
> **Principle 6** Forest School uses a range of learner-centred processes to create a community for development and learning.
>
> Source: Forest School, 2011

An important aspect of Forest School is in developing the area of risk and challenge in children and young people. Activities are developed which:
- are appropriate to the age of the learners
- allow them to take supported risks in a safe environment.

This is valuable, as being able to assess risk helps to develop children's confidence, resilience and self-esteem and prepares them for adult life.

Margaret McMillan

'The best classroom and the richest cupboard is roofed only by the sky'

Margaret McMillan

Margaret McMillan (1860–1931) was an educator who carried out extensive work with deprived children in London and Bradford, and pioneered the importance of holistic education for children.

She felt that it was important for us to understand the whole child and to care for every aspect of their development, including their health and wellbeing. She believed that outdoor play:
- was essential for children's health and wellbeing
- supported children's learning
- developed a play-centred approach.

> **Reflect**
>
> How has Margaret McMillan's work influenced the way in which our curriculum is structured today?
>
> Can you see a link to any specific areas?

K1.7 What distinctive qualities are offered by the outdoors as an educational environment compared to traditional classroom environments

As we have already seen, the outdoors offers different qualities to the teaching and learning experiences of pupils, while also giving them freedom from the physical constraints of the classroom. The table on the following page shows the key distinctive qualities and what they offer to pupils.

▲ Why is it important for children and young people to have opportunities to explore the outdoors as a learning environment?

Distinctive quality	What it offers pupils
Greater opportunity for risk and challenge	The outdoor environment offers pupils a greater opportunity to recognise and understand risks and challenges for themselves. The environment should be as safe as possible for pupils to explore, and health and safety checks should be made by adults to check equipment and any areas which are hazardous to children. However, the outdoor environment does offer more opportunities for pupils to assess for themselves the kinds of risks they are taking when going into different situations.
Space	Being in an outdoor space offers children and young people freedom from the normal confines of the classroom. It enables them to learn in a situation where they are not limited by four walls, and where the space is larger and constantly changing.
Animals, plants and lifecycles	The outdoors enables pupils to look at plants and animals in their natural habitat. It gives them a greater opportunity to understand the importance of nurturing and preserving the natural environment, and showing them how it relates to their own lives, for example through farming.
Changing seasons/ changing weather	Being outside gives pupils the opportunity to: • look closely at features which change with the seasons • experience the changes in weather and how they affect plants and nature.

Reflect

Watch a 4-minute promotional video for Farms for City Children, about residential trips where children from urban environments stay for a week to experience life on a working farm. This can be found on their website: https://farmsforcitychildren.org/about-us/
- Which of the distinctive qualities in the table does the farm residential offer children?
- Give three examples of what the children are learning during their time on the farm.
- How does the outdoor environment enhance the learning experience of all children, whatever their needs?

Skills practice

1 What age are children at the end of Key Stage 2?
2 What is the difference between teacher- and student-led provision?
3 Explain what is meant by inquiry-based learning.
4 How might constructivist theories underpin teaching and learning?
5 Give an example of when it may be necessary to work one-to-one with a pupil.
6 Why is group work an effective method of learning?
7 Explain the importance of giving feedback to pupils.
8 Explain the importance of giving feedback to teachers.
9 How does learning outside the classroom positively enhance children's education and development?
10 What is the central idea in Margaret McMillan's work?

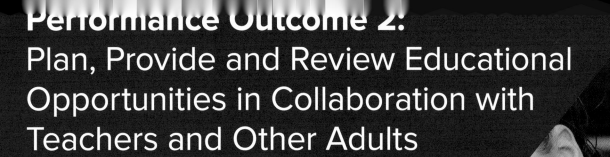

Performance Outcome 2:
Plan, Provide and Review Educational Opportunities in Collaboration with Teachers and Other Adults

In your role as a teaching assistant, you will need to work closely with teachers and other colleagues to plan, provide and review educational opportunities. This means that you should collaborate when planning and reviewing learning activities, and when considering different types of assessment.

You will need to look at the different factors which may impact on children's learning and development, and ways in which you might recognise that a pupil needs additional support. You also need to be aware of the kinds of strategies which might be used to promote mathematical thinking and literacy, as these are key areas which you will be asked to support through interventions.

Learning outcomes

This chapter covers the following knowledge outcomes for Performance Outcome 2.

K2.1	Different approaches to planning for learning and how they are used in practice
K2.2	Different types of assessment and their purpose
K2.3	How biological and environmental factors may impact on children's learning and development
K2.4	Factors which may indicate a pupil is in need of additional support
K2.5	How a range of strategies are used to promote mathematical thinking
K2.6	A range of strategies used to promote literacy

K2.1 Different approaches to planning for learning and how they are used in practice

The planning cycle

As we have already discussed in Core Chapter 8 on observation and assessment, it is important to know and understand that planning and assessment are part of a cycle.

Planning, delivering and reviewing learning activities lead into one another. This means that they must be considered together and cannot be looked at in isolation.

As you become more experienced, it will be helpful for colleagues if you can join in the planning process so that:
▶ when you support learning activities, you have a clearer idea about what is expected in advance
▶ you can contribute your own knowledge about the needs and abilities of pupils.

> See also Core Chapter 8, Section 8.3.

The planning cycle can be adapted and used for long-, medium- and short-term planning, as it helps us to review and think about our approach to teaching and learning.

Short-, medium- and long-term planning

Teachers usually create different types of plan that are used at different stages of the academic year. These are known as short-, medium- and long-term plans. Schools and individual teachers devise their own formats so that they use the one which works best for them.

There might be some overlap between the different plans, for example a plan for the week could come under medium- or short-term planning.

Type of plan	How these support learning
Long-term plans and schemes of work (also known as schemes of learning)	These are usually compiled well in advance and might be reused every year, with some amendments. You are unlikely to be involved with these as a teaching assistant, because they are set by year groups in primary schools and by subject or department areas in secondary. Depending on the size of the school, they are also likely to be created by more than one person as part of a team. Long-term plans might be created at the beginning of the school year so that: • it is clear what is going to be covered in the curriculum • staff can plan for the resources and equipment which will be needed, particularly if a large team will need to use them. They are usually stored in school computer systems so that staff can refer to them, and can be printed out if necessary.
Medium-term plans	These plans might be for the term or half-term, as well as for the week. • Termly or half-termly plans are broken down into weeks and show progression over time. • They have more details about individual learning activities and learning objectives, and should include space for notes or amendments depending on pupils' learning outcomes. Again, these are likely to be stored on school computer systems and placed in class or subject planning folders.
Short-term plans	These are plans for the week or for the day. They are detailed and include timings, objectives, assessment information and details about additional resources and support. • You might be involved with these if you are invited to planning meetings with teachers. This could be a formal arrangement with time set aside each week to plan together, or it could happen through informal discussions and conversations before and after the activities take place. • Teachers are also likely to have more detailed **lesson plans**, particularly in the core subjects, which might include pupil groups, information for support staff and the resources that will be needed. You need to know about the way in which teachers plan so that you can contribute and offer your own suggestions.

Research

If you have not seen them, ask to look at copies of long-, medium- and short-term plans for the pupils or class you support.

▶ How do they feed into each other?

▶ What key information can you find in each?

Science Medium-Term Planning

YEAR: 6	Teacher: Mrs B Support staff for first 30 mins of session: Mrs L	Term: 2 Topic Title: Reversible and Irreversible Changes/Changing Circuits	Time: Tuesday 1.30–3.30

WEEK	LEARNING OBJECTIVES	LEARNING ACTIVITY	Evaluation/Next steps
1 5/01/18	To recognise that mixing materials with water can cause them to change and that some changes are reversible.	• Start with quick quiz on work done last term. • Revise work done last term on dissolving and go over important vocabulary – solution, suspension, evaporation. • Go through homework from end of last term and think about what happened to the solutions on the windowsill and write up. • Important to recognise that dissolving is only one type of change. Is it reversible or irreversible? Ask pupils to assess their learning from last term with support from Mrs L. • Ask what they would do to separate a) salt and b) sand from water. Introduce the word 'reversible' to describe the changes. Show interactive BBC clip as a refresher. • Carry out investigation using plaster of Paris, some cement, cornflour, salt, flour, powder paint, baking powder, Andrews Salts/water and observe what happens. Mix them up and then try to separate them. • If they finish this try to think of some of their own which are reversible/irreversible.	• Kelly very good with quiz and especially definition of forces. • Mia did not give good example of food chain. • Josh remembered photosynthesis. • Alex not clear on how to get a solid back from a liquid. • All seemed to understand reversible/irreversible. • Adam/Elijah absent.
2 12/01/18	To recognise that heat ing materials can cause them to change and new materials to be formed.	• Remind students about last week and ask them to check back over their work after marking, particularly the write up of the investigation. Mrs L to support/note down any issues. • Put a series of objects on each table – egg, chocolate, water, wood, wax, paper, popcorn one at a time and ask children to answer questions on whiteboards about what will happen when they are heated. • Show photos and discuss fact that irreversible changes often caused by heating. • Move on to discuss what happens when you mix things together to cook them – what is this change? Discuss difference between physical and chemical changes – physical can be reversed, chemical cannot and a new substance can be made. • Complete test base questions, no time to do last week. • Talk about their ideas and ask them to suggest materials that are changed by cooling and decide whether these changes are reversible or irreversible. Make sure to distinguish the difference between burning and heating. • Discuss the kinds of materials and watch video on reversible and irreversible changes at end of lesson (15 mins).	All very impressed by video and understood concept of an irreversible change.

▲ A medium-term plan

Practice points

▶ Always plan with teachers if possible, or ask them to email you short-term plans in advance.

▶ Ask to see long- and medium-term plans, or look on the school's system so that you understand how lessons fit into the overall plans.

▶ Check planning and your role before the lesson so that you can prepare.

▶ Don't be afraid to put forward your own suggestions at the planning stage.

▶ Check with teachers before bringing any resources from home.

Planning according to the needs of the pupils

Planning alongside teachers and tutors is beneficial for everyone – pupils, teachers and support staff:
▶ It opens a dialogue between staff.
▶ Ideas and resources can be shared.

Planning should be accessible, transparent and easy to use, with clear objectives.

Class and setting

Although there are no set formats for school plans, staff need to use the school's planning format so that:
▶ planning is consistent between classes, subjects or year groups
▶ all those who need to see the plans can find key information quickly and easily.

Work for classes should be planned in a way which shows progression through different subjects and topics, and provides extension activities and a wider development of ideas.

Groups and individuals

Planning together also ensures that colleagues plan for the needs of individual pupils and support inclusion.

As staff work closely with pupils and groups, you and your colleagues will know about pupils' individual needs and interests, and will be able to discuss the best approach to learning activities. This will help you to meet everyone's needs effectively and engage pupils in their learning.

In some cases:
▶ you might know more about individual students than the teachers do, particularly if you work to support one pupil every day as an **individual support assistant**
▶ you will also know which pupils work well together and those who might be better off in different groups.

It is important to share your knowledge of how individual pupils learn with teaching staff, so that plans can be personalised and **differentiated** to provide appropriate strategies for them.

Key terms

Individual support assistant: an assistant who supports one pupil with specific needs.

Differentiation: setting work at an accessible level for each pupil and their needs.

The purpose, strengths and weaknesses of different approaches to assessment

For more on types of assessment used in the classroom and their purpose, you can look back at Core Chapter 8.

You will need to be able to understand and use different forms of assessment, both during and after teaching and learning activities. These give us different ways of finding out information about what pupils know and understand, and each has strengths and weaknesses.

Over time, you will probably use every method of assessment shown in this table.

Type of assessment	Strengths	Weaknesses
Observation	• A quick way to find out about pupils' learning and development • Helps to plan how to meet pupils' individual needs • Staff might observe things they do not usually see due to other commitments	• Making notes can be time-consuming • Staff presence can be a distraction for pupils, so observation might not be a true representation • Staff need to be very clear on what they are observing and the type of observation they are carrying out to use time effectively
Question and answer	• Staff can question pupils directly to find out exactly what they know • Questions can be targeted to individuals • Careful questioning is also a way of scaffolding and extending pupils' learning	• There can be a temptation to 'over-lead' teaching and learning through the questions • Poorly worded or closed questioning can shut down learning
Group tasks	• Staff can assess how pupils interact with and respond to each other • There are opportunities to self- and peer-assess • Group tasks might give some individuals more confidence	• It might be difficult to capture all assessment opportunities as learning is fast-paced • Might not be able to assess individual pupils

Type of assessment	Strengths	Weaknesses
Tests/written exams	• Tests and written exams are a way of gathering information about what pupils know at a specific time (e.g. end of a topic or key stage)	• Testing and written exams might not suit some pupils – they may become anxious or be unable to write down information under pressure. So this might not give a true representation of what they know
Assessment for learning	• Enables pupils to peer- and self-assess • Supports independent learning and self-evaluation • Feeds into planning and helps to set targets	• Adults need to provide pupils with initial support and monitor progress • Not a substitute for teacher assessment

K2.2 Different types of assessment and their purpose

The different types of assessment include:
▶ diagnostic
▶ formative
▶ benchmark (interim)
▶ summative
▶ statutory.

We looked at this knowledge outcome in Core Chapter 8. You will need to reread page 142 to check that you understand different types of assessment and their purpose.

Test yourself

1 What is the purpose of assessment?
2 Explain the difference between formative and summative assessment.
3 Name three types of statutory assessment used in schools.
4 Outline the strengths and weaknesses of two types of assessment.
5 How does questioning pupils support assessment?
6 What is assessment for learning?

K2.3 How biological and environmental factors may impact on children's learning and development

As we have seen in Core Chapter 7, children's development usually follows an expected pattern of development related to their age as they grow up. Areas of development are usually defined as:
▶ physical
▶ cognitive
▶ social and emotional
▶ communication and language.

However, there are a range of influences on children's development, and they will not all reach the same milestones at the same time. Some of these factors might have a more significant impact, either positive or negative.

Biological factors

Biological factors are linked to events that occur before or during birth. They include:
▶ factors directly linked to a child's genetic inheritance
▶ changes to the genes as a result of a faulty egg or sperm.

In some cases, biological factors are immediately apparent, such as where a child is born with a heart condition. In other cases, something in the environment may be a trigger. A good example of this is asthma:
▶ A child might be born predisposed to asthma, but as a result of living in an area with high levels of pollution, the asthma is triggered.

The table on the next page shows some examples of biological factors.

Factor	Impact on physical, cognitive or social and emotional development
Physical/mental health – these may be linked to genetic inheritance	Pupils will find it hard to concentrate in school if they are: • not in good health, either physically or mentally • suffering from pain due to physical conditions. They might have regular absences from school if they have medical conditions, which could impact on their work in school and affect their cognitive development. If they are unwell, they are less likely to want to join in with activities and be sociable with their friends. They might lose confidence, which in turn can affect their social and emotional development. Mental health issues can also have an impact on children's and young people's development – socially, emotionally and academically. The most recent survey of mental health in children and young people (gov.uk, October 2019) found that 12.5% of 5- to 19-year-olds had at least one mental disorder when assessed, and that 5% met the criteria for two or more mental health conditions.
Special educational needs and disabilities (SEND)	• Some SEND are more likely as a result of genetic inheritance, such as autism spectrum disorders or dyslexia. • Others might occur during pregnancy and birth, such as foetal alcohol syndrome or a lack of oxygen at birth. Children with SEND might need more support to master some skills, both physical and cognitive. Some children with social learning difficulties might find it harder to make friends. This will therefore impact on their social and emotional development.
Disabilities	Disabilities affect physical or sensory development. • Some disabilities are linked to genetic inheritance. • Others may occur during pregnancy and birth. Children with a disability might need additional support or equipment to join in activities. They might feel different to other children, which will affect their social and emotional development. Some children might have more absences from early years settings or schools as a result of medical or other appointments. If they have repeated absences, this might impact on their learning, as well as their social and emotional development.
Stage and rate of development/ atypical development	Children's and young people's stage and rate of development directly impacts on their learning and development. • Many milestones such as learning to walk and talk, learning to read, being able to share with others and so on will happen at a broadly similar age. • While all children pass through different stages, they might do so at different rates. This means that although children reach developmental milestones at similar times, they will not always be the same. • Development is 'atypical' when it is happening at a very different rate or pattern to others.

Environmental factors

Environmental factors are those things that happen around and to us. Our development is shaped by:
▶ where we live
▶ the size of our family
▶ all of our early experiences, including our
  relationships with parents.

Factor	Impact on physical, cognitive, or social and emotional development
Access to play spaces and the outdoor environment	We have already seen in Performance Outcome 1 in Sections K1.6 and K1.7 that access to the outdoor environment gives children and young people the benefits of developing all areas, particularly physical and social and emotional development. Fresh air and exercise: • benefit children's physical and mental wellbeing • enable them to learn to assess risks and develop confidence and independence.
Financial	Sadly, there is a link between growing up in a poor family and the learning and development of children. This is because having enough money gives families more options. They might: • live in safer and larger homes • be able to buy healthier food (which can improve health and development) • have more opportunities to do things that provide stimulation and enjoyment, e.g. going on holidays, music and swimming lessons.
Parental support	It is now recognised that parents who have access to support and advice might find it easier to: • make early attachments • cope with some of the demands of parenting. The stress levels of parents who feel supported are lower. This reduces stress in children, which is known to affect brain development and health.
Care status	Children who spend time in care or foster homes might: • not form secure attachments • have been removed from their main attachment without forming a new one. This can have an effect on their social and emotional development because they are likely to show signs of separation anxiety or clinginess, and also regression, particularly if they are continually being moved around. There is more information on care status and attachments in Core Chapter 7.
Early attachments	As we saw in Core Chapter 7, early attachments are highly important. Research has shown that babies and children who have strong first attachments will go on to have positive relationships themselves. If these early attachments are not secure, this might: • cause them to have lower self-esteem • affect their behaviour and ability to trust others.
Interpersonal relationships	Children and young people are likely to have good confidence levels and high self-esteem if they have positive relationships with their: • families and friends from an early age • teachers and other adults in school. Children who do not have opportunities to interact regularly with adults might also be affected in the area of speech and language development.

▲ How do early attachments affect children's development?

Test yourself

1 How does having access to the outdoor environment support children's development?
2 What biological factors have an impact on children's social and emotional development?
3 What is the significance of early attachment on children's development?

K2.4 Factors which may indicate a pupil is in need of additional support

Your role as a teaching assistant

As a teaching assistant, you might be regularly asked to work with pupils who have already been identified as needing additional support for their work or behaviour. These pupils might have a diagnosis which relates to their special educational need, such as dyslexia or autism spectrum disorder, or have learning needs in a particular subject area.

In this situation, you should be:
- ▶ told about any areas of difficulty
- ▶ given strategies and ideas to support their learning and development, and their progress towards specific targets.

You might work with them through specific intervention sessions or through additional support in class.

It is also part of your role in class to look out for signs that a pupil might need additional support. This might be for academic work, behaviour or mental health issues.

The sooner this need is recognised, the sooner interventions and additional provision can be put in place to support the child:
- ▶ Research on development of the brain has shown that early learning forms the basis of all future learning.
- ▶ Pupils who have SEND are at greater risk of falling behind their peers in reaching their potential, so action should be taken as soon as possible to support them through interventions.
- ▶ If pupils' needs are related to their behaviour or are due to social and emotional or mental health needs, staff will need to find out about the causes so that they are able to provide effective support.

If you are working with a pupil and have a cause for concern in any of these areas, you should speak to teachers and your SENDCo as soon as you can. If this is not possible for any reason, make a note of your observations so that you can back up what you have noticed with examples and tell colleagues about them.

▲ What should you do if you have a concern about a pupil's needs?

Factors indicating additional support is required

Delayed speech and language skills

You might notice over time that pupils are not making the same progress as their peers in the area of speech and language. The kinds of things you may notice include:
- ▶ reluctance to talk
- ▶ difficulty in making friends and socialising
- ▶ limited vocabulary
- ▶ difficulty in expressing themselves (using expressive language)
- ▶ difficulty in understanding others (using receptive language)
- ▶ frustration and poor behaviour when trying to get thoughts and ideas across
- ▶ problems articulating some speech sounds.

Delayed speech and language can be caused by a range of factors. It is important to assess this as soon as possible, because the development of language supports teaching and learning as well as enabling us to socialise and express ourselves. If pupils' speech is delayed, it can have an impact on other areas of development.

In some cases, pupils might not speak at all.
- ▶ This is known as selective mutism and is usually caused by severe anxiety.
- ▶ They might speak to their peers but not with adults, or speak at home but not in school, depending on where they feel most confident.

It is important for selective mutism to be treated and managed sensitively so that the child's anxiety can be reduced, rather than by putting them under pressure to speak.

If you are asked to work with a pupil who has delayed speech and language skills, you should have help from other professionals such as a speech therapist and your school SENDCo, so that you can support them effectively.

> For more on language development in children, how to support pupils and how it impacts on learning, see Core Chapter 7.

Good to know

Children and young people on the autism spectrum often find communication and social interaction difficult, as this is one of the features of the condition. In some cases, they do not see a need to communicate with others so they might avoid these kinds of situations and prefer to 'zone out'.

Staff working with pupils on the autism spectrum need to follow the advice of specialist teachers and speech and language therapists to support the development of their communication skills.

Not meeting academic milestones or finding work more challenging than others

You might find that:
▶ a pupil you are working with finds work more difficult than their peers
▶ teachers tell you which pupils are not meeting academic milestones, after completing summative assessments.

In these situations, pupils might need to be monitored more closely and given extra support to enable them to continue to make progress.

If you have concerns about a pupil, always highlight specific issues or things which have happened, so that you can provide examples to support what you are saying when you speak to colleagues.

Case study

You are working in a Year 2 class as a teaching assistant to support a small group of four pupils during maths lessons. You have got to know them well during the term and have some additional concerns about Emma, who is in your group and has always found maths challenging. You have noticed that:
▶ although she was trying very hard at the beginning of term, she has lost interest and is not making the same progress as others in the group
▶ she has become quite withdrawn and doesn't want to contribute to group conversations.

The pupils will have Key Stage 1 teacher assessments in a few months. You decide to speak to the teacher about her.
▶ Give two reasons why it is important to outline your concerns to the teacher.
▶ What specific issues would you highlight to the teacher?
▶ Write down two suggestions for further support you could offer Emma to discuss with the teacher.

Social, emotional and mental health factors

In some cases, pupils display behaviour which may cause staff to suspect social, emotional and mental health factors. The kind of behaviour which can cause concern could include:
▶ finding it very difficult to manage or regulate their emotions, for example having regular outbursts
▶ disrupting their own and others' learning with their behaviour
▶ a lack of confidence or withdrawn behaviour which is different from how they normally behave
▶ being unable to stay focused on activities, or hyperactivity
▶ immature social skills
▶ increased dependence on adults.

Children and young people might occasionally display some of these behaviours without raising concern, but if these are regular or ongoing behaviours, you should speak to teachers so that strategies can be put in place to support them.

> For more on supporting pupils with social and emotional needs, and on managing self-regulation, revisit Core Chapter 4 on page 64.

Sensory and/or physical factors, such as hearing loss or visual impairment

Pupils who have sensory or physical needs might not need additional support, and might have adapted well to the classroom environment with additional resources such as hearing loops, additional technologies or other adaptations. However, additional support might be needed if:

▶ their needs change as they grow older and the school curriculum becomes more complex
▶ they have a health condition which is progressive or newly diagnosed

▶ they have suffered a trauma such as an accident which has restricted their physical movement and affected their mental health.

As you get to know pupils, you will become aware of how they can manage their own needs and whether they need adult intervention.

Case study

Shella is in Year 2 and has recently been diagnosed with juvenile rheumatoid arthritis. She is able to take part in all learning activities with her peers including PE.

Lately you have noticed that she is finding her work more difficult in the afternoons and she says that her joints are hurting more. You know that the condition makes her tired and that she is on medication.

Amal is in Year 7 and has a visual condition called nystagmus which means that he cannot control the movement in his eyes. He also has very limited vision and needs quite bright light to be able to see anything.

Amal never had support in his small primary school, but now he has been provided with additional equipment and written materials made larger. Amal has

coped well with the transition to secondary school; he has made friends, and staff and pupils are aware of his needs. His parents have said that they would like him to be as independent as possible.

You are based in Year 7 and have noticed that Amal finds it difficult to arrive at lessons on time as he is still finding his way around. You have also noticed he has some problems with organisation – several times he has not completed his homework. You are concerned that he will start to fall behind with his work.

In each case, your role is that of a general classroom assistant.

▶ Do either of these pupils need additional support in your view? Explain why or why not.
▶ What should you do first in each case?

K2.5 How a range of strategies are used to promote mathematical thinking

When you are working with pupils to promote and develop mathematical thinking, you should know some of the different strategies which you can use.

▶ As maths is a broad and often abstract subject, it can sometimes be difficult for pupils to quickly pick up on and remember new concepts and ideas.

▶ Maths is a subject where pupils build on what they know. They need to understand and be confident with simpler concepts before moving on to more abstract ones.

As you become more experienced, you may also develop some strategies of your own to support them.

Strategy to promote mathematical thinking	How this may be used
Use of real-world examples and incidental learning to highlight maths concepts	Using real-world examples is very important, particularly for primary-aged children, as they need to develop an understanding of the significance of maths to their own experiences. Ways in which we use maths in everyday life include: • using timetables • converting temperatures • managing time • recipes • estimating costs and budgeting • making things. Problem-solving activities are therefore a useful way of using and applying maths in real-life situations. It can also be helpful to relate maths skills to other subjects, so that pupils develop an awareness of its relevance to them. • Looking for opportunities to include maths in subjects such as PE can engage older pupils and motivate them. • You could do this with topics such as estimating, keeping scores and measuring distances, and the language and vocabulary associated with position and direction.

Practical everyday tasks to reinforce concepts	Using practical tasks is often helpful when you are working on maths activities. This should also be used where possible to help pupils consolidate their use of maths. For example: • Food technology or cooking with pupils is an excellent way of reinforcing the concepts of weighing and their use of numbers. • Being able to read and understand a mobile phone bill or understand the different ways in which statistics can be used can engage older pupils.
A language-rich environment that includes mathematical vocabulary	Classrooms and other areas in the learning environment should include displays which involve mathematical language so that pupils can refer to them and develop their use of mathematical vocabulary. • Being able to talk about ideas and to reason is an important aspect of maths, and pupils who do not have an adequate vocabulary or who have poor speech and language skills will be at a disadvantage. • Displays can also include the stages to use when carrying out specific activities, or when learning about a particular topic or working on new concepts. This can help pupils to remember specific words or phrases.
Appropriate resources and equipment	As with all curriculum subjects, it is very important for pupils to have access to the appropriate resources and equipment during the lesson. • There must be enough for all of them to use so that teaching and learning is not interrupted. • Look at plans and resources in advance, along with the requirements of other year groups or classes so that you know there will be enough for everyone at the required time.
Scaffolding mathematical learning	When supporting maths, it is very important for you to be confident and understand concepts yourself, so that you can scaffold pupils' learning. Scaffolding means developing and extending children's existing knowledge, so you will need to know what came before and what comes afterwards. This will help you to: • extend the learning of pupils who grasp new ideas quickly • support the learning of those who find it more difficult, as they might need to go over the previous step again.
Repetition to reinforce concepts	Repeating and going over mathematical tasks helps to reinforce new concepts so that pupils remember the process and feel more secure in their learning. • Repetition is a way of consolidating and strengthening learning, because we need to practise and repeat experiences to help us remember them and develop confidence. • Talking about maths with pupils is a good way of going over what they have done and checking their understanding. • Asking pupils to talk about what they are doing while they are doing it is also a way of reinforcing and remembering the steps they are going through.

Questioning and prompting pupils to check learning	To check and assess learning in any subject, we need to question pupils about what they know.
	
	In a maths context, at the start of an activity this could include revising what they have done in previous sessions and, following teaching input, talking through what they are going to do next. For example:
	• When talking about percentages, pupils might talk through and remember easy tips for working them out.
	• You might need to prompt to help them remember, such as:
	  – reminding them about what they did last time
	  – asking them what they need to do first.
	
	You should not give them the answers, but help pupils by leading or directing them when they don't know what to do next.

Praise and feedback to promote self-esteem	When supporting pupils, particularly on maths activities where they can lack confidence, it is important to give them some feedback as they are working. • Where they are progressing well, the use of praise will give them encouragement and motivation to keep going. • If they have made errors, it is better to notice the effort that they are making while gently asking them to check their work. For example, you could praise their use of the method and steps in a calculation but ask them to look closely at a part they have done incorrectly. In this way, pupils will be looking both at the process and the actual calculation.

▲ How does the learning environment in your school support mathematical learning?

Remember to use opportunities to develop maths skills when you are working in other areas of the curriculum, particularly if you find that there is a clear overlap. For example, you might use maths skills in science or geography.

Reminding pupils about their maths skills while they work on the wider curriculum helps them to consolidate and practise what they already know.

▶ Unplanned opportunities might be easier to do with younger children – for example 'How many children are here today if there are three missing?'

▶ You can also find opportunities with older age groups – for example, when putting on a play at the school and working out how many seats are needed as well as catering or parking needs.

Case study

Jenna works in a secondary school and supports Maya, who has mild learning difficulties and a long-term medical condition requiring medication. Jenna is with Maya for 15 hours a week in the mornings.

Maya missed some of her primary school education due to her health needs and lacks confidence in maths. In her history lesson, Year 8 are presenting some information in the form of a line graph. Jenna knows that the class have recently been working on data collection in maths and that Maya might have some difficulty in presenting the information.

▶ How should Jenna approach this?
▶ What steps could she take to encourage Maya and to support the development of her maths skills?

Research

Investigate the National Curriculum for mathematics in the age group you support.

▶ Look at the headings for different aspects of mathematics. Why do you think it is divided in this way?

▶ Choose one aspect of mathematics (for example, geometry) and look at the progression between Year 1 and Year 9. How does the curriculum build on what pupils already know?

K2.6 A range of strategies used to promote literacy

As well as mathematics, you might be asked to work with pupils to develop their literacy skills. This will not just be in literacy lessons but also across the curriculum, as pupils might need support with their written work or their ability to articulate what they want to say.

English itself is also a very broad subject:

▶ It incorporates reading and writing as well as spoken language.

▶ According to the National Curriculum document, 'Spoken language underpins the development of reading and writing' (Source: National curriculum in England: English programmes of study 2013, page 3).

▶ Language is the basis of our ability to think and reason. It is very important that pupils hear a good quality and variety of language and vocabulary, so that they are encouraged to talk and discuss things in different contexts. This will support the development of all their literacy skills.

▲ Literacy skills

As literacy encompasses so many skills, reading and writing can prove challenging for many pupils in different ways. You will need to be able to support and encourage them throughout all key stages. Even as adults we are always refining these skills and learning new vocabulary.

Literacy strategies

The use of systematic synthetic phonics

All pupils are taught the use of phonics when learning to read and write, and you might need to remind or encourage them to do this when carrying out learning activities.

Phonics encourages the use of 'sounding out' or hearing the sounds within words, and children are taught to name the different phonemes as well as diagraphs and trigraphs, and to use these terms. Make sure that you know the different terms that are used to describe different aspects of the phonics system.

The phonics system is used throughout Key Stages 1 and 2 and beyond to support the development of reading and writing.

If you are working with the youngest pupils, try to observe or find out how they are taught at the initial stages, as many schools use specific programmes to teach phonics. You can then incorporate this into what you are doing, for example 'Do you remember using "p" for "puff out the candles"?'

> **Good to know**
>
> Staff working with younger pupils will need to be consistent to ensure that they pronounce or say phonemes in the same way. For example:
> ▶ When saying the sounds 's' or 'm' they should be pronounced 'sssssssss' or 'mmmmmmm' rather than 'suh' or 'em'.
> ▶ This is important because pupils will not be able to blend the sounds together to form words if they pronounce phonemes incorrectly.

Reading for meaning and enjoyment

Classrooms and libraries in schools should have a wide range of reading material available for pupils on a wide variety of topics.
▶ This should be accessible and well organised so that pupils can find what they need.
▶ As pupils develop their reading skills, they become more independent and use books for reference and enjoyment.

Listening to stories and reading fiction and non-fiction books with adults from an early age:
▶ enables children to have conversations and discussions about people, places and events
▶ develops their knowledge and understanding about things which they may not have seen for themselves.

Reading should be seen as a pleasure and something which they want to learn to do as it sparks their curiosity, and you should role-model reading so that children see you enjoying it.
▶ At the earliest stages, adults should regularly talk to children about what they are reading, questioning them to check their understanding and sharing ideas about books.
▶ Parents should also be encouraged to do this on a regular basis.
▶ As they develop their reading skills, children can explore topics which interest them in more detail, and this develops their confidence and motivates them.

See also the section on improving pupils' confidence in reading and writing on page 243.

Research

Speak to your school's literacy coordinator about the ways in which your school encourages pupils to read for meaning and enjoyment.
▶ What resources are available?
▶ How else does the school give pupils opportunities to share their reading experiences?

Providing specific feedback on the accurate use of spelling, punctuation and grammar

When supporting pupils' learning, you will need to be able to give pupils specific feedback on their use of spelling, punctuation and grammar. (Sometimes this is called SPaG in school during literacy sessions.)

This means that you will need to be sure about it yourself, and if you are in any doubt you should always ask teachers.

Spelling, punctuation and grammar is likely to be taught separately, and pupils need to use and apply what they have learned in their writing in literacy as well as other written subjects. You might need to:
▶ gently remind them if they forget that they have learned about something recently
▶ praise them for remembering to apply a grammatical, spelling or punctuation rule.

Before telling them the spelling or grammar rule, always give pupils the opportunity to recall and apply previous learning, or check back over their work.

	Strategy/feedback
Spelling	There are a few ways that you can give feedback about a pupil's spelling rather than telling them their spelling is incorrect. • Always encourage pupils to sound words out if they can or look around the classroom if it is a word on a display. • Encourage pupils to use dictionaries or word banks if they are unsure about a spelling. • If you know they have recently learned the word, for example in a spelling test, or they have used it before, ask them if they can remember any memory tricks, or remind them of a particular spelling rule.

| Punctuation/ grammar | The use of punctuation and grammar can be difficult for some pupils to remember, particularly rules such as the use of apostrophes, reported speech or correct tenses.
• There might be displays in the classroom to help.
• If they have had a lesson on it previously, you could ask them to check in their books. |

Pupils should also be taught the correct terms to use for different grammatical rules or identifying words, for example:
▶ the difference between a prefix and a suffix
▶ what a possessive pronoun is.

This means that all adults working with them should be comfortable with these terms and rules, and be able to use them too.

Research

Look at the National Curriculum for literacy for the key stage of the pupils you support. At the end of each key stage document you will find a glossary containing technical grammatical terms.
▶ Which ones do pupils find the hardest to identify and learn?
▶ What strategies can you think of to help them, based on the information here?
▶ Can you identify and name the grammatical terms for your age group?

Widening pupils' vocabulary

An important part of the National Curriculum for English is to encourage pupils to 'acquire a wide vocabulary'. When supporting pupils in doing this, you should look for opportunities to identify new words as they are working on learning activities or when talking to them.
▶ If you know the meaning of an interesting word which comes up, it is good practice to tell them about it.
▶ If they ask you about a word, instead of telling them straight away, encourage pupils to look it up in a dictionary or online if they can.
▶ Remember that you are a role model for the way in which pupils communicate with others, and that although you should use language and vocabulary which they will understand and which is appropriate for their age and stage of development,

you should also try to extend their knowledge. This can be done in a fun way, for example:

- a 'word of the week' with younger pupils
- word challenges for older pupils so that they have to find out the meaning of new words and phrases and use them.

When working on new topics or subjects, there will be opportunities for learners to discuss the new vocabulary they will need to know. Widening pupils' vocabulary is also particularly important if you are working with pupils who speak English as an additional language (EAL).

Case study

Alan is working outside on a field study with a group of Year 9s, including two pupils who speak English as an additional language. He has talked them through what they need to do and explained the process using specific vocabulary.

The pupils start their work and as he moves between them, he encourages them to talk through what they are doing and to tell him about it. Where they use vocabulary which is specific to geography and to the activity, he praises them and acknowledges this.

One of the pupils calls out that he has found something in the rocks, so Alan asks him if he can identify what it is. As he isn't sure, Alan comes back and the pupil tells him he thinks it is a fossil. They also discuss the type of rock and where he has found it.

- ▶ Give two examples of how Alan is supporting the pupils' literacy skills and their geographical skills during this activity.
- ▶ How else could Alan support the pupils who speak EAL during the activity?

Improving pupils' confidence in reading and writing

The development of reading, writing, speaking and listening skills supports the self-esteem and confidence of students in many ways, which will be felt on a daily basis.

- ▶ The process of communicating with others enhances a pupil's self-esteem.

- ▶ This is self-perpetuating as it enables them to express their own thoughts and feelings, feel acknowledged, and to develop relationships with others.
- ▶ It also gives children a starting point for reading and writing. Some of the strategies given above help to improve pupils' confidence in reading.

▲ How can you ensure that you develop children's confidence when reading with them?

Supporting reading

When listening to pupils read, particularly at the early stages, you can develop their confidence by showing that you are engaged and interested in what they are saying, and talking about the text with them.

- ▶ Talk to the pupil about what they are reading and encourage them to make predictions, explain facts or summarise the text at different stages.
- ▶ Ask them about what characters may be feeling or to retell parts of a story.
- ▶ If the book is non-fiction, question them about any interesting facts, remembering to use open questions. This is important because some pupils might be able to decode the words but be unable to talk about what they have read and what it means.
- ▶ When they reach an unknown word, encourage pupils to use picture cues, phonic cues and context cues. If they still have no idea, you might have to tell them the word. NEVER cover up pictures to try to catch them out – this can be demoralising.

Hearing pupils read

▶ Make sure the pupil is holding the book – not you.
▶ Encourage the pupil to point to the words to help them keep focused.
▶ Ask the pupil to use the initial sound of a word (**phonetic cues**) to help them guess a word if they need to.
▶ Encourage pupils to make substitutions that make sense in context if they are unable to decode them (**context cues**).
▶ If pupils are able readers, don't correct any mistakes too quickly. Give them time to realise that what they have read themselves doesn't make sense, and allow them to self-correct.
▶ If pupils make mistakes, ask them to check whether the word makes sense, or ask them to look again, rather than saying 'that's wrong'.
▶ Encourage them to 'word build' simple words if they have enough sounds to do this.
▶ Use plenty of praise, particularly if they have decoded an unfamiliar or difficult word.

Phonetic cues: sounds which are found in the word and help to identify it.

Context cues: cues which are suggested by the context of the text.

Supporting writing

Learning to write is a complex process. In order to be successful writers, pupils need to:
▶ know what they want to say
▶ be able to apply skills in phonics, spelling, punctuation and grammar
▶ be able to physically form the letters.

Lessons will be dedicated to each of these different aspects of writing, but pupils also need to be able to combine these skills when they are asked to write about something.
▶ To develop and improve pupils' confidence in writing, activities should be set at a level which is achievable for them, as it is very easy to damage their confidence at an early stage.

▶ Plenty of praise and encouragement is important, as is recognising effort as well as achievement. As writing incorporates so many different skills, pupils can become overwhelmed with what they are being asked to do.

You might have opportunities to 'rehearse' with pupils what they want to say before they try to write it. This is helpful for pupils who lack confidence with their writing, or are unsure about what they want to say, as they have an opportunity to practise and talk it through. It also means that they are sure about it before trying to write it down.

In some cases, you might be asked to **scribe** for pupils, if they find it difficult to write or to get their ideas down in time during the lesson.

Scribe: a person who writes or word processes a pupil's answers.

Supporting writing

▶ Draw attention to the formation of letters in contexts other than handwriting sessions.
▶ Use other opportunities and encourage pupils to talk about spellings, such as through the use of mnemonics, dictionaries and displays.
▶ If you see a relevant opportunity, remind pupils about teaching points from literacy lessons in other written work. For example: you know pupils have been thinking about the use of punctuation and then see they are writing a list during a history session.
▶ Encourage pupils to read back what they have written to check for meaning.
▶ Note their progress and relate their written work to writing targets if you can. For example: 'Well done Jack, your target is to make sure you use capital letters correctly and you have done it well throughout this piece of writing.'
▶ Do not correct every error as this will discourage pupils from trying. Choose the most important or representative errors to correct.

▲ How can you support the development of writing in pupils?

1 Explain two ways of developing reading for meaning.
2 How should you provide feedback to pupils on the accurate use of spelling?
3 Give three ways in which you can widen pupils' vocabulary.

Christopher is in Year 2 and lacks confidence with writing, although he is making progress with his reading. He tries very hard but finds the process of handwriting particularly difficult even though he has lots of ideas. He is constantly rubbing his work out and says that his mum has told him his writing is messy.

The teacher has asked you to support Christopher as he is repeatedly telling her he has finished but has only completed two lines of writing and says he 'can't do any more'.

▶ How might you approach the support you offer Christopher?
▶ What else could you do to help him with his confidence when approaching written work?

Skills practice

You are working in Year 3 and have been asked by the class teacher to deliver a phonics intervention programme to a group of four pupils twice a week, as they are finding reading and spelling more challenging than their peers.

You have been given a series of lesson plans for 15-minute sessions. These set out what needs to be taught. This is mainly revisiting previously taught phonics sessions, although you have been asked to go at a pace which works for the pupils.

You will also need to monitor and assess the pupils' learning as you go, to ensure that you are meeting their needs.

The teacher has given you the phonics sounds, which the children need to revise each day, and then games and consolidation activities to support their learning. These include 'Sound snap', 'Sound bingo', and other matching and sounding-out games. At the end of each session, the pupils will also need to check their own knowledge against a chart of the sounds which they have found it hard to learn.

The four pupils are:
▶ Hiromi – a very quiet pupil who lacks confidence and needs plenty of encouragement
▶ Tariq – a pupil who speaks English as an additional language, and who started at the school in September

▶ Maisie – a pupil who has a poor knowledge of high frequency and 'tricky' words, and who has been referred for speech and language therapy due to her difficulty in processing language
▶ Stanley – a lively pupil who finds it difficult to focus on written work and has a short attention span.

All four pupils have difficulty in segmenting and blending words.

As well as using the lesson plans from the teacher, write an outline of how you would continue to meet each pupil's needs during the intervention programme.

You should include:
▶ the kinds of resources you might use
▶ how you will use assessment to meet each pupil's needs
▶ how you will encourage the pupils to self- and peer-assess their learning during and after each session
▶ how you will use a range of strategies to enable pupils to engage with their learning and plan next steps.

Explain how you would ensure that you made note of each pupil's progress. What would you do if one or more of the pupils did not make any progress after several sessions?

Key term

Segmenting: breaking words up into individual sounds.
Blending: merging sounds together within words.

Performance Outcome 3:
Safeguard and Promote the Health, Safety and Wellbeing of Children and Young People

This chapter looks at how you can support safeguarding and the health, safety and wellbeing of pupils. Read it alongside Core Chapter 3, which covers the legislation and guidelines surrounding safeguarding, and the signs that a child or young person might be at risk.

We will look at the factors which contribute to a pupil's wellbeing and the importance of meeting their physical needs, alongside a range of common illnesses and infections and how you can respond to these. You will also need to know about the way in which individuals develop self-esteem and self-concept, and how you can use opportunities to develop their independence and control, promoting resilience within and outside the learning environment.

Learning outcomes

This chapter covers the following knowledge outcomes for Performance Outcome 3.

K3.1	How different factors can contribute to a pupil becoming physically or psychologically at risk, and the channels for reporting concerns
K3.2	Why it is important to share relevant information in a timely manner with the safeguarding lead
K3.3	How to promote the safe use of the technology and the web with pupils, including recognising and dealing with signs of cyber bullying and cyber grooming
K3.4	A range of signs of common illnesses/infections and the associated symptoms
K3.5	How illnesses and infections are spread
K3.6	The difference between accidents, injuries and emergency situations
K3.7	How a range of factors contribute to children's wellbeing
K3.8	A range of transitions that a pupil will experience through school and the possible positive and negative effects on pupils' wellbeing
K3.9	Why stable adult and peer relationships are important and the impact of disruption, including placement disruption, on a pupil's development and behaviour
K3.10	How a range of factors, in relation to family context, may impact on parenting
K3.11	Why physical care needs of pupils are important and the impact they may have on health and development, in accordance with Maslow's hierarchy of needs
K3.12	The positive impact of helping pupils to develop self-care skills and the strategies that can be used to support this
K3.13	The connection between pupils relating to others and their emotional resilience and wellbeing
K3.14	The possible impact of negative behaviours and the approaches to their management
K3.15	The strategies to help pupils understand, express and manage their feelings
K3.16	The positive effects of encouraging pupils to challenge and test their abilities
K3.17	Why the following policies and procedures are important within a school: first aid; health and safety; recording and reporting incidents
K3.18	How a range of factors can affect a pupil's self-concept
K3.19	Why it is important to give pupils independence and control
K3.20	How a range of factors impact on pupils' behaviour, and linking to attachment and emotional security as outlined in theories of attachment
K3.21	Why it is important to recognise and reward positive behaviour with reference to behaviourist approaches
K3.22	The expected levels of self-reliance and social behaviour at different ages and developmental stages

K3.1 How different factors can contribute to a pupil becoming physically or psychologically at risk, and the channels for reporting concerns

There are a large number of factors that can contribute to a pupil becoming physically or psychologically at risk of harm or abuse, and there can also be a combination of these factors present.

Pupils come from a range of backgrounds and families, and some individuals may be more vulnerable than others. Remember that:

▶ There may also be other risk factors.
▶ The presence of a factor does not necessarily mean that a pupil is at risk.

Identifying the factors

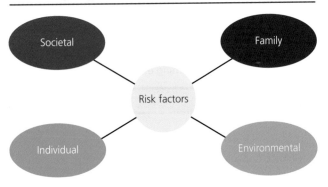

▲ Risk factors

Family and environmental factors

Research shows that many abusers are known to a child or young person, and that the abuse takes place either within the home or is carried out by a close family member or friend.

A background which is unstable because of one or more of the factors in the table below might mean that:

▶ abuse is less likely to be noticed, or
▶ the child suffers from neglect because parents or carers are preoccupied with their own needs.

Family risk factors	Reason for potential risk
Family breakdown	Family breakdown might mean that: • adults in the home are around the child or young person less, or • they are less likely to notice if a child or young person is withdrawn or anxious due to abuse, and put it down to the family break-up. At this time a child needs love and reassurance, so might also suffer emotional harm when they need care the most.
Harmful relationships	Harmful relationships within the home may mean that children and young people do not see role models for their close relationships. This means they are less likely to think that what is happening to them is wrong.
Physical or psychological abuse	If this type of abuse is happening within the home, it may make a child or young person feel that they are worthless, or that this is 'normal' behaviour.
Mental health issues	Having mental health issues might mean that a parent has difficulty in looking after their own needs, so the needs of the child or young person are less likely to be addressed. This could lead to issues of neglect or psychological abuse.
Criminality	Being brought up in or surrounded by criminal activity makes it harder for a child or young person to have the right moral influences or to distinguish between right and wrong. They might also have more contact with people who may harm them.

Family risk factors	Reason for potential risk
Substance addiction	A substance addiction within the home might again mean that: • the child's or young person's needs come second to those of the parent • the parent is not able to meet the child's or young person's needs. This can lead to the child being neglected.
Bereavement	A bereavement within the family might: • make a family member more vulnerable • act as the trigger for them to abuse a child or young person in a moment of anger or upset.
Domestic violence	If one of the partners in a family is a victim of domestic violence, it is more likely for a child or young person to be caught up in physical abuse.
Hereditary conditions	A parent or carer who has a hereditary condition, such as a chronic disease or illness, might find it more difficult to care for a child or young person. This can impact on the care and support the parent or carer is able to give, and may result in neglect.

Environmental risk factors	Reason for potential risk
Unsuitable housing	Unsuitable or inadequate housing might cause stress or frustration to the family, and mean that children or young people are more likely to suffer abuse.
Employment issues	If parents or carers have employment issues or are worried about their income, they might neglect to take care of the child's or young person's needs as they are unable to do this without support.
Low income	See both previous factors.
Care status	Looked after children or those who have lived in different foster or residential care homes might be more likely to suffer abuse.

Individual risk factors

Individual risk factors are due to the pupil's individual circumstances or needs. This means that the likelihood or risk of something happening to them is increased because of their situation.

Individual factors	Reason for potential risk
Special educational needs and disabilities (SEND)	According to the NSPCC: • Children and young people with SEND are at higher risk of being abused. • They are also more likely to be bullied. • They might find it more difficult to disclose or report what is happening to them.
Young carer	Young carers might be more likely to suffer from neglect and be more vulnerable as they focus on caring for their parent rather than on their own needs. Parents who have chronic conditions or illnesses might find it more difficult to focus on the needs of their children.
Health and wellbeing issues	If the child or young person has health or wellbeing issues, they might feel that they are not valued by others, or have low self-esteem. This could make them more vulnerable to abuse.
Mental health issues	If the child or young person has mental health issues or depression, they might: • be unable to report or realise what is happening to them • feel that they are worthless, which can lead to others seeing them in this way. This could make them more vulnerable to abuse.

Societal risk factors

Societal risk factors may exist due to cultural norms or expectations within a family or social group.

▶ In some cases, a family, culture or group may wish to continue to act in a way which is traditional to them, despite the requirements of UK laws.

▶ In others, friendship or social groups might have expectations which not all individuals wish, or are able, to conform to.

Societal risk factors	Reason for potential risk
Female genital mutilation (FGM)	FGM is a form of abuse and a criminal offence. • If parents or carers are responsible for arranging or assisting it, they are breaking the law. • If parents or those with parental responsibility fail to protect their child from FGM, they could also be convicted. • If a girl has been the victim of FGM, it is more likely for her to suffer other forms of abuse. See also Core Chapter 3, Section 3.1.
Forced marriage	In some cultures, forced marriages occur. • A forced marriage is when at least one of the couple does not consent. The young person is compelled to marry through pressure and coercion. • This pressure can take the form of physical violence or emotional and psychological pressure. These are all forms of abuse. It should be noted that forced marriage is different from arranged marriage. In an arranged marriage, both parties agree and the marriage is consensual and legal.
Honour killings	An honour killing takes place if a child or young person is killed by a member of their family. This might take place if the family believes that the child or young person has brought shame on the family or community for some reason. This reason is usually for not complying with the requirements of their culture, for example: • dressing in an 'inappropriate' way • refusing to agree to an arranged marriage • becoming pregnant outside marriage.
Social isolation	If a child or young person is socially isolated, they might be more vulnerable to, or at risk from, bullying from groups of children or young people.
Peer pressure	Peer pressure can cause abuse or bullying to take place. • In social situations, children and young people might not be confident enough to refuse to take part or report it. • If this happens, the abuse is likely to continue.
Gender inequalities	A child or young person might be more open to forms of psychological abuse if: • there is a culture of gender inequality • they are constantly told they will not be able to do or achieve something because they are male/female • the school or home does not believe in equality of opportunity.
Bullying	Bullying is a form of abuse which can escalate if not reported. It could take place: • within the home • outside the school • on social media through cyber bullying.
Anti-social behaviour	A child or young person could be more at risk if their friendship or social groups are taking part in anti-social behaviour. They could be easily led or get into groups which prey on more vulnerable individuals.

Societal risk factors	Reason for potential risk
Use of social media	Social media can put pressure on children or young people to abuse others.
	It allows them to do this anonymously, which can make their behaviour more cruel and harmful.

In many cases, a child or young person does not report abuse because:

▶ they are worried about what will happen or what their abuser will do
▶ they do not know who to tell or how to report it.

You should ensure that you are approachable and develop good relationships with pupils so that they are more likely to talk to you and disclose any concerns or worries that they have.

Associated signs of abuse

Sadly, there are a number of different types of abuse, and all adults who work with children and young people have a responsibility to be aware of and look out for signs of these in order to protect children and keep them safe.

According to the NSPCC, some children and young people might also be more at risk, for example:

▶ those in care
▶ those who are suffering neglect
▶ those with disabilities.

Abuse is likely to be very traumatic. It can cause outward signs in children and young people and can have long-term effects on them.

You should also know the steps to take according to your setting's safeguarding or child protection policy if you have any concerns about a child.

Physical abuse

This is when a child or young person is physically hurt or harmed by the actions of an adult. It can be tricky to detect this, particularly in older pupils, and because young children often have bumps and bruises. There are some things, however, that you should look out for:

▶ Repeated illnesses and/or medical investigations, particularly if a pupil is regularly absent from an early years setting.
▶ Bruising, bites, burns and non-accidental injuries, particularly if you notice them on a regular basis, or regular fractures or broken bones.
▶ Reluctance to remove clothes or change for PE or sports activities in case marks are seen.
▶ Flinching or cowering when adults make a sudden movement.

Practice points

What to do if you spot a suspicious injury

▶ When the pupil is not with the parent, ask them about how the injury happened.
▶ Mention the injury to the parent, and note their reaction and explanation.
▶ Keep a note of the injury and explanation, in case the setting is accused of having caused the injury.
▶ Report the injury to the designated safeguarding lead (DSL) in your setting.

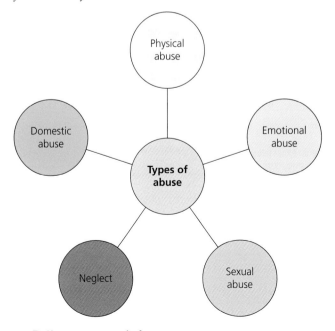

▲ Different types of abuse

Emotional abuse

This is when a child is continually emotionally mistreated over time, affecting their emotional development.

Emotional abuse occurs when a child is regularly and repeatedly made to feel worthless, unloved or frightened. It might be the only form of abuse a child suffers, but it can occur alongside other forms of abuse.

Emotional abuse is harder to detect than other forms, as there are no outward or obvious signs. However, signs may include:

▶ Withdrawal: The child is quieter and backs away from involvement in activities or being with friends.
▶ Changes in behaviour: For example, behaviour associated with comfort-seeking such as thumb sucking.
▶ Toileting problems: The child forgets to go and has regular 'accidents', when they didn't before.
▶ Developmental regression: For example, behaving in a way normally associated with a younger child.
▶ Poor concentration and inability to stay focused on tasks and activities.
▶ Difficulty in relating to others and making friends.
▶ Being affectionate to lots of different people, and needing more adult attention.

▲ Can you identify signs of emotional abuse in children?

Sexual abuse

This is when sexual activity is forced upon a child or young person. It includes both physical and non-physical contact, such as forcing the victim to look at pornographic material or taking sexual photographs. Signs might include:

▶ Sexualised behaviour or language: Children may display signs of knowing more than is appropriate for their age, for example simulating a sexual act in their play or talking in a way which is not expected.
▶ Sexually transmitted diseases (STDs – sometimes known as STIs, sexually transmitted infections), urinary infections, swelling, soreness, discharge: Sometimes young children might be reluctant to use the toilet or say that it hurts. They may also have increased toileting accidents.
▶ Self-harming behaviour: This is caused by anxiety in older children and young people, and can be a sign of sexual abuse although it may also be caused by other issues in the child's life.
▶ Eating disorders: Again, this is likely to be in older pupils but can be caused by a range of factors.
▶ The child being easily upset, clingy or seeming more anxious than usual.

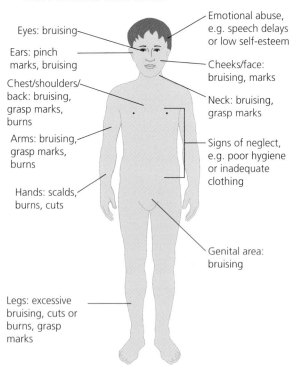

▲ Areas where abuse may be seen or detected

Neglect

This is when a child's or young person's needs are persistently not met by those who have parental responsibility. The child or young person might have:

▶ insufficient food
▶ inadequate clothing or living space
▶ a lack of medical care or emotional support when needed.

This can impact on their physical and emotional development and, depending on their age and the extent of the neglect, their ability to make friends.

Signs of neglect might include:

▶ **Failure to thrive**, grow and develop normally.
▶ **Poor hygiene**: Regularly coming to the setting with a dirty appearance, such as dirty clothes.
▶ **Inadequate clothing**: Regularly coming to the setting without appropriate clothing, for example no coat in rainy weather.
▶ **Untreated health problems**: The child or young person is regularly unwell, and health issues seem to be neglected.
▶ **Hunger/thirst**: The child or young person is always hungry or thirsty, or is regularly asking for food from adults or other children.
▶ **Failure to attend setting**: The child or young person is often absent, possibly with no explanation given.
▶ **Housing issues**: The child is regularly moved around, often without informing the setting, or is living in cramped or inadequate accommodation.

Domestic abuse

This is when there is violent behaviour within a relationship or family: a child or young person witnessing regular abuse is also child abuse. Domestic abuse also includes 'honour'-based violence within a family. Signs might include:

▶ Aggression in the child and possibly witnessed in the parent or carer: Young children might also, when they play, show the aggression that they have seen at home.
▶ Anti-social behaviour: The child or young person acts in ways that are not linked to expected development for behaviours.

▶ Depression or anxiety: The child or young person appears withdrawn and unhappy.
▶ Problems in the setting: They might have problems in their relationships with others within the setting, or other issues such as problems forming friendships or responding to staff.

Remember that this list is not exhaustive, and that there might be other signs of abuse.

Radicalisation

Radicalisation has become a serious issue in recent times. It involves an individual or group being coerced into a set of extreme political, social or religious aspirations.

Although it will not happen to younger children, staff should consider that younger parents or older pupils might be at risk of radicalisation.

Radicalisation might take place over a long period or can happen reasonably quickly. Those who have been radicalised are likely to show signs such as:

▶ becoming more argumentative and angry
▶ not listening to another's point of view or being unwilling to discuss it with them
▶ spending much more time online and showing increased secrecy
▶ expressing sympathy for more extremist views.

The DfE has a helpline so that school staff can raise concerns about extremism directly: 0207 340 7264. You can also email: counter.extremism@education.gov.uk

It is important to remember that the above list is not exhaustive and that there may be other signs of abuse.

Test yourself

1 Who is responsible for safeguarding in your school?
2 Name the five different types of abuse.
3 What type of abuse might you suspect if a pupil was dirty and constantly hungry?
4 Why is emotional abuse difficult to detect?

The procedures for reporting concerns

We looked at this knowledge outcome in Core Chapter 3, Section 3.5. You will need to reread pages 57–59 to check that you know:

▶ the policies and procedures you should follow
▶ how to report any concerns within your setting
▶ who you should report concerns to.

Inform the police or local child protection services if you:

▶ need to take your concerns out of the setting, or
▶ have concerns about a member of staff or someone who works with children and young people.

See also Section K3.2.

Research

The NSPCC website – www.nspcc.org.uk – has information and training on what to do in different situations under 'What is child abuse – Spotting the signs'.

▶ What kinds of signs do they list?
▶ What are their suggestions for reporting?

Good to know

All schools and early years settings are required to have regular safeguarding awareness training as part of whole staff development. This training ensures that staff are up to date and know the appropriate policies and procedures to follow.

Find out about your setting's procedures for ensuring that staff have met these statutory requirements.

K3.2 Why it is important to share relevant information in a timely manner with the safeguarding lead

We looked at this knowledge outcome in Core Chapter 3. You will need to reread pages 47–52 to check that you understand why it is important to share relevant information in a timely manner with the safeguarding lead.

Practice points

Safeguarding

▶ Always act on any concerns.
▶ Make notes and write things down if this helps you to remember what you have seen/heard.
▶ Make sure you know the identity of your school's DSL.
▶ Make sure you report to the appropriate person.
▶ Remember confidentiality – only speak to the DSL.
▶ Follow your school's policies and procedures correctly.

K3.3 How to promote the safe use of the technology and the web with pupils, including recognising and dealing with signs of cyber bullying and cyber grooming

For pupils who have grown up with the internet, it is a way of life. It is a very useful way of finding out information and of learning about the world. It is also a very quick and effective way of communicating.

However, due to the increased use of the internet in recent years, and the fact that many children and young people now have access to a phone, computer or tablet, it is even more important that adults talk to them about e-safety or how to keep safe online.

▶ As children and young people start to use these devices independently, they might make assumptions that everyone they talk to online is telling them the truth.
▶ Very young children sometimes have social media accounts and see it as a way of being more 'grown up', but they may not understand the potential dangers.

As adults we need to be able to talk to them about:

▶ why it is not always safe online
▶ what they should do if anyone bullies them or tells them to do something that they are uncomfortable with.

Research

Find out about your school's initiatives to ensure digital safety and protect against cyber bullying.

What can pupils tell you about the importance of staying safe online and the kinds of resources available to them?

There are three main areas of risk for pupils online, shown in the table below.

Area of risk	What it means
Content	Being exposed to illegal, inappropriate or harmful material. For example: • pornography • 'fake news' • racist or radical and extremist views. This material can be found on social media sites or in other internet mainstream content.
Contact	Being subjected to harmful online interaction with other users. For example: • commercial advertising • adults posing as children or young adults on social media or messaging sites.
Conduct	Personal online behaviour that causes harm or increases the likelihood of it. For example: • making, sending and receiving explicit images • online bullying, through sharing personal details with strangers and being unaware of potential issues.

▲ How do you know that pupils in your school are safe when they are online?

Promoting safe use of technology and the web

You can help pupils to be aware of these risks by demonstrating ways of keeping safe online. Some schools might have dedicated lessons or talks around internet safety and cyber bullying, while others have regular reminders, posters or information which highlight potential problems. The table below gives examples of different approaches and how these can be used to promote safe use of technology.

Approach	How to promote safe use of technology
Discuss appropriate online behaviour	Encourage pupils to talk about any concerns that they have. Have regular conversations about the risks involved with online activity.
Report concerns	Make sure that pupils know: • they can report any worries to an adult • it is not OK to be threatened or bullied in any way. You must report any concerns that you have about a pupil. See page 257 for signs of cyber bullying and cyber grooming.
Identify trustworthy sources	Ensure that pupils understand: • the risks of responding to emails or clicking on links which might come from an untrustworthy source • how they can identify these.

Approach	How to promote safe use of technology
Explain online security	Help pupils become aware of: • online security • the importance of checking any sites that they regularly use. For example: making sure that privacy settings are appropriate.
Share appropriate search techniques	Adults should work with pupils to show them appropriate online search techniques and share those which are safe.
Explain copyright infringement	Teach pupils about what **copyright** means when accessing materials online, particularly when looking up information for research. It is also important that pupils understand **plagiarism** and why this is not permitted.
Recognise techniques used for persuasion	Online scams and phishing are using increasingly realistic ways of encouraging people to reveal personal information. Children and young people might be particularly vulnerable to these. For example: • emails that may seem to be from real companies and that encourage the user to click on a link.
Discuss online risks when sharing personal information	Make sure that pupils know: • the risks of sharing personal information, such as their address • who they are talking to online if they do share information.

Key terms

Copyright: the legal right to intellectual property. Copyright is usually owned by the creator of materials and those authorised to use them.

Plagiarism: the use of work or materials which are protected by copyright as someone else's property.

Case study

Jackie is working with a group of Year 9 boys who are working in pairs using laptops. They have been asked to find out about a historical event for a piece of work they are handing in. She notices that two of the pupils are copying and pasting a lot of information straight into their own document.
▶ What should Jackie say to the boys?
▶ Why is this important?
▶ How can schools discourage the use of plagiarism?

The difference between cyber bullying and cyber grooming

It is also important to know the difference between cyber bullying and cyber grooming, so that you can share this with pupils and support them in coming forward if they are victims of either.

Cyber bullying

This is the bullying of another person using electronic means. It can follow the pupil wherever they go and is usually repeated and can be subtle.

Children and young people can be particularly vulnerable, and cyber bullying can cause mental health issues if it is not picked up.

According to the charity Bullying UK, 56 per cent of young people have seen others bullied online. Schools can support pupils by raising awareness of cyber bullying and encouraging pupils to come forward in confidence if they are victims.

Cyber bullying can take different forms, as shown in this table.

Form of cyber bullying	Description
Threats and intimidation	Individuals might use online messages or texts to threaten or intimidate others, often anonymously. This can cause deep upset and anxiety, and can damage the confidence and self-esteem of children and young people.
Harassment and stalking	Harassment means sending regular offensive comments or insults to the victim. Stalking is the act of regularly sending threats or other comments. This scares the victim as they feel they are being watched and in some cases fear for their safety.

Form of cyber bullying	Description
Defamation	This means damaging someone's reputation using spoken or written words.
	In the case of cyber bullying it might mean posting untrue information about them online.
Rejection and exclusion	Individuals might bully their peers online and make unkind comments, saying that they cannot join in with social events or be with particular people.
	They may also be more subtle, causing them to feel rejected by: • excluding them from activities • leaving them out of group messages.
Identity theft	Identity theft is stealing personal information about another person and then using it as your own.
	Children and young people can be vulnerable to this if they: • do not keep their personal information safe • pass it to others without being sure that it will be used appropriately.
Publicly posting personal information about others	This might include posting online photos that the person has not given their permission to be publicised.
	It can be very upsetting and hurtful.
Manipulation	This is when the bully tries to make the victim do or say something to their advantage, by threatening them or spreading rumours about them.

Cyber grooming

As well as cyber bullying, pupils might be victims of cyber grooming. This is the act of building a relationship with a child or young person online to be abused, exploited or trafficked. Groomers might:

▶ target vulnerable children and young people anonymously – they might not be visible to the victim

▶ pose as children and post false photographs of themselves

▶ give the victim regular attention and build up trust so that they can trick or pressurise them into doing something which they do not want to do.

Unfortunately, even if you keep channels of communication open and are approachable, some pupils will still become victims of cyber bullying or cyber grooming. It is important to understand the potential signs of these offences so that you can report any concerns to the DSL immediately.

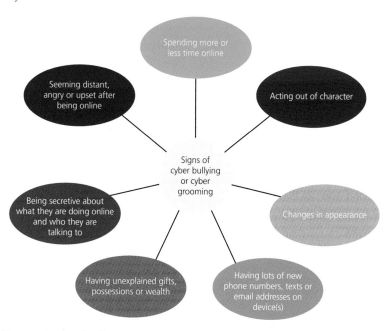

▲ Signs of cyber bullying or grooming

Case study

You are working in a secondary school in the food technology department to support practical sessions in class. You have noticed that Emilio, who is in one of the Year 10 classes, has changed a great deal in the past few weeks. He has become quiet and withdrawn and does not arrive prepared for classes. In the past he always had his money and equipment ready, and arrived with a smile.

You have asked him if he is OK and he just nods and moves away. You notice that others in the group seem to be teasing him more than usual about his name and his Italian accent, and he is spending a lot of time on his own. At break time you find him just walking around the school.

▶ Should you be concerned about Emilio?
▶ Should you take any more action and if so, why?
▶ What steps would you take to take this further?

Test yourself

1 What are the three areas of risk which pupils may fall into online?
2 How might someone use the internet to bully another person?
3 What are three potential signs of cyber bullying or cyber grooming?

K3.4 A range of signs of common illnesses/infections and the associated symptoms

Working in a school means that you will come into contact with a wide range of common illnesses, conditions and infections, as children and young people are more vulnerable to them.

You might be able to identify many of these, such as the spots associated with chickenpox or the signs of head lice.

You should be aware of:
▶ your school's policy when caring for ill children
▶ what to do if a pupil needs to be sent home due to illness

▶ illnesses or infections which may present a risk to those who are pregnant.

While older pupils are likely to talk about how they are feeling, you might need to be alert to some of these symptoms in younger pupils, in cases when they are lethargic or have a fever or temperature.

You should know the identity of first aiders in your school so that you are able to call on them if you need to. In some cases, illness can come on rapidly and you should be prepared to act quickly if needed. Some observable signs of the more common illnesses are listed in this table.

Type of illness/ infection and cause	Signs, symptoms and treatment
Chickenpox (virus)	You can identify chickenpox by a rash of pink, itchy spots and blisters over the body as well as a slight or moderate fever and headache.
	These symptoms usually appear between ten days and three weeks after the patient has been in contact with someone who has the illness.
	The rash may be mild or spread over the whole body, and the person is infectious until the spots have become scabs.
	Treatment involves painkillers and calamine lotion to cool the itchiness.

Type of illness/ infection and cause	Signs, symptoms and treatment
Measles (virus)	Signs of measles are similar to those of the common cold. With measles, after a few days, a rash of raised spots will spread from the head downwards and may last for up to a week.
	The child or young person may also have grey/white spots inside their cheeks and throat, and sore, watery eyes as well as a cough and fever.
	Measles is highly infectious, and although many pupils have now been vaccinated, some may not.
	Measles is treated by taking painkillers to relieve the symptoms and by having plenty of rest and fluids.
Mumps (virus)	Mumps is a painful swelling of one or both of the salivary glands, which are located under the ears.
	Patients might also be tired and achy and have a fever, and chewing may be uncomfortable, so soft foods are advised.
	It is highly contagious and should be treated by isolating the patient and giving them painkillers and rest.
	The infection should pass in a week or two.
Slapped cheek syndrome (virus)	Slapped check is characterised by a bright red rash on the cheeks and is caused by a virus.
	The rash may be itchy and may spread over the body and be accompanied by a headache, runny nose and fever.
	It can sometimes last up to a month.
	The child or young person should rest and take painkillers and antihistamines if the skin is very itchy.
Rubella (virus)	Rubella or German measles is caused by a virus.
	It is characterised by a slight pink rash of flat spots which starts behind the ears and on the forehead and then spreads to the body. The rash is not itchy.
	The patient is likely to also have a mild fever and symptoms of a slight cold and sore throat. They may have swollen glands behind the ears.
	Rubella is treated with plenty of rest if necessary and treating the symptoms and taking paracetamol to reduce the temperature.
	Complications can occur if a woman is in the first three months of pregnancy as it may cause harm to the unborn baby.
Whooping cough (bacteria)	Whooping cough might start with a slight cough and cold, or a mild fever.
	It develops into a characteristic whooping cough and coughing fits. These might cause vomiting or choking.
	The child or young person may have difficulty in breathing and become very tired due to continued coughing.
	It can cause problems in babies due to breathing difficulties, and is less severe in older children and adults, although care should be taken in pregnancy.
	Antibiotics should be given to treat whooping cough as soon as possible.
	Other treatments include rest and plenty of fluids.
Common cold (virus)	Common colds and coughs are the most common types of illness and children and young people may catch them fairly regularly.
	They are caused by a virus and are spread easily.
	They affect the nose, throat and lungs.
	In some cases they also affect the ears, which can temporarily affect the child's or young person's hearing.
	The throat might be sore and the patient might also have a runny nose, a headache and aching muscles.
	In some cases, young children might also have a temperature.
	There is no cure for the common cold, although pain relief and decongestants might help, along with rest.

Type of illness/ infection and cause	Signs, symptoms and treatment
Conjunctivitis (virus/allergy)	Conjunctivitis is highly contagious if caused by an infection and if the eyes are producing a yellow pus which sticks to the eyelashes. Symptoms also include bloodshot, burning or itchy eyes. If it is caused by an allergy such as hay fever, conjunctivitis might make the eyes red but it is not contagious. Treatment for conjunctivitis: • Clean off any pus using a cold flannel or pad. • Use eye drops. • Use antihistamines for hay fever.
Ear infections (virus)	Ear infections may be characterised by ear pain and difficulty hearing. There may also be discharge from the ear, along with itchiness as well as a temperature and sickness. Babies and young children are likely to pull at or rub their ear. Younger children might suffer from inner ear infections, which are caused by a virus. Older children are more prone to outer ear infections, which might be caused by irritation in the ear canal. Treatment for inner ear infections includes painkillers, or antibiotics in more severe cases.
Viral infections	A viral infection is any disease or condition which is caused by a virus, such as a cold, chickenpox, Covid-19 or flu. Viruses usually start before the symptoms occur or the person begins to feel unwell, so they are often spread without the person knowing as they can be hard to identify. Symptoms of a viral infection can include diarrhoea, stomach pain, sickness, loss of appetite, constipation, and a temperature, among others. Treatments may vary according to the infection but rest and plenty of water help, and the child should be monitored in case further symptoms appear.
Head lice or nits	Head lice are spread by head-to-head contact, and are very common in young children. Lice move onto another scalp and lay their eggs. Signs of head lice include an itchy scalp and noticeable white eggs on the hair shaft. There is no need for pupils to be kept off school, but parents should be informed so that they can check for signs. Lice and eggs can be treated without medical intervention using a wet nit comb or by using over-the-counter medicated lotions.
Hand, foot and mouth disease (virus)	This is an infection which is characterised by a sore throat and high temperature, along with mouth ulcers and a rash which develops into blisters on the hands and feet. It can also cause a loss of appetite. It is common in children but can also affect adults, and the blisters can be painful. There is no specific treatment, but painkillers and plenty of fluids can help as well as gels for mouth ulcers and soft foods to make eating more comfortable. It will usually pass in seven to ten days. Care should be taken in pregnancy.

➡

Type of illness/ infection and cause	Signs, symptoms and treatment
Meningitis (bacteria or virus)	Meningitis is caused by an infection of the membranes which surround the brain and spinal cord.
	It can be spread virally or through bacteria, and is more common in babies, children and young people.
	Bacterial meningitis is more serious and can be life-threatening if it is not treated quickly. It can also come on very rapidly.
	There are a wide range of symptoms, which include: • a dislike of bright light • a high temperature • severe headache and confusion • muscle pain and stiffness • sickness • cold hands and feet • pale blotchy skin • a rash which does not fade when a glass is pressed against it.
	The patient may not have all of these symptoms but should be taken to hospital to test whether they have bacterial or viral meningitis.
	In the case of bacterial meningitis, they need to take antibiotics and drink fluids.
	Meningitis can sometimes result in long-term problems, including hearing or vision loss.
	Viral meningitis can be treated at home with rest, fluids and painkillers.

There are also more general signs and symptoms of ill health which you should be aware of, particularly if you work with very young pupils, as they may not be able to tell you what is wrong.

These signs are indicators that their immune system is fighting an illness, and it is important to recognise these so that:

▶ children can be given opportunities to rest and receive medical attention

▶ children can be separated from other children and sent home in order to prevent the spread of infection.

Signs that require immediate medical intervention

As well as being aware of these signs and symptoms, you should know about those which require immediate medical attention. This might include allergic reactions, for example anaphylactic shock, or severe asthma.

In the case of unresponsiveness or difficulty breathing, call 999 immediately and contact your first aider.

Sign or symptom	Potential cause/treatment
Raised temperature	A raised temperature is one which is 38°C or more. It is usually the body's response to an infection.
	Depending on other symptoms, it can be a cause for concern.
	If you think a pupil has a temperature, check with a digital thermometer.
	A child with a raised temperature should: • rest • be given plenty to drink • be sent home, if they are in school.
	Their temperature should be checked regularly.
	Seek urgent medical attention if a very young child (up to six months old) has: • a raised temperature • a rash • other signs of illness.

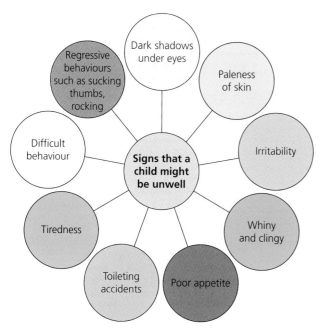

▲ Signs that a child might be unwell

Sign or symptom	Potential cause/treatment
Rash	A rash can be caused by: • an allergy such as heat rash or hives, or • an illness such as slapped cheek syndrome. If you know that the pupil has an allergy and they have medication in school, they should get the medication (see below). Seek urgent medical attention if: • the pupil has other symptoms such as a stiff neck or temperature • the rash does not fade when a glass is pressed against it. These can be signs of meningitis.
Unresponsive	If you find a pupil or adult who is unresponsive, for example who has difficulty in staying awake, seek immediate medical attention and call the emergency services.
Difficulty breathing	This might be caused by an allergic reaction. Seek medical attention and call the emergency services straight away.

Administering medication

You should also be aware of your school's policy for administering medication, particularly if you work with a pupil who regularly needs it due to their medical needs or who has an education, health and care (EHC) plan or an allergy. This might be part of the school's health and safety policy or be a policy on its own.

It is important that:
▶ the medication is stored only in its original container
▶ prescribed medicines show the name of the child or young person and the required dose.

The child or young person must know:
▶ where their medicine is stored
▶ who has the key, particularly in the case of emergency medicines such as asthma inhalers and **adrenaline autoinjectors** (i.e. EpiPen®), so they can be accessed quickly.

The school will also need to keep records including parental consent forms and any instructions, and staff should always record the date and time as well as the dose following administration.

Older children might be given responsibility for administering their own medication, although it should still be locked away centrally until needed.

Key term

Adrenaline autoinjector (often known as EpiPen ®): a device to administer adrenaline to decrease swelling in the case of an acute allergic reaction.

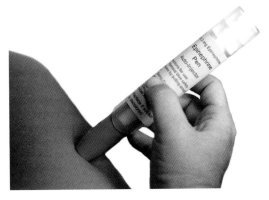

▲ An adrenaline autoinjector, EpiPen®

K3.5 How illnesses and infections are spread

Many illnesses and infections can be treated with rest and painkillers, but in some cases they might be life-threatening.

Illnesses and infections are spread mainly through close contact with those who already have an infection, through:
▶ breathing in airborne particles, or
▶ directly touching a surface which has been recently touched by an infected person.

In many cases, those who have an illness or infection might not know that they are contagious, as this stage often occurs before the symptoms of the illness appear.

For this reason, it is a good precaution to take steps to avoid the risk of passing on infections. This includes:
▶ regular handwashing
▶ paying attention to good hygiene, particularly when preparing food.

The term 'infection control' usually applies to the kinds of precautions that the school needs to take to avoid the spread of infection; for example:
▶ when clearing up a spillage of blood or other body fluids
▶ while putting dressings on wounds.

Follow these other examples of good practice:
▶ Cover your mouth when you cough.
▶ Sneeze into a tissue.

▶ Keep fingernails short.
▶ Cover wounds with a plaster.
▶ Dispose of any waste in appropriate containers.

Schools should have processes and procedures for minimising illness and infection, and you should check your health and safety policy for more information.

If pupils or staff have not been immunised against a particular illness, this increases the likelihood of their catching it. Schools may ask parents and carers if pupils' immunisations are up to date before they start school.

How to prevent and control infection

There are some very simple ways to prevent and minimise the risk of infection, given in the table below.

How to minimise illness and infection	Strategy
Modelling and encouraging effective hygiene practice to pupils	Point out and talk about the steps you are taking which show that you are using effective hygiene practice.
	When talking to younger pupils, ask them why it is important. For example, you could ask, 'Why do we need to wash our hands before we have lunch?'
	Always model good practice in your day-to-day behaviour so that pupils can see you using it yourself.
Promoting immunisation	Talk about the importance of immunisation so that pupils and staff are kept safe.
	There has been some discussion in recent years about the safety of the **MMR vaccine**. • These concerns have been disproved, but they led to some parents not having their children immunised, and cases of measles have risen as a result. • As this disease is dangerous and can be fatal to children, it is important for everyone to be aware of the importance of having up-to-date vaccinations.
Removing unwell pupils or staff members from the setting	As soon as it is clear that an individual is unwell or infectious, they should be sent home so that the infection is not passed on to others.
	In schools it is easy for infections to be passed around very quickly, and this risk should be minimised as much as possible.
Following hygiene processes and procedures	Always ensure that you follow your school's policy and procedures for hygiene, so that you can be sure you have minimised your risk of infection.
	This might include wearing personal protective equipment (PPE), such as disposable gloves when clearing up vomit or blood from a cut.
Being aware of the required exclusion periods	Most illnesses have required exclusion periods or the amount of time a pupil needs to be off school once diagnosed.
	Check with your local authority or your school office for more information about exclusion periods.
Reporting notifiable diseases to the local authority	Some illnesses need to be reported to local authorities so that they can be monitored in case of local or national outbreaks.
	These are called notifiable diseases and a list of them may be found on the government webpage 'Notifiable diseases and causative organisms' at: www.gov.uk/guidance/notifiable-diseases-and-causative-organisms-how-to-report

Key term

MMR vaccine: a vaccination for measles, mumps and rubella which is currently given to young children in two doses, at one year and at three years four months old.

HOW TO
WASH YOUR HANDS

1 Apply soap on wet hands

2 Rub the palm of your hands

3 Don't forget the back!

4 Interlace your fingers

5 Rub thumbs

6 Pay attention to your nails and fingertips

7 Use water to rinse your hands

8 Dry with paper towel

▲ It is important to know how to wash your hands thoroughly when working with children

Practice points

Illness and infection

▶ Know the identity of first aiders in your school and how to find them quickly.
▶ Find out what to do if a pupil tells you that they are feeling unwell.
▶ Be aware of pupils you work with who have allergies or medical conditions.
▶ Always follow your school's hygiene procedures and encourage pupils to follow and talk about them. You should also model the procedures to pupils, particularly the youngest children.
▶ Make sure you wear disposable gloves when cleaning up any body fluids.
▶ Know your school's policy for administrating medication.
▶ The younger the pupils, the more spare clothes you should keep in the setting so that pupils can change if necessary.

Test yourself

1 What might cause you to think a pupil is unwell?
2 What are the main ways in which illnesses and infections are spread?
3 What illnesses might cause a rash?
4 When should you call for immediate medical attention?

K3.6 The difference between accidents, injuries and emergency situations

Even if your school carries out regular risk assessments and health and safety checks in the learning environment, there is the potential for accidents, injuries and emergency situations to occur at some point.

You should be familiar with your school's health and safety policy so that you know what to do and how to respond if you are first on the scene.

This table describes the different types of accidents, injuries and emergency situations that may occur in education settings.

Type of incident	Response
Accident/injury	• **Accidents** are unintended incidents which might be caused by a spillage, breakage, burn, trip, slip or fall. • **Injuries** range from a graze, small cut or bump to a broken bone or serious head injury. In both cases you should: • Reassure the casualty. • Ensure that other pupils keep well out of the way and out of danger, particularly if there is a breakage or a spillage which could cause further accident or injury. • Send someone for help and a first aider straight away. • Follow your school's first aid policy until they arrive.
Emergency situation	Emergency situations are those which can potentially endanger life. Examples of these include: • fires • gas leaks • serious burns • choking • any loss of consciousness caused by a head injury • strangers on the premises or breaches of security, with a threat of harm or violence • missing children or young people • life-threatening allergic reactions or illness (see Section K3.4) • lockdown, e.g. due to bomb threat. There should be regular evacuation drills and meetings so that staff and pupils know the correct procedure in these situations. • If you are a volunteer in the school or a new member of staff, make sure that you find out this information as soon as possible, particularly if you have not been present for a fire drill. • Make sure that you know how to raise the alarm quickly, in case you discover any of these situations. • If you are first on the scene in a medical emergency, make sure that you call for a first aider straight away.

▲ Do you know what you should do if a pupil is hurt or injured?

How to respond to accidents, injuries and emergencies

Policies and procedures for dealing with the situations within the setting

Your school will have procedures for dealing with accidents and emergencies in the setting, and these will usually be in the health and safety or first aid policy.

There should always be a first aider to accompany pupils on school trips and off-site visits. All adults should be aware of who they are. First aiders also need to have regular training to keep up to date.

For more on first aid, see Section K3.17 on page 280.

According to legislation set out by **RIDDOR**, all serious workplace accidents and dangerous occurrences must be reported.

Research

For more details and guidance on how schools should do this, search the Health and Safety Executive website: **www.hse.gov.uk**

Key term

RIDDOR: Reporting of Injuries, Diseases and Dangerous Occurrences Regulations.

Responsibilities and limitations of your role

It is very important that all staff are aware of their own responsibilities towards others, and the limitations of their roles.

This should be stated in the setting's health and safety or first aid policy.

Remember that you should not treat an emergency unless you are a trained first aider, in case you cause more harm to the casualty.

Recording and reporting requirements

You should know about your school's recording and reporting requirements. All accidents and emergencies which take place on the school site must be recorded as soon as possible by the staff who were present at the time. This is so that:
▶ as much information as possible is written down
▶ if it is needed later on, it is easy to find.

The format might vary between schools, but there should be established recording and reporting methods in place.

In this situation you should ensure that information is:
▶ recorded appropriately
▶ stored confidentially and in line with school procedures.

For more on recording and reporting, see Section K3.17.

Research

If you do not know already, find out about your school or college policy for responding to:
▶ accidents
▶ injuries
▶ emergencies.

Find out the school's policy for recording and reporting any incidents or accidents.
▶ Ask to see the documentation that is used and where it is kept.
▶ Make sure you are fully aware of your own role in the event of accidents and emergencies.

Practice points

Health and safety policy
▶ Always be vigilant in all areas of the school.
▶ Know your school's policy so that you are ready for emergency situations.
▶ Remove pupils from immediate danger straight away.
▶ Call for help if you are first on the scene of an emergency.
▶ Familiarise yourself with fire or safety procedures if you have not already been told.
▶ If dealing with an injury, always send for a first aider as soon as possible.

For more on first aid and health and safety, see also Section K3.17 on page 280.

K3.7 How a range of factors contribute to children's wellbeing

As we have discussed in Core Chapters 4 and 7, a range of influences support the development and wellbeing of children and young people. Adults must support this by looking out for signs that children's needs are not being met.

From a physical point of view, children and young people:
▶ have health and nutrition needs
▶ need to have enough sleep and rest
▶ require regular physical activity to guarantee the development of their wellbeing.

Although they do not have dedicated time for sleep and rest in school, young pupils in reception and Year 1 in particular may sometimes show signs of tiredness and may need to have some quiet time.

You should also look out for signs that pupils are not eating, particularly if they appear to be losing weight. In older pupils, this may be a sign of **bulimia**.

> **Key term**
>
> **Bulimia:** a condition in which the person has an obsessive desire to lose weight, and self-induces vomiting.

For more on the physical needs of pupils, see Section K3.11 on page 272.

As discussed in Core Chapter 7, emotional wellbeing is dependent on the following physical and emotional factors:
▶ stable and safe environments
▶ adult care
▶ secure attachments
▶ interpersonal relationships.

This table includes signs which might indicate a lack of one or more of these factors.

Sign or indicator	Potential cause and action
Poor appearance and hygiene	If a pupil has poor physical appearance or does not seem to have good hygiene, this might be an indicator of: • neglect, or • a lack of care and unmet nutrition or health needs. You should raise your concerns with the DSL as soon as you notice it.
Recurring health problems	These might be caused by: • lack of nutrition • an undiagnosed medical condition • stress or anxiety if a pupil is going through challenges in their emotional life. Teachers might speak to parents or carers to find out if there is a reason for the pupil's heath issues. If they are ongoing and the child is not being checked out by medical professionals, this is a cause for concern and should be reported to the DSL.
Not meeting milestones	Children or young people who are not meeting developmental milestones might not be receiving enough nutrition or having their health or emotional needs met. You should: • flag this up to parents or carers in the first instance • discuss it with the SENDCo and teachers so that action can be taken to support them.
Negative self-concept	Children and young people who have a negative **self-concept** are likely to lack confidence and are often reluctant to join in with or try new activities. They might have this perception due to negative or unstable attachments and relationships in their lives. • This may have happened over time, but if it is a recent development, you should talk though your concerns with the DSL and with teachers. • Work with colleagues to support the pupil in case there is an underlying change in circumstances. For more on self-concept and the factors affecting it, see Core Chapter 4.
Changes in behaviour	Changes in a pupil's normal behaviour – such as becoming withdrawn or lacking concentration – might be caused by: • temporary changes in their lives, for example a bereavement or another type of unexpected transition • stress or anxiety, for example if it is close to exam time, or if they are moving on to secondary school. Teachers should speak to pupils to find out whether there is a direct cause so that they can support them. If the behaviour continues, it should be reported in case it is caused by safeguarding issues.

Sign or indicator	Potential cause and action
Inappropriate behaviour	Pupils whose physical or emotional needs are not being met in some way may show inappropriate behaviour, such as: • attention-seeking • stealing • emotional instability, among others. If the pupil's needs continue to be unmet and the behaviour is ongoing, parents or carers should be informed and involved alongside other professionals to support the pupil in making better choices.

Key term

Self-concept: the idea and belief which an individual has of themselves.

Case study

You work in a primary school in a Year 2 class. You have some concerns about Rani. She lives with her parents and older brother, and regularly comes to school looking dirty and uncared for. She is always very quiet and does not have many friends.

Her older brother, Luay, is in Year 4 and you have worked with him previously. He has many friends and a strong personality. He can be badly behaved and needs lots of attention.

You have noticed that the children's mother does not seem as interested in Rani when she collects the children from school, although she greets Luay and always addresses him first. You have never seen the children's father. You ask the teacher about Rani and Luay but she says that they are just very different children and there is nothing to worry about.

▶ How do you think Rani sees herself?
▶ What could you do to support her in class?
▶ Should you have any concerns and if so, who should you speak to?

K3.8 A range of transitions that a pupil will experience through school and the possible positive and negative effects on pupils' wellbeing

We looked at this knowledge outcome in Core Chapter 7. You will need to reread pages 134–5.

Practice points

Transitions

▶ Reactions to transitions vary from pupil to pupil – remember that what works for one might not work for another.
▶ Work with colleagues to manage transitions which pupils experience when moving classes, changing key stages or moving schools.
▶ Be aware of transitions which can be unexpected and are not common to all pupils, such as a bereavement or a new step-parent.
▶ Keep checking in with pupils and keep lines of communication open, particularly with quieter pupils.
▶ Be approachable and always make time if a pupil needs to talk.

K3.9 Why stable adult and peer relationships are important and the impact of disruption, including placement disruption, on a pupil's development and behaviour

We looked at this knowledge outcome in Core Chapter 4. You will need to reread pages 68 and 74.

K3.10 How a range of factors, in relation to family context, may impact on parenting

Pupils come from a wide range of backgrounds and family structures and contexts. You will need to be aware of the influence of these factors on:

▶ the way in which parents and carers raise their children
▶ how this might affect their learning and development.

The range of factors

Family structure

In Core Chapter 5, we looked at different types of family structure. You will need to reread pages 92–93 to remind yourselves of these and what they mean, as they significantly influence pupils' holistic development.

Another aspect to consider is how the number of parents and type of family affects the time available for parents or carers to engage in their child's education. Research in a range of areas has consistently shown that children who have more adult time and interaction are likely to have better outcomes. However, you should remember that this might not always be the case.

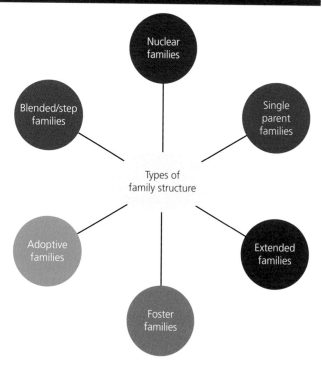

▲ Types of family structure

Reflect

Consider the following family structures:
▶ Ramina lives with her twin brother Romesh and a large extended family.
▶ Jake lives with his dad who is a widower and works full time.
▶ Nilaya and her two siblings live with their foster parents.
▶ Danny lives in a nuclear family with his parents, who both work although his mum works from home.
▶ Maddie and her sister live with their mum and stepdad, and go to stay with their dad every weekend.

Answer these questions:
1 Which of these children do you think has the least amount of time with their parents? Which children might have sufficient time with their family?
2 How might the family structure in each case influence the children's development?
3 Why is it important not to make assumptions about pupils and their families?

Parenting style

We have also looked at parenting styles in Core Chapter 5. You may wish to reread page 96.

Parenting style refers to the way in which parents and families bring up their children. They may vary from authoritarian, with strict rules and boundaries, to uninvolved, where parents are detached and uninterested in their children's lives.

The type of parenting style used impacts on the types of boundaries and interactions which parents have with their children. Remember that:

▶ different parenting styles work better with some children than with others

▶ parents might use a mixture of styles as children grow up and families change.

Parenting style	Impact of parenting and effect on the child
Authoritarian	An authoritarian parent is likely to: • have very high expectations of their children • use control and a 'because I said so' approach. They apply strict discipline and expect their child to fall into line without explanation. In the most extreme cases, this can lead to physical or emotional abuse. Children might be well-behaved and high achievers but not as happy and balanced as other children. The effect of this approach on a child can be to: • reduce confidence and self-esteem • lead to a feeling of powerlessness. Children of authoritarian parents are more likely to have anxiety and depression.
Permissive	A permissive parent is likely to be lenient with their child and avoid confrontation and any kind of discipline. • They might not have any expectations or demands, and can appear to be more of a friend than a parent. • They are however warm and want to care for their children. This kind of parenting may cause problems within families, as children grow up without any limits or expectations. The effect of this approach on the child is that: • although they can choose to do what they like, they can feel insecure without consistency or boundaries • they might not understand what is acceptable behaviour, or may behave in an immature way due to a lack of age-related expectations.
Authoritative	The authoritative or response approach is different from the authoritarian style: • Although there are boundaries and rules, parents show children how they can achieve and give them support and guidance to do so. • Parents listen to their children and explain to them why they have asked them to behave in a particular way. • They show a caring and warm approach to parenting. • Parents might adjust their expectations depending on their child's needs, and focus on the balance between the child's rights and responsibilities. This parenting style is accepted as the one which creates the best outcomes for children. The effect of this approach is that the child is able to: • develop independence and assertiveness • understand the need for self-discipline and social responsibility.
Instinctive	This parenting style is heavily influenced by parental instinct. • Parents tend to use methods which are influenced by their own childhood and upbringing. • They react to the needs of the child and are less driven by rules. Children who are parented in this way differ in their reactions to this style, as it is a personal choice which varies between individuals.

Parenting style	Impact of parenting and effect on the child
Uninvolved/detached	Uninvolved parents know very little about what their children are doing at any time or who they are with. • This type of parenting style might be a result of other pressures on parents, but it means that they do not show any interest in or spend time with their children. • In more extreme cases, uninvolved parents can neglect the physical and emotional needs of the child. The children of uninvolved parents might have behaviour problems and struggle with self-esteem.
Helicopter	Helicopter parents are those who are closely involved with every aspect of their child's life and experiences. • Although it is usually well-intentioned, this style of parenting can mean that the child does not learn to be independent or manage disappointments, as their parent has over-protected them and prevented them from learning to do things for themselves. • Helicopter parenting might result in children who struggle to solve problems. From the child's point of view, it can result in: • an over-reliance on others and a lack of confidence • frustration at being unable to work things out for themselves.

In some cases, parents within the same family might decide to use different parenting styles: one parent might be authoritarian while another is permissive or uninvolved. This can cause problems for the child because there is a lack of consistency between parents.

▲ How might different parenting styles affect children's development?

Income

The amount of income which a family has influences the opportunities and time available for parents to spend with their children. This might be positive or negative, particularly if parents are not aware of how it may affect their children.

Large income

When pupils grow up in families with plenty of money, sometimes this is because both parents have well-paid jobs and might have to spend a lot of time away from home. This could impact on the development of attachments with their children.

However, having a larger income can be beneficial if it allows families to have more experiences together and provides more opportunities for children.

Lack of income

Income can also affect families negatively:
▶ If there is not enough money for a nutritious diet, this will have an impact on children's health and wellbeing.
▶ Lack of income might cause stress and anxiety in adults, which can also affect the home environment.

Education

The level of education which parents have achieved is likely to affect:
▶ the way in which they view educational experiences
▶ the importance which they place upon it and their expectations for their child.

A parent who has had a positive experience of education themselves is more likely to engage with their child's education and want to be involved in it.

On the other hand, parents might not see school experiences as important, and might pass this opinion on to their children. They might not realise how much their opinions influence their children and how this can affect their development, particularly when children are under five years old.

Culture

Parents from different cultures might have different approaches to parenting.

They might also have different sets of values and norms to those of the school. This can mean that:

▶ beliefs or methods which are set out in school policies are not in line with those of some cultures

▶ parents from some cultures might favour a more authoritarian parenting style, and schools should be sensitive to this.

These are important points, as a pupil's beliefs and relationships are heavily influenced by their culture and family background.

Stress and mental health

In situations where one or both parents have problems with their own mental health or have stress-related illnesses, family life and parenting might be neglected. This may be in the short or long term, depending on the situation.

Stress in parents may be due to a large number of factors, including: lack of income, housing issues, illness or disability, domestic violence, substance or alcohol abuse, divorce or refugee status.

Parents suffering from mental health problems might:

▶ feel unable to go out or to interact socially with others

▶ discourage their children from going out so they can care for the parents

▶ fear for their own safety if they have been victims of threats or violence, and feel that they need to keep their children at home.

This impacts on children's and young people's opportunities and social relationships, and might influence their self-esteem and confidence.

K3.11 Why physical care needs of pupils are important and the impact they may have on health and development, in accordance with Maslow's hierarchy of needs

The physical care needs of pupils are highly important, as they have a direct influence on their health and development.

In Core Chapter 2, we looked at the work of the theorist Abraham Maslow, who believed that people need to meet their physical needs before they are able to pay attention to other needs. You might like to reread this section on pages 35–36 and look again at the diagram of his hierarchy of needs.

Adults who work in schools need to be mindful of this in their day-to-day practice, and with pupils of all ages. It is very hard for pupils to concentrate if they are tired, hungry or upset.

▲ Why do children and young people need access to physical activity during the day?

How to support physical care for pupils appropriate to age and stage of development

Physical need	Impact on health and development and the role of the adult

Nutrition	A balanced diet is important in order to meet pupils' physical needs. The correct nutritional balance will enable children to grow, develop and keep healthy. Adults will need to ensure that the food and snacks which children and young people have in the setting are as far as possible healthy and well balanced.
	
	Some pupils might have a consistently poor diet, perhaps as a result of low income or lack of time or resources. This can:
	• affect pupils' physical development by
	  – restricting their growth
	  – causing them to gain weight and develop unhealthy eating habits
	• lead to poor mood and behavioural problems
	• reduce their energy levels, which will restrict their cognitive development.
	
	In adulthood it can also lead to obesity and chronic diseases.
	
	As part of your teaching assistant role, you should ensure that you talk to pupils about the importance of good nutrition when discussing food. Schools are likely to work with catering firms who provide school meals to ensure that they are healthy and balanced. When young children start school, they should be encouraged to make healthy food choices where possible, particularly when eating school meals. Healthy snacks such as fruit are provided to primary-aged pupils. Pupils who bring packed lunches will be asked to bring healthy foods as far as possible and staff may be asked to monitor this.

Hydration	Regular hydration is vital for everyone. Pupils should always have access to water in the learning environment and when on school trips. You should ensure that pupils have access to enough water and do not become dehydrated, particularly when they are: • outside in hot weather • undertaking physical activity • leaving the setting for any reason.
Rest/sleep	Children and young people need to have enough rest and sleep in order to be able to concentrate in school. Younger pupils might become tired in the afternoon if they: • are still getting used to being in school all day • attend breakfast clubs or after-school clubs. Older pupils might also be tired if they stay up late. • Teenagers' body clocks are known to change around puberty. • They might be online and looking at blue light late at night. This can interfere with sleep and make it harder for them to concentrate during the day. If you notice that a child or young person is excessively tired, you should let teachers know when you can. Very young children, for example Reception and Year 1, may be able to sleep in a quiet corner of the classroom if they need to, although parents should also be informed. In the case of older pupils, parents may need to be informed if tiredness is affecting their learning, and the importance of getting enough rest should be highlighted to pupils.

Physical need	Impact on health and development and the role of the adult
Physical activity	The need for physical activity and access to the outdoors is a fundamental part of a child's physical development. As such, it is a good reason for them to get outside and have some fresh air and exercise during a day in school. In addition to PE lessons and breaktimes, many schools offer physical activities such as the 'Daily Mile', which is a brief exercise break from the classroom during the day. Pupils need to be able to develop and refine their **fine** and **gross motor skills**, as well as their coordination and confidence. Physical activity is also important for: • developing muscles and bone density • building physical strength. It also means that children and young people are more likely to be physically active as they grow up and mature. Children and young people with poor physical skills may be affected in all areas, as physical activity: • develops confidence • supports their social and emotional development through the development of teambuilding and communication skills • supports better mental health and development of the brain through forming new connections and improving memory and concentration. Children and young people who find these skills more challenging may need to have support and more practise from adults, for example during playtimes and PE lessons. In addition, if pupils have not had a chance to get outside or have exercise, on a bad weather day for example, adults may need to give them the opportunity of moving and increasing their heart rate at some point during the day. This will also help to support their concentration at all ages.
Suitable clothing for activities	Pupils should always have the correct clothing for the activities they are being asked to undertake. While younger children may be provided with these by parents, those who are older may forget them or not have them in school. • Schools should ensure that parents are aware of what is needed, both for extremes of temperature and for rain if pupils are asked to work outside. • If pupils are going on school trips or residential activities, a list of suitable clothing should always be provided. • Even if notification has been given, there might be a pupil who does not have suitable clothing, so schools might need to take extra items. Schools are likely to have a store of spare clothing or kit for pupils, and you should know where to find this so that you can access it quickly if needed.
Safety needs	The safety needs of pupils are always of the utmost importance. • Adults should remember that they are acting 'in loco parentis', or in place of parents. • Where there is any possibility of real danger to pupils, they should not carry out an activity or be exposed to it. • Where there is an element of risk in some outdoor and off-site activities, these should be checked using a risk assessment and appropriate measures put in place. For more on the requirements of a risk assessment, see page 207. The age and developmental stage of pupils is also an important consideration here: younger pupils will not have so much awareness of hazards in the environment and online. You should always talk to pupils about potential dangers if they carry out activities which may be different, ensuring that age-appropriate language is used.

Physical need	Impact on health and development and the role of the adult
Consideration for medical conditions	Schools have a statutory responsibility to ensure that they have appropriate arrangements in place to support pupils who have medical conditions. These ensure that: • they have the same opportunities as other pupils • they are not put at unnecessary risk. Staff must be aware of those pupils who may need support, particularly in the case of younger children. Appropriate measures must be in place to administer medication and manage emergency procedures. The government has produced a guidance document, 'Supporting pupils with medical conditions at school', which is available at: www.gov.uk

Key terms

Fine motor skills: the skills needed to hold and manipulate smaller objects with the fingers, such as holding a pencil or doing up a zip.

Gross motor skills: the skills needed to control and develop the movement of the arms and legs, such as throwing and catching, or running and skipping.

Reflect

Consider the times when pupils in your school have been unable to go outside and have physical exercise during the day, perhaps because of the weather.
▶ What impact has this had on their behaviour, mood or ability to concentrate?
▶ Why is it important to meet pupils' physical needs during the day through exercise?
▶ What other areas of development are supported through physical activity?

K3.12 The positive impact of helping pupils to develop self-care skills and the strategies that can be used to support this

Whatever their age, pupils should be encouraged to develop the skills and independence to meet their own self-care needs. This is because, as educators, we should encourage them to try to do things for themselves, rather than doing things for them. This will both benefit them through developing their own skills, as well as reducing the pressure on adults.

Although it is not possible to completely avoid hazards and ill health, pupils should be able to develop routines and habits so that they:
▶ minimise illness and infections
▶ learn to keep themselves safe, both within and outside school.

The positive impact of developing independence skills means that pupils gradually take over responsibility for their own self-care as they mature.

Strategies to support self-care skills

Promoting good hygiene routines

Encourage and remind pupils to use good hygiene and handwashing routines to minimise the spread of infection and to protect those around them, for example:
▶ after using the toilet
▶ before eating
▶ before working on food technology activities.

You should also talk to all pupils about the importance of good general hygiene, such as bathing and hair care, particularly as they enter puberty. This is likely to form part of the PSHE (personal, social, health and economic education) curriculum.

Encouraging self-care and independence

Where possible, you should emphasise the importance of self-care in pupils so that they do not rely too much on others to do things for them.

The move to secondary school or to college/university are specific points which some students find difficult, particularly if their parents have given them fewer opportunities to develop self-help skills.
▶ This is an ideal point to give pupils more responsibility if they have had limited experience up to then. However, they will still need support in order to do this.

▶ A good way of promoting and encouraging independence is through a pupil's hobbies and interests, as they will be motivated to be organised for something they enjoy. This will also support their mental wellbeing.

Case study

Joe has just started Year 7 at a large comprehensive school which is just under a mile from his home. He is an only child and his parents have taken him to school by car since he was in reception. In primary school, Joe's mum went through his spelling and maths homework with him and checked that he had done it.

She relies on the parental engagement app that the school uses and the school's learning platform for information about what her son is doing in school, and regularly talks to Joe about it. Joe's new school has given him a planner with his timetable and access to the school's learning platform so that he can communicate with teachers and look at his homework calendar. His mum also has access to this information and checks it regularly through the portal.

Joe is a keen member of the Year 7 football team, and information about matches is sent to him directly.
▶ How can Joe's mum and the teaching staff support him while encouraging him to take over some responsibility?
▶ In your view, should parents and carers have access to learning platforms such as this once pupils move to secondary school? Give reasons for your answer.

Promoting healthy food choices

Schools usually promote healthy food choices:
▶ through the PSHE/RSE (relationships and sex education) and health education curriculum
▶ when talking about food and nutrition during the day.

Opportunities to discuss the nutritional value of foods can also occur in canteens at lunchtimes and in food technology lessons. This will encourage pupils to make healthier choices and to think about the impact of these foods on their bodies.

Older pupils should also be made aware of the impacts of a poorly balanced diet, such as:
▶ obesity
▶ high blood pressure
▶ long-term health conditions.

These types of strategies should encourage pupils to make healthy choices for themselves as they grow up and make their own decisions about what they eat.

Research

Find out about the healthy food plate and the Eatwell Guide.
▶ Is this used in your school?
▶ What opportunities do children and young people have to discuss diet and healthy eating?

Encouraging care of belongings

Care of belongings is an important part of developing responsibility and independence. Pupils should learn the value of taking care of items which they use and need on a daily basis. This can start at the earliest stage, when pupils have book bags or lunch boxes to take into school.
▶ Pupils should see these as their responsibility, rather than giving them to parents as soon as they meet at the end of the day.
▶ If pupils are encouraged to think about this for themselves, they will quickly learn to be responsible for their own belongings.
▶ Items should be marked with their name so that if they are lost, they can be traced.
▶ Pupils should be discouraged from bringing anything of value into school.

Understanding how to keep themselves safe

Schools need to work with parents to develop pupils' understanding of how to keep themselves safe as they become older and carry out more activities independently. By developing their understanding and awareness, pupils will be more protected from harm.
▶ Very young children need support to develop their understanding of keeping safe in their immediate environment.
▶ Older pupils need guidance and support in knowing what to do if they are affected by issues such as internet safety, substance abuse or violence.

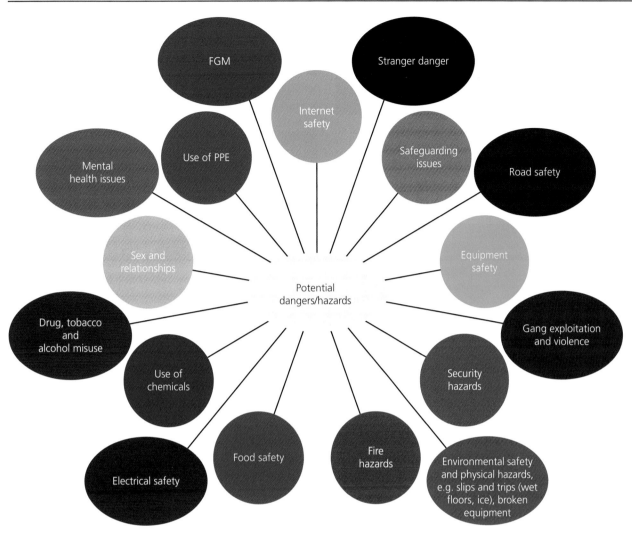

The following elements surround "Potential dangers/hazards":
- FGM
- Stranger danger
- Internet safety
- Use of PPE
- Safeguarding issues
- Road safety
- Mental health issues
- Sex and relationships
- Equipment safety
- Drug, tobacco and alcohol misuse
- Gang exploitation and violence
- Use of chemicals
- Security hazards
- Electrical safety
- Food safety
- Fire hazards
- Environmental safety and physical hazards, e.g. slips and trips (wet floors, ice), broken equipment

▲ Children and young people need to be aware of potential hazards and dangers in their environment

It is important that children and young people know what to do if they are affected by any of these situations, so that they can receive appropriate support.

▲ What opportunities do pupils have to discuss personal safety?

Research

Schools teach pupils about many of these issues at an age-appropriate stage through the PSHE and RSE curriculum. This gives them opportunities to discuss and understand the importance of keeping safe, both physically and mentally.

Look at the statutory guidance on the **www.gov.uk** website, and answer the following questions:
▶ Why is it important that pupils are made aware of these kinds of issues in school?
▶ Give three examples of ways in which the PSHE curriculum supports pupils' wellbeing.

K3.13 The connection between pupils relating to others and their emotional resilience and wellbeing

In order to develop emotional **resilience**, pupils should have as many opportunities as they can to develop strong relationships and support systems with others.

Resilience is a strength which is linked to confidence and self-esteem, as it helps pupils to:
▶ believe in their own abilities
▶ deal with stress and anxiety
▶ meet the challenges they will face as they grow up
▶ be able to respond to difficult situations.

> **Key term**
>
> **Resilience:** the capacity and ability to recover quickly from difficulties, or 'bounce back'.

How resilience supports children and young people	Explanation
Resolving problems	Resilience helps pupils to: • solve problems • face and resolve challenges. These types of challenging situations occur throughout life, so we have to adapt our thinking and amend or change what we are doing. Being able to resolve problems or break them down is important: • It enables us to face up to and work through difficulties. • It stops us from avoiding or blocking out difficulties in other ways, such as by using drugs or alcohol.
Developing empathy	Empathy is an important human quality as it enables us to see things from another's point of view rather than just from our own. Empathy also enables us to put others' needs ahead of our own, which: • makes us better listeners and communicators • improves our relationships.
Communicating needs	Individuals who are more resilient are likely to be more confident at: • putting their own needs forward • being able to listen to the responses of others. They are less anxious about being liked or about others disagreeing with them, as they can listen to others' points of view.
Developing a support network	Support networks could be at home, at school or in the wider community. Pupils can be supported by parents, families, communities and other networks. Having a support network gives pupils a feeling of belonging. The ability to relate to other people means that they can: • see how others cope with challenges • learn from them.
Understanding right and wrong	Developing resilience also helps pupils to develop their understanding of right and wrong, as it encourages them to: • weigh up different situations • think about positive and negative aspects • make choices for themselves.
Listening to feedback and advice	Individuals who are resilient are more able to listen to feedback and advice from others, as they are less likely to see it as a negative, and more likely to see it as constructive criticism. However, you also need resilient children to know that it is OK to ask for help and support if they need it.

1 Copy and complete this table to show:
  – the opportunities that pupils in your school have for developing resilience. Think about on- and off-site activities, learning activities and extracurricular activities.
  – how these activities support the development of the skills linked to resilience.

Skill	Opportunity to develop	Helps develop skills by
Resolving problems		
Developing empathy		
Communicating needs		
Developing a support network		
Understanding right and wrong		
Listening to feedback/advice		

2 What evidence have you seen of how developing resilience has helped pupils' confidence?

K3.14 The possible impact of negative behaviours and the approaches to their management

We looked at this knowledge outcome in Core Chapter 4. You will need to reread pages 70–75 and 79–83.

Practice points

Managing behaviour

▶ Build positive relationships with pupils.
▶ Make sure they are aware of expectations for behaviour.
▶ When managing negative behaviour, listen to each side.
▶ Make sure you are following the school's behaviour policy and apply sanctions if needed.
▶ Always reinforce good behaviour.
▶ Always send for help if the behaviour is violent or pupils have lost control.

▲ Are you clear about the way in which behaviour should be managed in your school?

K3.15 Strategies to help pupils understand, express and manage their feelings

We looked at this knowledge outcome in Core Chapter 4. You will need to reread pages 64–87.

K3.16 The positive effects of encouraging pupils to challenge and test their abilities

We looked at this knowledge outcome in Core Chapter 4. You will need to reread Sections 4.9 and 4.13.

K3.17 Why policies and procedures are important within a school

As well as knowing how to keep pupils and staff safe and secure, you should know and understand the importance of school policies and procedures in this area.

In particular, you should be familiar with these policies:
- first aid policy
- health and safety policy
- recording and reporting policies.

When you start at the school, your induction should include information about your day-to-day responsibilities under the policies. You should know where to find them so that you can refer to them when needed.

The policies

First aid policy

Many schools now have a dedicated first aid policy, although for some it is written within the health and safety policy. In any case, the school needs to have procedures for first aid of which all staff need to be aware.

There are four main reasons for having this policy:
1 To preserve life
2 To apply first aid treatment and prevent the condition from getting worse
3 To promote recovery
4 To know the appropriate actions to take, according to school policy.

The school should have first aid kits which should be regularly checked and restocked, for example every half-term, by a named person.
- Typically, kits are kept in the school office, kitchen and other central points in the school such as a first aid room.
- Staff should know the location of first aid kits or who to ask if they are unsure.

In 2019 it was announced that first aid classes would become compulsory in state-funded English primary and secondary schools from September 2020 as part of the health curriculum. This initiative came about following the Manchester Arena terrorist attack in 2017, when many members of the public were unable to help casualties.
- Pupils in primary schools are now taught basic first aid, and how to deal with common injuries and call the emergency services.
- Pupils in secondary schools are taught further first aid, including how to administer **cardiopulmonary resuscitation (CPR)**.

> **Key term**
>
> **Cardiopulmonary resuscitation (CPR):** an emergency procedure which involves applying chest compressions and breaths to an individual who has had a cardiac arrest.

Health and safety policy

The health and safety policy is a key document. It should set out all the requirements for the health, safety and security of pupils, staff and visitors while on site and during off-site visits.

Purpose of policy	Explanation
Protects the wellbeing of pupils and staff	Governors, senior managers, and the health and safety officer are responsible for keeping staff, pupils and visitors safe. The health and safety policy should be at the forefront of all school practice and procedures to ensure that this is the case.
Knowing the requirements and boundaries of own role	All staff should be clear on: • their responsibilities under the policy • when and how they report to others.
Knowing the appropriate actions to take	All staff should know what to do in potentially hazardous situations, for example: • a broken fence • an unidentified visitor in school.
Knowing who to report to and lines of responsibility	The policy should identify: • the health and safety officer in your school • others in the school who may have responsibilities, such as the site manager • how to report hazards.

Recording and reporting incidents

Your school's health and safety policy should also contain the school's procedures for recording and reporting incidents.

The Health and Safety Executive (HSE) has produced guidance for reporting incidents such as accidents, diseases and dangerous occurrences under RIDDOR.

Comply with legislation

RIDDOR

RIDDOR is the UK's health and safety legislation with regard to recording and reporting incidents. It places a responsibility on all employers, including schools, to report all work-related accidents to staff, pupils and visitors while in the school setting.

A RIDDOR report is required for the following types of incidents:
▶ the death of anyone from a work-related accident
▶ injuries (from a specified list, including serious burns, fractures and head injuries causing lack of consciousness)
▶ accidents where the casualty is taken to hospital for treatment (although not if there is no injury).

Parents and carers must also be informed of any accidents, injuries or first aid which has been given to pupils while they are on the school premises.

A full list of reportable incidents is available on the RIDDOR website: www.hse.gov.uk

When recording incidents, it is important to follow the school's policy for doing this, so that you comply with confidentiality and data protection requirements.

See also K3.6 on page 265.

GDPR

All schools and colleges need to comply with the General Data Protection Regulation 2018 (GDPR) when collecting and storing information. This is because they hold a large amount of data on pupils and staff. This includes personal information on all individuals and anything that is relevant to the welfare and educational needs of pupils, such as:
▶ medical records or information
▶ records of any SEND
▶ records from social services
▶ records from previous schools
▶ records of accidents and emergencies.

Records are usually kept on file and computer in the school, and those who have access to them need to be aware of **confidentiality** requirements:
▶ If any information needs to be passed on to others (for example, to other professionals) parents or carers might need to complete a consent form to authorise this.
▶ If you are working with an individual pupil, be careful about how much you discuss them with others, and do not take any files off the school premises.

> **Key term**
>
> **Confidentiality:** the importance of keeping information private.

Research

Find out who is your school's health and safety officer. Ask them about:
▶ procedures for reporting accidents and injuries
▶ location and storage of information when recording and reporting
▶ school health and safety checks and how regularly they occur
▶ risk assessments and how to complete them.

Help complete future risk assessments and develop solutions to potential risks

For the purpose of this qualification, you will need to understand **risk assessments** and understand how to complete these to ensure pupils' safety.

Although they are not required for every activity in the classroom, risk assessments should be considered before anything which could potentially be hazardous, such as using:
▶ chemicals in science
▶ tools in design and technology.

By completing a risk assessment, you will consider the kinds of precautions you need to take and develop solutions to potential risks.

Key term

Risk assessment: a check for potential risks so that measures can be put in place to control them.

For more on this and support on completing a risk assessment, see Core Skill 4 on page 207.

Practice points

Risk assessments
▶ Identify the type of hazard (physical, security, fire, food safety, or personal safety).
▶ Make sure you have all the information and documents you need.
▶ Record who might be harmed and how.
▶ Evaluate the level of risk and decide on the precautions you should take.
▶ Record your findings.
▶ Implement your plan.
▶ Review and update your assessment.

K3.18 How a range of factors can affect a pupil's self-concept

We looked at this knowledge outcome in Core Chapter 4. You will need to reread pages 71–72.

Research

Find out about the different ways in which your school celebrates pupils' diversity and individuality.
▶ How is role modelling used successfully?

▶ What type of praise and reward strategies are there in your school?
▶ How effective do you think they are at supporting self-concept?

K3.19 Why it is important to give pupils independence and control

We looked at this knowledge outcome in Core Chapter 4. You will need to reread pages 64–87.

K3.20 How a range of factors impact on pupils' behaviour, and linking to attachment and emotional security as outlined in theories of attachment

We looked at this knowledge outcome in Core Chapter 4. You will need to reread pages 64–87.

Reflect

Consider each of the following situations:
▶ Pupil A is withdrawn.
▶ Pupil B is attention-seeking.
▶ Pupil C is anxious.
▶ Pupil D is always tired.
▶ Pupil E is self-harming.

How would you respond in each case?

Could the behaviour in each case be a sign of a larger problem?

K3.21 Why it is important to recognise and reward positive behaviour with reference to behaviourist approaches

We looked at this knowledge outcome in Core Chapter 4. You will need to reread pages 70–72 and 75–79.

K3.22 The expected levels of self-reliance and social behaviour at different ages and developmental stages

We looked at this knowledge outcome in Core Chapter 7. You will need to reread Core Chapter 7, Sections 7.1 and 7.5.

Skills practice

You are working in a boys-only secondary school, usually based in the art and design and technology department to support pupils from all age groups in these subjects.

One of the pupils you regularly work with in Year 9, Adam, has recently become quieter and more withdrawn than usual. He is less focused on his work and hardly engaging with you. You have noticed this over the past three weeks although you have not said anything to other staff or asked him what is wrong. He usually talks to you as you know his parents outside school, although you are always careful to keep a professional distance. You are the only male member of staff in the department.

This morning Adam has come to you before the lesson and is clearly upset. He tells you that he is being bullied via text messages and social media by a group of classmates and others from the local football club he belongs to. One of these boys has

also been sending Adam inappropriate material which he has deleted and tried to ignore, but this is not making any difference. This messaging has gone on for several months but is becoming increasingly upsetting and hurtful, and he is anxious that it will get worse.

Adam says that he is trying to be resilient and show them that he is not going to react, but that this is becoming too difficult. He is asking you for your help. He has also requested that you do not talk to the other pupils or tell his parents, as the content of the messages is embarrassing and he does not want to show anyone. He says he doesn't know what to do, and it is making him feel sick and lose sleep.

Give a clear outline of the steps you would take to support Adam in this situation, being sure to consider your responsibilities and both national and school-based systems.

Performance Outcome 4:
Recognise, Adapt and Respond to Individual Children's Needs, including those with SEND, to Support Development and Access to the Curriculum

This chapter looks at how you can support pupils who have additional needs, as well as their families; we looked at some aspects of this in Core Chapter 11.

You will need to be able to recognise when pupils may need additional support, as well as know how to adapt to meet their needs. The chapter looks at the differences between areas of special educational need and how these areas may affect pupils and their families. It also covers the support which is available to help these pupils and the services which schools and parents are able to access. Finally, we will look at the potential barriers which these pupils may face in the learning environment, and how you can support them to access the curriculum.

Learning outcomes

This chapter covers the following knowledge outcomes for Performance Outcome 4.

K4.1 Theories of language acquisition and why communication and speech play such an important part in pupils' development

K4.2 A range of cognitive difficulties and how they may impact on language development, communication, behaviour and education

K4.3 The relationship between pupil self-esteem and self-management and how this can impact on their education, both positively and negatively

K4.4 How a range of services can support pupils who have been abused, bullied, persecuted, who are at risk of harm or danger, or of becoming involved in offending behaviour

K4.5 The definition of a parent and carer

K4.6 The possible practical and emotional impacts of having a child with a disability or special educational need on a family

K4.7 The potential barriers pupils may face in the learning environment and how to overcome them

K4.8 A range of strategies that support pupils to access the curriculum

K4.1 Theories of language acquisition and why communication and speech play such an important part in pupils' development

The knowledge from this element also corresponds with the material which was covered in Core Chapter 7, Section 7.3; see page 121.

Test yourself

1 How might speaking English as an additional language (EAL) affect communication and speech development in children?
2 What did the theorist Lev Vygotsky say about the development of language?
3 Why is language so closely linked to learning?
4 How does autism spectrum disorder affect the development of children's language?
5 How can adults support the development of language in the early years?

K4.2 A range of cognitive difficulties and how they may impact on language development, communication, behaviour and education

A pupil who has special educational needs and disabilities (SEND) might have a range of cognitive difficulties. Each difficulty might affect:
▶ how they approach learning
▶ their progress in the classroom
▶ their language and other areas of development.

▲ The impact of cognitive difficulties

Cognitive difficulties include the following:
▶ Dyslexia: Difficulty in learning to read or interpret words, letters and other symbols
▶ Dyscalculia: Difficulty in learning and understanding mathematics
▶ Dysgraphia: Difficulty with basic writing skills, such as handwriting, typing and spelling
▶ Dyspraxia: A condition affecting physical coordination
▶ Attention deficit hyperactivity disorder (ADHD): A condition which affects behaviour through inattentiveness, hyperactivity and impulsiveness.

Cognitive difficulties can include a range of impacts, as shown in this diagram.

If a pupil has a specific diagnosis of a cognitive difficulty, it can help you to approach the way in which you support them and to focus more on their needs. For example:
▶ A pupil who has dyslexia is likely to experience difficulties in many areas of the curriculum, as so much of it is based on written work and organising their thoughts.

This table shows the impact of cognitive difficulties on children's development in more detail.

Area of difficulty	Impact on language development, communication, behaviour and education
Dyslexia and dysgraphia	In some cases, pupils might have a specific learning difficulty such as dyslexia. This affects the part of the brain which: • processes language • identifies and decodes words and sounds. It might also cause difficulties such as dysgraphia, or problems with handwriting and spelling. Pupils who find these activities difficult might try to avoid them or complete them quickly, so they may practise and develop these skills less often. As reading and writing are central to accessing the curriculum, difficulties in this area will affect pupils' ability to access the curriculum in many ways. • They might also become frustrated and suffer anxiety or low self-esteem if they are unable to make progress over time, as they will find it so much more difficult to express what they want to say. • This can cause behaviour problems or withdrawal in some cases if it is not addressed.
Dyscalculia	Dyscalculia is a cognitive difficulty which is specific to understanding numbers and making calculations. Pupils who find mathematical concepts challenging might also need support to be able to talk through the steps as they work things out.
Dyspraxia	Dyspraxia, otherwise known as developmental coordination disorder, affects the brain and nervous system. It is a specific learning difficulty which can affect many different areas of learning and development. • It can make a child or young person 'clumsy' or lack physical coordination, and sometimes affects their organisational skills. • Children might find it hard to communicate and organise their thoughts, which also affects how they approach learning activities.
ADHD	If a pupil has a condition that affects behaviour, such as ADHD: • Their hyperactivity might prevent them from concentrating, which can affect their academic work and their ability to complete tasks. • The condition affects their relationships with others, and they might find it difficult to communicate what they want to say. In some cases, ADHD can be controlled by medication. See also Core Chapter 11, Section 11.7. You need to support pupils by breaking tasks into shorter and more manageable chunks so that they are able to achieve smaller targets. This helps their self-esteem as they will feel that they are able to complete tasks.

Research

▶ Choose one of the areas of cognitive difficulty in the table and find out more about it.
▶ If you can, talk to your SENDCo about how pupils in your school with similar difficulties are supported and the strategies which are used.

K4.3 The relationship between pupil self-esteem and self-management and how this can impact on their education, both positively and negatively

Self-esteem, or the extent to which we value ourselves, is something which develops and evolves over time. As we have explored in Core Chapter 4 and Performance Outcome 3, it is directly related to self-concept.

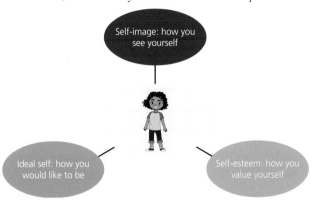

A pupil's view of themselves affects how they think and behave. For this reason, self-esteem also affects **self-management** and can impact on a pupil's education.

> ### Key terms
>
> **Self-esteem:** how we value ourselves.
>
> **Self-management:** how we organise ourselves.

The impact of low self-esteem

A pupil who has low self-esteem might:
▶ feel that they are unable to complete a learning activity, even if adults tell them they can do it
▶ feel that they are not good enough
▶ lack motivation to carry out a task
▶ be less organised in their learning
▶ be less likely to ask for help, as they do not feel that they can complete it, even with support.

However, in some cases, those with low self-esteem might ask an adult for help before even attempting a task themselves, as they might feel that there is no point in trying to do it without help. If this continues over time, it might also affect their social and emotional development and mental health.

Pupils who have low self-esteem usually need tasks to be broken down into small, achievable steps and benefit from plenty of praise and encouragement as they are working to build up their confidence.
▶ For younger pupils, stickers and charts can help motivation.
▶ For older pupils, house points or other forms of positive recognition can be effective in rewarding effort as well as achievement.

> ### Practice points
>
> #### Building self-esteem
> ▶ Use verbal and other forms of praise when you notice a pupil has done well, to support their self-esteem.
> ▶ Check in with those you know might be finding tasks challenging, and break activities into smaller chunks for them.
> ▶ Find out about and use your school's reward system to recognise pupils' efforts in the classroom.
> ▶ Encourage pupils to complete work independently if they can, but offer reassurance and encouragement where needed.

▲ How can you support pupils who are struggling with low self-esteem?

Case study

Chloe has a diagnosis of dyslexia and is in Year 4. You work with her in the mornings to support her during literacy lessons. The teacher differentiates the work for Chloe, but she always looks at her work and compares it to that of other children, saying she can't ever be like them and work so quickly.

Chloe has very low self-esteem and you feel that this is becoming more of a problem. She always looks to you before starting a learning activity and says she doesn't know what to do or where to start.
▶ How is Chloe's self-esteem affecting her learning?
▶ What should you do in this situation?
▶ Why is it important to try to change the way in which Chloe approaches learning activities?

The impact of high self-esteem

A pupil who has good level of self-esteem and self-worth might be:
▶ highly motivated in learning situations
▶ able to effectively manage their learning
▶ able to organise themselves and feel a sense of achievement in what they are doing
▶ progressing well in their learning and development.

In more extreme cases, those with a highly developed level of self-esteem might be over-confident and even feel superior to others.
▶ This is also likely to impact on their education and the way in which they approach learning activities, as well as their relationships with their peers.
▶ They may approach a task in a way which is rushed, or leave their learning to the last minute as they are sure that they can complete it.

▶ This can lead to frustration or anger when they find that this is not the case.

If you find that you are working with a similar pupil, you might need to speak to them as well as the teacher to find ways of addressing it.

As you are working with pupils, you will start to recognise those who may have higher or lower self-esteem. Although there are extremes, there will also be pupils who have a tendency towards one or the other, which can also be damaging to the learning process, and you should look out for this so that you can support them more effectively.

Case study

Joel is in Year 6 and is a competent sportsman. He is in the school team for football and has regularly brought medals from his club to assembly to show the rest of the school.

Your class has a supply teacher in today, and she has taken them outside to play rounders. You are with the group. Before the lesson, Joel told the teacher how good he is at rounders, and was extremely confident in his behaviour. He also told you and others that he was going to score several rounders today.

During the match, Joel was unable to hit the ball and his team lost. His behaviour deteriorates following the lesson when the class go back indoors to get changed – he starts lashing out and calling those in the other team names.
▶ Why is Joel behaving like this?
▶ Do you think that this is likely to affect his self-esteem?
▶ What could you or the teacher say to him to help the situation?

K4.4 How a range of services can support pupils who have been abused, bullied, persecuted, who are at risk of harm or danger, or of becoming involved in offending behaviour

Unfortunately, during your career working with children and young people, you are likely to come across situations in which some of them are mistreated or are at greater risk of harm or danger.

As well as looking out for the signs of abuse and risk, you should be aware that there are different services available to support these pupils, shown in the table below.

See also Core Chapter 3 and Performance Outcome 3.

In most cases, your SENDCo will be the link between these services and pupils and their families.

Organisation or professional body	Support available
Charities	Charities such as the NSPCC, Barnardo's and the Child Exploitation Online Protection Centre (CEOP) work directly with children and young people to support those at risk of harm. Their websites offer information about the kind of support they can give in situations where children and young people have been abused.
Healthcare professionals	GPs and other healthcare professionals might be involved in discussions and meetings about a pupil's physical or emotional wellbeing. They will also provide reports and information towards the creation of a child's or young person's education, health and care (EHC) plan, and will be involved in reviews for these pupils.
LSCP (previously LSCB)	Local Safeguarding Children Partnerships are a statutory requirement in each local area following the Children Act 2004. The purpose of these multi-agency partnerships is to ensure that organisations and local agencies work together effectively to protect children and young people from harm, and to promote their welfare. Section 14 of the Children Act 2004 lists these two objectives: a to coordinate what is done by each person or body represented on the Board for the purposes of safeguarding and promoting the welfare of children in the area; and b to ensure the effectiveness of what is done by each such person or body for those purposes.
CAMHS	The Child and Adolescent Mental Health Services (CAMHS) are the NHS services which assess and treat children and young people with a range of emotional and behavioural difficulties. They also provide support for children and young people who: • have been abused • need help with their mental health.
School or college	In the first instance, particularly in cases of bullying or where pupils have turned to the teacher for help, schools should refer these internally to the SENDCo, who should arrange support. However, where there have been cases of abuse, bullying or other behaviour which causes concern, or where children or young people are at risk, schools should refer these directly to the appropriate professionals. These may include the local Children's Services, CAMHS or LSCP.
Children's Services	Local Children's Services include social services and local provision for families and vulnerable children and young people. • They provide a range of services, including foster and residential care for children and young people when needed. • Social workers work with other professionals to assess and work with children, young people and their families, to offer support and advice and to intervene in cases of safeguarding. For more on Children's Services, see Core Chapter 11.
Youth offending team (YOT)	Youth offending teams work with young people who have offended, or are at risk of offending or reoffending. • They work alongside the police and probation officers, Children's Services, charities and schools, and build relationships with young people and stay in touch with them if they are sentenced. • Although they are separate from the police, the teams are usually made up of representatives from a range of community services to ensure a joint approach. • They also sometimes work with victims of crime to show young people how their behaviour has affected others.

▲ What do you know about your local YOT, and how often they meet?

K4.5 The definition of a parent and carer

Parents and carers should be respected by all professionals as the pupil's primary educators and nurturers. Their rights and responsibilities should always be taken into account.

In your work with pupils, you should be aware that:
▶ there are many definitions of a parent depending on the context
▶ education law and family law recognise this in different ways.

It is important to find out how parents and caregivers are defined when working in schools, as there might be issues of confidentiality, data protection and child safeguarding. You should be aware of this when passing on any information.

How the law defines a parent

According to section 576 of the Education Act 1996, a parent includes:
1 All biological parents, whether they are married or not.
2 Any person who, although not a biological parent, has **parental responsibility** for a child or young

person – this could be an adoptive parent, a step-parent, a guardian or another relative.
3 Any person who, although not a biological parent and who does not have parental responsibility, has care of a child or young person, for example a grandparent.

Non-biological parents, or those who do not have parental responsibility or live with the child, are unlikely to be recognised as parents under education law.

Key term

Parental responsibility: the legal rights, responsibilities and duties which by law a parent has when bringing up a child, including choice of school, religion and managing a child's financial affairs.

The legal rights of parents and carers

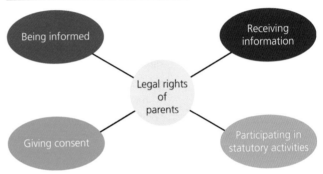

▲ The legal rights of parents

The diagram shows that under education law, parents and carers have several legal rights:
▶ **To receive information from the school**:
All parents and carers should receive regular information from the school about their child's progress, for example through school reports. It is important to keep contact details up to date, especially in cases where biological parents or those who share parental responsibility are separated. Items such as school newsletters and any bulletins should also be sent to both parents where necessary.
▶ **To participate in statutory activities**: Sometimes parents and carers are asked to take part in activities such as voting for parent governors. They should be invited to take part and given all the information they need.
▶ **To be asked to give consent**: It is important that parents and carers give consent in situations where:
– the school day may be different to usual, for example when pupils are going on school trips
– medication needs to be given to pupils
– someone different is collecting their child.

▶ **To be informed about meetings involving the child**: Parents should be kept informed about any meetings which take place concerning their child's progress. These may include parents' evenings or educational reviews which take place for pupils with SEND.

Case study

You are working in a primary school, and a person you have not met before has come to collect Oscar, who is in Year 3. The man says that he is Oscar's stepfather. Oscar is keen to go with him.

You are on the door as the teacher has had to go and speak to another parent. The man tells you that Oscar has to come home with him today, but you have not been informed about this and it has not been written in the 'home' book.

▶ Would you let Oscar go home with this man?
▶ What would you say to Oscar?
▶ Why is it important to do the right thing in this situation?

Research

Look at the government guidance on issues relating to parental responsibility in schools at: **www.gov.uk**

Use the guidance to answer the following questions:
▶ Who has parental responsibility for a child or young person?
▶ Can a same-sex couple both have parental responsibility?
▶ What does the guidance say about foster carers?

The responsibilities parents and carers have in their children's lives

This table shows the rights and responsibilities which parents and carers have in their children's lives.

Parental responsibility	What this means in practice
Providing a home for the child/young person and meeting their emotional needs	All parents are responsible for ensuring that their child has a home where they are loved and cared for. Meeting children's and young people's emotional needs includes making sure that they feel safe, valued and listened to, and acknowledging their feelings.
Protecting and maintaining the child/young person	Parents are responsible for protecting their child, and for looking after their day-to-day needs. Protection in this context means: • keeping them safe • teaching them about the kinds of hazards they might face, so that they can learn to evaluate risk themselves.
Disciplining the child/young person	Part of parents' responsibility is to teach their child about the kinds of behaviours which are acceptable and those which are not, and to understand the consequences of their actions. It is important for children to have boundaries but also to feel loved and accepted whatever they do. Consistency between both parents is also very important, whether or not they live together.
Choosing and providing for the child's/young person's education	Parents are responsible for choosing their child's school and for ensuring that they have what they need during the education process. They should also support their child's education and engage with what they are doing.
Agreeing to the child's/young person's medical treatment	Part of a parent's responsibility is looking after their child's medical needs and any treatment which they need to have. Parents need to ensure that their child has medical attention when it is needed.
Looking after the child's/young person's property	Parents should support their child in looking after their property and keeping it safe. When children take their own things to school, for example in the case of clothes and lunchboxes, these should be named to stop them getting lost.

The concept of 'parental responsibility' in family law

According to the Children Act 1989, the term 'parental responsibility' means all the rights, duties, powers, authority and responsibility that parents have regarding their child and their child's property.

▶ Mothers automatically have parental responsibility and will not lose it if divorced.
▶ Married fathers automatically have parental responsibility and will not lose it if divorced.
▶ Unmarried fathers do not automatically have parental responsibility but can apply for it through a court order or 'parental responsibility agreement' between themselves and the child's mother. Alternatively, they can gain it by registering the birth jointly with the child's mother, or by marrying the mother.
▶ Stepfathers and stepmothers do not automatically have parental responsibility.
▶ Grandparents do not automatically have parental responsibility.

Test yourself

1 What does the term 'parental responsibility' mean?
2 What is the difference between parental responsibility under education law and family law?
3 Name four responsibilities of a parent.
4 What are the situations in which parents might be asked to give consent to the school?

K4.6 The possible practical and emotional impacts of having a child with a disability or special educational need on a family

In Core Chapter 11, we looked at the effects of disabilities and chronic health conditions on a child's or young person's emotions and quality of life.

As well as being aware of the needs of pupils with SEND, you should also recognise the potential practical and emotional impacts which these needs may have on a family.

Parents, carers and other siblings might have known from the time of the child's birth that they had a disability or area of SEN, but in some cases it may have been caused by an accident, health condition or illness which happened more recently. As each situation is different, so is the impact on those closest to the pupil.

Practical impact

There may be a number of different practicalities to consider with a pupil who has a disability, although this will depend on the nature and severity of the SEND.

▶ The family home and car might need to be adapted with equipment and made accessible for the child to enter and exit easily.
▶ The house might need to be adapted so that they are able to go upstairs or so they can meet their everyday needs, such as toileting and showering.
▶ There will be a financial impact on the family, to pay for:
  – these adaptations and equipment
  – specific training, foods or medicines.
▶ There are a range of everyday challenges or situations that are likely to occur regularly, for example knowing the best course of action when making decisions concerning their child. This could include:
  – deciding the best school to send them to
  – whether they should change their medication.
▶ Parents might also need to juggle work commitments or other increased demands on their time with an increased likelihood of hospital appointments. This will impact on their relationships both with one another and also with their other children, as their focus is more likely to be on the child with the SEND.
▶ The family might meet challenges in the way others respond to their child, particularly if they have a condition which is not visible such as autism spectrum disorder.

Case study

Anya has cerebral palsy and is in Year 1. She lives with her mum and twin brother Andrew. Although she does not have any learning difficulties, Anya has problems swallowing and eating, and needs support for toileting. She sometimes needs to use a wheelchair as she has weak muscle tone. Her mum has a part-time job locally, and both children are brought to school and collected by their grandmother.
▶ What kinds of everyday challenges do you think Anya's mum faces?
▶ What impact might these challenges have on Anya's mum and brother?
▶ What kind of support might the school be able to offer Anya's family?

Emotional impact

There may be many emotional impacts on families where children and young people have a disability or have been diagnosed as having an SEN.

▶ Parents have to come to terms with the idea that their child has a disability, health condition or learning need which may be lifelong.

▶ They might blame themselves, for example in the case of inherited genetic disorders. This could affect people differently, depending on the level of support they have from their extended family or through other networks.

▶ The emotional impact on other children in the family may be subtle and can happen over time.

 – It may mean that parents have less time and money to spend on them so they may become jealous.

 – They might resent their sibling for being the centre of their parents' attention, and feel that they are not noticed as much.

▶ Parents will be concerned about their child and affected by the emotions surrounding this, but they might also find that the practicalities of caring for their child lead to increased tiredness, anxiety or depression. This can affect relationships with their partner and with their other children.

▶ Parents might have other concerns such as housing issues, employment or financial problems, which can make the situation feel worse.

Schools might be able to put parents and families in touch with organisations such as charities or local groups, who can offer support to families in challenging situations.

Research

Speak to your SENDCo to find out what kind of additional support the school can offer parents and carers in the following situations:

▶ A Year 8 pupil has just returned to school in a wheelchair following a serious traffic accident.

▶ A Year 2 pupil with dyspraxia and ADHD has been refused additional support in school through the EHC process.

▶ A Year 10 pupil has a progressive health condition which has worsened considerably recently.

▶ A Year 6 pupil with autism spectrum disorder has severe anxiety about starting secondary school.

K4.7 The potential barriers pupils may face in the learning environment and how to overcome them

Unfortunately, all pupils are likely to face potential barriers to learning at some time, although there may be more to consider for those who have SEND.

It is important for us as adults to:
▶ look out for these barriers
▶ make the environment as inclusive as possible when working with pupils and setting up activities for them.

The environment

Staff should ensure that the learning environment is appropriate for the needs of all pupils. For example:
▶ It should be the correct temperature so that pupils can concentrate.
▶ Lighting and noise levels should not prevent them from being able to do their work.

All pupils, whatever their needs, should be able to access the resources and materials without any distractions.

Ensuring that lighting and noise levels are appropriate

Although you might be prepared for the activity, and have checked that the space will be available:

▶ There might be a last-minute disruption or noise, such as workmen or gardeners outside. You should ask the pupils if they will be able to concentrate and then monitor the situation closely. If they are unable to, you should move and wait until the disturbance has finished or find an alternative space.

▶ There might also be another group of pupils making a noise close by which disrupts what you are doing. In this situation you should wait until they have moved past or see if there is an alternative working space.

Light levels are also important.
▶ Pupils should have an appropriate amount of light.
▶ You should check whether blinds are available, for example, if the area is in full sun.
▶ Adverse weather such as snow or thunderstorms also causes disruption, and pupils are unlikely to be able to concentrate on their work. In this situation it may be better to move if possible or postpone what you are doing.

Making adjustments to the physical space to accommodate disabilities

The learning environment may need to be adapted so that pupils with disabilities or sensory needs are able to access the curriculum. They need to be able to:

▶ move around as independently as possible
▶ have access to any additional equipment which is needed.

Ensuring availability of appropriate resources

There should be enough resources for the whole group to work with.

▲ How do you ensure that the physical environment is accessible to all pupils?

If the resources are shared with other groups or classes, or if you need batteries or instructions on how to make an item work, make sure you have tried this out before starting the activity so that it does not interrupt teaching and learning.

Teaching and learning

The quality of teaching and learning is important as this will clearly affect how easily pupils are able to access the curriculum.

If teaching is of poor quality, with poorly planned, disorganised and undifferentiated teaching, or if pupils are not supported in achieving learning objectives, learning will become more difficult.

The following table shows routine ways in which we as adults can ensure that all pupils are given the best possible opportunities to achieve.

Overcoming barriers to learning	How to do this
Clarifying learning objectives	At the start of any learning activity, all pupils should be made aware of learning objectives.
	Adults should make sure that the objectives are displayed or written at the top of the page, or are close by so that pupils can refer to them if needed during the activity. Pupils can then remind themselves what they should be able to do by the end of each session.
	If this is not possible due to the pupils' needs, check with them during the activity to make sure that they are still working towards the objectives.
Adapting learning activities to pupils' individual needs	Depending on the individual needs of the pupils, you might need to adapt learning activities for them. This could mean:
	• talking them through what they need to do
	• providing additional materials or support so that they can carry out the activity as independently as possible.
	For information on augmentative and alternative communication (AAC) and other specific equipment, see Section K4.8 and Core Chapter 11, Section 11.11.

Overcoming barriers to learning	How to do this
Providing bilingual resources to pupils with EAL	Pupils who speak English as an additional language might need bilingual resources to help them access the curriculum. • Although these pupils might need some additional support, you should remember that they do not have SEN unless you have been told this by the teacher or SENDCo. • If you are not sure of their level of understanding, check that they have understood the learning objectives to ensure that they have everything they need when carrying out activities. • If you do not know what additional resources are available for pupils who speak English as an additional language (EAL), check with teachers to ensure that you are providing as much support as is needed. See also Core Chapter 12, Section 12.5.
Ensuring resources are understood and prepared in advance	Before starting work with pupils on any learning activity, make sure that you are clear on exactly what they need to do and the resources they need to do it. • Check that what you need is available, and that you understand how to use it. • Make sure that you have access to power if it is needed or have enough batteries where necessary. • If resources need to be prepared (such as photocopied), try to do this before the time that you need them, as this could take longer than you think. • If you can, ask teachers for plans in advance so that you have enough time to prepare and think about what you need to do.
Providing appropriate feedback to support progression	You need to provide pupils with feedback and encouragement to support their progression. This means: • asking them to check their progress against learning objectives • giving them support where needed. This could be in the form of appropriate questioning to direct their thinking, or scaffolding their learning so that they can make progress. See Performance Outcome 1, Section K1.4 for more on how feedback supports learning.
Including all pupils in the activity	Always make sure that every pupil is included in learning activities. • Due to differences in personalities, there will always be children who are more keen to put their ideas forward and be involved, particularly when working as part of a group. However, make sure you involve quieter and less confident pupils, and question them about their progress and ideas. • You can also use what you know about pupils, for example if they have a particular interest or skill, to involve them further. Involving all pupils is important, to make them feel part of the activity and allow you to find out about their learning.

The pupil

Barriers to learning might come from the pupil themselves. For example:

▶ They might find learning challenging due to low ability or self-esteem.
▶ If they have learning or behavioural difficulties, it might be harder for them to focus on the activity.
▶ They might be affected by home circumstances if these are difficult; for example if they are distracted by something which is happening at home, or if they are anxious or hungry.
▶ Peer pressure can also make it harder for them to concentrate; for example if they want to do what others are doing and are keen to be seen to act in the same way.

For more on factors affecting learning and development, see Performance Outcome 2, Section K2.3.

As a teaching assistant, you might be well placed to notice when a pupil is not 'themselves', or they might confide in you if something is worrying them. However, if their behaviour or what they are doing is interfering with their learning or that of others, you should always take action. This action can take different forms, as shown in the table on the following page.

Method of support when pupils are faced with barriers	What you should do
Intervening to manage disruptive behaviour	This is important. You should intervene straight away so that disruptive behaviour does not interrupt teaching and learning. • Remind pupils about the agreed expectations for behaviour in the class or school. • If the disruptive behaviour continues, act in line with your school's policy and use the sanctions which have been agreed.
Keeping pupils focused on tasks	It can be easy for pupils to become distracted or for the conversation to move away from learning, particularly if you are working in a small group. Always be mindful of this and refocus pupils where necessary.
Encouraging pupils to participate	Pupils might need encouragement to participate in activities, particularly if they find the activities challenging or they have low self-esteem. Make sure you note which pupils are not taking part, and check on those who might be vulnerable.
Breaking down learning into smaller steps	If pupils find tasks difficult, they might need you to break them down into smaller steps, so that they can work on the tasks in stages.
Following a pupil's EHC plan	If you are working with pupils who have an EHC plan, you should know about their needs and be aware of their targets and areas for development so that you can support them more effectively. Depending on your level of involvement with specific pupils, you might also be involved in meetings to set targets and discuss a pupil's progress.
Referring any concerns to appropriate colleagues or professionals	Make sure you note down any concerns about pupils' learning or behaviour so that you can pass these on to teachers or the SENDCo where necessary.
Developing confidence and self-esteem	All pupils need praise and encouragement at school. This is particularly important if they are finding the task or class challenging. Noticing what pupils have done and building on their successes will develop their confidence and encourage them to keep going.

Test yourself

1 What is meant by a 'barrier to learning'?
2 Are barriers to learning more likely for pupils with SEND? Explain your answer.
3 What aspects of the environment at school are potential barriers to learning?
4 How might a pupil's self-esteem affect their learning?
5 Why is it important for you to know about a pupil's EHC plan?

K4.8 A range of strategies that support pupils to access the curriculum

As a teaching assistant working with individuals and groups of pupils, you need to be able to use a range of different teaching and learning strategies in order to support them to access the curriculum. This applies to all pupils, and not just those who have SEND.

In order to do this, you will need to know about individual pupils, their needs and personalities. Being able to use different strategies is important so that you do not need to keep referring back to the teacher about what to do next during lesson time, as they are likely to be working with a group themselves.

The strategies you use will vary according to the needs of the pupils, the situation and the focus of the lesson. In all cases, you should have a clear understanding of each strategy so that you can support pupils effectively.

The strategies

Modifying or adapting learning activities

If you are working with an individual pupil who has SEND, you might need to **modify** or adapt the activity for them so that they can access the curriculum more easily.

This may happen sometimes if pupils are finding the tasks too difficult, or if they complete them quickly and have time to spare. In order to do this, you will need to have a good understanding of the needs of the learners you are supporting and the kinds of activities which are appropriate for them.

You should also ensure before the start of the lesson that teachers are happy with you adapting the activity. Usually, if work has been well differentiated and pitched at the right level, the pupils should have the right amount of time to complete the tasks that have been set. However, there will be times where you need to provide further work or modify learning activities.

> **Key term**
>
> **Modify:** adapt or make minor changes or adjustments.

In addition, you might need to modify or adapt activities for pupils with SEND by providing them with additional resources to support their learning. For example, some pupils with dyslexia find that it helps to have coloured overlays when they are reading.

▲ How might you need to adapt learning activities for pupils with SEND?

If pupils find the task too challenging

If you are supporting a pupil who has SEND, you might need to explain the activity again and break it down into smaller steps so that they find it more achievable.

You could:
▶ take the activity back a few steps, or
▶ give them fewer goals to ensure that they make progress during the lesson.

This will also help to support the pupil's self-esteem and confidence when approaching learning activities.

If pupils complete the task quickly

If possible and appropriate for the age and needs of the pupil:

1 First ask them to check it through and self-assess, to make sure that they have met the learning objectives and looked through their work for grammatical or other errors.
2 If more than one pupil has finished the task, they could peer-assess each other's work.
3 If you are satisfied that they have done this, give them an extension activity. This should be based on the subject or topic which is being studied. In some classrooms, teachers have extension activities which pupils can move on to, or in some cases an ongoing project or task which they can return to.

Using targeted interventions

Teachers might ask you to use targeted **interventions** to help some pupils progress with their learning. These interventions are likely to be for literacy or numeracy, and will be for pupils who need additional support in particular aspects of these subjects.
▶ Several intervention sessions are likely to be timetabled over a period of weeks, and might be for one pupil or a small group.
▶ Teachers should provide you with materials for each session so that it is clear how to use the interventions to close the gaps in pupils' learning and help them to progress.

Key term

Intervention: an activity or strategy which is used in addition to those which have already been carried out in the classroom, designed to support children who are working below national expectations but who should reach them with the right support.

Using accessible resources to support learning

Pupils who have SEND should have access to the same resources as their peers, so that they have the same opportunities in the classroom. There should be an inclusive environment for all, and those who have SEND should be able to find their own resources independently when required.

Providing individual attention or support

As you get to know the pupils you work with, you will learn which of them are likely to need some support, and you will be able to look out for them during lessons.

You might need to provide a pupil with individual attention or support to ensure that they can keep making progress.

See also Performance Outcome 2 for more on strategies to support teaching and learning.

Providing motivation and encouragement

All pupils are likely to need motivation and encouragement from time to time, and those with SEND might need it more than other pupils. Depending on their needs, they might become tired and disheartened, or lack confidence in themselves about what they have been asked to do.
▶ Look out for these pupils, particularly if they are making an effort to work hard.
▶ Make sure that you provide them with encouragement, even if just verbally.

Use of specific equipment, materials, resources and skills including communication systems

In some cases, pupils with SEND might need to have specific equipment, materials and resources to help them to communicate and access the curriculum.

There are many different types of equipment and resources available, which can make a dramatic difference to the way in which you can enhance the teaching and learning experience for pupils you support.

If you have been asked to work with a pupil who needs this type of equipment, you should know how to use it before the lesson. Your SENDCo and other professionals working with the pupil will be able to give you (and the teachers involved) help and training in how to use any necessary resources or technology, such as hearing loops and AAC.

For more on AAC, see Core Chapter 11, page 191.

This table shows resources that can help overcome or reduce the impact of sensory or physical impairment.

Area of SEND	Type of equipment or resource
Cognition and learning needs	Computer software and equipment for specific needs such as dyslexia
	Life skills software
Behavioural, emotional and social development needs	Social stories software
	Puppets to help discuss emotions
	Circle-time games
Speech and language needs	Text-to-speech software
	Recording devices
	Speaking and listening games
	Speech amplifiers
	AAC
Sensory needs	Hearing aids, microphones, hearing loops
	Visualisers, magnifiers, speech software, Braille embossers
	Light source and sensory tubes
	Sensory bags
Physical needs	Computer equipment such as adapted mice and keyboards
	Programs to aid fine motor skills
	Touchscreen technologies

Knowing about and working towards pupils' individual targets

If you are working with pupils who have SEND, they will probably be working towards individual learning targets in one or more areas. For example:

▶ A pupil who has an EHC plan should have agreed targets with their teachers, SENDCo and other professionals as well as their parents.

▶ They should know how they are to achieve these targets.

▶ The targets should be reviewed at least once a year, and the younger the pupil, the more often this should take place.

▶ All pupils are likely to have targets for maths and English, particularly in primary school, and they should know what these are so that they know what they are working towards.

When you have been working with pupils on learning activities, it is very important to feed back to teachers afterwards about the strategies you have used and pupils' learning outcomes, so that the teachers know how the pupils are progressing and can plan the next steps.

▶ This feedback could be verbal, through written feedback sheets, or emailed to teachers at the end of the day.

▶ Make sure that you comment in particular on any learners who have found the activity very straightforward and have completed it easily, as well as those who have found it challenging, and reasons in each case.

Skills practice

You work with Lidia, a pupil in Year 6, and you have been asked by the SENDCo to prepare for an EHC plan review meeting for her. This will also act as a transfer meeting for her new secondary school in a few months' time. Lidia has SEN which are outlined below. The following people will be at the meeting:

- Lidia and her parents
- her current school's SENDCo
- Lidia's current class teacher
- Lidia's speech therapist, physiotherapist and occupational therapists
- the SENDCo from the new secondary school.

All of the professionals who have been invited to the meeting have also been asked to prepare a report.

Here is a list of Lidia's needs:

- She has a disability which means that she has limited mobility on her left side and uses a wheelchair.
- She also has a speech and language disorder, and although her articulation is good, she has difficulty in understanding and using some aspects of language.
- This disorder means that she needs more time to process information during lessons, and requires support to go over what has been said and to organise her thoughts in class.
- Lidia's reading was last assessed at Level 3 of the National Curriculum, and her writing and maths at Level 2.
- Lidia's fine motor skills and handwriting are poor, and she sometimes uses technology to support her writing.
- She needs some support with self-care such as eating, dressing and toileting but manages as much as she can independently.

- Lidia works hard but lacks confidence and can become anxious about her work as she always wants to do her best. Her medication can also mean that at times she becomes tired, particularly during the afternoon.

Lidia's first language is Polish, and she speaks English as an additional language. This is not an area of SEN, but alongside the speech and language disorder it means that she does not always pick up on all cues when listening to others.

Lidia has been very settled in primary school but is anxious about the transfer to the large local secondary school where she has accepted a place. She is worried about being able to find her way around and getting to lessons on time. She has been to the school once for the open day, but has not yet been back for her transition visit with others who will be going into Year 7, to meet her teachers and find out more about the school.

Lidia loves music and enjoys singing. She has several close friends, and two of them will be going to the same school.

Using the information above, write a report for the meeting. Your report should include:

- details about the support Lidia needs in the classroom and around the school
- suggestions for the ongoing help she will need for the transfer to secondary school
- ways in which the school can support her.

You should consider:

- Lidia's physical and mental health needs
- her educational needs
- her speech and language needs
- resources required
- secondary transfer considerations.

ASSESSMENT

Types of assessment

This qualification is assessed in several ways.
- Core Component:
  - Papers A and B
  - Employer-set Project (specific to your occupational specialism)
- Occupational Specialism Component:
  - Synoptic assessment

Core Component assessment: Papers A and B

In order to complete the Core Component assessment, you will have to sit two question papers made up of multiple-choice, short-answer and extended-response questions. These are called Paper A and Paper B, and are directly linked to the Core Elements covered by Chapters 1–12 of this book. Each paper is worth 35 per cent of your grade for the Core Component. Paper A covers knowledge from Core Elements 1–6, and Paper B covers knowledge from Core Elements 7–12.

The 'Assessment practice' or 'Skills practice' feature at the end of each chapter will help you revise for these papers. In addition, your tutor may give you some practice papers to help build your confidence in completing them.

There are two opportunities each year to sit these papers. Visit the NCFE website for more details and an up-to-date assessment timetable.

Question types

There are three types of question in Papers A and B. It is a good idea for you to become familiar with each type of question and also to practise answering them.

Multiple-choice questions

Some questions in the exam will be multiple choice, requiring you to select the correct answer from four options. For example:

> Which of these is the function of Ofsted?
> a) To regulate and maintain standards in examinations
> b) To regulate the higher education system in England
> c) To inspect services providing education for children and young people in England
> d) To provide data and information for parents

When answering multiple-choice questions, start by reading the question carefully. In the example we have given above, you are required to focus on the function of Ofsted. Read through each of the answers carefully before making a decision. You need to start by ruling out answers that you know not to be correct. These questions are designed to have answers that look plausible, but one will always be the best fit.

Short-answer questions

Short-answer questions always have at least one command verb, such as 'describe' or 'identify', in them. You need to look carefully at these before writing an answer as the length and depth of your answer will depend on the command. 'Identify', for example, could require a single word answer, whereas 'describe' requires you to provide more detail.

Here is an example:

> Identify and describe one piece of health and safety legislation. (2 marks)

Read the question carefully and underline each of the command words. In the example given above, you need to do two things: identify and also describe.

Extended-response questions

Both Paper A and Paper B will have a small number of questions that require a longer answer, with more marks available for these questions. As with the short-answer questions, you should note the command words and read each question carefully. Extended-response questions usually require you to show that you can analyse and evaluate, not just that you know something. This is a different skill to simply describing or explaining.

For example:

> Evaluate how a setting's approach to supporting children and young people with EAL may affect their overall development and learning. (12 marks, plus 3 marks for QWC)
>
> Your response should demonstrate:
> ▶ how children and young people develop English as an additional language
> ▶ specific practice that would support the development of English as an additional language
> ▶ the range of factors that might influence an individual child's or young person's acquisition of English as an additional language.

Take a moment to read through the question and plan your answer. This may help you to structure your answer more effectively and will allow you to gain additional marks for QWC (quality of written communication).

Here is a sample answer:

> A setting's approach to supporting a child or young person with EAL can make a significant impact on other areas of their development as well as language. This is because a person's fluency and level of vocabulary can affect their levels of literacy, as well as the development of new concepts. Being able to communicate and articulate emotions also affects social development and how easily friendships are formed and maintained. Children and young people who are not supported to develop English effectively may withdraw socially and also from their learning.
>
> In order to support a child or young person, a setting would need to assess how much English has already been acquired. While some children and young people may already be nearly fluent, others may be new to a language. It is important for a setting to use strategies that are appropriate to the individual. A young person who is nearly fluent may need specific support in understanding the meaning of vocabulary before writing about, for example, a poem. A four year old who is new to English may need to stay near, and interact mainly with, one adult when they start in a nursery. There are many strategies that settings can use, including the use of technology and specialist staff, as well as encouraging children's and young people's peers to support them. These strategies

> as part of an overall approach are only effective if the individual needs of the child or young person are met. This is because a range of factors can affect language acquisition. These factors not only include age, but also personality and motivation. A child or young person who is outgoing may try harder to make friends and be more confident to use their language, while a child or young person who prefers playing or studying alone may not make as much progress. By adjusting their approach and using a range of strategies, settings can be more effective.

Comments on the sample

The question required that the learner should demonstrate how children and young people develop English as an additional language. The learner did not cover this in their answer although they did mention that the setting should assess children's and young people's level. More marks would be awarded if the learner had clearly demonstrated that they understood the stages of EAL language development.

The learner gained marks by showing that they understood the link between language and development and learning. They also showed that they understood the impact if support was not provided by settings.

The learner showed, with relevant examples, that they understood a range of strategies that settings could use, as well as some of the factors that affect how children and young people acquire language.

The learner's level of language was good and the answer showed that they recognised the importance of meeting individuals' needs.

Core Component assessment: Employer-set Project

As well as Paper A and Paper B, you will need to complete an Employer-set Project (ESP). This is worth 30 per cent of your grade for the Core Component of this qualification and relates to the four Core Skills.

> The four Core Skills are discussed in the Core Skills chapter (pages 202–210).

The ESP is split into several parts. In this section we look at the structure of the project and how you can prepare for each part of it.

Pre-release activity

You will be given a pre-release activity to look at. Using the information provided, you need to carry out some research that you can then use to help you in the actual task.

Here is an example of a pre-release activity:

> The secondary school you work in has been asked to be involved in a project that has allocated additional funding to support pupils in deprived areas. This funding is for pupils who are not making expected progress in core subjects following the transition to secondary school.
>
> You have been asked to work with teachers to support a pupil in Year 7 with specific needs. You are therefore required to undertake research that will inform your practice to effectively support the pupil's development.
>
> You should particularly focus on the following:
> ► developmental norms and strategies that would be appropriate to support development
> ► the curriculum and selection of suitable resources
> ► the role of observation, reflection, assessment and planning
> ► partnership working with parents, practitioners and other professionals
> ► safe working practices and risk assessment
> ► education theories, concepts and pedagogies.

Analysing the pre-release activity

It is a good idea when looking at the pre-release activity to note down the age of the pupil(s), as they will be the focus of the next tasks. In this example the pupil is 11. You should also look at the type of school or college that the pupil or pupils are in. In this example, the pupil is in a secondary school. You should note what information is provided about the pupil at this point. In this example, the brief tells you that the pupil is not making expected progress in core subjects. The pre-release activity also indicates that you will be required to plan some activities for this pupil. Finally, the activity suggests areas where you might focus your research.

Planning research

You will use the notes from your research as a basis for answering the two next tasks. You are only allowed to have four pages of research. (Your tutor will provide you with information about how they should be presented.) This means that you need to plan your research carefully. Here are some things that you should focus on.

Developmental norms

You will need to research the developmental norms for the age of the pupil mentioned in the brief. In this example the pupil is 11 years old. We also know that the pupil is working below the expected level in core subjects. It will be important to know what is typical for a pupil of this age in each of the core subjects, but also what development might be shown by a pupil who is at an earlier age and stage.

Role of the adult and strategies

Bearing in mind the age of the pupil or pupils mentioned in the brief, you should also look at some teaching and learning strategies to support the core subjects of English, maths and science.

National Curriculum

You will need to link your planning to the National Curriculum, and in this case, specifically to one of the core subjects (English, maths and science).

> We looked at the structure of the National Curriculum in Core Chapter 2.

You may also, however, like to look in more detail at the requirements for the different core subjects in this age range, particularly how they are broken down into different areas – for example, reading, writing, speaking and listening for English.

Resources and activities for pupils within this age range

It is likely that you will need to plan an activity for the pupil or pupils mentioned in the brief as part of the actual assessment. It will be helpful to have identified in advance resources and activities that can be used with the age range mentioned. If the pre-release activity suggests that the pupil has some developmental needs, you should also research resources and activities typically used for pupils at an earlier stage of learning and development.

Observation and assessment

It is likely that, for the next task, you will be given examples of a summative and formative assessment on the pupil or pupils mentioned in the pre-release activity. This will provide you with more detailed information about them. Make sure that you are confident in analysing information from a range of summative and formative assessments.

> We look at observation and assessment in Core Chapter 8 and also in Performance Outcome 2.

Examples of planning formats

It is likely that you will need to show that you can plan for pupils' development and also for specific activities. It will be worth looking at different ways in which schools use plans for individuals and groups of pupils. Ideally, you should practise filling them in. You should also look at other examples from your work placement and on the internet.

As planning formats take up a lot of space, you could, in your notes, just write some of the key headings, e.g. name of pupil, age and year group, learning objectives, and so on.

Safe working practices and risk assessment

As your next tasks are likely to involve planning, you will need to look at some of the potential hazards and safe working practices to consider when working with the age range mentioned in the pre-release activity.

> We look at risk assessment in the Core Skills chapter.

In addition, you can talk to your work placement about how, when planning and providing activities, practitioners consider safety. You may not need to take detailed notes about this, but you might want to write a reminder to yourself in your notes to mention it when writing the plans.

Approaches to how children and young people learn, and how best to support them

As part of the project, you need to show that you have understood some theories relating to how pupils learn, and also different approaches to teaching and learning.

> We look at theories of learning in Core Chapter 7, and consider different approaches to teaching and learning in Performance Outcome 1.

To help you prepare for the tasks, it will be worth identifying two or three theories of learning. You will need to know what they are and how they apply to working with children and young people. A good example is social learning theory. This is the idea that children and young people can learn some skills and behaviours by watching adults.

Completing the Employer-set Project

▶ In exam conditions, you will be given a more detailed scenario about the pupil or pupils mentioned in the pre-release activity.

▶ You are also likely to be given details of assessments and reports about the pupil or pupils.

▶ You will then have two tasks to complete by yourself, and two other tasks involving others.

▶ The tasks are likely to ask you to plan for one or more aspects of the pupil's or pupils' development.

Here is an example of the type of information that you may be given:

You are employed in a large secondary school in a deprived area. You work in Years 7 and 8, and support pupils with additional learning needs in English and maths. The Year 7 pupils have been in school for four weeks and you have recently been working with teachers to identify pupils who will benefit from additional support.

You have been asked to work closely with Khalid, who lacks confidence in maths and has very poor number skills. He is not able to use and apply these skills in different situations and often seeks adult support in maths lessons.

At the end of Year 6, Khalid completed National Curriculum tests to measure his competency in a range of areas. An extract from the school results, along with Khalid's results, is provided for you. Some background information on Khalid has also been sent from his primary school, Oak Tree Primary School.

The teacher has asked you to analyse the data and profile notes in order to plan a comprehensive approach to meet and support the development of Khalid's maths skills; the approach will be shared with and approved by the maths teacher and Khalid's form tutor.

Regular informal reviews with the maths teacher will take place to monitor Khalid's ongoing progress and the teacher will also formally review his maths skills towards the end of the autumn term.

Pupil profile	
Setting:	Oak Tree Primary School
Name:	Khalid
Age:	11 years
Family background notes:	Khalid has attended Oak Tree Primary school since the age of four. However, he did not attend a pre-school or nursery. He has always been quiet and reserved, both with his peers and with adults. Khalid has two younger sisters and lives at home with them and both parents, as well as his grandmother. English is the family's spoken language in the home.
Health and wellbeing notes:	Khalid had some intervention for his speaking and listening skills as well as English and maths during Key Stage 2. He was referred to the speech and language therapist and had two blocks of speech and language therapy when he was in Year 2.
Other professional involvement:	SENDCo
Teacher comments:	Khalid is very good at music and drama, as well as art and technology subjects. He plays the guitar and keyboards, and belongs to a local football club. Khalid can be distracted during lessons, and often seems to be 'in his own little world', staring out of the window rather than focusing on his work. He lacks confidence in academic subjects but enjoys more creative aspects of the curriculum. He excels in drama, where he seems to lose his inhibitions and has an ability to take on different characters. Khalid often scores poorly in maths tests and has never been able to remember his tables. He has difficulty in organising himself and remembering to revise for tests. He finds it hard to remember number facts and how to apply these in different situations. He becomes very frustrated with using number, although he has a better understanding of the shape, space and measures aspect of maths. Although a cautious pupil, Khalid interacts politely with teachers and other pupils. He is quiet in class although he does have a small circle of friends that he plays football with, both within and outside school. He has recently started attending a local theatre group and has begun speaking about how much he enjoys it on a Thursday after school. During some of our transition activities, it became clear that Khalid was very anxious about the transfer to secondary school. We have spent time in small groups with him and other pupils talking through some of the expectations and he seemed a little less worried following the taster days.

End of Key Stage 2 NCTs results 2019	Khalid's performance	Oak Tree Primary's performance	National average
Mathematics – Expected Standard		68%	79%
Mathematics – High Standard (Scaled Score of 110+)		59%	27%
Mathematics – Average Scaled Score	90	110	105
Writing – Expected Standard (Scaled Score of 103+)		88%	78%
Writing – Greater Depth (High Standard/Scaled Score of 113+)		16%	20%
Writing – Average Scaled Score	95	110	103
Reading – Expected Standard (Scaled Score of 100/100±)		97%	78%
Reading – High Standard (Scaled Score of 110+)		55%	30%
Reading – Average Scaled Score	100	108	106

Task 1

1 Create an intervention plan proposal that you would use to meet Khalid's development needs for his skills in mathematics.

You should make reference to your research findings in your plan.

2 Create an activity plan that you could use to support Khalid.

You should include an explanation of how the planned activity:
- links to the wider curriculum
- is underpinned by theory, concepts and pedagogy.

Preparing for the tasks

Read through the two parts of the task carefully. Underline key phrases and, as you work, keep referring back to the information you have been given, as well as the requirements of the task.

You may find that you are asked in at least one of the tasks to refer directly to your research findings. You may also find that, for at least one of the plans, you have to show that you can link it to educational theories as well as the wider curriculum. There are many ways that you can make these references as part of your planning. Here are a couple of suggestions you might like to consider.

- **Add in a rationale section:** You could create a rationale section. In this section you would explain the reasons behind your choice of strategies, activities or resources. For example: 'According to Vygotsky's theory of learning adults need to understand a child's current capabilities and then look for ways of slightly challenging them. Based on the assessments provided, I believe that the activity I have chosen will extend Khalid's knowledge, but it will be achievable.'
- **Add in a commentary section:** You may wish to create a section titled 'Commentary'. This will contain your comments about your decisions. You might write comments such as 'As Khalid is not confident in his maths skills, I have suggested that most intervention activities will take place with the same adult. This will build his confidence with maths and help to support his self-concept.'
- **Links to the National Curriculum:** It will be important to explain how an activity links to the National Curriculum. If the planning requires that you show how an activity or a series of activities

links to the wider curriculum, you could put this as a separate section.

- **Add in a safety and safeguarding section:** Depending on the actual tasks, it might be helpful to add in a safety and safeguarding section. For example, if you were planning an activity outside the classroom, you might draw attention to the need for the area to be checked for hazards beforehand. In the same way, if the activity was an outing, you might write that there would need to be a risk assessment, including taking any medication for pupils with you.

Task 2

This task requires you to share your responses to Task 1 with other students. You will need to talk to them about your ideas and justify them. You will also be looking at their work and making comments and suggestions. Task 2 is split into different parts.

Preparation

To prepare for Task 2, your tutor will give you back the work you did for Task 1. You will also be given other students' work and a form to help you prepare. You will have plenty of time to carry out this preparation. During this time you need to:
- think about the key points you need to say about your plan
- practise speaking aloud
- take time to analyse the other students' plans, and jot down your ideas and comments
- practise phrasing questions and comments in ways that appear fair and thoughtful.

2a Peer discussion

Your tutor will put you into a group with other students. You will be given back Task 1 as well as your preparation form. You will also be given a form to write down the feedback you are given from the other students. You will then take it turns to talk about, listen to and give feedback on one another's plans.
- Do not take the suggestions and comments of others personally.
- Take careful notes about everything that is said.
- If you are not sure what point someone is trying to make, you can ask questions to clarify.

2b Amending your plan, with justifications

After the peer discussion, you will be given an opportunity to revise your plan using the feedback you have been given. Your revised plan should show what changes you have made, and you will need to explain why you have made them.

You must reference the notes you wrote on the peer discussion feedback form. If points were raised that you have chosen not to act on, you should explain what these were and why you decided not to act on them. If you have a 'Rationale' section in your plan, you could use this heading to include this information. For example, 'According to the notes I took, one of my peers suggested that the activity could work better outdoors. I have not made this change to the plan as there is a danger that the pupil might be distracted and it might be easier to focus their attention in a smaller space.'

Task 3

Task 3 is completed with your tutor. It is divided into two sections: a presentation of your plans followed by a discussion with your tutor.

3a Presentation

The idea of this task is to show that you know how to present information to another professional. During your presentation, you will need to explain your planning and the rationale behind it. Some learners find it easier to do this by preparing a slide show.

It is important to remember that a presentation is not a conversation or a chat. You will need to be ready to talk without interruption for around ten minutes. It is important that you do not simply read out what is on the plan. Instead, imagine that you are explaining something new to someone who does not know about the National Curriculum and planning.

To prepare for the presentation, you might like to write a list of points that you could talk about. Here are some examples:

▶ Your identification of the pupil's needs, and how you arrived at these judgements.
▶ Factors that you took into account when drawing up the different plans, such as resources or educational theories.
▶ The amendments you made following the peer discussion, and why these were made.

Practising your presentation

You will have two hours to prepare for your presentation. This means that you will have time to practise your presentation, prepare a slide show if you wish, and also to check that you have sufficient to say for ten minutes – it is worth remembering that most people, when they are nervous, speed up. It can be useful to divide your presentation into three parts: introduction, middle and conclusion. Make sure you have a clear introduction and practise saying this aloud.

This is important, as you have to get used to hearing your own voice.

Carrying out the presentation

Giving a presentation can make some people nervous. Here are a few tips:

▶ Remember that your tutor is on your side.
▶ Take a deep breath and smile as you start.
▶ Make a definite start by saying something like 'Good morning/afternoon. My name is _____. Today I am going to present my _____.'
▶ Try to make some eye contact while you are talking – even if briefly.
▶ Write simple notes to remind you of what you want to say and the order you want to say it in – you can put these on cards.
▶ Avoid reading from a script.
▶ Don't worry if your tutor is writing things down. This is not a bad sign.
▶ Wear a watch so you can keep an eye on the time.
▶ End your presentation by saying something like 'I hope that you have found this useful' or 'Thank you for taking the time to listen to me.'

3b Discussion with your tutor

For this task you need to show that you can communicate well with another adult. Your tutor may take the part of a professional such as a key person, health visitor or parent. You will be given a form that you can use to help you prepare for the discussion. You should expect your tutor to ask questions or ask you to justify what you have said. As part of this discussion, you will talk about how you reviewed your plans as a result of the peer discussion.

Task 4: Reflection

The final task for the Employer-set Project is to write a reflective account. Your tutor will give you a form to complete and you will have two hours to complete the activity.

Your account should include the following sections:

Analysis
▶ Did each of the tasks meet the required outcomes?
▶ How do you know?

Evaluation
▶ What went well and not so well with each of the tasks?
▶ Why do you think this was the case?

Reflection
▶ What have you learned from completing the project?
▶ How might you approach the project differently if you were to do it again?

Occupational Specialism Component: Synoptic assessment

As part of the assignments for your occupational specialism, you will also need to complete a synoptic assessment at the end of the year, in the form of two written assignments. The purpose of the synoptic assessment is to draw together the knowledge from the different performance outcomes and relate it to practical situations or scenarios. It will also give you the opportunity to apply your knowledge and skills in greater depth.

Synoptic assessments will take the form of actual workplace scenarios or longer case studies, which are linked to your area of specialism. These question papers will be longer and you will need to consider all of the material you have been given, and ensure that you have answered each part of the instructions.

During your time in placement, even when you are in your first year, try to relate what you are seeing and doing to the knowledge that has been covered in the units you have studied. For example, in a maths lesson, can you identify how differentiation is being used to support individual pupils' learning? Thinking like this will help you to practise for the assessment.

Glossary

Abstract conceptualisation (AC) This is when the learner has a new idea or has changed their thinking due to their experience.

Accountable Required or expected to justify actions or decisions.

Active experimentation (AE) The learner applies their new way of thinking to a future experience.

Adrenaline autoinjector (often known as EpiPen®) A device to administer adrenaline to decrease swelling in the case of an acute allergic reaction.

Affluent Being wealthy, having a relatively large amount of money and/or material possessions.

Alternative provision settings Education providers for pupils who are unable to go to a mainstream school. This may be, for example, due to exclusion or illness.

Anaemia A health condition in which there are not enough red blood cells in your body, which means that your body may not get enough oxygen.

Animism Ascribing feelings and personality to inanimate objects, e.g. 'my car is happy'.

Assessment for learning Information from assessment is used to raise the achievement of pupils in finding out what they need to do to improve.

Barrier to learning Anything that prevents a child or young person from taking part fully in the activities or experiences that are offered by the school or early years setting.

Benchmark A point of reference for checking standards.

Bilingualism The ability to use two languages.

Blended learning A style of teaching that uses a blend of online and face-to-face teaching.

Bulimia A condition in which the person has an obsessive desire to lose weight, and self-induces vomiting.

Cardiopulmonary resuscitation (CPR) An emergency procedure which involves applying chest compressions and breaths to an individual who has had a cardiac arrest.

Code switching Using a word or phrase from one language when speaking another.

Concrete experience (CE) This is when the learner encounters an activity or experience for themselves.

Confidentiality The importance of keeping information private.

Consolidate To review or reinforce learning.

Context cues Cues which are suggested by the context of the text.

Continuing professional development (CPD) Ongoing professional training and development to keep up to date.

Copyright The legal right to intellectual property. Copyright is usually owned by the creator of materials and those authorised to use them.

Core subjects English, maths and science.

DBS Stands for Disclosure and Barring Service, part of the suitability checks that must be made on individuals in the UK involved in the care of children and young people under 18 years of age. These specifically look at any criminal convictions recorded against an individual and are an important feature of safeguarding (see Core Chapter 3). You will find out more about DBS processes as you prepare for placement, as it is likely you will be required to undertake a DBS check yourself.

Designated safeguarding lead (DSL) The person in a school or early years setting who is responsible for all safeguarding issues.

Differentiation Setting work at an accessible level for each pupil and their needs.

Disability 'A physical or mental impairment which has a substantial or long-term negative effect on your ability to do normal activities' (DfE, 2010).

Discrimination Unfair treatment of a group of people due to prejudice.

Diversity Recognising our individual differences.

Early Help Assessments (EHAs) A tool to identify and discuss support for children and families with local partners.

Early identification Quickly recognising that a child or young person may need additional support.

Early production Being able to say or repeat some words.

Education, health and care (EHC) plan An EHC plan is for children and young people aged up to 25 who need more support than is available through special educational needs support; it is drawn up to outline provision for a child or young person following an assessment of special educational needs (see Core Chapter 11, page 172). EHC plans identify educational, health and social needs, and set out the additional support to meet those needs. Find out more here: www.gov.uk/children-with-special-educational-needs/extra-SEN-help

Equality Being equal in status, rights and opportunities.

Esteem Having a positive self-concept and having feelings of competence. Feeling recognised and valued by others.

Experiential learning theory (ELT) The theory that knowledge is created through experience.

EYFS *Development Matters* Non-statutory guidance to support early years practitioners with observation, assessment and planning.

Fine motor skills The skills needed to hold and manipulate smaller objects with the fingers, such as holding a pencil or doing up a zip.

Fixed mind-set When a person believes that their intelligence and ability to learn cannot be altered.

Fluency Being able to use a language easily and to an advanced level.

Formal observations Structured observations taking place within a set time in which the observer has specific criteria to look for.

Formative assessment Frequent, often informal, assessment that is designed to generate ongoing evidence of children's and young people's progress and attainment, and is used to inform the next steps.

Formative feedback Verbal or written information that helps children or young people to work out how they can improve.

Further education colleges Include general FE and tertiary colleges, sixth-form colleges and specialist colleges, as well as adult education provision. You can find out more on the government's website.

Gender transition When a child or young person wants to change from their biological gender to the one that they identify with.

Gestures Actions involving fingers, hands or feet, used when communicating.

Gross motor skills The skills needed to control and develop the movement of the arms and legs, such as throwing and catching, or running and skipping.

Growth mind-set When a person believes that they can control their learning and outcomes through hard work, practice and by asking for help.

Hazard Something in the environment that could cause harm.

Health and Safety Executive (HSE) An independent regulator for the prevention of work-related death, injury and ill health.

Heel prick test This is a blood test that is carried out on all babies when they are a few days old to test for serious conditions.

Holistic Overall or all round; the idea that the parts of something are interconnected so looking at the whole rather than each individual part. For example all-round care needs, with an appreciation of the contribution of each care need to overall wellbeing.

Inclusion The process of identifying, understanding and breaking down barriers to participation and belonging.

Inclusive practice Developing an approach that recognises the diversity of children and young people, and promotes positive attitudes, differentiation and respect.

Individual support assistant An assistant who supports one pupil with specific needs.

Informal observations Simple observations that take place during the course of the day, which may look at behaviour, relationships or confidence.

INSET day In-service training day, or day when teaching staff meet in term time, without pupils, for additional training.

International Baccalaureate Two-year international programme leading to an internationally recognised diploma, which prepares students for higher education.

International GCSE (sometimes iGCSE) International General Certificate for Secondary Education. The iGCSE is available internationally.

Intervention An activity or strategy which is used in addition to those which have already been carried out in the classroom, designed to support children who are working below national expectations but who should reach them with the right support.

Learning journal In the EYFS, individual learning journals may be used as a record of a child's progress and achievements during the year. They may include observations, photos and quotes from the child.

Lobby When an individual or organisation sets out to influence governmental decisions.

Looked after child (LAC) A child who has been in the care of their local authority for more than 24 hours, sometimes also referred to as children in care. This can include children living with foster parents, in a residential children's home, hostel or secure accommodation.

Love and belonging Feeling part of a group, having family and friends; for adults this may include a life partner.

Mindfulness A technique of reducing stress that involves acknowledging emotions and sensations.

MMR vaccine A vaccination for measles, mumps and rubella which is currently given to young children in two doses, at one year and at three years four months old.

Mnemonic A system for improving and helping memory.

Modify Adapt or make minor changes or adjustments.

Motor skills Physical movements.

Multidisciplinary team A team that consists of professionals working together from across the sector who have different roles. For example, a health visitor and a social worker may work together with an early years practitioner to bring together their specialist expertise in order to support a child and their family at a particular time.

Neurological Relating to or affecting the brain and nervous system.

Non-verbal Communication that takes place without words being said.

Non-verbal cues Prompts using body language, e.g. facial expression, eye contact or gestures.

Ofsted Stands for the Office for Standards in Education, Children's Services and Skills. Ofsted inspects and regulates services providing education and skills for learners of all ages, including those who care for babies, children and young people.

Open question A question that cannot be answered with a yes or no response.

Parallel play Two or more children engaged in their own individual play but in close proximity to each other.

Parental responsibility The legal rights, responsibilities and duties which by law a parent has when bringing up a child, in relation to the child and their property.

Pedagogical Educational, or related to teaching.

Phonetic cues Sounds which are found in the word and help to identify it.

Physiological needs Things that the human body needs to survive, including clean water, shelter, food and also being at a comfortable temperature.

Picture exchange communication systems (PECS) A method of communication that uses simple pictures.

Plagiarism The use of work or materials which are protected by copyright as someone else's property.

Planning, learning and assessment cycle The process through which children's needs and abilities are identified, which enables teachers to plan for next steps.

PPE Personal protective equipment – equipment to protect the user from risk. Examples of PPE might be helmets, eye protection, gloves or gowns, and high-visibility (hi-vis) jackets.

Prejudice A set of preconceived negative ideas about a particular group of people.

Primary disability A physical or mental impairment that has a negative effect on a person's ability to carry out normal activities.

Proximity The distance between the child or young person and the adult.

Pupil premium An amount of money given to the school each year by the government in order to raise the attainment of disadvantaged pupils.

Ratify To vote on or sign a written agreement to make it official.

Receptive language The ability to understand what is being said through language.

Reflective observation of a new experience (RO) This stage is when the learner thinks back, or reflects on, their experience.

Regulated activity Unsupervised activities when teaching, training, instructing, caring for or supervising children.

Regulation Control of a process by a set of rules.

Reliable Able to be trusted.

Resilience The capacity and ability to recover quickly from difficulties, or 'bounce back'.

RIDDOR Reporting of Injuries, Diseases and Dangerous Occurrences Regulations.

Risk The chance, whether high or low, that someone could be harmed by a hazard.

Risk assessment A check for potential risks so that measures may be put in place to control them.

Role model Someone who is looked to by others as an example.

Safeguarding Action taken to promote the welfare of children and protect them from harm (NSPCC, 2018).

Safety needs People know that they are not in danger.

Scaffolding The way an adult supports children's and young people's learning through questions and comments.

Schema A pattern of thought or behaviour.

Scribe A person who writes or word processes a pupil's answers.

Self-actualisation The ability to think and be creative without worrying what others might think.

Self-concept The idea and belief which an individual has of themselves.

Self-esteem How we value ourselves.

Self-management How we organise ourselves.

SEND (sometimes called SEN) 'A child or young person has SEN if they have a learning difficulty or disability which calls for special educational provision to be made for him or her' (SEND Code of Practice, 2015).

Sequential language learning Where a language is learned after a home language has been established.

Simultaneous language learning Where children are exposed to two or more languages in their first three years.

Social mobility Movement of individuals or groups between different social classes or levels.

Social referencing How babies and young children look at adults' responses as a guide to how they should themselves react.

Spiral curriculum The concept that a subject may be repeatedly taught but in increasing depth.

State funded Money that the government provides for something.

Statutory Something that is required by law.

Summative assessment A final assessment, usually occurring at the end of a period of study, which is used to sum up children's and young people's overall level of attainment, and to provide data for stakeholders.

Tailored intervention Designing support to help a child or young person pick up a specific skill or piece of knowledge.

Tertiary college An institution that provides general and vocational FE for students aged 16–19. Such colleges provide the next stage of education, after primary and secondary. They are distinct from general FE colleges in that they cater for a specific age group, and offer a less extensive and varied curriculum.

Upskirting Taking a photo up a person's skirt or dress without their knowledge or consent.

Valid Worth consideration; should be recorded.

Verbal The use of words as well as how the words are said.

Verbal cues Prompts that help the listener to answer, e.g. speaking more slowly or emphasising particular words.

Vicarious experience Learning about behaviours and attitudes through observing others and imagining yourself in same situation.

Index